THEORY OF FILM

SIEGFRIED KRACAUER

THEORY
OF FILM

THE REDEMPTION OF PHYSICAL REALITY

WITH AN INTRODUCTION BY
MIRIAM BRATU HANSEN

PRINCETON UNIVERSITY PRESS · PRINCETON, NEW JERSEY

Published by Princeton University Press
41 William Street, Princeton, New Jersey 08540
In the United Kingdom: Princeton University Press, Chichester, West Sussex

Reprinted by arrangement with Oxford University Press

Library of Congress Cataloging-in-Publication Data
Kracauer, Siegfried, 1889–1966.
    Theory of film : the redemption of physical reality / Siegfried
Kracauer ; with an introduction by Miriam Bratu Hansen.
        p. cm.
    Originally published: London ; New York : Oxford University Press,
1960.
    Includes bibliographical references and index.
    ISBN 0-691-03704-3 (pbk. : alk. paper)
    1. Motion pictures. I. Title.
PN1994.K7   1997
791.43 — dc21   97-23804

Princeton University Press books are printed on acid-free paper and meet the
guidelines for permanence and durability of the Committee for Production
Guidelines for Book Longevity of the Council on Library Resources

First Princeton Paperback Printing 1997

http://pup.princeton.edu

Printed in the United States of America

10   9   8   7   6

ISBN-13: 978-0-691-03704-2

ISBN-10: 0-691-03704-3

TO MY WIFE

INTRODUCTION

Miriam Bratu Hansen

The turn to photography is the *go-for-broke game* of history.
— Kracauer, "Photography," October 1927

Film brings the whole material world into play; reaching beyond theater and painting, it for the first time sets that which exists into motion.
It does not aim upward, toward intention, but pushes toward the bottom, to gather and carry along even the dregs. It is interested in the refuse, in what is just there — both in and outside the human being. The
face counts for nothing in film unless it includes the *death's-head* beneath. "Danse macabre." To which end? That remains to be seen.
— Kracauer, notes toward a book on film aesthetics, November 1940

So the cinema may well weather the crisis. Its potentialities are far from
being exhausted, and the social conditions which favored its rise have
not yet changed substantially. . . . Germs of new beginnings may develop within a thoroughly alienated environment.
— Kracauer, *Theory of Film*, 1960

IN THE PREFACE to the original edition of this book, Siegfried Kracauer sums
up the key assumption underlying his "*material* aesthetics" of film: "that film
is essentially an extension of photography and therefore shares with this medium a marked affinity with the visible world around us. Films come into
their own when they record and reveal physical reality."[1] Kracauer conceives
of film as a medium of representation whose realistic potential is grounded in
its photographic technology. In the photochemical process, visual data are
inscribed on a celluloid strip at a particular moment in time, the instant of
exposure. Whatever may be done to them through syntactic procedures such

vii

as editing or sound mixing, these images are fixed once and for all, and their meanings will be actualized only in belated perceptions and readings. In semiotic terms, one might say that, by insisting on film's "photographic nature," Kracauer stresses the *indexical* dimension of film, the trace of a material bond with the world represented (the camera having been there at a certain point in time, light rays having linked the object with the photochemical emulsion for fractions of a second). This linkage is key to — but also qualifies and circumscribes — the *iconic* dimension of film, its ability to represent something as "real" through a relation of resemblance or analogy.[2]

It is a commonplace of contemporary media criticism that films no longer function quite that way; more precisely, the material conditions under which films are shot — the work of the camera, variables of film stock and mise-en-scène — are no longer as essential in determining the way films eventually look and affect their viewers. Digital technologies such as computer enhancement, imaging, and editing have shifted the balance increasingly toward the postproduction phase, thus further diminishing the traces of photographic, indexical contingency in the final product. Not only can "mistakes" made during shooting be "corrected" and recorded effects be maximized, but on the very level of production live-action images and sounds can be generated independently of any referent in the outside world. In short, traditional models of representation have given way to the reign of simulation. Whether one believes that these events are a good thing for cinema or the end of cinema as we know it, and whether one thinks these technological innovations have actually inspired new cinematic styles and genres, the impact and implications of this shift, which marks Hollywood products since the late 1970s, can hardly be ignored.

What, then, in light of these developments, is the significance of a theory of film that insists on film's "photographic nature"? Has technological progress reduced Kracauer's reflections, as a German critic recently proclaimed, to the status of "beautiful ruins in the philosophical landscape"?[3] What, if anything, can historical film theory tell us about the practice of cinema today? Are there fragments amid the ruins with which we could reconstruct a new "material aesthetics" that might address the practice of cinema today?

In the history of film theory, *Theory of Film* holds an important place. The book ranks as a canonical work of classical film theory, the tradition of theoretical writings on film that begins in the 1920s (with Béla Balázs, Jean Epstein, Rudolf Arnheim, and Hans Richter, to name just a few) and is concerned preeminently with questions of the medium's "specificity" — what film can do that the traditional arts cannot, and what kind of film practice succeeds best in utilizing the aesthetic possibilities of the cinematic medium. In relation to this tradition, *Theory of Film* is a somewhat belated offspring. But the

book is also a contemporary of post–World War II theories of cinematic realism, notably the work of André Bazin (whose essays were collected and published in French around 1960, in English a decade later), and of writings
accompanying and promoting stylistic movements such as Italian neorealism.
For Kracauer, the specificity of film is rooted emphatically in its photographically based ability to "record and reveal physical reality" (also referred to
as "material reality," "the visible world," "nature," "life," or "camera-reality"
[p. 28]), and he offers a vast catalogue of functions, "inherent affinities," and
objects (urban crowds, the street; things normally unseen, the small and the
big, the quotidian and the marginal, the fortuitous and the ephemeral) to
illustrate his claim. But, as Kracauer well knows, film's "affinity" with "the
transitory world we live in" is an "elective" one (to use Tom Levin's para-
phrase): It has to be translated into an aesthetic effect by means of cinematic
techniques such as framing and editing; in other words, the "potentialities" of
the medium can only be implemented through particular stylistic choices.[4]

Kracauer's plea for a cinematic realism of everyday life fell on fertile
grounds during the high cold war, a period that saw counterpublic stirrings in
various artistic and cultural media and among disparate social and political
constituencies. In this sense, it might be productive to think of *Theory of Film*
as contemporaneous with the magazine *Film Culture* and developments in
independent film production and distribution; with existentialism in philosophy and life-style, minimalism in art and music; with Susan Sontag's essay
"Against Interpretation," Miles Davis's *Kind of Blue*, Lawrence Ferlinghetti's *A
Coney Island of the Mind*, and movies such as *Shadows* and *The Hustler.*[5]
Likewise, on a more international scale, Kracauer's book, like Bazin's writings,
has to be seen as part of the cinéaste environment that spawned and supported
New Wave movements in France, Germany, Eastern Europe, India, and other
parts of the world.

Whatever its subterranean resonances and impact may have been, Kracauer's book became the object of critical demolition early on; in fact, *Theory
of Film* did not have to wait for the digital revolution to be laid in ruins.
Intellectual attacks on the book assumed an unusually condescending tone,
from Pauline Kael's smug polemics against the author's Germanic pedantry
(1962) and Andrew Tudor labelling the book a "teutonic epic" (1974);
through Dudley Andrew's indictment of its normative ontology (1976) and
"naive realism" (1984) and similar charges raised from a semiotic perspective
in the pages of *Screen*; to the standard German new-left argument that, with
the shift in emphasis to "physical reality," Kracauer had abandoned his earlier
preoccupation with the cinema's relation to social and political reality.[6] No
doubt many of these criticisms have a point, to which the present reader may
add yet other objections. Whatever these may be, however, I want to empha-

size that this book is anything but "utterly transparent" or "direct," as Andrew asserts, nor is it "a huge homogeneous block of realist theory."[7] On the contrary, much as *Theory of Film* strives toward transparency and systematicity, the text remains uneven, slippery, and occasionally inconsistent, defying any attempt to deduce from it a coherent, clear-cut, and univocal position. And perhaps the insights that the work still yields are to be found in this unevenness and do not depend upon its status as logically consistent, "solid" theory nor, for that matter, upon claims to transhistorical and transcultural validity.[8]

What *Theory of Film* can offer us today is not a theory of film in general, but a theory of a particular type of film experience, and of cinema as the aesthetic matrix of a particular historical experience. To reconstruct that theory, however, and to "redeem" it in Kracauer's idiosyncratically materialist inflection of that word, we have to take a double detour: one through his early writings, dating back to the Weimar period, and another through the beginnings of this book, dating back to 1940–1941 in Marseille. (A further route, productively pursued by others, goes through Kracauer's book *History: The Last Things Before the Last*, published posthumously in 1969, which builds on and spells out key philosophical implications of the film theory book.)[9]

From the early twenties until his forced exile from Germany in 1933, Kracauer published close to two thousand articles and reviews (about seven hundred on film), almost all in the *Frankfurter Zeitung*, a liberal daily of which he became feuilleton editor in 1924.[10] In this body of writings, film and cinema figure as part of a whole array of phenomena, ranging from the habitual and marginalized spaces of the modern metropolis (train stations, bars, homeless shelters, arcades); through objects of quotidian use (maps, inkwells, typewriters, suspenders, umbrellas); to the media and rituals of an emerging mass culture of leisure and consumption (photography, radio, advertisement, tourism, dance, revues, amusement parks, entertainment malls). Whether defined by the ephemeral glamor of distraction or the less conspicuous, normalized misery of the everyday, these phenomena attracted Kracauer to the degree that they eluded the optics of dominant bourgeois culture or were acknowledged by that culture only to be denounced as harbingers of moral and spiritual decline. Against pessimistic critiques of modern civilization and idealist assertions of lost values, Kracauer insisted that intellectuals should engage the yet unnamed, untheorized realities of contemporary life and try to register them in their material density and multiplicity, to read them as indexes of history in the making.

Kracauer's own engagement with the cinema was bound up with his philosophically and theologically motivated project to "determine the place" that the present "occupies in the historical process," a project that entailed a materialist inquiry into the meanings and directions of modernity.[11] Like few

other Weimar writers, Kracauer saw in film and cinema the matrix of a specifically modern episteme, at once an expression of and a medium for the experience of a "disintegrating" world.[12] For much as the cinema participated in and
advanced the process of modernization (mechanization, standardization, dis-
embedding of social relations), it also emerged as the single most accessible
institution in which the effects of modernization on human experience could
be acknowledged, recognized, negotiated, and perhaps reconfigured and transformed. Thus, in his more utopian moments, Kracauer understood the cinema as an alternative public sphere — alternative to both bourgeois institutions
of art, education, and culture and the traditional arenas of politics — a discursive horizon through which, however compromised by its capitalist foundations, something like an actual democratization of culture seemed to be taking shape: the possibility of a "self-representation of the masses subject to the
process of mechanization."[13] The cinema suggested this possibility not only
because it attracted and made visible to itself and society an emerging, heterogeneous mass public (consisting in large part of the mushrooming class of
white-collar workers); the cinema also offered an alternative because it engaged the contradictions of modernity at the level of the senses, the level at
which the impact of modern technology on human experience was most palpable and irreversible. In other words, the cinema's heuristic, cognitive function for a history of the present was bound up with its pivotal role in the
restructuring of sense perception, of the very conditions of experience and
subjectivity.

Kracauer discerned in cinema's decentering mode of reception ("distraction"), in its peculiar forms of mimetic identification and psychoperceptual
mobility (and, not least, the liberating anonymity of moviegoing), a practical
critique of the sovereign subject, of outdated notions of personality, interiority,
and self-identity, and of the traditional subject-object dichotomy. The critique
of the subject that Kracauer, Benjamin, and others sought to theorize through,
in, and for the cinema, however, has to be understood in more specific terms
than those by now familiar from poststructuralist recyclings of Nietzsche. The
crisis of the subject that mandated such a critique was precipitated by a particular historical experience: the experience of modernity as living on the brink
of catastrophe (rather than in the trajectory of progress, as which it had been
touted for decades), a catastrophe that threatened the very bases of day-to-day
existence. From the trauma of industrial warfare and mass death in World War
I, the failed revolution, and political assassinations; through the great inflation,
rationalization, labor struggles, and mass unemployment; to the remilitariza-
tion of German society and the rise of the National Socialists (to name just a
few of the cumulative disasters that became synonymous with the fate of the
Weimar Republic), the flip side of the liberating, exuberant topoi of Weimar

modernism was the widespread experience of violence, instability, and fear, magnified by the political volatility of an emergent mass society.

In this situation, the photographic media were playing an increasingly important role, as much from the long view of a philosophy of history as from the perspective of daily political battles and cultural trench warfare. As early as 1927, in his great essay on photography, Kracauer credits the medium with having "provoked the decisive confrontation [of consciousness with nature] in every field": "The turn to photography is the *go-for-broke game* of history."[14] As I will elaborate below, Kracauer analyzed the social uses and abuses of photography in terms of the fear, confrontation, and denial of death. The photographic media (illustrated magazines, newsreels, "society films") could advance society's frantic evasion of its material foundations ("the flight of the images is the flight from revolution and from death"[15]), but they could also translate their medium-specific affinities with contingency and temporality into a conscious aesthetic and political practice. Film could continue to lend itself to the circulation of outdated emotions, noble personalities, and armored bodies—thus transmuting the fears of modernity into new myths—but it could also realize its photographically based capacity for "stir[ring] up the elements of nature" to establish "the *provisional status* of all given configurations."[16] Like Benjamin, Kracauer invested the mass media's double-edged implication in the crisis of modernity with therapeutic or cathartic intentions: the hope that a public, and sensory, recognition or "innervation" (Benjamin's term) of contemporary reality could deflect the fatal course of history, so that the final catastrophe in this crisis could yet be averted.[17]

The concept of history underlying Kracauer's writings on film, mass culture, and modernity is no doubt tinged with an apocalyptic urgency, a perception of modernity as an accelerating process of the world going to pieces (*Weltzerfall*). Like Benjamin, Ernst Bloch, Leo Löwenthal, and others, Kracauer was part of a secular revival of Jewish Messianism (though he was more skeptical toward that tradition than most and gave it a distinctly Gnostic inflection).[18] In this mode, he refused to envision any real change as historically immanent (whether brought about through liberal reform or a socialist revolution); rather, it could only come with and as a total break. His redemptive project of exploring, recording, and archiving the scattered fragments of contemporary life was fueled by the utopian-nihilist idea that modernity had to be overcome—and would ultimately overcome itself—only by fully realizing its disintegrating and destructive potential: "America," the period's contested symbol of disenchanted modernity, "will disappear only when it completely discovers itself."[19] Paradoxically, the metaphysically inspired goal of transcending modernity turned increasingly into immanent critique, especially by the end of the 1920s, the more Kracauer immersed himself in the micropolitical analysis of contemporary mass culture — as the crucial site at which the battle over the fate of modernity, the *go-for-broke game* of history," was being fought. Whatever its theological roots, Kracauer's confrontation with the catastrophic features of Weimar modernity took on a radical political edge in his practice of film criticism as "social critique" and in his acute and relentless pinpointing of the discrepancies between reactionary cultural productions and the mounting crisis.[20] At the same time, he continued to single out efforts — in German, Soviet, French, and even Hollywood films — that resisted ideological complicity with nationalist and class fantasies and succeeded in keeping alive some of the cinema's alternative possibilities.

Theory of Film was published at a fundamentally different point in history: The all-out gamble of the historical process had been lost on an unprecedented scale, the catastrophe had happened, but the messiah had not come. With the triumph of fascism, brute nature, to use an image from Kracauer's photography essay, "[sat] down at the very table that consciousness had abandoned."[21] But fascism was eventually defeated, and Kracauer, unlike millions of others (including his mother and aunt), survived, if only, like so many, at the price of exile. In the wake of postwar affluence and cold war stability, the catastrophic features of capitalist industrial modernity were increasingly normalized or marginalized (both within Western societies and on a global scale) or, for that matter, aestheticized and spectacularized (as in Hollywood disaster films). The view of history that arises from the pages of *Theory of Film* no longer ticks to the countdown of a self-destructing modernity but keeps time with an "open-ended limitless world," the proverbial "flow of life."[22] The subject that seeks refuge in the movie theater no longer acts out the crisis of the Subject but has become the stoically cool, postapocalyptic "subject of survival" (in Heide Schlüpmann's words). And Kracauer's attempt, in the notorious epilogue to the book, to sketch "modern man's intellectual landscape" (287) could easily be construed as anticipating the postmodern, neoconservative topos of "the end of ideology" and other proclamations of the *posthistoire*.

One might say that history disappears from *Theory of Film* in a double repression: on the level of theory, inasmuch as the specifically modern(ist) moment of film and cinema is transmuted into a medium-specific affinity with physical, external, or visible reality; and, in the same move, on the level of intellectual biography, in that Kracauer seems to have cut himself off completely from his Weimar persona and the radical "love of cinema" that inspired him at that time.[23] (With a few minor exceptions, there are no references at all to his earlier texts, even in places, especially those concerning photography and the "photographic approach," that call out for such a genealogy.)[24] This double repression can be — and has been — linked to Kracauer's near elision of the trauma around which his "psychological history of German film," *From Caligari to Hitler* (1947), still revolved somewhat more explicitly: the unimaginable, systematic mass annihilation of European Jewry. In *Theory of Film*, Kracauer alludes to the Shoah only briefly, in the section entitled "The Head of the Medusa," where he mentions films made of the Nazi death camps as examples of how film, like Perseus's shield, could mirror unspeakable horrors "and thus incorporate into [the spectator's] memory the real face of things too dreadful to behold in reality" (306).[25] Proceeding from this passage, both Gertrud Koch and Heide Schlüpmann have argued that the impossibility of representing mass death, conjoined with the stubborn hope that film might be the medium to register that horror, constitutes the epistemic and ethical vanishing point of *Theory of Film*; the elided historical object of the book is not film as a phenomenon of late capitalism but, more specifically, the question of film after Auschwitz.[26]

The effort to restore this dimension of history *in* and *to* the book is supported by a second detour, relating to the history *of* the book. The project itself was actually conceived in the midst of the catastrophe, under the threat of annihilation — "during those months [in 1940/1941]," as Kracauer told Theodor W. Adorno in a later letter, "that we spent in anguish and misery in Marseille."[27] Like many other refugees, Kracauer and his wife Lili were stranded in the French port city waiting for papers to escape extradition by the Vichy government and to emigrate to the United States. Benjamin, whom Kracauer had known since 1924 and seen regularly during their years of exile in Paris, arrived in Marseille in mid-August and stayed through the end of September, up to his failed attempt to cross the Spanish border and his tragically premature suicide.[28] During that summer, Kracauer began taking "copious notes" toward a "book on film aesthetics,"[29] which Benjamin, shrewdly if a bit ungenerously, interpreted as a single-minded strategy of survival. Soma Morgenstern, novelist and former Vienna correspondent of the *Frankfurter Zeitung*, describes how he and Benjamin, on their way to the prefecture, ran into Kracauer, seated in front of a café, scribbling eagerly. At the end of the familiar desperate conversation about expired transit visas and the perpetually delayed French exit visa, Morgenstern recalls asking Kracauer, "What will become of us, Krac?" To which the latter replied, without thinking twice, "Soma, we will all have to kill ourselves here," and quickly returned to his notes. As they reached the prefecture, Benjamin turned to Morgenstern and remarked, "What will happen to us cannot be easily predicted. But of one thing I'm sure: if anyone will *not* kill himself, it's our friend Kracauer. After all, he has to finish writing his encyclopedia of film. And for that you need a long life."[30]

If Benjamin (according to Morgenstern) is right, and Kracauer's immersion into the project at this point represents a stubborn ruse of self-preservation, the strategy of disavowal involved is a rather curious one. For the fetishistic gesture that averts the gaze from the threat of annihilation onto the precious object that was to become a major book paradoxically embraces, in its conception of the cinematic experience, the very undoing of fetishistic wholeness, perfection, distance, and control. Kracauer incorporates the threat of annihilation, disintegration, and mortal fear into his film aesthetics — as a fundamental historical experience of modernity. He also incorporates his by-then dead friend's memory and legacy in the first major outline for the book, consisting of three fat notebooks dated November 16, 1940, after Benjamin's suicide and before Kracauer's own rescue. To the extent that they can be read as a coherent text, these notebooks take up Benjamin's vision of modernity at its bleakest, harking back to his early treatise on the *Origin of German Tragic Drama* (1925). This vision is adapted, however, not only to the medium of film but to the prospect of confronting life after the apocalypse.[31]

Kracauer did not return to the project until November 1948, after his narrow escape to the United States, after difficult years of settling in New York, after the publication of his *Caligari* book. Sources relating to this phase of the project include a "Preliminary Statement on a Study of Film Aesthetics" in English (November 6, 1948), a mixed English-German excerpt from the Marseille notebooks (May 8–12, 1949), and a "Tentative Outline" dated September 8, 1949, typed with marginalia recording critical comments by Adorno, Rudolf Arnheim, and Robert Warshow. Kracauer signed an advance contract with Oxford University Press in August 1949. The first full-length draft of the book, 192 typed pages in English, was probably written in 1954, when Kracauer received another grant. While this lengthy essay contains some of the basic arguments of the later book, it hardly attempts to forge them into generalizable oppositions (such as the "realistic" versus the "formative tendency"). Kracauer did not try to systematize in this manner until 1955, in response to readings from film historian Arthur Knight and Eric Larrabee, his editor at Oxford University Press. Only then did he begin to organize and reorganize the material in what he referred to as his "syllabus," of which there are three draft versions and several schematic synopses. During this last phase, the process of revision assumes an anxious, if not obsessive, quality that contrasts with the final text's aspiration to a detached, Olympian vision and its display of the well-turned, idiomatic phrase.[32]

Had it been completed at a time closer to the stage of its conception, Kracauer's virtual book on film aesthetics would have gone a long way toward restoring the history that seems to have disappeared in the later book. For the unpublished material, especially the Marseille notebooks (including summaries and proposals dating from 1948 and 1949), furnishes a bridge between *Theory of Film* and Kracauer's Weimar writings. It thus helps reconstitute a violently fractured intellectual biography. What is more, the way in which the virtual book both modifies and preserves the defeated, lost perspective of the Weimar essays allows us to recast and rehistoricize key concepts of the book as published. I will try here to trace some of the hidden lineages that have shaped and, I believe, will reactualize the argument of the book.

At first sight, the Marseille notebooks suggest a clear break with the concerns of Kracauer's earlier writings on film and mass culture: "The dimension which defines the phenomenon of film at its core lies below the dimension in which political and social events take place."[33] If, before 1933, Kracauer had attempted to avert the defeat of German democracy on the level of a journalistic (that is, public and local) critique of ideology and society, he now retreats onto a more general, philosophical plane. The eschatological urgency of his early essays gives way to a different temporality: film is no longer the medium of a self-reflecting, self-sublating, self-destructing modernity as the vanishing point of history but rather figures as the episteme of a postmodern, postmetaphysical, postanthropocentric universe of death. Paradoxically, this radical shift of perspective still makes the Marseille notebooks a more historically conscious project than the later book. For one thing, Kracauer was planning to develop his key categories in three chapters on early film history, in a manner quite distinct from the analogous move in Theory of Film: Instead of the infamous section on the "two main tendencies" (Lumière versus Méliès, realistic versus formative), there was to be an emphasis on early cinema's diversity of genres and appeals and on preclassical modes of film experience that have more recently been theorized in terms of a "cinema of attractions" and an "aesthetic of astonishment."[34] For another, despite the initial disclaimer, the Marseille notebooks resume Kracauer's concern with the cinema's role in the crisis and restructuring of subjectivity, as part of an irreversible transformation and reconfiguration of social relations. In other words, while proleptically shifting to a different time and temporality, the philosophical perspective of the virtual "Theory of Film" is still anchored in the historical experience of modernity, revolving around the traumatic impact of technology, the emergence of mass society, and the threat of mass annihilation.

What the trajectory of Weimar through Marseille illuminates is that, even in the published book, Kracauer's concept of realism — his insistence on film's affinity with "material," "physical," "external reality," "existence," and "environment" — is bound up with the problematic of the subject (rather than simply film's referential relation to the material world). This concern underpins Kracauer's attempts, throughout the notebooks, to delineate the particular ways in which film in its "basic layer" (Grundschicht) engages the "material dimension." While somewhat underconceptualized, the notion of the material dimension is far more comprehensive than the term "physical reality" that appears to govern the later book; it certainly does not reduce to the "visible world around us" (p. xlix). When Kracauer contends that, "in contrast with the theater, . . . film mixes the *whole world* into play, be that world real or imagined," he includes not only a limitless range of objects of representation but also the basic cinematic materials: "the whole world in every sense: from the beginning film strove toward sound, speech, color" (MN, 1:16). Kracauer's concern is not with authenticity or verisimilitude but rather with film's ability to discover and articulate materiality, to enact "the process of materialization" (MN, 2:9). This is to say, his love of cinema pivots on the aesthetic possibilities of film to stage, in a sensory and imaginative form, a fundamental experience of the twentieth century — an experience that has been variously described in terms of reification and alienation, fragmentation and loss, but that for Kracauer no less held a significant share of exhilarating and liberatory impulses.

Film "enacts the historical turn to materiality," Kracauer asserts throughout the Marseille notebooks, because like hardly any other art form it has the ability to confront "intention with being," with existence, facticity, and contingency. The direction of this confrontation is downward ("film looks *under* the table" [MN, 1:5]), with the effect of deflating myths and ideals, conventions and hierarchies that have lost their material basis, if they ever had one, in social reality — an effect for which Kracauer uses the shorthand *dégonflage*.[35] As in his Weimar writings, film's materialist capability not only undercuts the sovereign subject of bourgeois ideology but with it a larger anthropocentric worldview that presumes to impose meaning and control upon a world that increasingly defies traditional distinctions between the human and the nonhuman, the living and the mechanical, the unique (integrated, inner-directed) individual and the mass subject, civilization and barbarism. Hence his polemic against the theater (bourgeois drama rather than popular and experimental forms) and against films that adapt dramatic standards of individual psychology, thorough motivation, and closure; hence his preoccupation with the actor in film (one of the earliest chapters in draft form) as a "thing among things," sharing the screen with inanimate objects come to life; and hence his interest in early cinema ("Horses Galloping," "Archaic Panorama"), its scientific and inventorizing drives, its relative "indifference" vis-à-vis a given hierarchy of objects, its "jumble" of subjects and styles.

Most effectively, the cinema undermines idealist and anthropocentric positions on the level of reception, in the ways it engages the material reality of the spectator — the human being "with skin and hair [*mit Haut und Haar*]." In contrast to the "referential subject of the theater," the spiritually determined and psychologically integrated individual Kracauer dubs "the human being in long shot" (*Totale*), film addresses its viewer primarily as a corporeal

Wohin?   BEMERKUNGEN   BEISPIELE:

1

The first double-page of Siegfried Kracauer's Marseille notebooks. Photo: Deutsches Literaturarchiv, Marbach am Neckar.

16. XI. 40

EINLEITUNG

A) Eine Darstellung des Inhaltsrahmens des Films bezieht ihren Reiz aus der __Natur seines Materials__ wegen Schwierigkeiten.

1) Die Fülle des Filma : Je mehr man kennt, desto unerschöpflicher scheint ihre Menge zu sein : es ist, als ob man in den gestirnten Nachthimmel sähe.

Man sieht diese Filme noch nicht alle zu gleicher Zeit.

Viele von ihnen sind zerstört oder werden wie noch möglich laufend. Hinweis auf die Cinémathèques

[Marginal left:] Cinémathèque

[Marginal right:] Vorschlag?: Katharisches Version d. „Freudlose Gasse"

2) Einen Film sich so zu merken, daß man ihr wirklich durchstimmen können, ist es wirklich schwer. Der Film ist kein Stück. Das man nur zergliedern könnte. Erinnerung an die Mit-Aufgaben d Zeugenaussagen : auch der Talbestand des Films aufgezeichnet.

[Marginal left:] 3) Angaben über Herstellung abzuwägen

Es Original : festen Talbestand Verständnis Ke Brasillach. Vincent (s. Kollektion) Hinweis auf meine KOLLEKTION.

[Marginal right:] Endlich suchen!

B) Zur Möglichkeit einer Geschichte des Films

1) Die Gründung der Cinémathèques. Sie vollzieht sich wunderfarbte ihrer Füll ungefähr für in die Jahre 33 - 34. Was besagt ihre Entstehung? Daß der Film als historisches Phänomen zu werden begann — werden will.

[Boxed:] Film als historisches Phänomen.

[Marginal right:] Wann sind die Cinémathèques entstanden?

2) Das heißt nicht, daß man bereits seine Geschichte schreiben könne. Der Film ist noch keine 50 Jahre alt, seine technische Entwicklung noch im Fluß (Farbe, Plastik) das noch abzuschließen.

— Nur die Stummfilme liegt vergangaben aus, wenn man es nicht recht zu tun in die Gegenwart finden, um historisch fortschritt zu sein.

3) Diese These zu illustrieren an der Filmgeschichte von Bra u Vincent. Ihre Disposition:

Bra geht die historisch neuen Material Fruchtbare ; Vin schreibt die Filmgeschichte der verschiedenen Produzentenländer.

Je mehr sie sich der Gegenwart nähern, desto leichter werden sie — die Geschichte zerfällt in die Entwicklung einzelner Regisseure, in eine pure Aufzählung, auch geschichtlichen

[Marginal left:] Gründungszeit der Cinémathèques

[Marginal right:] Bei spiele prüfen!

[Marginal bottom left:] 72 3562

19. November 1940

(A)

1) Pferdegalopp
2) Archaisches Panorama
3) . Film d'ART"
4) Mit Haut und Haaren (Musik / Propaganda)
5) Grundsehicht (Photographie / Das Grauen / Groteske)
6) Grundschicht, von Bedeutung angestrahlt
7) Griffith

(B)

8) Die Filmhandlung ist endlos (Gag / Zufall)
9) Documentaire und Spielfilm
10) Bild - Wort - Farbe →
11) Grammatik / 2-3 Filmanalysen: Montage, Figuren, Übergänge usw.
12) Tragödie und Historie

(C)

13) Panorama von Spielfilmen
14) Produzenten - Publikum - Kinos
15) Film und Gesellschaft
   a) Querschnitt: STARWESEN / DARSTELLERTYPEN
   b) Längsschnitt: - durch die deutsche Entwicklung
16) Nationale Charaktere
17) Handlung unter der Handlung

(D)

18) Miteinander: Ince / Schweden / Pagnol
19) Bewegung : Herrschaft über Technik zu Zeichenfreu, RC., Avantgarde
20) Groteske → Chaplin — David gegen Goliath - Märchen
21) Degonflage, aus Sein gegen Intention (Strohheim)
22) Massen - bei den Russen zum Sinn entwickelt
23) Das materielle Grauen : zum Spiel !

24) Kermesse funèbre (Danse macabre?)
    Russische Manen zu ...
    Film operateure nehmen den Krieg auf.
    Pferdegalopp .

2
Draft table of contents for Kracauer's book on film aesthetics. Photo: Deutsches Literaturarchiv, Marbach am Neckar.

being. "The material elements that present themselves in film directly stimulate the *material layers* of the human being: his nerves, his senses, his entire
physiological substance." While traditional theater maintains perspectival unity
and tends to mediate emotional responses with consciousness, the cinema
assaults the viewer on the level of sensory, bodily perception, shattering the
boundaries of individual identity: "The 'ego' [*Ich*] of the human being assigned to film is subject to *permanent dissolution*, is incessantly exploded by
material phenomena" (MN, 1:23).

Nothing could be further from more recent attempts to theorize cinematic spectatorship in terms of the pleasures of perceptual (imaginary, disembodied) mastery and identification, or for that matter, from cognitivist conceptions of film viewing as an operation of "scanning," of processing hypotheses
relevant for the construction of a story from the film's representational materials.[36] Kracauer participates in an alternative tradition that locates the film
experience in psychic regions closer to those explored by Freud in *Beyond the
Pleasure Principle* (1920), particularly through concepts of shock, primary
masochism, and the death drive.[37] Benjamin, theorizing the shock experience
as the signature of technological modernity, stresses the defensive mechanism
triggered by an increased exposure to shock, its numbing and anaesthetizing
effects on human consciousness and the concomitant increase in phan-
tasmagoric thrills designed to pierce that protective shield.[38] Kracauer, by contrast, seems more interested in the possibilities of masochistic self-abandonment and dissociation, in the cinema's ability to subject the viewer, in an
institutionally bounded form of play, to encounters with contingency, lack of
control, and otherness. The object of such play, however, is not an aesthetic-
ization of horror and violence, let alone a cult of death, but an aesthetic
experience on a par with the historical crisis of experience.

Complementing the concepts of *shock* and *dégonflage* in the Marseille
notebooks is the concept of *chance*; the genre that brings these terms together
in an exemplary way is American slapstick comedy, to which Kracauer refers
by the German term "*Groteske*." From his earliest reviews, slapstick comedy,
with its physicality and kinetic energy, its clashes between human beings
turned into things and objects assuming a life of their own, ranked high in his
attempt to theorize film as a discourse of modernity. Extolling shorts of the
Mack Sennett and Hal Roach variety over pretentious feature films (mostly of
German origin), Kracauer perceived in slapstick comedy an anarchistic critique of, and relief from, the discipline of capitalist rationalization and Tay-
lorized work processes.[39] When he resumes his discussion of slapstick in the
Marseille notebooks, this reflexive and critical dimension seems to have re-
ceded; what matters now is the genre's systematic confrontation of intentionality with "material life at its crudest" ("the shock troops of unconquered

nature"). The sole purpose of the slapstick genre is "to perform games in the material dimension" (MN, 1:39f.). With its "shock-like," "discontinuous" sequence of gags, which Kracauer compares to the "sputtering of a machine gun," slapstick comedy not only affects the viewer "with skin and hair," riddling fictions of an integral, identical subject with the involuntary mechanics of laughter; it also counters the protocols of narrative development and closure with patterns of seriality and a potentially "endless action" (MN, 2:2–3).

The games slapstick comedy performs take place "on the brink of the abyss" (MN, 1:39); the genre engages, in a ludic form, the threat of annihilation. "The leitmotif of slapstick comedy is the play with danger, with catastrophe, and its prevention in the nick of time" (MN 1:37). The last-minute rescue in slapstick comedy, as Kracauer points out, is not brought about by divine intervention or melodramatic coincidence, but simply by chance, by accident—the same principle that sets into play the anarchic transactions between people and things in the first place. Like shock, chance for Kracauer is a historical category, another signature of modernity: It arises with "the entry of the masses into history," with the emergence of a public sphere that is unpredictable and volatile, with public spaces such as the urban street and movie theaters (MN, 2:28–30). The concept of chance, which affiliates Kracauer with both the surrealists and, proleptically, a figure like John Cage, emerges as a historicophilosophical alternative to the closed dramaturgy of fate or destiny (which Kracauer associates with the work of Fritz Lang); in fact, chance alone offers a tiny window, at once hope and obligation, of survival, of continuing life after the grand metaphysical stakes have been lost.

As in his earlier writings on Chaplin, Kracauer links the comic rescue in the nick of time to the rescue in the fairy tale, the hero's escape against all odds, and the counterfactual victory of the weak and powerless over brute force (David versus Goliath). In both genres, the rescue is a happy ending under erasure, containing both the appeal of a utopian humanity and its impossibility, the realization that "the fairy tale does not last, that the world is the world, and that home [die Heimat] is not home."[40] But this realization also entails the insight that the world "could be different and still continues to exist."[41] In the Marseille notebooks, Kracauer reads the happy endings of Chaplin's films as injunctions that say, "we must go on living" (MN, 2:33), and that entail reimagining the conditions of experience, memory, and interaction after the catastrophe.

While the notion of chance and Kracauer's defense of happy endings under erasure have survived into the published Theory of Film (as has the David versus Goliath motif), slapstick comedy no longer commands the paradigmatic significance it had in the earlier version. The fact that it ended by and large with the silent era—a point Kracauer dwells on in relation to the

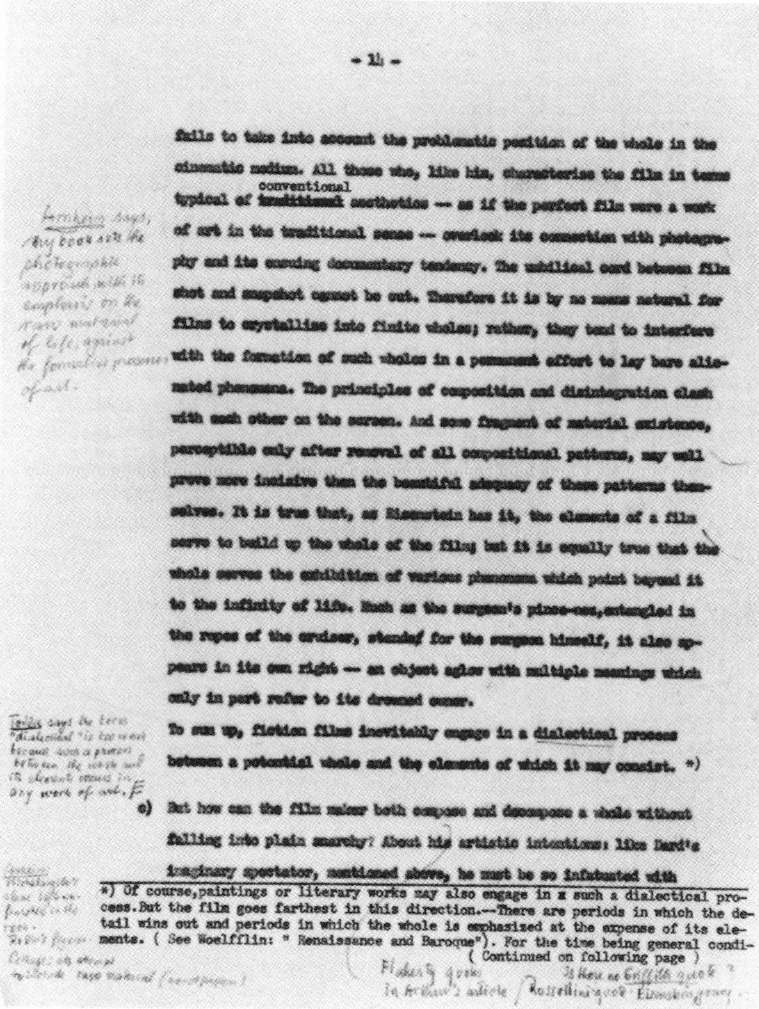

- 14 -

fails to take into account the problematic position of the whole in the cinematic medium. All those who, like him, characterise the film in terms typical of ~~traditional~~ conventional aesthetics — as if the perfect film were a work of art in the traditional sense — overlook its connection with photography and its ensuing documentary tendency. The umbilical cord between film shot and snapshot cannot be cut. Therefore it is by no means natural for films to crystallise into finite wholes; rather, they tend to interfere with the formation of such wholes in a permanent effort to lay bare alienated phenomena. The principles of composition and disintegration clash with each other on the screen. And some fragment of material existence, perceptible only after removal of all compositional patterns, may well prove more incisive than the beautiful adequacy of these patterns themselves. It is true that, as Eisenstein has it, the elements of a film serve to build up the whole of the film; but it is equally true that the whole serves the exhibition of various phenomena which point beyond it to the infinity of life. Much as the surgeon's pince-nez, entangled in the ropes of the cruiser, stands for the surgeon himself, it also appears in its own right — an object aglow with multiple meanings which only in part refer to its drowned owner.

To sum up, fiction films inevitably engage in a dialectical process between a potential whole and the elements of which it may consist. *)

c) But how can the film maker both compose and decompose a whole without falling into plain anarchy? About his artistic intentions: like Dard's imaginary spectator, mentioned above, he must be so infatuated with

*) Of course, paintings or literary works may also engage in x such a dialectical process. But the film goes farthest in this direction.—There are periods in which the detail wins out and periods in which the whole is emphasized at the expense of its elements. (See Woelfflin: " Renaissance and Baroque"). For the time being general condi-

(Continued on following page)

Arnheim says; My book sets the photographic approach with its emphasis on the raw material of life, against the formative process of art.
Tyler says the term "dialectical" is too weak because such a process between the whole and its elements occurs in any work of art. F
Flaherty quote in Arnheim's article / Rossellini quote
Is there no Griffith quote?

3
From Kracauer's "Tentative Outline," 8 Sept. 1949. Photo: Deutsches Literaturarchiv, Marbach am Neckar.

question of sound — is not the only reason for this shift. Rather, the genre's gamble with catastrophe, like the idea of the photographic turn as the "go-for-broke game of history," could no longer be thought through to the end, not even imagined on the level of aesthetics. What is marginalized along with slapstick comedy is Kracauer's earlier concern with the problematic of death, with film's ability to stage encounters with horror, mortality, and the other. The desire for film to "include the death's head beneath the face" — the allegorical impulse from Benjamin's *Trauerspiel* book — had presided over the Marseille project as an epigraph and a never realized final chapter, to be called, variably, "Kermesse funèbre," "Danse macabre," or "The death's head."[42] Kracauer's 1949 outline specifies that this chapter was to center "around an analysis of DEATH DAY, a short assembled from Eisenstein's Mexican material" and asserts that it "will not only summarize the whole of the book but formulate certain ultimate conclusions." In an "attempt at general organization" dated November 1954, the last chapter heading still reads, "'Death Day' and (contemporary Am. Film)," followed by a note in which Kracauer records discussing the Eisenstein film with Jay Leyda as late as January 6, 1955. But in the contents page dated January 15, 1955, the title of the last chapter has been changed to "Epilogue: The redemption of physical existence."[43]

The historical rupture of the Holocaust irrevocably changed the terms under which film could still be imagined as a publicly available medium for experiencing and acknowledging the precariousness of the sovereign, identical self. If the death of the subject, troped in various ways by the 1920s modernists, still referred to a nineteenth-century conception of the individual, the Holocaust presented the problematic of what Edith Wyschogrod calls "manmade mass death" in a world historically unprecedented dimension: the possibility of the annihilation of a collective subject, an entire genus.[44] *Theory of Film* assumes the aporias of that history, but from its postapocalyptic landscape even the traces of the annihilated subject seem to have been effaced. The utopian motif of the last-minute rescue (*Rettung*) — the rescue of suffering individuals, of a people threatened with annihilation — has given way to a more modest project of redemption (*Errettung*), a term that no longer promises critical-allegorical readings (as in Kracauer's Weimar texts) but rather seems to entail a mimetic adaptation to the world of things. Whether we read this retreat as a lack of "indignation about reification" (as Adorno does in his ambivalent homage to Kracauer) or as linked to the theological motif of an "anamnestic solidarity with the dead" (as Koch suggests), a sense of displacement is undeniable.[45]

And yet, *Theory of Film* is fully worth reading and fully relevant to a material aesthetics of cinema today, in part because that displacement is not complete, because there are traces, and more than traces, of history — both of the earlier project and of history — in the published book. This is particularly the case for Kracauer's insistence on "the photographic approach," which is often misread as ordaining a "naively realist" theory of film. As I remarked initially, Kracauer's investment in the photographic basis of film does not rest on the iconicity of the photographic sign, at least not in the narrow sense of a literal resemblance or analogy with a self-identical object. Nor, for that matter, does he conceive of the indexical, the photochemical bond that links image and referent, in any positivist way as merely anchoring the analogical "truth" of the representation. Rather, the same indexicality that allows photographic film to record and figure the world also inscribes the image with moments of temporality and contingency that *dis*figure the representation. If Kracauer seeks to ground his film aesthetics in the medium of photography, it is because photographic representation has the perplexing ability not only to re-semble the world it depicts but also to render it strange, to destroy habitual fictions of self-identity and familiarity. It is in this sense that the slippery term "affinity" (of the medium with material reality) includes both film's ability to *record* and its potential to *reveal* something in relation to that world.[46]

The chapter on photography in *Theory of Film* belongs to the earliest layers of the text and provides the strongest link with Kracauer's Weimar writings.[47] To illustrate his notion of the photographic approach, he quotes a passage from Proust's *The Guermantes Way*, in which the narrator, after a long absence, enters, unannounced, the drawing room of his grandmother. Instead of the beloved per-son, he sees "sitting on the sofa, beneath the lamp, red-faced, heavy and common, sick, lost in thought, following the lines of a book with eyes that seemed hardly sane, a dejected old woman whom I did not know." Proust's narrator compares this terrifying sight of his grandmother to a photograph, the opposite of a vision charged with familiarity, intimacy, and memory. The arbitrary, split-second expo-sure through the photographic apparatus, which for a moment suspends habit, interpretation, and intention, epitomizes the emotionally detached view of a stranger, of "eyes that obviate our love."[48] While Kracauer revises Proust regarding the conscious and unconscious factors that condition even the most automatic photographs (the limit case being aerial reconnaissance photos), he stresses the insight into the differential moment, the blind spot of mechanical recording that unsettles and defies our habitual modes of seeing or, rather, not-seeing. What the camera, unlike the loving grandson, sees and what Kracauer barely names is the grandmother's closeness to death. It is no coincidence that Kracauer goes on to link the photographic approach to a "state of alienation," to a psychic disposition of melancholy and self-estrangement. This disposition, however, advances "identi-fication with all kinds of objects": it makes the individual "lose himself in the incidental configurations of his environment, absorbing them with a disinterested intensity no longer determined by his previous preferences" (p. 17).[49]

These themes resonate with the concerns of Kracauer's early essay, "Photography," which is one of the curiously unmentioned intertexts of *Theory of Film* but one that is key to understanding how Kracauer's notion of "physical reality" or "camera-reality" is still a fundamentally historical category. In the 1927 essay, the image of the grandmother appears in juxtaposition with another kind of image, the photograph of a "demonic diva," twenty-four years old, on the cover of an illustrated magazine. Kracauer reads the photograph of the film star as exemplary of the new culture of industrial image production that proliferates in the illustrated magazines and newsreels. This "blizzard" (*Schneegestöber*) of photographic images is indifferent toward the particular meanings and history of the things portrayed; instead, it extends laterally to create a presence effect of imperial, global dimensions. Photographibility has become the condition under which reality is constituted and perceived: "The world itself has taken on a 'photographic face.'"[50] Kracauer analyzes society's devouring of photographic images as a sign of the fear of death and, simultaneously, its repression. Seeking to eternalize its objects in all spatial dimensions, however, the photographic present does not banish the thought of death but has succumbed to it all the more.

The photograph of the grandmother, also at the age of twenty-four, both extends and complicates this critique. Kracauer contrasts the photographic image of the grandmother (likely his own) with the "memory image," which is ultimately condensed in the "monogram of a remembered life." For those who still knew the grandmother, the memory image fleshes out and revises the photographic image. But later generations perceive in the photograph of the grandmother only a specter in an outmoded costume, a bad amalgamation of disintegrated elements. It is not the preserved presence of the grandmother that moves the beholder but, on the contrary, her reduction to a spatialized, arbitrary configuration of time. This is what "makes the beholder of old photographs shudder" and makes the grandchildren giggle in defense. Like Proust's involuntary sight of his grandmother, the photograph of Kracauer's is disturbing because it alienates both object and beholder, because it ruptures the web of intimacy, memory, and interpretation. What makes the beholder shudder is ultimately the shock of his or her own material contingency and temporality: "Those things once clung to us like our skin, and this is how our property still clings to us today. Nothing of these contains us, and the photograph gathers fragments around a nothing."[51] The photograph thus in fact may trigger, rather than prevent, a momentary encounter with mortality, an awareness of a history that does not include us. It is in such moments of almost physical recognition that Kracauer grants photography the potential to offer an antidote to its own positivist ideology.

By the end of the essay, the very negativity of photography, its role in corroding the "memory image," assumes a key function in the historical confrontation of human consciousness with nature. For photography provides a "general inventory," a "central archive" that assembles "in effigy the last elements of a nature alienated from meaning." This "unexamined *foundation of nature*" includes, above all, the reality of a society generated by capitalist production, a "reality that has slipped away from [consciousness]." In reflecting this reality in its randomness and disorder, by suspending "every habitual relationship among the elements of nature," photography can assist consciousness in pointing up the provisionality of all given, presumably natural, arrangements. Kracauer finds this possibility prefigured in the works of Kafka, which he invokes — along with the fragmentary logic of dreams — to suggest ways in which film, playing games "with the pieces of disjointed nature," could turn photography's radical potential into an aesthetic and political practice.[52]

Yet Proust, rather than Kafka, is the literary figure presiding over *Theory of Film* (as over the posthumously published *History*), and the late Kracauer seems more concerned with the "continuum" of material life than with modernist practices of discontinuity, fragmentation, and negation. As in the 1927 essay, photography is seen as a medium of alienation or estrangement, thus allowing for both expression and enactment of a particular historical experience.[53] But if the early Kracauer discerned film's potential to radicalize photographic negativity in its constructive and syntactic procedures (techniques of framing and editing), he now locates the principle of cinematic alienation *within* the unit of the shot. As Schlüpmann points out, the single frame becomes the basis of montage because it already contains, *in nuce*, the disjuncture or difference that makes for montage: "The estranged picture of the grandmother that presents itself to the Proustian narrator is itself already a continuum which emanates from an interruption, namely the interruption of the normal process of vision."[54]

Unlike Sergei Eisenstein (who is the subject of a running polemic in *Theory of Film*), Kracauer does not conceive of this montage principle within the shot as a compositional effect (for instance, a graphic conflict within the frame),[55] but as an effect of de-composition — of a fissure between psyche and physis that is made visible by the photographic apparatus and from which a materialist film aesthetics takes its cue. The difference that erupts within the image is not one between minimal units within an oppositional system of signs (the realm of semiotics) but one between discourse and the realm of material contingency, between the implied horizon of our "habits of seeing," structured by language, narrative, identification, and intentionality, and that which perpetually eludes and confounds such structuring. Nor does photographic alienation simply destroy or set aside, let alone dialectically sublate, habitual vision. Rather, as Kracauer says regarding the same passage in *His-*

tory, Marcel's troubling vision makes for a kind of "palimpsest," in which the stranger's observations are "superimposed upon the lover's temporarily effaced inscription." He goes on to compare this palimpsestic vision with the disjunctive temporality of the experience of "exile" and of "extra-territoriality," in other words, with a diasporic sensibility.[56]

The fissure that erupts within the filmic image still revolves, at whatever remove, around the question of the subject. Accordingly, the photographic qualities that bring these disjunctures into play register only at the level of reception, as an effect on the viewer. I would not go as far as to call *Theory of Film* an aesthetics of reception, although the earlier versions certainly point in that direction. In the 1960 book, the Marseille notebooks' systematic reflections on the "referential subject" of film are distilled into a single chapter on "The Spectator," and the notion of the "basic layer," which in the 1940s included the human being with "skin and hair," is ontologized into "basic properties of the medium." And yet, when Kracauer lists one example and aspect after another of film's affinity with "physical existence" or "physical reality," he more often than not describes these moments in terms of their effect on the viewer, as the experiential instance of the fractured, "shrinking" subject.

Among the particular ways in which the cinema affects its viewer, Kracauer continues to stress the physiological impact of film, including moments of shock, panic, and suspense and kinesthetically induced reflexes. Whether it is the "compulsory attractiveness" of movement or the impact of material phenomena never seen before (or never seen in this particular way), the film experience calls into play "not so much [the spectator's] power of reasoning as his visceral faculties," his "sense organs" (not just vision and hearing), as well as "his innate curiosity" pp. 158f., that is, the twin drives of scopophilia and epistemophilia. Consequently, the psychoperceptual process that Kracauer is concerned with is not one of identification with individual characters and the narrating gaze of the camera but, in a different conscious or subconscious register, a form of mimetic identification that pulls the viewer into the film and dissociates rather than integrates the spectatorial self. "In the theater I am always I," Kracauer quotes an anonymous French woman saying , "but in the cinema I dissolve into all things and beings."[57] By the same token, this state of self-abandonment and dissociation becomes the condition of a perceptual movement in the opposite direction, away from the film, when a material detail assumes a life of its own and triggers in the viewer associations, "memories of the senses," and "cataracts of indistinct fantasies and inchoate thoughts" that return the "absentee dreamer" to forgotten layers of the self (pp. 165–66). Film viewing thus not only requires a "mobile self," as Kracauer says of the historian's "job of sightseeing," but it also provides a framework for mobilizing the self.

With its interplay of alienating and mimetic effects, the cinema "assists us in discovering the material world with its psychophysical correspondences," a world that "we are free to experience . . . because we are fragmentized" (p. 300). The concept of "psychophysical correspondences," through which Kracauer resumes his earlier interest in what we might call a negative physiognomy, ranges from Proust's mystical (gnostic) speculations about how objects retain traces of past looks, events, and habits (and therefore can induce moments of *mémoire involontaire*) to Benjamin's metaphor of an "optical unconscious." As I have elaborated elsewhere, the trope of the "optical unconscious" hovers between a celebration of the human sensorium's imbrication with technology ("innervation") and a persistence, in Benjamin's writing, of the model of auratic experience, the idea of investing a phenomenon "with the capability of returning the gaze."[58] For both Kracauer and Benjamin, the only historically and politically viable method of adapting the magic of Proust's madeleine for postbourgeois society is through the alienating intervention of the apparatus. The technically mediated gaze of dead things — furniture, clothes, architecture — may "spirit" the viewer "away into the lumber room of his private self" (p. 56), but this is not a comfortable resting place, let alone cause for nostalgia.[59] For Kracauer, even more than for Benjamin, the nature that returns the gaze through the camera's defamiliarizing lens is an alien *physis*, which comes across in the very passage that refers to Benjamin's account of the "optical unconscious": "Any huge close-up reveals new and unsuspected formations of matter; skin textures are reminiscent of aerial photographs, eyes turn into lakes or volcanic craters. Such images blow up our environment in a double sense: they enlarge it literally; and in doing so, they blast the prison of conventional reality, opening up expanses which we have explored at best in dreams before" (p. 48). While echoing the avant-gardist, iconoclastic, liberatory thrust of the "optical unconscious" in Benjamin's artwork essay, this passage suggests that the dreamworld film allows us to explore may well be one of nightmares.

And yet, if Kracauer's notion of "psychophysical correspondences" gravitates toward the melancholic, haunting, uncanny side of such encounters, it no longer entails the sense of crisis, of demonic self-confrontation that one finds in his Weimar writings and, for that matter, in Benjamin's speculations on the "aura."[60] The alienated physis may still return the gaze and may jolt the viewer from/into/with a long forgotten past, but the wounding, unsettling effect no longer translates into any allegorical meaning. Kracauer repeatedly invokes Proust's image of the "ghostly trees that seem to impart a message to him,"[61] an image that serves ultimately to distinguish film's capability of triggering involuntary memories from the language-bound elaboration of memories in the novel: "[Proust's] affinity for the cinema makes him sensitive to transient impressions, such as the three trees which look familiar to him; but when he identifies the trees as yet undeciphered phantoms of the past 'appealing to me to take them with me, to bring them back to life' he exchanges the world of cinema for dimensions alien to it" (pp. 238–39). Kracauer wants those trees to remain trees, rather than "rebuses" or decipherable messages. If cinema has the power to stage encounters with the other, it can also, like no other medium, register material phenomena in their otherness, in their opaque singularity. "Snatched from transient life, they [these ideograms] not only challenge the spectator to penetrate their secret but, perhaps even more insistently, request him to preserve them as the irreplaceable images they are" (p. 257).

During the Weimar period, Kracauer's attention to the "surface," as the site where contemporary reality appeared in an iridescent and contradictory multiplicity, was still coupled with the ideal of "transparency" (a term of rather more theological than logical valence); accordingly, the project of registering and transcribing the surface phenomena of everyday life was often linked to an allegorizing mode of reading and critiques of ideology.[62] In *Theory of Film*, Kracauer is concerned with surface reality, "the outer skin of things" (Artaud, quoted below, p. 189), the "flow of life" as the locus of opacity and indeterminacy — not just a multiplicity and changeability of meanings but the possibility of a basic indifference to sense and legibility. This "return of an opaque thisness," to adapt Friedrich Kittler's phrase, is not necessarily a romantic "nostalgia for life as such" (p. 169), nor is it, as Adorno imputes, a yearning for "things" in a "state of innocence."[63] To be sure, Kracauer speaks of film's ability to capture "nature in the raw," to discover "physical existence in its endlessness," and he repeatedly insists on a "resemblance between cinematic and scientific procedures" (pp. 68, 71, 52). But the fringe of indeterminacy that surrounds "camera-reality" is as much a product of overdetermination as it is one of underexposure: It is the aura of history's vast refuse or debris, the snowy air reflecting the perpetual blizzard of media images and sounds, the "hyperindexicality" that at once distinguishes and threatens to defeat cinematic representation.[64]

In her essay on Freud's and Etienne-Jules Marey's distrust of the cinema, Mary Ann Doane links Kracauer's alarm over "photography's and film's inscription of a spatial and temporal continuum without a gap, of a 'blizzard' or 'flood' of images," to widespread "anxieties of total representation generated by the new technological media." This may or may not be the case for Kracauer in 1927, but in the 1960 book the cinema's (initial) penchant for hyperindexicality, its striving "for the status of total record," and its "refusal of a distinction or differentiation that would insure legibility" provokes anything *but* anxiety.[65] The late Kracauer confronts, if not embraces, the cinema's pull toward material contingency with a remarkable stoicism, a disposition that Heidegger, around the same time though from a different political trajectory, referred to as "*Gelassenheit.*"[66] Helmut Lethen has called attention to the ways in which Kracauer participates in the topos of "coldness" (or "ice-age folk-lore") common in avant-garde intellectual discourse on modernity from the 1920s on.[67] The "cooling process" Kracauer observes in his epilogue is "irre-versible"—the blizzard will never cease—but this is "the world that is ours," and film has "the power of deepening and rendering more intimate 'our rela-tion to this Earth which is our habitat' [Gabriel Marcel]" (pp. 295f., 304). Occasionally, the snow will melt or reconfigure itself, and the "blind drive of things" (Laffay) will turn up "random coincidences" and "unforeseeable possi-bilities" (pp. 58, 138, 170). Whether this sensibility connects Kracauer "sub-terraneously" with postmodern theories, as Lethen suggests, or whether it is the discontinuous legacy of his own stubborn brand of modernism, the mech-anisms by which the cinema yields moments of chance, improvisation, and unpredictability are closely related to its photographic affinity with contin-gency, otherness, and death. It is no coincidence that the section on "Mo-ments of Everyday Life," on film's transcultural ability to explore "the ordinary business of living," is followed by the section on "The Head of Medusa," on film's ability to "incorporate" into our memory the horror of industrialized mass killing and dying.

Kracauer's insistence on indeterminacy should not be understood as a romantic defense of the irrational nor as an abdication of principles of coher-ence and intelligibility. What is at stake is the possibility of a "split-second meaninglessness," as the placeholder of an otherness that resists unequivocal understanding and total subsumption.[68] What is also at stake is the ability of the particular, the detail, the incident, to take on a life of its own, to precipi-tate processes in the viewer that may not be entirely controlled by the film. These twin concerns are at the core of Kracauer's critique of the hegemony of narrative, as of the hegemony of dialogue and vocality in the realm of sound—that is, his critique of any attempt to subordinate the material, sensory qualities of film to a tight and a priori discursive structure.[69]

For Kracauer, the narrative film is an intrinsically "problematic genre"; it presents an "insoluble dilemma" (p. 230). The tension between "formative" and "realistic tendencies" that links the history of photography with that of the cinema is not simply a binary opposition, let alone a stylistic alternative, but a "genuine antinomy." The tradition of narrative film predicated on drama (from bourgeois tragedy to the well-made play) conflicts with a material aes-thetics of film because it imposes the closed structure of a "finite, ordered cosmos" upon the heterogeneous, heteronomous, open-ended flow of life. As far as a sense of "endlessness" and attention to ephemeral details and random

incidents are concerned, narrative films have a more acceptable literary model
in the novel, in particular the modern novel (Proust, Virginia Woolf, James
Joyce, as read through Erich Auerbach's *Mimesis*). "But the two media also
embrace different worlds" (p. 237): The continuum the novel evokes is a
"mental" — emotional, intellectual, discursive — continuum rather than a material one, and tracing its subtle movements the camera would again risk losing touch with the "basic layer" of physical, sensory reality.

This does not mean, however, that film could, and should, entirely renounce narrative (quite apart from the question of popularity). For one thing,
even the films Kracauer considers "cinematic" do not exhaust themselves in
capturing "small material phenomena," nor does he think that fleeting impressions, overwhelming sights, or the alienation of sights too familiar can "be
expected to fill the bill" (p. 271). For another, any film literalizing the medium's "chimerical desire to establish the continuum of physical existence" —
Kracauer cites Fernand Léger's idea of a "monster film . . . record[ing] painstakingly the life of a man and a woman during twenty-four consecutive
hours" — would expose everyday life's "widely ramified roots in crude existence" and thereby send us into a state of horror and panic (pp. 63–64).
Kracauer recognizes and acknowledges the need for storytelling, for structures
organizing time and space, action and subjectivity; he even gives a qualified
approval to the convention of "happy," or rather "nontragic," provisional endings (pp. 268–70). The point is that some types of narrative are more apt than
others to mobilize the medium's purchase on material contingency, to maintain an awareness of the tensions involved in their own construction.

Kracauer is undoubtedly one of the major theorists of the nonnarrative
aspects of cinema, a tradition that runs from phenomenological and physiognomic approaches in 1920s film theory, often entwined with the artistic avant-
garde and experimental film practice, through more recent and systematic
studies such as the work of Gilles Deleuze and Tom Gunning.[70] Yet it would
be a mistake to label Kracauer's stance as *anti*-narrative; if anything, it has to
be called anti-*classical*. *Theory of Film* may well be one of the most substantial
attempts to gather the cross- and countercurrents, as it were, *below* the paradigm of "classical cinema," the system of norms governing narrative film practice in Hollywood (and elsewhere) from about 1917 to 1960 and beyond;
indeed, the book could be read as an *avant-la-lettre* critique of scholarly approaches that implicitly assert that paradigm as a natural, universal form.[71]
Classical principles of thorough motivation centering on individual characters,
causal coherence and continuity of space and time, compositional harmony,
unity and closure — any stylistic and ideological effort to press cinematic materiality into a "whole with a purpose" — appear to Kracauer as a relapse into
traditional (neo-Aristotelian, neo-Kantian) aesthetics, at odds with the histori-

cal contemporaneity of film as a medium of modernity, of mass society, serial production, distracted consumption, and chance developments.

Against the tightly knit plots of classical ("theatrical") narrative, Kracauer extols the loosely composed, "porous," "permeable," open-ended narratives of the episode film and the found story, types of narrative that leave "gaps into which environmental life may stream" (pp. 255–56). To the "false unity" of artistic productions he prefers the "fragmentized whole" and improvisational effects of the musical, the repetitive gag structure of comedy, and the "sensational incidents" of melodrama that allow films of that genre to preserve a "relative autonomy of [their] parts" (pp. 149, 272). He praises D. W. Griffith for his "admirable nonsolution," in particular his insertion of images that "retain a degree of independence of the intrigue and thus succeed in summoning physical existence" (p. 231). (He repeatedly cites the close-up of Mae Marsh's hands in *Intolerance* that makes us "forget that they are just ordinary hands": "Isolated from the rest of the body and greatly enlarged, the hands we know will change into unknown organisms quivering with a life of their own" [p. 48].) What these semiautonomous details succeed in summoning is not exhausted by a functionalist concept of "motivation," whether realistic, artistic, or compositional;[72] their "intoxicating effect" derives from the very moment of contingency, which is also a moment of freedom, that exceeds such motivation. "Street and face . . . open up a dimension much wider than that of plots which they sustain" (p. 303). This excess of sensory experience not only blurs the boundaries of narrative space but also involves a temporal disjunction ("strange shapes shine forth from the abyss of timelessness," p. 235). If narrative cinema, as Doane contends, responds to the antinomy between the ideals of total storage and legibility by "content[ing] itself with producing time as an effect," Kracauer reminds us that such "shaped time" is only a compromise, a necessary fiction through and against which we may experience moments of another temporality, the time of history, everyday living, and mortality.[73]

The centrifugal tendency that Kracauer emphasizes on the level of the filmic text is, most importantly, the condition for another movement, this one away from the filmic text and into the cinema — that is, into the social, public space of reception. The gaps and fissures in the filmic text that allow for moments of contingency and indeterminacy are essential to the circulation between the film on the screen and what Alexander Kluge calls "the film in the viewer's head."[74] Kracauer's view of spectatorial activity is diametrically opposed to a cognitivist conception of film viewing as scanning, of "executing the operations relevant to constructing a story out of the film's representation."[75] Films may *try* to direct our attention more forcefully than a play or a novel, but they may also afford us an opportunity to meander across the screen and away from it, into the labyrinths of our own imagination, memories, and dreams. This process takes the viewer into a dimension beyond — or below — the illusory depth of diegetic space, beyond/below even the "intersubjective protocols" and particular kinds of knowledge that govern our understanding of narratives, into the slippery realm of experience, the heterogeneity of social space, the unpredictable dynamics of public life. It is in Kracauer's insistence on the possibility of such openings that we can hear an echo, albeit a muted one, of his earlier vision of cinema as an alternative public sphere, a sensory and collective horizon for people trying to live a life in the interstices of modernity.

The figure of centrifugality, finally, returns us to the "problematic genre" of the book itself, its palimpsestic and uneven quality, and the question of its relation to the future, which includes the practice of film and cinema today. In addition to and alongside the lineages with Kracauer's earlier writings that I have tried to highlight, *Theory of Film* still contains remarkable insights into particular aspects of the medium, both its aesthetic possibilities and its empirical diversity. There are, for instance, reflections on film sound that point not only in the direction of an "acoustic unconcious" but also toward experimental uses of sound ("anonymous noises," multilingual speech, etc.) from Lang through Clair and Pabst (discussed in the book) to New Wave and New Hollywood practices of the 1960s and 1970s (Jean-Luc Godard, Kluge, Marguerite Duras, Yvonne Rainer, Robert Altman); there is an awareness of genre and of the ways in which generic specificities modify and challenge the norms of classical narrative; and there are surprising observations and assessments, such as the singling out of Hitchcock as an authority in the twilight zone of "psychophysical correspondences" (p. 276).

Above all, there is Kracauer's own faith in happy endings under erasure that makes him considerably more open toward possibilities within mass and media culture than his Frankfurt School colleagues, especially Max Horkheimer and Adorno. True to twenties avant-garde iconoclasm, Kracauer is more likely to be irritated by the falsity of "cultural aspirations" than by the commercialization of art per se: "Many a commercial film or television production is a genuine achievement besides being a commodity. Germs of new beginnings may develop within a thoroughly alienated environment" (pp. 217–18). Nor does he panic over the "crisis" of cinema, the drop in attendance that preoccupied Hollywood during the 1950s, but takes the very fact that both films and audiences have migrated to television as a sign of cinema's survival capacities: "Its potentialities are far from being exhausted, and the social conditions which favored its rise have not yet changed substantially" (p. 167). The conditions, needs, and pressures that shaped the cinema, at least in Western Europe and the United States, are those of modern mass society. And Kracauer's penchant for terms such as anonymity, isolation, alienation, and dissociation, but also receptivity, flexibility, improvisation, and openness toward strangers, is no doubt indebted to modern mass sociology, in particular David Riesman's *The Lonely Crowd* (1950), a study that in turn fleshes out, for a different context, the contours of new forms of subjectivity and interaction that Kracauer saw emerging in Weimar employee culture.[76]

To return to my initial question, then, what, in the age of video and the digital, are we to do with a film theory that insists on the "photographic nature" of the medium? Which fragments from this quarry, which layers of this palimpsest can help us reconfigure the place of the cinema within contemporary (audio-)visual culture? One could easily suggest, for instance, that Kracauer's aesthetics of seriality, dissociation, and kinetic affect is vindicated by postclassical film practices inspired by television commercials and MTV, practices that would certainly have aroused his curiosity. But in doing so we would have to be careful not to surrender the philosophical and political concerns that fueled his insistence on the ambivalence of photographic representation — as the material layer in which temporality and history could leave a trace, as momentary islands of contingency and indeterminacy that show up the blizzards of seemingly transparent, universally fungible sights and sounds. One could also argue that since the photographic approach in Kracauer's theory of film is as much a matter of aesthetic effect as one of material specificity, it is already understood as a translation or troping of the principle of photographic alienation into another medium — that is, as a matter of stylistic and rhetorical choices involving particular cinematic techniques (of framing, editing, sound, mise-en-scène, and trick) rather than as a matter of medium ontology.[77] If this is the case, we might read *Theory of Film* as an impulse to identify and envision comparable "chances of alienation" in the new media, in whatever hybridized forms and formats the cinema may assume.

Quite apart from the problem of technological teleologies that lay claim to our future, Kracauer's book elucidates the tremendous significance of cinema, the love it inspired along with new forms of knowledge and experience, in a period that may well be past, but that is very much part of our history. As we embrace, endure, or resist the effects of the digital, the cinematic still remains the sensorial dominant of this century, of a modernity defined by mass production, mass consumption, and mass destruction. At the very least, *Theory of Film* may help us understand the experience that cinema once was and could have been, whatever may become of it.

NOTES

For readings and discussions that helped shape this introduction, I wish to thank Bill Brown, Michael Geyer, Joel Snyder, Lesley Stern, and Yuri Tsivian. In the effort to redeem Kracauer from — and for — film theory and criticism, I am greatly indebted to my friend Karsten Witte, to whose memory this text is dedicated.

1. Siegfried Kracauer, *Theory of Film: The Redemption of Physical Reality* (New York: Oxford University Press, 1960), ix.

2. The distinction between "indexical," "iconic," and "symbolic" functions of the sign goes back to Charles Sanders Peirce; it has found a somewhat reductive adaption in structuralist-semiotic film theory, notably the work of Christian Metz. These terms (in particular the notion of indexicality) are mobilized here for heuristic purposes but not to suggest that Kracauer's approach to photographic and filmic representation can be conflated with the project of semiotics.

3. Norbert Bolz, "Die Zukunft der Zeichen: Invasion des Digitalen in die Bilderwelt des Films," in Ernst Karpf, Doron Kiesel, Karsten Visarius, eds., *Im Spiegelkabinett der Illusionen: Filme über sich selbst*, Arnoldshainer Filmgespräche, vol. 13 (Marburg: Schüren, 1996): 57. Bolz also includes Walter Benjamin's film theory in this assessment.

4. Thomas Y. Levin, "Iconology at the Movies: Panofsky's Film Theory," *Yale Journal of Criticism* 9 (1996): 35.

5. A version of chapter 14 of *Theory of Film*, "The Found Story and the Episode," was first published in *Film Culture* 2 (1956): 1–5, with a portrait of the author.

6. Pauline Kael, "Is There a Cure for Film Criticism? Or: Some Unhappy Thoughts on Siegfried Kracauer's *Nature of Film* [sic]," *Sight and Sound* 31 (spring 1962): 56–64, rpt. in Kael, *I Lost It at the Movies* (Boston: Little, Brown and Co., 1965), 269–92; Andrew Tudor, *Theories of Film* (London: Secker and Warburg, 1974), 79; J. Dudley Andrew, *The Major Film Theories* (London: Oxford University Press, 1976), chap. 5; J. Dudley Andrew, *Concepts in Film Theory* (Oxford: Oxford University Press, 1984), 19; on the German reception of *Theory of Film*, see Helmut Lethen, "Sichtbarkeit: Kracauers Liebeslehre," in Michael Kessler and Thomas Y. Levin, eds., *Siegfried Kracauer: Neue Interpretationen* (Tübingen: Stauffenburg, 1990), 196ff.

7. Andrew, *Major Film Theories*, 106.

8. This is the standard against which Noël Carroll reads the book; see Carroll, "Kracauer's *Theory of Film*," in Peter Lehman, ed., *Defining Cinema* (New Brunswick: Rutgers University Press, 1997).

9. Siegfried Kracauer, *History: The Last Things Before the Last*, ed. Paul Oskar Kristeller (New York: Oxford University Press, 1969); 2d ed. (Princeton: Markus Wiener, 1995). On the relationship between *History* and Kracauer's film theory, see David Rodowick, "On Kracauer's *History*," *New German Critique* 41 (spring 1988): 109–39; and Gertrud Koch,

"'Not Yet Accepted Anywhere': Exile, Memory, and Image in Kracauer's Conception of History," trans. Jeremy Gaines, *New German Critique* 54 (fall 1991): 95–109.

10. For a complete annotated listing of these writings, see Thomas Y. Levin, *Siegfried Kracauer: Eine Bibliographie seiner Schriften* (Marbach am Neckar: Deutsche Schillergesellschaft, 1989). The majority of Kracauer's articles from the *Frankfurter Zeitung*, many of which were published under pseudonyms or even anonymously, can be found in his own scrapbooks, Kracauer Papers, Deutsches Literaturarchiv (DLA), Marbach am Neckar. A large selection of these articles is reprinted in Kracauer, *Schriften* vol. 5, ed. Inka Mülder-Bach (Frankfurt: Suhrkamp, 1990). For a selection of his film reviews, see Kracauer, *Kino*, ed. Karsten Witte (Frankfurt: Suhrkamp, 1974), and vol. 2 of Kracauer's *Schriften*, ed. Karsten Witte (Frankfurt: Suhrkamp, 1979). So far, the only collection of Kracauer's early writings in English translation is *The Mass Ornament: Weimar Essays*, trans., ed., and with an introduction by Thomas Y. Levin (Cambridge, Mass.: Harvard University Press, 1995); see also Kracauer, "Loitering: Four Encounters in Berlin," *Qui Parle* 5 (spring/summer 1992): 51–60, and various texts in translation in Anton Kaes, Martin Jay, Edward Dimendberg, eds., *The Weimar Republic Sourcebook* (Berkeley and Los Angeles: University of California Press, 1994).

11. Kracauer, "The Mass Ornament" (1927), in *Mass Ornament*, 75.

12. Michael Schröter, "Weltzerfall und Rekonstruktion: Zur Physiognomik Siegfried Kracauers," *Text + Kritik* 68 (Munich: Beck, 1980): 18–40. See also Miriam Hansen, "Decentric Perspectives: Kracauer's Early Writings on Film and Mass Culture," *New German Critique* 54 (fall 1991): 47–76.

13. S. Kracauer, "Berliner Nebeneinander: Kara-Iki — Scala-Ball im Savoy — Menschen im Hotel," *Frankfurter Zeitung*, 17 February 1933; see also Kracauer, "Cult of Distraction" (1926), in *Mass Ornament*. On Kracauer's recognition of the cinema as "public" see Heide Schlüpmann, "Der Gang ins Kino — ein Ausgang aus selbstverschuldeter Unmündigkeit: Zum Begriff des Publikums in Kracauers Essayistik der Zwanziger Jahre," in Kessler and Levin, *Siegfried Kracauer*, 267–84; as well as Hansen, "America, Paris, the Alps: Kracauer (and Benjamin) on Cinema and Modernity," in Leo Charney and Vanessa Schwartz, eds., *Cinema and the Invention of Modern Life* (Berkeley and Los Angeles: University of California Press, 1995) 362–402, esp. 374ff.

14. "Photography" (1927), in *Mass Ornament*, 62, 61.

15. Kracauer, *Die Angestellten: Aus dem neuesten Deutschland* (1929), rpt. in Kracauer, *Schriften*, vol. 1, ed. Karsten Witte (Frankfurt: Suhrkamp, 1978), 289. An abbreviated translation of the chapter in which this phrase occurs, "Shelter for the Homeless," from Kracauer's groundbreaking so-

cioethnographic study of white-collar employees, can be found in Kaes, Jay, and Dimendberg, *The Weimar Republic Sourcebook*, 189–91.

16. Kracauer, "Photography," 62; for examples of Kracauer's critique of the ideology of contemporary film production, see "The Little Shopgirls Go to the Movies" and "Film 1928," in *Mass Ornament*.

17. On Benjamin's concept of "innervation," see Susan Buck-Morss, "Aesthetics and Anaesthetics: Walter Benjamin's Artwork Essay Reconsidered," *October* 62 (fall 1992): 3–41; on his argument for mass cultural catharsis, see Hansen, "Of Mice and Ducks: Benjamin and Adorno on Disney," *South Atlantic Quarterly* 92 (January 1993): 27–61.

18. See Anson Rabinbach, "Between Enlightenment and Apocalypse: Benjamin, Bloch and Modern German Jewish Messianism," *New German Critique* 34 (winter 1985): 78–124.

19. Kracauer, "Der Künstler in dieser Zeit," *Der Morgen* 1 (April 1925), rpt. in *Schriften*, 5.1:305.

20. See Kracauer, "The Task of the Film Critic" (1932), in Kaes, Jay, and Dimendberg, *Weimar Republic Sourcebook*, 634–35; see also n. 16, above. As a result of his outspoken stance, Kracauer's influential position at the *Frankfurter Zeitung* was hemmed in, and his salary cut, as early as 1930 and 1931; he was officially dismissed in 1933.

21. Kracauer, "Photography," 61. See also Heide Schlüpmann, "The Subject of Survival: On Kracauer's *Theory of Film*," trans. Jeremy Gaines, *New German Critique* 54 (fall 1991): 116.

22. See below, 71f. It is important to note that Kracauer makes these terms overlap with phrases such as "everyday life" and, in *History*, the "zone of inertia." While he dissociates himself explicitly from the "nostalgia for life as such" in the tradition of *Lebensphilosophie* (169), he is no doubt linked to that tradition, especially through Georg Simmel (but also Henri Bergson and Wilhelm Dilthey), by a logic of materialist revisionism.

23. The term "love of cinema" is used by Heide Schlüpmann to capture the intellectual and erotic investment in theorizing the cinema in analogy with the root meaning of "philo-sophy," after, against, and with Nietzsche; see her essay, "Am Leitfaden der Liebe: Philosophie und Kino," in Hartmut Böhme and Klaus Scherpe, eds., *Literatur- und Kulturwissenschaften: Positionen, Theorien, Modelle* (Reinbek bei Hamburg: Rowohlt, 1996).

24. The reference to the essay on "Photography" resurfaces in Kracauer's introduction to *History*, where he notes with amazement that he had already observed "parallels between history and the photographic media," in particular between the rise of photography and that of historicism, in an article in the 1920s. He marvels whether his previous "blindness" was

effected by the "strange power of the subconscious" but finds that his (re)discovery of the essay justified, "after the event," all the years he had spent on *Theory of Film* (3–4).

25. There are actually other, less overt references to the Shoah in the book, as when Kracauer remarks on Buñuel's *Land Without Bread / Las Hurdes* (1932), a work in which the filmmaker "reverted from his surrealist ventures to the monstrous core of reality itself": "this terrifying documentary bared the depth of human misery, prefiguring the near future with its unspeakable horrors and sufferings" (181).

26. Koch, "'Not Yet Accepted Anywhere'"; Schlüpmann, "The Subject of Survival."

27. Kracauer to Theodor W. Adorno, February 12, 1949, in Ingrid Belke and Irina Renz, *Siegfried Kracauer 1889–1966, Marbacher Magazin* 47 (1988): 107.

28. In addition to their personal contact, Kracauer and Benjamin reviewed each other's publications and exchanged letters: see Kracauer, "On the Writings of Walter Benjamin," in *Mass Ornament*; Benjamin, "Ein Außenseiter macht sich bemerkbar," *Die Gesellschaft* 7 (1930): 473–77, and "S. Kracauer, Die Angestellten [. . .]," *Die Literarische Welt* 6 (June 16, 1930): 5, in Benjamin, *Gesammelte Schriften*, 3:219–28; Benjamin, *Briefe an Siegfried Kracauer* (Marbach am Neckar: DLA, 1987). On the refugees' harrowing experience in Marseille and Benjamin's failed crossing of the Franco-Spanish border, see Lisa Fittko, *Escape through the Pyrenees*, trans. David Koblick (Evanston, Ill.: Northwestern University Press, 1991).

29. Letter to Adorno, February 12, 1949.

30. Soma Morgenstern to Gershom Scholem, December 21, 1972, excerpts in Hans Puttnies and Gary Smith, eds., *Benjaminiana* (Gießen: Anabas, 1991), 202–3. See also Klaus Michael, "Vor dem Café: Walter Benjamin und Siegfried Kracauer in Marseille," in Michael Opitz and Erdmut Wizisla, eds., *"Aber ein Sturm weht vom Paradise her": Texte zu Walter Benjamin* (Leipzig: Reclam, 1992), 203–21. Kracauer makes reference to his and his wife's own plans for suicide in a letter to Max Horkheimer, June 11, 1941, Kracauer Papers, DLA.

31. Accompanying the notebooks are hand-written and typed outlines of different degrees of elaboration, as well as drafts for a chapter on film and theater. The vast amount of materials relating to *Theory of Film* are deposited, along with Kracauer's other papers, at DLA. For a more detailed discussion of these materials, see Hansen, "'With Skin and Hair': Kracauer's Theory of Film, Marseille 1940," *Critical Inquiry* 19 (1993): 437–69; and Michael, "Vor dem Café."

32. This impression is confirmed by Kracauer's correspondence with Adorno, Leo Löwenthal, Rudolf Arnheim, and Erwin Panofsky, in the Kracauer Papers, DLA.

33. Marseille notebooks (hereafter MN), 1:3.

34. See Tom Gunning, "The Cinema of Attraction[s]," *Wide Angle* 8 (1986): 63–70, and "An Aesthetic of Astonishment: Early Film and the (In)credulous Spectator," *Art & Text* 34 (spring 1989): 31–45.

35. In the Marseille notebooks, the term *dégonflage* (letting the air out, deflating) is often coupled with the shorthand of "Sancho Panza," referring to the Cervantes character through the lens of Kafka's "The Truth on Sancho Panza": "Insofar as film, by representing materiality, promotes the work of disenchantment, it can be called the Sancho Panza who exposes the Donquichoteries of ideologies and intentional constructions" (MN, 1:42; also see 1:5). Kracauer reuses Kafka's Sancho Panza aphorism in *History*, 216–17.

36. See, for example, texts by Jean-Louis Baudry, Christian Metz, Laura Mulvey, Stephen Heath et al. reprinted in Philip Rosen, ed., *Narrative, Apparatus, Ideology: A Film Theory Reader* (New York: Columbia University Press 1986); as well as David Bordwell, *Narration in the Fiction Film* (Madison, Wisc.: University of Wisconsin Press, 1985).

37. This alternative tradition has been resumed more recently by, among others, Gaylyn Studlar, *In the Realm of Pleasure: Von Sternberg, Dietrich, and The Masochistic Aesthetic* (Urbana, Ill.: University of Illinois Press, 1988); Kaja Silverman, *Male Subjectivity at the Margins* (New York: Routledge, 1992); Linda Williams, "Film Bodies: Gender, Genre, and Excess," *Film Quarterly* 44 (summer 1991): 2–13; and Steven Shaviro, *The Cinematic Body* (Minneapolis: University of Minnesota Press, 1992).

38. See Buck-Morss, "Aesthetics and Anaesthetics."

39. In a 1926 review, for instance, Kracauer writes: "One has to hand this to the Americans: with slapstick films they have created a form that offers a counterweight to their reality: if in that reality they subject the world to an often unbearable discipline, the film in turn dismantles this self-imposed order quite forcefully" (*Frankfurter Zeitung*, January 29, 1926). Twenty-five years later, the anarchistic critique of capitalist rationalization has all but vanished from Kracauer's reading of slapstick comedy; see his article on "Silent Film Comedy" in *Sight and Sound* 21 (August/September 1951): 31–32.

40. Kracauer, "Chaplins Triumph," *Neue Rundschau* 42 (April 1931): rpt. in Kracauer, *Kino*, 179.

41. Kracauer, "Chaplin: Zu seinem Film 'Zirkus,'" *Frankfurter Zeitung*, February 15, 1928, rpt. in Kracauer, *Kino*, 169.

42. English-German summary, May 8–12, 1949; first chapter outline dated Nov. 19, 1940.

43. The parenthetical mention of contemporary American film most likely refers to film noir, which Kracauer discerned as a distinct tendency in postwar cinema; there are numerous notes to that effect in his letters and unpublished papers. On links between Weimar conceptions of urban modernity and American film noir, in particular the cinematic topos of the street, see Edward Dimendberg, "Down These Seen Streets A Man Must Go: Siegfried Kracauer and Film Noir" (paper presented at the Society for Cinema Studies conference, Dallas, March 1996).

44. Edith Wyschogrod, *Spirit in Ashes: Hegel, Heidegger, and Man-Made Mass Death* (New Haven: Yale University Press, 1985), esp. chap. 4.

45. Theodor W. Adorno, "The Curious Realist: On Siegfried Kracauer" (1964), trans. Shierry Weber Nicholsen, *New German Critique* 54 (fall 1991): 177; Koch, "'Not Yet Accepted Anywhere,'" 98.

46. I am indebted to Joel Snyder for helping me think about this particular twist in Kracauer's understanding of photographic representation.

47. A version of this chapter, entitled "The Photographic Approach," was published in *Magazine of Art* 44 (March 1951): 107–13.

48. This phrase appears only in the German translation, on which Kracauer himself worked extensively: "wenn unsere Augen unserer Liebe zuvorkommen" (*Theorie des Films: Die Errettung der äußeren Wirklichkeit*, in Kracauer, *Schriften*, vol. 3, ed. Karsten Witte, trans. Friedrich Walter and Ruth Zellschan [Frankfurt: Suhrkamp, 1985], 286). The quotation from Proust first appears in "Tentative Outline," September 8, 1949, 1; Marcel Proust, *Remembrance of Things Past*, trans. C. K. Scott Moncrieff, 1: 814–15, quoted below, 14.

49. Rudolf Arnheim registered, and was quite troubled by, Kracauer's advocacy of a melancholy aesthetics (which is one of the traces of the book's original resumption of Benjamin's treatise on the baroque *Trauerspiel*); see Arnheim's review of *Theory of Film*, "Melancholy Unshaped," *Journal of Aesthetics* 21 (spring 1963): 291–97.

50. Kracauer, "Photography," 58. Such formulations prefigure, though not necessarily with the same implications, the key insight of Heidegger's essay begun in 1938, "Die Zeit des Weltbildes." See Martin Heidegger, *Holzwege* (Frankfurt: Klostermann, 1950); translated as "The Age of the World Picture," trans. William Lovitt, in *The Question Concerning Technology* (San Francisco: Harper and Row, 1977), 115–54.

51. Kracauer, "Photography," 56. This is just one of the many moments in Kracauer's essay that resonate in Roland Barthes's *Camera Lucida: Reflections on Photography*, trans. Richard Howard (New York: Hill and Wang, 1981) 64f., 92f., and passim.

52. Kracauer, "Photography," 63. See Kracauer's review of Kafka, *The Castle*, a year earlier (*Frankfurter Zeitung*, November 28, 1926), which reads like

a blueprint for a gnostic-utopian film aesthetics. Underlying Kracauer's argument about photography's historical function in relation to nature is the concept of "*Naturgeschichte*," a key concept of Critical Theory indebted to Georg Lukács and Benjamin and developed by Adorno (in his programmatic lecture of 1932, "Die Idee der Naturgeschichte"); see Susan Buck-Morss, *The Origin of Negative Dialectics* (New York: The Free Press, 1977), 52–57 ("Natural History and Historical Nature").

53. The notion of exposing a historical state of alienation (*Entfremdung*) through aesthetic means of estrangement (*Verfremdung*) had, of course, a wide currency during the interwar period, notably in the work of Brecht, but also in the experiments and writings of the Russian Formalists.

54. Schlüpmann, "Subject of Survival," 119.

55. See Sergei Eisenstein: "The Cinematographic Principle and the Ideogram" (1929), in *Film Form*, trans. Jay Leyda (New York: Harcourt, Brace, Jovanovich, 1949), 28–44; rev. trans.: "Beyond the Shot," in Eisenstein, *Writings 1922–1934*, ed. and trans. Richard Taylor (London: BFI, 1988), 138–50.

56. Kracauer, *History*, 83f.; see also 92f. This diasporic sensibility is in turn linked, later in the book, with the notion of "anteroom thinking" as a form of historical knowledge — prefigured in the ambivalent structure of photographic representation — that forgoes the certainties and purities of philosophical and aesthetic truth in favor of a "radical compromise" (Rodowick, "On Kracauer's *History*," 138): the "side-by-side" principle of timeless and temporal, transcendental and immanent registers. On the significance of "extra-territoriality" for Kracauer, see Martin Jay, "The Extraterritorial Life of Siegfried Kracauer" (1975) in *Permanent Exiles* (New York: Columbia University Press, 1986), 152–97; and Inka Mülder-Bach, "'Mancherlei Fremde': Paris, Berlin und die Extraterritorialität Siegfried Kracauers," *Juni: Magazin für Kultur & Politik* (Mönchengladbach) 3 (1989): 61–72.

57. See below, 159. It is precisely this dimension of mimetic identification in Kracauer's concept of "camera-reality" that eludes Arnheim when he criticizes the following sentences from the epilogue as a "bold *nonsequitur*": "The moviegoer watches the images on the screen in a dream-like state. So he can be supposed to apprehend physical reality in its concreteness" ("Melancholy Unshaped" 295).

58. Benjamin, "On Some Motifs in Baudelaire," *Illuminations*, trans. Harry Zohn (New York: Schocken, 1969), 188; the passage continues with a reference to Proust: "This experience corresponds to the data of the *mémoire involontaire*." On the relation between "aura" and "optical unconscious," see Hansen, "Benjamin, Cinema and Experience: 'The Blue

Flower in the Land of Technology,'" *New German Critique* 40 (spring 1987): 207ff.

59. Kracauer's fascination with films that stage such uncanny encounters through physiognomic explorations of the quotidian harks back to his discovery of this tendency in French cinema, in particular René Clair and Jacques Feyder (see his review of the latter's *Thérèse Raquin, Frankfurter Zeitung*, March 29, 1928; rpt. in Kracauer, *Kino*, 136f.). Interestingly, he extols the same aesthetic power in contemporary Russian films, in particular those of Dziga Vertov, who in turn must be considered one of the sources of Benjamin's notion of the optical unconscious. The obvious precursor for a physiognomic conception of film is Béla Balázs (see Gertrud Koch, "Béla Balázs: The Physiognomy of Things," *New German Critique* 40 [1987]: 167–77), yet Schlüpmann is right to distinguish Kracauer's interest in photographic alienation from Balázs's basically Romantic approach ("Subject of Survival," 118–20).

60. See, for instance, Kracauer "Der verbotene Blick," *Frankfurter Zeitung*, April 9, 1925, rpt. in *Schriften*, 5.1: 296–300; "Erinnerung an eine Pariser Straße," *Frankfurter Zeitung*, November 9, 1930, rpt. in *Schriften* 5.2:243–48. On the darker, personal side of Benjamin's "aura" (as distinct from the notion of aura one might derive from a reductive reading of the artwork essay), see Gershom Scholem, "Walter Benjamin and His Angel" (1972), in *On Jews and Judaism in Crisis* (New York: Schocken, 1976), 236; and Scholem, *Walter Benjamin: The Story of a Friendship*, trans. Harry Zohn (Philadelphia: Jewish Publication Society of America, 1981), 186ff.

61. Kracauer, *History*, 6; see also 78f.

62. Lethen, "Sichtbarkeit," 218; on the status of the ideal of "transparency," see also Susan Sontag, *Against Interpretation* (New York: Delta, 1964), 13.

63. Friedrich Kittler, *Discourse Networks 1800/1900*, trans. Michael Metteer, with Chris Cullens (Stanford: Stanford University Press, 1990), 338; Adorno, "The Curious Realist," 177.

64. Mary Ann Doane, "Temporality, Storage, Legibility: Freud, Marey, and the Cinema," *Critical Inquiry* 22 (winter 1996): 313–43: "The threat was one of overpresence, of excessive coverage, of a refusal of a distinction or differentiation that would insure legibility. To the extent that cinema strove for the status of the total record, strove to confirm the senses and their potential apprehension of anything and everything, it constituted itself as a failure of representation" (343).

65. Ibid.

66. Martin Heidegger, *Gelassenheit* (Tübingen: Neske, 1959).

67. Lethen, "Sichtbarkeit," 201–5; Lethen, *Verhaltenslehren der Kälte: Lebensversuche zwischen den Kriegen* (Frankfurt: Suhrkamp, 1994), trans.

forthcoming (Berkeley and Los Angeles: University of California Press); see also Lethen, "Refrigerators of Intelligence," *Qui Parle* 5 (spring/summer 1992): 73–101.

68. Kracauer's observation that film is for "a split second meaningless" occurs in "Tentative Outline for a Book on Film Aesthetics (Title not yet fixed)," dated September 8, 1949, 5; it was removed on the advice of Robert Warshow.

69. Kracauer's *bête noire* in this regard is again Eisenstein (specifically the later, "totalitarian" Eisenstein), whose idealist urge to impose meaning on every image ("his upward drive toward the significant" [208]) is wedded to an organicist conception of the work of art as a closed economy, "a whole with a purpose" (221). As emerges from his extensive correspondence with Arnheim during the period, as well as the latter's review of the book, Kracauer must have had a similar problem with Arnheim's notion of "significant form," although this issue was not confronted overtly. He is more outspoken in his critique of organicist norms in his correspondence with Erwin Panofsky; see especially the letter dated November 6, 1949.

70. Gilles Deleuze, *Cinema 1: The Movement Image*, trans. Hugh Tomlinson and Barbara Habberjam (Minneapolis: University of Minnesota Press, 1986), and *Cinema 2: The Time-Image*, trans. Hugh Tomlinson and Robert Galeta (Minneapolis: University of Minnesota Press, 1989); Gunning, "The Cinema of Attraction[s]" and "An Aesthetic of Astonishment."

71. See in particular, David Bordwell, Janet Staiger, and Kristin Thompson, *The Classical Hollywood Cinema: Film Style and Mode of Production to 1960* (New York: Columbia University Press, 1985). While this book gives an impressive account of classical Hollywood cinema as a *historical* formation, interrelating industrial organization with the elaboration of stylistic norms, the emphasis on the flexibility and stability of the "system" tends to reproduce classicism's traditional self-image as a timeless, natural, and universal norm.

72. Ibid., 19–23.

73. Doane, "Temporality, Storage, Legibility," 343. See also Kracauer's discussion of competing registers of time and temporality in *History*, esp. chap. 6, "Ahasuerus, or the Riddle of Time."

74. See, for instance, Kluge, "On Film and the Public Sphere," trans. Thomas Y. Levin and Miriam Hansen, *New German Critique* 24–25 (fall/winter 1981–1982): 206–20.

75. Bordwell, *Narration in the Fiction Film*, 30.

76. Kracauer invokes Riesman's phrase, "suburban sadness," below, 180. Riesman analyzes the emergence of a new, "other-directed" character type in

terms of the "radar" or X-ray metaphor he borrows from the Marxist economic historian Karl August Wittfogel, a collaborator of the Frankfurt (later New York) Institute for Social Research from the 1920s on. On this connection, see Lethen, "Radar-Typ," *Verhaltenslehren der Kälte*, 235–43.

77. Kracauer stresses the active, interventionist, rhetorical manner in which film translates the photographic approach into cinematic terms more clearly in the Marseille notebooks (1:19f., 2:2). In the published book, the notion of "camera-reality" seems to vacillate between rhetorical and ontological assumptions (Joel Snyder's distinction) but is never purely either.

It would be fair to advise the reader at the outset that this book does not include all the things he may be looking for. It neglects the animated cartoon and avoids broaching problems of color. Certain recent developments and extensions of the medium are left undiscussed also. There are doubtless still other omissions; indeed, some of the topics which loom large in most writings on film have either been relegated to the background or completely dropped. But the reader himself will not be slow in discovering these gaps, if gaps they are.

What then does the book deal with? Its exclusive concern is the normal black-and-white film, as it grows out of photography. The reason I confine myself to it is rather obvious: Film being a very complex medium, the best method of getting at its core is to disregard, at least temporarily, its less essential ingredients and varieties. I have adopted throughout this sensible procedure. And by the way, is the ground thus covered really so limited? From Lumière's first film strips to Fellini's Cabiria, from The Birth of a Nation to Aparajito, and from Potemkin to Paisan, practically all important cinematic statements have been made in black and white and within the traditional format.

In sum, my book is intended to afford insight into the intrinsic nature of photographic film. If it halfway serves the purpose, as I dare hope it does, it must of course apply to all elements and derivatives of the medium. So one might all the more argue that, in the interest of completeness, I should have brought to bear my theory also on color, the wide screen, television, and what not. Now note that color, for example, involves numerous issues which cannot be apprehended in a cursory manner. To mention one such issue, experience shows that, contrary to what should be expected, natural colors, as recorded by the camera, tend to weaken rather than increase the realistic effect which black-and-white movies are able to produce. The wide screen too raises many a question which requires special treatment. On the one hand, these subsidiary matters undoubtedly "belong"; on the other, they invite inquiries which, perhaps, are too heavy a burden for a book centering on the basic characteristics of film. Evidently, I am caught in a dilemma. Or rather, I would be caught in it did I not feel strongly against rushing through places which ought to be dwelt in. It is my considered opinion that color and other related subjects had better be discussed separately. Why indeed should one say everything at the same time?

At this point I might as well anticipate another possible objection. Perhaps the reader will wonder why, in substantiating my views, I do not limit myself to the testimony of current films which still stand out in his memory, but refer him so often to movies he has long since forgotten or never heard of. This old stuff, he may maintain, is very difficult to check, not to mention that it is probably outmoded in various ways. In consequence, he is likely to question the validity, or the range of validity, of many of my arguments and conclusions. Would they not offer greater interest, I hear him ask, if they were mainly derived from contemporary achievements?

I believe this line of reasoning to be fallacious. Even had I kept my material completely up to date, yet I would still be accused of relying on outdated examples within a few years. What is the talk of the town today will have sunk into oblivion tomorrow; the cinema voraciously devours its own children. Nor can it be said that the most recent films always represent the last word of film making. We know, alas, that technical innovations need not involve advances in design and execution; and the battle scenes in D. W. Griffith's THE BIRTH OF A NATION—a film dating as far back as 1915—have never been matched, let alone surpassed.

In addition, too strong an emphasis on modern practices would have been incompatible with my objectives. Since I aim at tracing the peculiar properties of the medium, I naturally depend, for supporting evidence, on a sample selected from among films of all periods. Hence my constant recourse to a random mixture of old and new instances. Frequently the seeming new is nothing but a variation of old models. All meaningful close-ups originate with AFTER MANY YEARS (1908), in which D. W. Griffith initiated their use for dramatic effect. Similarly, present-day experimental films contain little that cannot be found in the French *avant-garde* films of the 'twenties. In any such case I preferred to stick to the prototypes which, more vividly than all that follows, still vibrate with the intentions engendering them.

For the rest, these old pictures have by no means disappeared. Regular access to them is had in the film libraries of New York, Paris, London, and elsewhere; also, scattered moviehouses occasionally cultivate revivals or resort to them as stopgaps. If there were more such opportunities, people would be less inclined to mistake for a "new wave" what is actually an old story—which is not to say, of course, that new waves do not rise from time to time: think of the neorealistic movement in postwar Italy.

As for my approach to film, I shall certainly not attempt to outline it in advance. Yet I feel I should at least point here to some of its distinguishing features so that prospective readers will get a rough idea of what is awaiting them. My book differs from most writings in the field in that it is a *material* aesthetics, not a formal one. It is concerned with content. It rests upon the assumption that film is essentially an extension of photography and therefore shares with this medium a marked affinity for the visible world around us. Films come into their own when they record and reveal physical reality. Now this reality includes many phenomena which would hardly be perceived were it not for the motion picture camera's ability to catch them on the wing. And since any medium is partial to the things it is uniquely equipped to render, the cinema is conceivably animated by a desire to picture transient material life, life at its most ephemeral. Street crowds, involuntary gestures, and other fleeting impressions are its very meat. Significantly, the contemporaries of Lumière praised his films—the first ever to be made—for showing "the ripple of the leaves stirred by the wind."

I assume, then, that films are true to the medium to the extent that they penetrate the world before our eyes. This assumption—the premise and axis of my book—gives rise to numerous questions. For instance, how is it possible for films to revive events of the past or project fantasies and yet retain a cinematic quality? What about the role of the sound track? If films are to confront us with our visible environment, a good deal obviously depends upon the manner in which the spoken word, noises, and music are related to the pictures. A third question bears on the character of the narrative: Are all types of stories indiscriminately amenable to cinematic treatment or are some such types more in keeping with the spirit of the medium than the rest of them? In answering these and other questions, I am bringing out the implications of my assumption about the photographic nature of film.

It is two different things to espouse an idea and to realize, let alone endorse, all that is implied by it. Even though the reader will presumably agree that the cinema is engrossed in the physical side of life in and about us, he may not be prepared to acknowledge certain consequences of its preoccupation with externals. Consider the issue of story types: a majority of people take for granted that everything that can be staged in the theater or told in a novel can also be conveyed in terms of the cinema. Given a purely formal approach to film, this is a quite sensible expectation. Hence the widespread opinion that tragedy is not only as accessible to the screen as any other literary genre but belongs among the noblest pursuits of the medium—those raising it to the level of an art medium.

Accordingly, culture-minded moviegoers tend to prefer, say, Orson Welles's OTHELLO or Renato Castellani's ROMEO AND JULIET to the crudeness of a Hitchcock thriller. No doubt these two adaptations represent ingenious attempts to translate Shakespearean tragedy into cinematic language. But are they films in the sense that they would make one see and grasp things which only the cinema is privileged to communicate? Decidedly not. While admiring them, the spectator cannot help feeling that the stories which they impart do not grow out of the material life they picture but are imposed on its potentially coherent fabric from without. Even with these products of consummate craftsmanship the tragic is an addition rather than an integral element.

I submit that film and tragedy are incompatible with each other. This proposition, impossible to a formal aesthetics, follows straight from my initial assumption. If film is a photographic medium, it must gravitate toward the expanses of outer reality—an open-ended, limitless world which bears little resemblance to the finite and ordered cosmos set by tragedy. Unlike this cosmos, where destiny defeats chance and all the light falls on human interaction, the world of film is a flow of random events involving both humans and inanimate objects. Nor can the tragic be evoked by images of that flow; it is an exclusively mental experience which has no correspondences in camera-reality. . . .

I should also like to mention here that all implications of my emphasis on the photographic nature of film converge toward the issue of art. Once you start from the assumption that the cinema retains major characteristics of photography, you will find it impossible to accept the widely sanctioned belief or claim that film is an art like the traditional arts. Works of art consume the raw material from which they are drawn, whereas films as an outgrowth of camera work are bound to exhibit it. However purposefully directed, the motion picture camera would cease to be a camera if it did not record visible phenomena for their own sake. It fulfills itself in rendering the "ripple of the leaves." If film is an art, it is art with a difference. Along with photography, film is the only art which leaves its raw material more or less intact. In consequence, such art as goes into films results from their creators' capacity to read the book of nature. The film artist has traits of an imaginative reader, or an explorer prompted by insatiable curiosity.

All this means that films cling to the surface of things. They seem to be the more cinematic, the less they focus directly on inward life, ideology, and spiritual concerns. This explains why many people with strong cultural leanings scorn the cinema. They are afraid lest its undeniable penchant for externals might tempt us to neglect our highest aspirations in the kaleidoscopic sights of ephemeral outward appearances. The cinema, says Valéry, diverts the spectator from the core of his being.

Plausible as this verdict sounds, it strikes me as unhistorical and superficial because it fails to do justice to the human condition in our time. Perhaps our condition is such that we cannot gain access to the elusive essentials of life unless we assimilate the seemingly non-essential? Perhaps the way today leads from, and through, the corporeal to the spiritual? And perhaps the cinema helps us to move from "below" to "above?" It is indeed my contention that film, our contemporary, has a definite bearing on the era into which it is born; that it meets our inmost needs precisely by exposing—for the first time, as it were—outer reality and thus deepening, in Gabriel Marcel's words, our relation to "this Earth which is our habitat."

These few hints will have to do, for there is no short cut to the observations and thoughts on which my contention is based. I have tried to unfold them in the last chapter, which both completes and transcends the preceding aesthetic considerations. In fact, it reaches far beyond film proper. Just as, throughout the book, numbers of movies are analyzed with a view to exemplifying various points of my theory, so, in this chapter, the cinema itself is set in the perspective of something more general— an approach to the world, a mode of human existence.

Let me conclude with a personal reminiscence. I was still a young boy when I saw my first film. The impression it made upon me must have been intoxicating, for I there and then determined to commit my experience to writing. To the best of my recollection, this was my earliest literary project. Whether it ever materialized, I have forgotten. But I have not forgotten its long-winded title, which, back home from the moviehouse, I immediately put on a shred of paper. *Film as the Discoverer of the Marvels of Everyday Life*, the title read. And I remember, as if it were today, the marvels themselves. What thrilled me so deeply was an ordinary suburban street, filled with lights and shadows which transfigured it. Several trees stood about, and there was in the foreground a puddle reflecting invisible house façades and a piece of the sky. Then a breeze moved the shadows, and the façades with the sky below began to waver. The trembling upper world in the dirty puddle—this image has never left me.

SIEGFRIED KRACAUER

June 1960
New York City

FIRST OF ALL, I wish to express my profound gratitude to the Foundations which assisted me in preparing my book. Without the generous support of Bollingen Foundation I would not have been able to get immersed in this project to which I had given thought for years. Then Mr. John Marshall of the Rockefeller Foundation, to whom I am forever indebted for his sustained and active interest in my work, brought the project to the attention of Chapelbrook Foundation which continued to sponsor it with the same magnanimity as Bollingen. At a still later stage a grant I was awarded by the American Philosophical Society afforded me the coveted opportunity to complete my research in Europe.

I also should like to acknowledge my indebtedness to several institutions. Mr. Richard Griffith, Curator of the Museum of Modern Art Film Library, put the facilities of his Department at my disposal whenever I asked for help; and Mr. Bernard Karpel, the Museum's Librarian, never tired of supplying me with information and material difficult to trace. I need hardly add that the staff members of these Museum Departments were no less responsive to my frequent requests. At the British Film Institute in London I was received with heartwarming friendliness; indeed, the days I spent there abounded with film screenings and stimulating conversations. Mr. Henri Langlois and his associates at the Cinémathèque Française, old friends from my years in Paris, did everything they could to anticipate my wishes; I felt, somehow, like the prodigal son in their midst. Dr. Luigi F. Ammannati, Director of the Venice Film Festival, kindly invited me to be guest of the *Mostra* in 1958; it was a wonderful occasion for me to listen and talk, see and learn.

Furthermore, I wish to extend my most sincere thanks to all those whose good counsel contributed to the growth of this book. Professor Erwin Panofsky's comment on an early outline of my basic ideas proved very helpful indeed—not to mention that his interest was a source of comfort to me. The chapter on photography owes much to the suggestions of such authorities in the field as Mr. Beaumont Newhall and Mr. Edward Steichen. In long and repeated discussions with the late Erich Auerbach, Professor Meyer Schapiro, and Professor Rudolf Arnheim I greatly benefited by their scholarly experience and the views they held of many a relevant problem and controversial issue. To revert to Mr. Griffith, I drew heavily on his wide knowledge of film and its history. How can I sufficiently appreciate Mr. Paul Rotha's share in my work? He read my manuscript with a watchful eye to detail; and the exhaustive talks we had in New York, Wilmington (Vermont), and London—talks animated by professional concern and sympathetic understanding—echo throughout the book. Even though I am fully aware that my wife would prefer to remain in the background, I cannot possibly avoid naming her here: the sureness of her judgment and the breadth of her insight were invaluable to me.

In addition, I am deeply grateful to Mr. Arthur Knight and Mr. Eric Larrabee, both of whom went over my manuscript once it was virtually finished. The former took the trouble to comb it for factual inaccuracies, suggesting improvements in a number of places. Mr. Larrabee on his part edited the whole in a spirit of selfless friendship which moved him to treat the text with a strictness constantly mitigated by tenderness. Nor can I think without gratitude of the measure of personal devotion which Mr. Sheldon Meyer of the Oxford University Press manifested in readying the completed manuscript for publication.

Finally, I wish to thank the publishing houses which granted me permission to quote passages from the following works: Random House and Chatto and Windus, Ltd., from Marcel Proust's *Remembrance of Things Past*; Princeton University Press and Oxford University Press, London, from Erich Auerbach's *Mimesis*; Harcourt, Brace and Company and Dobson Books Ltd., from Sergei Eisenstein's *Film Form*; Harcourt, Brace and Company and Edward Arnold, Ltd., from E. M. Forster's *Aspects of the Novel*; and Arthur Geist Verlag, Bremen, from Wolfgang Wilhelm's *Die Auftriebswirkung des Films*.

S. K.

INTRODUCTION

Photography

This study rests upon the assumption that each medium has a specific nature which invites certain kinds of communications while obstructing others. Even philosophers of art concentrating on what is common to all the arts cannot help referring to the existence and possible impact of such differences. In her *Philosophy in a New Key* Susanne Langer hesitantly admits that "the medium in which we naturally conceive our ideas may restrict them not only to certain forms but to certain fields." [1]

But how can we trace the nature of the photographic medium? A phenomenological description based on intuitive insight will hardly get at the core of the matter. Historical movements cannot be grasped with the aid of concepts formed, so to speak, in a vacuum. Rather, analysis must build from the views held of photography in the course of its evolution—views which in some way or other must reflect actually existing trends and practices. It would therefore seem advisable first to study the historically given ideas and concepts. Now this book is not intended as a history of photography—nor of film, for that matter. So it will suffice for our purposes to scrutinize only two sets of ideas about photography. those entertained in the early stages of development and relevant present-day notions. Should the thoughts of the pioneers and of modern photographers and critics happen to center on approximately the same problems, the same essentials, this would bear out the proposition that photography has specific properties and thus lend vigor to the assumption about the peculiar nature of media in general. Such similarities between views and trends of different eras should even be expected. For the principles and ideas instrumental in the rise of a new historical entity do not just fade away once the period of inception is over; on the contrary, it is as if, in the process of growing and spreading, that entity were destined to bring out all their implications. Aristotle's theory of tragedy is still being used as a valid starting-point *great quote* →

for interpretation. A great idea, says Whitehead, "is like a phantom ocean beating upon the shores of human life in successive waves of specialization." [2]

The following historical survey, then, is to provide the substantive conceptions on which the subsequent systematic considerations proper will depend.

HISTORICAL SURVEY

Early views and trends

With the arrival of daguerreotypy, discerning people were highly aware of what they felt to be the new medium's specific properties, which they unanimously identified as the camera's unique ability to record as well as reveal visible, or potentially visible, physical reality. There was general agreement that photography reproduces nature with a fidelity "equal to nature itself." [3] In supporting the bill for the purchase of Daguerre's invention by the French government, Arago and Gay-Lussac reveled in the "mathematical exactness" [4] and "unimaginable precision"[5] of every detail rendered by the camera; and they predicted that the medium would benefit both science and art. Paris correspondents of New York newspapers and periodicals chimed in, full of praise for the unheard-of accuracy with which daguerreotypies copied "stones under the water at the edge of the stream,"[6] or a "withered leaf lying on a projecting cornice." [7] And no less a voice than Ruskin's was added to the chorus of enthusiasm over the "sensational realism" of small plates with views of Venice; it is, said he, "as if a magician had reduced the reality to be carried away into an enchanted land." [8] In their ardor these nineteenth-century realists were emphasizing an essential point—that the photographer must indeed reproduce, somehow, the objects before his lens; that he definitely lacks the artist's freedom to dispose of existing shapes and spatial interrelationships for the sake of his inner vision.

Recognition of the camera's recording faculty went together with an acute awareness of its revealing power. Gay-Lussac insisted that no detail, "even if imperceptible," can escape "the eye and the brush of this new painter." [9] And as early as 1839 a New York *Star* reporter admiringly remarked that, when viewed under a magnifying glass, photographs show minutiae which the naked eye would never have discovered.[10] The American writer and physician Oliver Wendell Holmes was among the first to capitalize on the camera's scientific potentialities. In the early 'sixties he found that the movements of walking people, as disclosed by instantaneous photographs, differed greatly from what the artists imagined they were, and on the grounds of his observations he criticized an artificial leg then popular with amputated Civil War veterans. Other scientists followed suit. For his *The Expression of the Emotions in Man and Animals* (1872) Darwin preferred photographs to engravings and snapshots to time exposures, arguing that he was concerned with truth rather than beauty; and snapshots could be relied upon to convey the "most evanescent and fleeting facial expressions." [11]

Many an invention of consequence has come into being well-nigh unnoticed. Photography was born under a lucky star in as much as it appeared at a time when the ground was well prepared for it. The insight into the recording and revealing functions of this "mirror with a memory" [12]— its inherent realistic tendency, that is—owed much to the vigor with which the forces of realism bore down on the romantic movement of the period. In nineteenth-century France the rise of photography coincided with the spread of positivism—an intellectual attitude rather than a philosophical school which, shared by many thinkers, discouraged metaphysical speculation in favor of a scientific approach, and thus was in perfect keeping with the ongoing processes of industrialization. [13]

Within this context, only the aesthetic implications of this attitude are of interest. Positivist mentality aspired to a faithful, completely impersonal rendering of reality, in the sense of Taine's radical dictum: "I want to reproduce the objects as they are, or as they would be even if I did not exist." What counted was not so much the artist's subject matter or easily deceptive imagination as his unbiased objectivity in representing the visible world; hence the simultaneous breakthrough of *plain-air* painting devoid of romantic overtones. [14] (Yet of course, despite their emphatic insistence on truth to reality, the intellectual *bohème* [15] would expect such truth to serve the cause of the revolution temporarily defeated in 1848; a few years later, Courbet called himself both a "partisan of revolution" and a "sincere friend of real truth." [16]) It was inevitable that this turn to realism in art—which gained momentum with Courbet's *Burial at Ornans* (1850) and had its short heyday after the scandal roused by *Madame Bovary* (1857)—should bring photography into focus. [17] Was the camera not an ideal means of reproducing and penetrating nature without any distortions? Leading scientists, artists and critics were predisposed to grasp and acknowledge the peculiar virtues of the emergent medium.

However, the views of the realists met with strong opposition, not only in the camp of the artists but among the photographers themselves. Art, the opponents held, did not exhaust itself in painterly or photographic records of reality; it was more than that; it actually involved the artist's creativity in shaping the given material. In 1853, Sir William Newton suggested that the photographic image could, and should, be altered so as to make the result conform to the "acknowledged principles of Fine Art."[18] His suggestion was heeded. Not content with what they believed to be a mere copying of nature, numerous photographers aimed at pictures which, as an English critic claimed, would delineate Beauty instead of merely representing Truth.[19] Incidentally, it was not primarily the many painters in the ranks of the photographers who voiced and implemented such aspirations.

With notable exceptions the "artist-photographers" of those days followed a tendency which may be called "formative," since it sprang from their urge freely to compose beautiful pictures rather than to capture nature in the raw. But their creativity invariably manifested itself in photographs that reflected valued painterly styles and preferences; consciously or not, they imitated traditional art, not fresh reality.[20] Thus the sculptor Adam-Salomon, a top-ranking artist-photographer, excelled in portraits which, because of their "Rembrandt lighting" and velvet drapery, caused the poet Lamartine to recant his initial opinion that photographs were nothing but a "plagiarism of nature."[21] Upon seeing these pictures, Lamartine felt sure that photography was equally capable of attaining the peaks of art. What happened on a relatively high level became firmly established in the lower depths of commercial photography: a host of would-be artist-photographers catered to the tastes of the *juste-milieu* which, hostile to realism, still went for romantic painting and the academic idealism of Ingres and his school.[22] There was no end of prints capitalizing on the appeal of staged genre scenes, historical or not.[23] Photography developed into a lucrative industry, especially in the field of portraiture in which Disdéri set a widely adopted pattern.[24] From 1852, his *portrait-carte de visite* ingratiated itself with the petit bourgeois, who felt elated at the possibility of acquiring, at low cost, his likeness—a privilege hitherto reserved for the aristocracy and the well-to-do upper middle class.[25] As might be expected, Disdéri too preached the gospel of beauty.[26] It met the needs of the market. Under the Second Empire professional photographers, no less than popular painters, sacrificed truth to conventional pictorialness by embellishing the features of their less attractive clients.[27]

All this means that such concern with art led the artist-photographers to neglect, if not deliberately to defy, the properties of their medium, as perceived by the realists. As far back as 1843, daguerreotypists renounced camera explorations of reality for the sake of soft-focus pictures.[28] Adam-Salomon relied on retouching for artistic effect,[29] and Julia Margaret Cameron availed herself of badly made lenses in order to get at the "spirit" of the person portrayed without the disturbing interference of "accidental" detail.[30] Similarly, Henry Peach Robinson encouraged the use of any kind of "dodge, trick, and conjuration" so that pictorial beauty might arise out of a "mixture of the real and the artificial."[31]

Small wonder that the champions of realism and their adversaries engaged in a lively debate.[32] This famous controversy, which raged in the second half of the nineteenth century, with no clear-cut solution ever being reached, rested upon a belief common to both schools of thought—that photographs were copies of nature. Yet there the agreement ended. Opinions clashed when it came to appraising the aesthetic significance of reproductions which light itself seemed to have produced.

The realists, it is true, refrained from identifying photography as an art in its own right—in fact, the extremists among them were inclined to discredit artistic endeavors altogether—but strongly insisted that the camera's incorruptible objectivity was a precious aid to the artist. Photography, as a realistic-minded critic put it, reminds the artist of nature and thus serves him as an inexhaustible source of inspiration.[33] Taine and even Delacroix expressed themselves in similar terms; the latter compared daguerreotypy to a "dictionary" of nature and advised painters diligently to consult it.[34]

Those in the opposite camp naturally rejected the idea that a medium confining itself to mechanical imitation could provide artistic sensations or help achieve them. Their contempt of this inferior medium was mingled with bitter complaints about its growing influence, which, they contended, lent support to the cult of realism, thereby proving detrimental to elevated art.[35] Baudelaire scorned the worshippers of Daguerre among the artists. He claimed they just pictured what they saw instead of projecting their dreams.[36] The artist-photographers shared these views with a difference: they were confident that photography need not be limited to reproduction pure and simple. Photography, they reasoned, is a medium which offers the creative artist as many opportunities as does painting or literature—provided he does not let himself be inhibited by the camera's peculiar affinities but uses every "dodge, trick, and conjuration" to elicit beauty from the photographic raw material.

All these nineteenth-century arguments and counterarguments now sound oblique. Misled by the naïve realism underlying them, both sides failed to appreciate the kind and degree of creativeness that may go into a photographic record. Their common outlook prevented them from penetrating the essence of a medium which is neither imitation nor art in the traditional sense. Yet stale as those old notions have become, the two divergent tendencies from which they drew strength continue to assert themselves.

Current views and trends

Of the two camps into which modern photography is split, one follows the realistic tradition. True, Taine's intention to reproduce the objects as they are definitely belongs to the past; the present-day realists have learned, or relearned, that reality is as we see it. But much as they are aware of this, they resemble the nineteenth-century realists in that they enhance the camera's recording and revealing abilities and, accordingly, consider it their task as photographers to make the "best statement of facts."[37] The late Edward Weston, for instance, highly valued the unique precision with which instantaneous photography mechanically registers fine detail and the "unbroken sequence of infinitely subtle gradations from black to white"[38] —a testimony which carries all the more weight since he often indulges in wresting abstract compositions from nature. It is evident that Weston refers to camera revelations rather than representations of familiar sights. What thrills us today then is the power of the medium, so greatly increased by technical innovations and scientific discoveries, to open up new, hitherto unsuspected dimensions of reality. Even though the late László Moholy-Nagy was anything but a realist, he extolled records capturing objects from unusual angles or combinations of phenomena never before seen together; the fabulous disclosures of high-speed, micro- and macro-photography; the penetrations obtained by means of infrared emulsions, etc. Photography, he declares, is the "golden key opening the doors to the wonders of the external universe."[39] Is this a poetic exaggeration? In his book, *Schoepfung aus dem Wassertropfen* (*Creation out of a Waterdrop*), the German photographer Gustav Schenk uncovers the Lilliputian world contained in a square millimeter of moving plain water—an endless succession of shapes so fantastic that they seem to have been dreamed rather than found.

In thus showing the "wonders of the external universe," realistic photography has taken on two important functions unforseeable in its earlier stages of development. (This may explain why, for instance, Moholy-Nagy's account of contemporary camera work breathes a warmth and a sense of participation absent in pertinent nineteenth-century statements.)

First, modern photography has not only considerably enlarged our vision but, in doing so, adjusted it to man's situation in a technological age. A conspicuous feature of this situation is that the viewpoints and perspectives that framed our images of nature for long stretches of the past have become relative. In a crudely physical sense we are moving about with the greatest of ease and incomparable speed so that stable impressions yield to ever-changing ones: bird's-eye views of terrestrial landscapes have become quite common; not one single object has retained a fixed, definitely recognizable appearance.

The same applies to phenomena on the ideological plane. Given to analysis, we pass in review, and break down into comparable elements, all the complex value systems that have come to us in the form of beliefs, ideas, or cultures, thereby of course weakening their claim to absoluteness. So we find ourselves increasingly surrounded by mental configurations which we are free to interpret at will. Each is iridescent with meanings, while the great beliefs or ideas from which they issue grow paler. Similarly, photography has effectively impressed upon us the dissolution of traditional perspectives. Think of the many prints picturing unwonted aspects of reality—spatial depth and flatness are strangely intertwined, and objects apparently well-known turn into inscrutable patterns. All in all, the realists among the modern photographers have done much to synchronize our vision with topical experiences in other dimensions. That is, they have made us perceive the world we actually live in—no mean achievement considering the power of resistance inherent in habits of seeing. In fact, some such habits stubbornly survive. For instance, the predilection which many people show today for wide vistas and panoramic views may well go back to an era less dynamic than ours.

Second, precisely by exploding perceptual traditions, modern photography has assumed another function—that of influencing art. Marcel Duchamp relates that in 1912, when he was painting his *Nude Descending the Staircase*, Paris art circles were stimulated by stroboscopic and multiple-exposure high-speed photographs.[40] What a change in the relationships between photography and painting! Unlike nineteenth-century photography, which at best served as an aid to artists eager to be true to nature—nature still conceived in terms of time-honored visual conventions—scientific camera explorations of the first decades of the twentieth century were a source of inspiration to artists, who then began to defy these conventions.[41] It sounds paradoxical that, of all media, realistic photography should thus have contributed to the rise of abstract art. But the same technological advance that made possible photographs bringing our vision, so to speak, up to date has left its imprint upon painters and prompted them to break away from visual schemata felt to be obsolete. Nor is it in the final analysis surprising that the achievements in the two media do coincide up to a point. Contemporary photographic records and painterly abstractions have this in common: they are both remote from the images we have been able to form of reality in a technically more primitive age. Hence the "abstract" character of those records and the surface similarity to them of certain modern paintings.

Yet, as in the old days, formative urges still vie with realistic intentions. Although Moholy-Nagy delights in the visual conquests of realistically handled photography and readily acknowledges their impact on art, he is nevertheless much more concerned with emancipating the medium from the "narrow rendering of nature." His guiding idea is that we should learn to consider photography, no less than painting, an "ideal instrument of visual expression."[42] "We want to create," he exclaims.[43] Consequently, he capitalized, as did Man Ray, on the sensitivity to light of the photographic plate to produce black-and-white compositions from purposefully controlled material. All modern experimental photographers proceed in essentially the same way. It is as if they suffered from their obligations toward nature in the raw; as if they felt that, to be artists, they would have to work the given raw material into creations of an expressive rather than reproductive order. So they use, and often combine, various artifices and techniques—among them negatives, photograms, multiple exposure, solarization, reticulation, etc.—in order to mount pictures which are palpably designed to externalize what Leo Katz, an experimental photographer, calls "our subjective experiences, our personal visions, and the dynamics of our imagination."[44]

No doubt these artistic-minded experimenters aspire to photographic values; significantly, they refrain from retouching as an interference with the alleged purity of their laboratory procedures.[45] And yet they are clearly the descendents of the nineteenth-century artist-photographers. Much as they may be reluctant to imitate painterly styles and motifs after the manner of their predecessors, they still aim at achieving art in the traditional sense; their products could also be patterned on abstract or surrealist paintings. Moreover, exactly like the early champions of pictorialism, they tend to neglect the specific properties of the medium. In 1925, it is true, Moholy-Nagy still referred to astronomical and X-ray photographs as prefigurations of his photograms,[46] but meanwhile the umbilical cord, tenuous anyway, between realistic and experimental photography seems to have been completely severed. Andreas Feininger suggests that "superfluous and disturbing details" should be suppressed for the sake of "artistic simplification"; the goal of photography as an art medium, he stipulates, is "not the achievement of highest possible 'likeness' of the depicted subject, but the creation of an abstract work of art, featuring composition instead of documentation."[47] He is not the only one to discount the "wonders of the external universe" in the interest of self-expression; in a publication on the German experimental photographer Otto Steinert, the latter's so-called "subjective" photography is characterized as a deliberate departure from the realistic point of view.[48]

All of this implies that the meaning of photography is still controversial. The great nineteenth-century issue of whether or not photography is an art medium, or at least can be developed into one, fully retains its topical flavor. When tackling this perennial issue, the modern realists are wavering. In their desire to highlight the artistic potentialities of their medium they usually draw attention to the photographer's selectivity, which, indeed, may account for prints suggestive of his personal vision and rich in aesthetic gratifications. But is he for that reason on a par with the painter or poet? And is his product a work of art in the strict sense of the word? Regarding these crucial questions, there is a great deal of soul-searching in the realist camp, affirmative testimony alternating with resignation over the limitations which the medium imposes upon its adepts. No such ambivalence is found among the experimental photographers. They cut the Gordian knot by insisting that renderings of chance reality, however beautiful, cannot possibly be considered art. Art begins, they argue, where dependence upon uncontrollable conditions ends. And in intentionally ignoring the camera's recording tasks, Feininger and the others try to transform photography into the art medium which they claim it to be.

Toward the end of 1951, the *New York Times* published an article by Lisette Model in which she turned against experimental photography, pronouncing herself in favor of a "straight approach to life." The reactions to her statement, published in the same newspaper, strikingly demonstrate that the slightest provocation suffices to revive hostilities between the defenders of realism and of unfettered creativity. One letter writer, who described himself as a "frankly experimental photographer," blamed Miss Model for arbitrarily curtailing the artist's freedom to use the medium as he pleases. A second reader endorsed her article on the strength of the argument that "photographers work best within the limitations of the medium." And a third preferred not to advance an opinion at all because "any attempt . . . to formalize and sharply define the function of our art can only lead to stagnation."[49] Skirmishes such as these prove that the belligerents are as far apart as ever before.

In sum, the views and trends that marked the beginnings of photography have not changed much in the course of its evolution. (To be sure, its techniques and contents have, but that is beside the point here.) Throughout the history of photography there is on the one side a tendency toward realism culminating in records of nature, and on the other a formative tendency aiming at artistic creations. Often enough, formative aspirations clash with the desire to render reality, overwhelming it in the process. Photography, then, is the arena of two tendencies which may well conflict with each other. This state of things raises the aesthetic problems to which we now must turn.

SYSTEMATIC CONSIDERATIONS

The basic aesthetic principle

It may be assumed that the achievements within a particular medium are all the more satisfying aesthetically if they build from the specific properties of that medium. To express the same in negative terms, a product which, somehow, goes against the grain of its medium—say, by imitating effects more "natural" to another medium—will hardly prove acceptable; the old iron structures with their borrowings from Gothic stone architecture are as irritating as they are venerable. The pull of the properties of photography is, perhaps, responsible for the inconsistent attitudes and performances of some photographers with strong painterly inclinations. Robinson, the early artist-photographer who recommended that truth should be sacrificed to beauty, at the same time eulogized, as if under a compulsion, the medium's unrivaled truth to reality.[50] Here also belongs the duality in Edward Weston's work; devoted to both abstraction and realism, he paid tribute to the latter's superiority only after having become aware of their incompatability and of his split allegiance.[51]

Yet this emphasis on a medium's peculiarities gives rise to serious objections, one of which may be formulated as follows: The properties of a medium elude concise definition. It is therefore inadmissible to postulate such properties and use them as a starting-point for aesthetic analysis. What is adequate to a medium cannot be determined dogmatically in advance. Any revolutionary artist may upset all previous speculations about the "nature" of the medium to which his works belong.

On the other hand, however, experience shows that not all media obstruct a definition of their nature with equal vigor. In consequence, one may arrange the different media along a continuum according to the degree of the elusiveness of their properties. One pole of the continuum can be assigned, for instance, to painting, whose varying modes of approach seem to be least dependent upon the fixed material and technical factors. (Lessing's great attempt, in his *Laocoön*, to delineate the boundaries between painting and poetry suffered from his inability to gauge the potentialities of either art. But this does not invalidate his attempt. Notwithstanding their near-intangibility, these boundaries make themselves felt whenever a painter or poet tries to transfer to his own medium statements advanced in the other.) "There are many things beautiful enough in words," remarks Benvenuto Cellini, roughly anticipating Lessing, "which do not match . . . well when executed by an artist."[52] That the theater is more restrictive than painting is strikingly demonstrated by an experience of Eisenstein. At a time when he still directed theatrical plays he found out by trial and error that stage conditions could not be stretched infinitely —that in effect their inexorable nature prevented him from implementing his artistic intentions, which then called for film as the only fitting means of expression. So he left the theater for the cinema.[53] Nor does, at least in our era, the novel readily lend itself to all kinds of uses; hence the recurrent quest for its essential features. Ortega y Gasset compares it to a "vast but finite quarry."[54]

But if any medium has its legitimate place at the pole opposite that of painting, it is photography. The properties of photography, as defined by Gay-Lussac and Arago at the outset, are fairly specific; and they have lost nothing of their impact in the course of history. Thus, it seems all the more justifiable to apply the basic aesthetic principle to this particular medium. (Since hybrid genres drawing on photography are practically nonexistent, the problem of their possible aesthetic validity does not pose itself.)

Compliance with the basic aesthetic principle carries implications for (1) the photographer's approach to his medium, (2) the affinities of photography, and (3) the peculiar appeals of photographs.

The photographic approach

The photographer's approach may be called "photographic" if it conforms to the basic aesthetic principle. In an aesthetic interest, that is, he must follow the realistic tendency under all circumstances. This is of course a minimum requirement. Yet in meeting it, he will at least have produced prints in keeping with the photographic approach. Which means that an impersonal, completely artless camera record is aesthetically irreproachable, whereas an otherwise beautiful and perhaps significant composition may lack photographic quality. Artless compliance with the basic principle has its rewards, especially in case of pictures adjusting our vision to our actual situation. Pictures of this kind need not result from deliberate efforts on the part of the photographer to give the impression of artistic creations. In fact, Beaumont Newhall refers to the intrinsic "beauty" of aerial serial photographs taken with automatic cameras during the last war for strictly military purposes.[55] It is understood that this particular brand of beauty is an unintended by-product which adds nothing to the aesthetic legitimacy of such mechanical explorations of nature.

But if candid shots are true to the medium, it would seem natural to imagine the photographer as a "camera-eye"—a man devoid of formative impulses who is all in all the exact counterpart of the type of artist proclaimed in the realist manifesto of 1856. According to the manifesto, the artist's attitude toward reality should be so impersonal that he might reproduce the same subject ten times without any of his copies showing the slightest difference.[56] This is how Proust conceives of the photographer in that passage of *The Guermantes Way*, where, after a long absence, the narrator enters, unannounced, the living room of his grandmother:

> I was in the room, or rather I was not yet in the room since she was not aware of my presence. . . . Of myself . . . there was present only the witness, the observer with a hat and traveling coat, the stranger who does not belong to the house, the photographer who has called to take a photograph of places which one will never see again. The process that mechanically occurred in my eyes when I caught sight of my grandmother was indeed a photograph. We never see the people who are dear to us save in the animated system, the perpetual motion of our incessant love for them, which before allowing the images that their faces present to reach us catches them in its vortex, flings them back upon the idea that we have always had of them, makes them adhere to it, coincide with it. How, since into the forehead, the cheeks of my grandmother I had been accustomed to read all the most delicate, the most permanent qualities of her mind; how, since every casual glance is an act of necromancy, each face that we love a mirror of the past, how could I have failed to overlook what in her had become dulled and changed, seeing that in the most trivial spectacles of our daily life our eye, charged with thought, neglects, as would a classical tragedy, every image that does not assist the action of the play and retains only those that may help to make its purpose intelligible. . . . I, for whom my grandmother was still myself, I who had never seen her save in my own soul, always at the same place in the past, through the transparent sheets of contiguous, overlapping memories, suddenly in our drawing room which formed part of a new world, that of time, saw, sitting on the sofa, beneath the lamp, red-faced, heavy and common, sick, lost in thought, following the lines of a book with eyes that seemed hardly sane, a dejected old woman whom I did not know.[57]

Proust starts from the premise that love blinds us to the changes which the beloved object is undergoing in the course of time. It is therefore logical that he should emphasize emotional detachment as the photographer's foremost virtue. He drives home this point by comparing the photographer with the witness, the observer, the stranger—three types supposed not to

be entangled in the events they happen to watch. They may perceive anything because nothing they see is pregnant with memories that would captivate them and thus limit their vision. The ideal photographer is the opposite of the unseeing lover. He resembles the indiscriminating mirror; he is
identical with the camera lens. Photography, Proust has it, is the product
of complete alienation.

The onesidedness of this definition is obvious. Yet the whole context
suggests that Proust was primarily concerned with the depiction of a state
of mind in which the impact of involuntary memories blurs the external
phenomena touching them off. And the desire to contrast, in the interest
of clarity, this state of mind with the photographer's may have led him to
adopt the credo of the extreme nineteenth-century realists, according to
which the photographer—any artist, for that matter—holds a mirror up to
nature.

Actually there is no mirror at all. Photographs do not just copy nature
but metamorphose it by transferring three-dimensional phenomena to the
plane, severing their ties with the surroundings, and substituting black,
gray, and white for the given color schemes. Yet if anything defies the idea
of a mirror, it is not so much these unavoidable transformations—which
may be discounted because in spite of them photographs still preserve the
character of compulsory reproductions—as the way in which we take cognizance of visible reality. Even Proust's alienated photographer spontaneously structures the inflowing impressions; the simultaneous perceptions
of his other senses, certain perceptual form categories inherent in his nervous system, and not least his general dispositions prompt him to organize
the visual raw material in the act of seeing.[58] And the activities in which
he thus unconsciously engages are bound to condition the pictures he
is taking.

But what about the candid photographs mentioned above—prints obtained almost automatically? In their case it falls to the spectator to do the
structuring. (The aerial reconnaissance photos referred to by Newhall interfere with the conventional structuring processes because of their unidentifiable shapes which cause the spectator to withdraw into the aesthetic
dimension.) Objectivity in the sense of the realist manifesto is unattainable. This being so, there is no earthly reason why the photographer should
suppress his formative faculties in the interest of the necessarily futile
attempt to achieve that objectivity. Provided his choices are governed by
his determination to record and reveal nature, he is entirely justified in
selecting motif, frame, lens, filter, emulsion and grain according to his
sensibilities. Or rather, he must be selective in order to transcend the
minimum requirement. For nature is unlikely to give itself up to him if
he does not absorb it with all his senses strained and his whole being

participating in the process. The formative tendency, then, does not have to conflict with the realistic tendency. Quite the contrary, it may help substantiate and fulfill it—an interaction of which the nineteenth-century realists could not possibly be aware. Contrary to what Proust says, the photographer sees things in his "own soul."

And yet Proust is right in relating the photographic approach to a state of alienation. Even though the photographer who acknowledges the properties of his medium rarely, if ever, shows the emotional detachment which Proust ascribes to him, he cannot freely externalize his inner vision either. What counts is the "right" mixture of his realist loyalties and formative endeavors—a mixture, that is, in which the latter, however strongly developed, surrender their independence to the former. As Lewis Mumford puts it: the photographer's "inner impulse, instead of spreading itself in subjective fantasy, must always be in key with outer circumstances."[59] Some early artist-photographers, such as Nadar, David Octavius Hill, and Robert Adamson, knew how to establish this precarious balance. Much as they were influenced by painting, they primarily aimed at bringing out the essential features of any person presented;[60] the photographic quality of their portraits, says Newhall, must be traced to the "dignity and depth of their perception."[61]

This means that the photographer's selectivity is of a kind which is closer to empathy than to disengaged spontaneity. He resembles perhaps most of all the imaginative reader intent on studying and deciphering an elusive text. Like a reader, the photographer is steeped in the book of nature. His "intensity of vision," claims Paul Strand, should be rooted in a "real respect for the thing in front of him."[62] Or in Weston's words, the camera "provides the photographer with a means of looking deeply into the nature of things, and presenting his subjects in terms of their basic reality."[63] Due to the revealing power of the camera, there is also something of an explorer about him; insatiable curiosity stirs him to roam yet unconquered expanses and capture the strange patterns in them. The photographer summons up his being, not to discharge it in autonomous creations but to dissolve it into the substances of the objects that close in on him. Once again, Proust is right: selectivity within this medium is inseparable from processes of alienation.

Let me insert here an observation on the possible role of melancholy in photographic vision. It is certainly not by accident that Newhall in his *History of Photography* mentions, on two different occasions, melancholy in connection with pictorial work in a photographic spirit. He remarks that Marville's pictures of the Paris streets and houses doomed under Napoleon III have the "melancholy beauty of a vanished past";[64] and he says of Atget's Paris street scenes that they are impregnated with the "melancholy that a good photograph can so powerfully evoke."[65] [Illus. 1] Now melancholy as an inner disposition not only makes elegiac objects seem attractive but carries still another, more important implication: it favors self-estrangement, which on its part entails identification with all kinds of objects. The dejected individual is likely to lose himself in the incidental configurations of his environment, absorbing them with a disinterested intensity no longer determined by his previous preferences. His is a kind of receptivity which resembles that of Proust's photographer cast in the role of a stranger. Film makers often exploited this intimate relationship between melancholy and the photographic approach in an attempt to render visible such a state of mind. A recurrent film sequence runs as follows: the melancholy character is seen strolling about aimlessly: as he proceeds, his changing surroundings take shape in the form of numerous juxtaposed shots of house façades, neon lights, stray passers-by, and the like. It is inevitable that the audience should trace their seemingly unmotivated emergence to his dejection and the alienation in its wake.

The formative tendency may not only become so weak that the resultant prints just barely fulfill the minimum requirement, but it may also take on proportions which threaten to overwhelm the realistic tendency. During the last few decades many a noted photographer has indulged in pictures which are either meant to explore the given raw material or serve to project inner images of their authors, or both. Characterizing a photograph of tree trunks with eye-like hollows in their bark, Moholy-Nagy observed: "The surrealist often *finds* images in nature which express his feelings."[66] Or think of Moholy-Nagy's own picture, *From Berlin Wireless Tower* [Illus. 2] and certain abstract or near-abstract compositions which on closer inspection reveal themselves to be rock and soil formations, unconventional combinations of objects, faces in big close-up, and what not. [Illus. 3]

In pictures of this type the balance between empathy and spontaneity is rather fragile. The photographer producing them does not subordinate his formative impulses to his realistic intentions but seems eager to manifest both of them with equal vigor. He is animated, perhaps without being aware of it, by two conflicting desires—the desire to externalize his inner images and the desire to render outer shapes. However, in order to reconcile them, he relies on occasional coincidences between those shapes and images. Hence the ambiguity of such photographs, which are a veritable *tour de force*. A good case in point is Mary Ann Dorr's photograph, *Chairs in the Sunlight*.[67] [Illus. 4] On the one hand, it does justice to the properties of the medium: the perforated chairs and the shadows they cast do exist. On the other, it is palpably intended as an artistic creation: the shadows and the chairs affect one as elements of a free composition rather than natural objects.

Unsettled borderline cases like these certainly retain a photographic quality if they suggest that their creators are devoted to the text of nature. And they are on the verge of losing that quality if the impression prevails that the photographer's "finds" merely reflect what he has already virtually found before training his camera on the external world; then he does not so much explore nature as utilize it for a pseudo-realistic statement of his own vision. He might even manufacture the coveted coincidence between his spontaneous imagery and actuality by slightly tampering with the latter.

The experimental photographer tends to trespass the border region marked by these blends of divergent intentions. Are his products still in the nature of photographs? Photograms or rayographs dispense with the camera; and those "creative" achievements which do not, radically consume —by molding it—the recorded raw material possibly going into them. The same holds true of photomontage.[68] It might be best to classify all compositions of this type as a special genre of the graphic arts rather than photography proper. Despite their obvious affiliations with photography, they are actually remote from it. Indeed, as we have seen, the experimental photographers themselves assert that their prints belong to a peculiar medium and, being artistic creations, should not be confused with such quasi-abstract records of reality as are, perhaps, no less attractive aesthetically.[69] But if these creations are no records, they do not fall into the dimension of paintings or drawings either. James Thrall Soby once remarked of them that they do not "wear well when hung as pictures."[70] It is as if the use of photography for strictly artistic purposes led into a sort of no man's land somewhere between reproduction and expression.

Affinities

Photographs in keeping with the photographic approach—where no misunderstanding is possible, they may just be called photographs—show certain affinities which can be assumed to be as constant as the properties of the medium to which they belong. Four of them call for special attention.

First, photography has an outspoken affinity for unstaged reality. Pictures which strike us as intrinsically photographic seem intended to render nature in the raw, nature as it exists independently of us. Now nature is particularly unstageable if it manifests itself in ephemeral configurations

which only the camera is able to capture.[71] This explains the delight of
early photographers in such subjects as "an accumulation of dust in a
hollow moulding,"[72] or a "casual gleam of sunshine."[73] (It is worth mentioning that Fox Talbot—it was he who exclaimed over the sunbeam—was
still so little sure of the legitimacy of his preferences that he tried to authenticate them by invoking the precedent of the "Dutch school of art.")
In the field of portraiture, it is true, photographers frequently interfere with
the given conditions. But the boundaries between staged and unstaged
reality are very fluid in this field; and a portraitist who provides a special
setting or asks his model to lower the head a bit may well be trying to
bring out the typical features of the client before his lens. What
counts is his desire to picture nature at its most characteristic so that his
portraits look like casual self-revelations, "instinct with the illusion of
life."[74] If, on the other hand, the expressive artist in him gets the better
of the imaginative reader or curious explorer, his portraits inevitably turn
into those ambiguous borderline cases dealt with above. They give you the
impression of being overcomposed in terms of lighting and/or subject
matter; they no longer catch reality in its flux, you feel, but arrange its
elements into a pattern reminiscent of painting.

Second, through this concern with unstaged reality, photography tends
to stress the fortuitous. Random events are the very meat of snapshots.
"We want to seize, in passing, upon all that may present itself unexpectedly
to our view and interest us in some respect," said a Frenchman about instantaneous photography nearly ten years before the first films appeared.[75]
Hence the attractiveness of street crowds. By 1859, New York stereographs
took a fancy to the kaleidoscopic mingling of vehicles and pedestrians,[76]
and somewhat later Victorian snapshots reveled in the same inchoate agglomerates. Marville, Stieglitz, Atget—all of them, as has been remarked,
acknowledged city life as a contemporary and photogenic major theme.[77]
Dreams nurtured by the big cities thus materialized as pictorial records of
chance meetings, strange overlappings, and fabulous coincidences. In portraiture, by the same token, even the most typical portraits must retain an
accidental character—as if they were plucked en route and still quivered
with crude existence. This affinity for the adventitious again implies that
the medium does not favor pictures which seem to be forced into an
"obvious compositional pattern."[78] (Of course, photographs of the compositional inventions of nature or man-made reality are quite another thing.)

Third, photography tends to suggest endlessness. This follows from
its emphasis on fortuitous complexes which represent fragments rather
than wholes. A photograph, whether portrait or action picture, is in character only if it precludes the notion of completeness. Its frame marks a

provisional limit; its content refers to other contents outside that frame; and its structure denotes something that cannot be encompassed—physical existence. Nineteenth-century writers called this something nature, or life; and they were convinced that photography would have to impress upon us its infinity. Leaves, which they counted among the favorite motifs of the camera, cannot be "staged" but occur in endless quantities. In this respect, there is an analogy between the photographic approach and scientific investigation: both probe into an inexhaustible universe whose entirety forever eludes them.

Fourth and finally, the medium has an affinity for the indeterminate of which Proust was keenly aware. Within the passage partially quoted, Proust also imagines the photograph of an Academician leaving the Institute. What the photograph shows us, he observes, "will be, instead of the dignified emergence of an Academician who is going to hail a cab, his staggering gait, his precautions to avoid tumbling upon his back, the parabola of his fall, as though he were drunk, or the ground frozen over."[79] The photograph Proust has in mind does not intimate that the Academician must be thought of as being undignified; it simply fails to tell us anything about his behavior in general or his typical attitudes. It so radically isolates a momentary pose of the Academician that the function of this pose within the total structure of his personality remains everybody's guess. The pose relates to a context which, itself, is not given. Photographs, implies Proust, transmit raw material without defining it.

No doubt Proust exaggerates the indeterminacy of photographs just as grossly as he does their depersonalizing quality. Actually the photographer endows his pictures with structure and meaning to the extent to which he makes deliberate choices. His pictures record nature and at the same time reflect his attempt to assimilate and decipher it. Yet, as in pointing up the photographer's alienation, Proust is again essentially right, for however selective photographs are, they cannot deny the tendency toward the unorganized and diffuse which marks them as records. It is therefore inevitable that they should be surrounded with a fringe of indistinct multiple meanings. (To be sure, the traditional work of art carries many meanings also. But due to its rise from interpretable human intentions and circumstances, the meanings inherent in it can virtually be ascertained, whereas those of the photograph are necessarily indeterminate because the latter is bound to convey unshaped nature itself, nature in its inscrutability. As compared with a photograph, any painting has a relatively definite significance. Accordingly, it makes sense to speak of multiple meanings, vague meaningfulness, and the like only in connection with camera work.)

Appeals

Products of a medium with so outspoken affinities may well exert specific appeals differing from those of the art media proper. Three such appeals are discernible.

We know, says Newhall, that subjects "can be misrepresented, distorted, faked . . . and even delight in it occasionally, but the knowledge still cannot shake our implicit faith in the truth of a photographic record."[80] This explains a common reaction to photographs: since the days of Daguerre they have been valued as documents of unquestionable authenticity. Baudelaire, who scorned both art's decline into photography and photography's pretense to art, at least admitted that photographs have the merit of rendering, and thus preserving, all those transient things which are entitled to a place in the "archives of our memory."[81] It would be difficult indeed to overestimate their early popularity as souvenirs. There is practically no family which does not boast an album crowded with generations of dear ones before varying backgrounds. With the passing of time, these souvenirs undergo a significant change of meaning. As the recollections they embody fade away, they increasingly assume documentary functions; their impact as photographic records definitely overshadows their original appeal as memory aids. Leafing through the family album, the grandmother will re-experience her honeymoon, while the children will curiously study bizarre gondolas, obsolete fashions, and old young faces they never saw.

And most certainly they will rejoice in discoveries, pointing to odd bagatelles which the grandmother failed to notice in her day. Or think of the satisfaction people are deriving from the scrutiny of an enlargement in which, one by one, things emerge they would not have suspected in the original print—nor in reality itself, for that matter. This too is a typical reaction to photographs. In fact, we tend to look at them in the hope of detecting something new and unexpected—a confidence which pays tribute to the camera's revealing faculty.

Finally, photography has always been recognized as a source of beauty. Yet beauty may be experienced in different ways. All those who do not expect a photograph to impress them as would a painting, are agreed that the beauty of, say, Nadar's portraits, Brady's Civil War scenes, or Atget's Paris Streets is inseparable from their being sensitive and technically impeccable readings rather than autonomous creations.[82] Generally speaking, photographs stand a chance of being beautiful to the extent that they comply with the photographic approach. This would account for the frequent observation that pictures extending our vision are not only gratifying as camera revelations but appeal to us aesthetically also—no matter, for the rest, whether they result from high selectivity or amount to purely mechanical products like the aerial reconnaissance photographs.

Fox Talbot called it one of the "charms" of photographs that they include things unknown to their maker, things which he himself must discover in them.[83] Similarly, Louis Delluc, one of the key figures of the French cinema after World War I, took delight—aesthetic delight—in the surprising revelations of Kodak pictures: "This is what enchants me: you will admit that it is unusual suddenly to notice, on a film or a plate, that some passer-by, inadvertently picked up by the camera lens, has a singular expression; that Mme X . . . preserves the unconscious secret of classic postures in scattered fragments; and that the trees, the water, the fabrics, the beasts achieve the familiar rhythm which we know is peculiar to them only by means of decomposed movements whose disclosure proves upsetting to us."[84] The aesthetic value of photographs would in a measure seem to be a function of their explorative powers.[*]

In our response to photographs, then, the desire for knowledge and the sense of beauty interpenetrate one another. Often photographs radiate beauty because they satisfy that desire. Moreover, in satisfying it by penetrating unknown celestial spaces and the recesses of matter, they may afford glimpses of designs beautiful in their own right.

The issue of art

At this point the controversial issue of whether or not photography is an art comes into view again. The controversy in its present form is strongly determined by the unwillingness of the champions of creativity to put up with the limitations which the photographic process imposes upon their formative urges. They consider any photographer who is following the photographic approach something less than an artist and, on their part, revolt against the recording duties he readily assumes. The issue, as they see it, could not be more poignantly characterized than by Moholy-Nagy's definition of the experimental photographer as an artist who "will not only select what he finds but . . . produce situations, introduce devices so far unused and neglected, which for him contain the necessary qualities of photographic expression."[85] The emphasis is on the elimination of accidental reality for the sake of art. Barbara Morgan, who builds a universe of

---

[*] Valéry, *Degas, dance, dessin*, p. 73, remarks that, in the case of flying birds, instantaneous photographs corroborate the prints of Japanese artists. For the resemblances between instantaneous photography and Japanese art, see Wolf-Czapek, *Die Kinematographie* . . . , pp. 112–13.

her own with the aid of synchroflash and speedlamps, declares that she is "grateful for man-made light and the creative freedom it gives."[86]

Yet much as the concept of art or creativity behind these statements applies to the traditional arts, it fails to do justice to the high degree of selectivity of which photographic records are susceptible. To be more precise, it overshadows the photographer's peculiar and truly formative effort to represent significant aspects of physical reality without trying to overwhelm that reality—so that the raw material focused upon is both left intact and made transparent. No doubt this effort carries aesthetic implications. Stieglitz's group of huddled trees is a memorable image of autumnal sadness. Cartier-Bresson's snapshots capture facial expressions and interrelationships between human figures and architecture which are strangely moving. [Illus. 5] And Brassai knows how to make walls and wet cobblestones eloquent.

Why, then, reserve the term "art" for the free compositions of the experimental photographers which, in a sense, lie outside the province of photography proper? This threatens to divert the attention from what is really characteristic of the medium. Perhaps it would be more fruitful to use the term "art" in a looser way so that it covers, however inadequately, achievements in a truly photographic spirit—pictures, that is, which are neither works of art in the traditional sense nor aesthetically indifferent products. Because of the sensibility that goes into them and the beauty they may breathe, there is something to be said in favor of such an extended usage.

I. GENERAL CHARACTERISTICS

Basic Concepts

LIKE THE EMBRYO in the womb, photographic film developed from distinctly separate components. Its birth came about from a combination of instantaneous photography, as used by Muybridge and Marey, with the older devices of the magic lantern and the phenakistoscope.[1] Added to this later were the contributions of other nonphotographic elements, such as editing and sound. Nevertheless photography, especially instantaneous photography, has a legitimate claim to top priority among these elements, for it undeniably is and remains the decisive factor in establishing film content. The nature of photography survives in that of film.

Originally, film was expected to bring the evolution of photography to an end—satisfying at last the age-old desire to picture things moving. This desire already accounted for major developments within the photographic medium itself. As far back as 1839, when the first daguerreotypes and talbotypes appeared, admiration mingled with disappointment about their deserted streets and blurred landscapes.[2] And in the 'fifties, long before the innovation of the hand camera, successful attempts were made to photograph subjects in motion.[3] The very impulses which thus led from time exposure to snapshot engendered dreams of a further extension of photography in the same direction—dreams, that is, of film. About 1860, Cook and Bonnelli, who had developed a device called a photobioscope, predicted a "complete revolution of photographic art. . . . We will see . . . landscapes," they announced, "in which the trees bow to the whims of the wind, the leaves ripple and glitter in the rays of the sun."[4]

Along with the familiar photographic leitmotif of the leaves, such kindred subjects as undulating waves, moving clouds, and changing facial expressions ranked high in prophecies. All of them conveyed the longing for an instrument which would capture the slightest incidents of the world about us—scenes that often would involve crowds, whose incalculable movements resemble, somehow, those of waves or leaves. In a memorable statement published before the emergence of instantaneous photography, Sir John Herschel not only predicted the basic features of the film camera but assigned to it a task which it has never since disowned: "the vivid and lifelike reproduction and handing down to the latest posterity of any transaction in real life—a battle, a debate, a public solemnity, a pugilistic conflict."[5] Ducos du Hauron and other forerunners also looked forward to what we have come to label newsreels and documentaries—films devoted to the rendering of real-life events.[6] This insistence on recording went hand in hand with the expectation that motion pictures could acquaint us with normally imperceptible or otherwise induplicable movements—flashlike transformations of matter, the slow growth of plants, etc.[7] All in all, it was taken for granted that film would continue along the lines of photography.*

To summarize: the preceding statements about photography also hold true of the cinematic medium; but they do not apply to it mechanically or go far enough to exhaust its potentialities. Elaborations and extensions are needed. They will be provided in the first three chapters, which represent an attempt to account for the general characteristics of the medium. The present chapter concentrates on the basic concepts underlying the subsequent analyses. The next chapter details the recording and revealing functions of film. The third deals with its particular affinities. This conceptual framework will later be filled in by inquiries into specific areas and elements of film and problems of film composition.

PROPERTIES OF THE MEDIUM

The properties of film can be divided into basic and technical properties.

The basic properties are identical with the properties of photography. Film, in other words, is uniquely equipped to record and reveal physical reality and, hence, gravitates toward it.

Now there are different visible worlds. Take a stage performance or a painting: they too are real and can be perceived. But the only reality we are concerned with is actually existing physical reality—the transitory world we live in. (Physical reality will also be called "material reality," or "physical existence," or "actuality," or loosely just "nature." Another fitting term might be "camera-reality." Finally, the term "life" suggests itself as an alter-

* Mr. Georges Sadoul, L'Invention du cinéma, p. 298, sagaciously observes that the names given the archaic film cameras offer clues to the then prevailing aspirations. Such names as vitascope, vitagraph, bioscope, and biograph were undoubtedly intended to convey the camera's affinity for "life," while terms like kinetoscope, kinetograph, and cinematograph testified to the concern with movement.

nate expression—for reasons which will appear in chapter 4.) The other visible worlds reach into this world without, however, really forming a part of it. A theatrical play, for instance, suggests a universe of its own which would immediately crumble were it related to its real-life environment.

As a reproductive medium, film is of course justified in reproducing memorable ballets, operas, and the like. Yet even assuming that such reproductions try to do justice to the specific requirements of the screen, they basically amount to little more than "canning," and are of no interest to us here. Preservation of performances which lie outside physical reality proper is at best a sideline of a medium so particularly suited to explore that reality. This is not to deny that reproductions, say, of stage production numbers may be put to good cinematic use in certain feature films and film genres.*

Of all the technical properties of film the most general and indispensable is editing. It serves to establish a meaningful continuity of shots and is therefore unthinkable in photography. (Photomontage is a graphic art rather than a specifically photographic genre.) Among the more special cinematic techniques are some which have been taken over from photography—e.g. the close-up, soft-focus pictures, the use of negatives, double or multiple exposure, etc. Others, such as the lap-dissolve, slow and quick motion, the reversal of time, certain "special effects," and so forth, are for obvious reasons exclusively peculiar to film.

These scanty hints will suffice. It is not necessary to elaborate on technical matters which have been dealt with in most previous theoretical writings on film.[8] Unlike these, which invariably devote a great deal of space to editing devices, modes of lighting, various effects of the close-up, etc., the present book concerns itself with cinematic techniques only to the extent to which they bear on the nature of film, as defined by its basic properties and their various implications. The interest lies not with editing in itself, regardless of the purposes it serves, but with editing as a means of implementing—or defying, which amounts to the same—such potentialities of the medium as are in accordance with its substantive characteristics. In other words, the task is not to survey all possible methods of editing for their own sake; rather, it is to determine the contributions which editing may make to cinematically significant achievements. Problems of film technique will not be neglected; however, they will be discussed only if issues going beyond technical considerations call for their investigation.

This remark on procedures implies what is fairly obvious anyway: that the basic and technical properties differ substantially from each other. As

* See pp. 73–4.

a rule the former take precedence over the latter in the sense that they are responsible for the cinematic quality of a film. Imagine a film which, in keeping with the basic properties, records interesting aspects of physical reality but does so in a technically imperfect manner; perhaps the lighting is awkward or the editing uninspired. Nevertheless such a film is more specifically a film than one which utilizes brilliantly all the cinematic devices and tricks to produce a statement disregarding camera-reality. Yet this should not lead one to underestimate the influence of the technical properties. It will be seen that in certain cases the knowing use of a variety of techniques may endow otherwise nonrealistic films with a cinematic flavor.*

THE TWO MAIN TENDENCIES

If film grows out of photography, the realistic and formative tendencies must be operative in it also. Is it by sheer accident that the two tendencies manifested themselves side by side immediately after the rise of the medium? As if to encompass the whole range of cinematic endeavors at the outset, each went the limit in exhausting its own possibilities. Their prototypes were Lumière, a strict realist, and Méliès, who gave free rein to his artistic imagination. The films they made embody, so to speak, thesis and antithesis in a Hegelian sense.[9]

Lumière and Méliès

Lumière's films contained a true innovation, as compared with the repertoire of the zootropes or Edison's peep boxes:[10] they pictured everyday life after the manner of photographs.[11] Some of his early pictures, such as Baby's Breakfast (Le Déjeuner de bébé) or The Card Players (La Partie d'écarté), testify to the amateur photographers's delight in family idyls and genre scenes.[12] And there was Teasing the Gardener (L'Arroseur arrosé), which enjoyed immense popularity because it elicited from the flow of everyday life a proper story with a funny climax to boot. A gardener is watering flowers and, as he unsuspectingly proceeds, an impish boy steps on the hose, releasing it at the very moment when his perplexed victim examines the dried-up nozzle. Water squirts out and hits the gardener smack in the face. The denouement is true to style, with the gardener chasing and spanking the boy. This film, the germ cell and archetype of all film comedies to come, represented an imaginative attempt on the part of Lumière to develop photography into a means of story telling.[13] Yet the

* See pp. 61–2, 87.

story was just a real-life incident. And it was precisely its photographic veracity which made Maxim Gorki undergo a shock-like experience. "You think," he wrote about TEASING THE GARDENER, "the spray is going to hit you too, and instinctively shrink back."[14]

On the whole, Lumière seems to have realized that story telling was none of his business; it involved problems with which he apparently did not care to cope. Whatever story-telling films he, or his company, made— some more comedies in the vein of his first one, tiny historical scenes, etc. —are not characteristic of his production.[15] The bulk of his films recorded the world about us for no other purpose than to present it. This is in any case what Mesguich, one of Lumière's "ace" cameramen, felt to be their message. At a time when the talkies were already in full swing he epitomized the work of the master as follows: "As I see it, the Lumière Brothers had established the true domain of the cinema in the right manner. The novel, the theater, suffice for the study of the human heart. The cinema is the dynamism of life, of nature and its manifestations, of the crowd and its eddies. All that asserts itself through movement depends on it. Its lens opens on the world."[16]

Lumière's lens did open on the world in this sense. Take his immortal first reels LUNCH HOUR AT THE LUMIERE FACTORY (*Sortie des usines Lumière*), ARRIVAL OF A TRAIN (*L'Arrivée d'un train*), LA PLACE DES CORDELIERS A LYON:[17] their themes were public places, with throngs of people moving in diverse directions. The crowded streets captured by the stereographic photographs of the late 'fifties thus reappeared on the primitive screen. It was life at its least controllable and most unconscious moments, a jumble of transient, forever dissolving patterns accessible only to the camera. The much-imitated shot of the railway station, with its emphasis on the confusion of arrival and departure, effectively illustrated the fortuity of these patterns; and their fragmentary character was exemplified by the clouds of smoke which leisurely drifted upward. Significantly, Lumière used the motif of smoke on several occasions. And he seemed anxious to avoid any personal interference with the given data. Detached records, his shots resembled the imaginary shot of the grandmother which Proust contrasts with the memory image of her.

Contemporaries praised these films for the very qualities which the prophets and forerunners had singled out in their visions of the medium. It was inevitable that, in the comments on Lumière, "the ripple of leaves stirred by the wind" should be referred to enthusiastically. The Paris journalist Henri de Parville, who used the image of the trembling leaves, also identified Lumière's over-all theme as "nature caught in the act."[18] Others pointed to the benefits which science would derive from Lumière's invention.[19] In America his camera-realism defeated Edison's kinetoscope with its staged subjects.[20]

Lumière's hold on the masses was ephemeral. In 1897, not more than two years after he had begun to make films, his popularity subsided. The sensation had worn off; the heyday was over. Lack of interest caused Lumière to reduce his production.[21]

Georges Méliès took over where Lumière left off, renewing and intensifying the medium's waning appeal. This is not to say that he did not occasionally follow the latter's example. In his beginnings he too treated the audience to sightseeing tours; or he dramatized, in the fashion of the period, realistically staged topical events.[22] But his main contribution to the cinema lay in substituting staged illusion for unstaged reality, and contrived plots for everyday incidents.[23]

The two pioneers were aware of the radical differences in their approach. Lumière told Méliès that he considered film nothing more than a "scientific curiosity,"[24] thereby implying that his cinematograph could not possibly serve artistic purposes. In 1897, Méliès on his part published a prospectus which took issue with Lumière: "Messrs. Méliès and Reulos specialize mainly in fantastic or artistic scenes, reproductions of theatrical scenes, etc. . . . thus creating a special genre which differs entirely from the customary views supplied by the cinematograph—street scenes or scenes of everyday life."[25]

Méliès's tremendous success would seem to indicate that he catered to demands left unsatisfied by Lumière's photographic realism. Lumière appealed to the sense of observation, the curiosity about "nature caught in the act"; Méliès ignored the workings of nature out of the artist's delight in sheer fantasy. The train in ARRIVAL OF A TRAIN is the real thing, whereas its counterpart in Méliès's AN IMPOSSIBLE VOYAGE (*Voyage à travers l'impossible*) is a toy train as unreal as the scenery through which it is moving. [Illus. 6, 7] Instead of picturing the random movements of phenomena, Méliès freely interlinked imagined events according to the requirements of his charming fairy-tale plots. Had not media very close to film offered similar gratifications? The artist-photographers preferred what they considered aesthetically attractive compositions to searching explorations of nature. And immediately before the arrival of the motion picture camera, magic lantern performances indulged in the projection of religious themes, Walter Scott novels, and Shakespearean dramas.[26]

Yet even though Méliès did not take advantage of the camera's ability to record and reveal the physical world, he increasingly created his illusions with the aid of techniques peculiar to the medium. Some he found by accident. When taking shots of the Paris Place de l'Opéra, he had to discontinue the shooting because the celluloid strip did not move as it should; the surprising result was a film in which, for no reason at all, a bus abruptly transformed itself into a hearse.[27] True, Lumière also was not disinclined to have a sequence of events unfold in reverse, but Méliès was the first to exploit cinematic devices systematically. Drawing on both photography and the stage, he innovated many techniques which were to play an enormous role in the future—among them the use of masks, multiple exposure, superimposition as a means of summoning ghosts, the lap-dissolve, etc.[28] And through his ingenuity in using these techniques he added a touch of cinema to his playful narratives and magic tricks. Stage traps ceased to be indispensable; sleights-of-hand yielded to incredible metamorphoses which film alone was able to accomplish. Illusion produced in this climate depended on another kind of craftsmanship than the magician's. It was cinematic illusion, and as such went far beyond theatrical make-believe. Méliès's THE HAUNTED CASTLE (*Le Manoir du diable*) "is conceivable only in the cinema and due to the cinema," says Henri Langlois, one of the best connoisseurs of the primitive era.[29]

Notwithstanding his film sense, however, Méliès still remained the theater director he had been. He used photography in a pre-photographic spirit—for the reproduction of a papier-mâché universe inspired by stage traditions. In one of his greatest films, A TRIP TO THE MOON (*Le Voyage dans la lune*), the moon harbors a grimacing man in the moon and the stars are bull's-eyes studded with the pretty faces of music hall girls. By the same token, his actors bowed to the audience, as if they performed on the stage. Much as his films differed from the theater on a technical plane, they failed to transcend its scope by incorporating genuinely cinematic subjects. This also explains why Méliès, for all his inventiveness, never thought of moving his camera;[30] the stationary camera perpetuated the spectator's relation to the stage. His ideal spectator was the traditional theatergoer, child or adult. There seems to be some truth in the observation that, as people grow older, they instinctively withdraw to the positions from which they set out to struggle and conquer. In his later years Méliès more and more turned from theatrical film to filmed theater, producing *féeries* which recalled the Paris Châtelet pageants.[31]

The realistic tendency

In following the realistic tendency, films go beyond photography in two respects. First, they picture movement itself, not only one or another of its phases. But what kinds of movements do they picture? In the primitive era when the camera was fixed to the ground, it was natural for film makers to concentrate on moving material phenomena; life on the screen was life only if it manifested itself through external, or "objective," motion. As cinematic techniques developed, films increasingly drew on camera mobility and editing devices to deliver their messages. Although their strength still lay in the rendering of movements inaccessible to other media, these movements were no longer necessarily objective. In the technically mature film "subjective" movements—movements, that is, which the spectator is invited to execute—constantly compete with objective ones. The spectator may have to identify himself with a tilting, panning, or traveling camera which insists on bringing motionless as well as moving objects to his attention.[32] Or an appropriate arrangement of shots may rush the audience through vast expanses of time and/or space so as to make it witness, almost simultaneously, events in different periods and places.

Nevertheless the emphasis is now as before on objective movement; the medium seems to be partial to it. As René Clair puts it: "If there is an aesthetics of the cinema . . . it can be summarized in one word: 'movement.' The external movement of the objects perceived by the eye, to which we are today adding the inner movement of the action."[33] The fact that he assigns a dominant role to external movement reflects, on a theoretical plane, a marked feature of his own earlier films—the ballet-like evolutions of their characters.

Second, films may seize upon physical reality with all its manifold movements by means of an intermediary procedure which would seem to be less indispensable in photography—staging. In order to narrate an intrigue, the film maker is often obliged to stage not only the action but the surroundings as well. Now this recourse to staging is most certainly legitimate if the staged world is made to appear as a faithful reproduction of the real one. The important thing is that studio-built settings convey the impression of actuality, so that the spectator feels he is watching events which might have occurred in real life and have been photographed on the spot.[34]

Falling prey to an interesting misconception, Emile Vuillermoz champions, for the sake of "realism," settings which represent reality as seen by a perceptive painter. To his mind they are more real than real-life shots because they impart the essence of what such shots are showing. Yet from the cinematic point of view these allegedly realistic settings are no less stagy than would be, say, a cubist or abstract composition. Instead of staging the given raw material itself, they offer, so to speak, the gist of it. In other words, they suppress the very camera-reality which film aims at incorporating. For this reason, the sensitive moviegoer will feel disturbed by them.[35] (The problems posed by films of fantasy which, as such, show little concern for physical reality will be considered later on.)

Strangely enough, it is entirely possible that a staged real-life event evokes a stronger illusion of reality on the screen than would the original event if it had been captured directly by the camera. The late Ernö Metzner who devised the settings for the studio-made mining disaster in Pabst's KAMERADSCHAFT—an episode with the ring of stark authenticity— insisted that candid shots of a real mining disaster would hardly have produced the same convincing effect.[36]

One may ask, on the other hand, whether reality can be staged so accurately that the camera-eye will not detect any difference between the original and the copy. Blaise Cendrars touches on this issue in a neat hypothetical experiment. He imagines two film scenes which are completely identical except for the fact that one has been shot on the Mont Blanc (the highest mountain of Europe) while the other was staged in the studio. His contention is that the former has a quality not found in the latter. There are on the mountain, says he, certain "emanations, luminous or otherwise, which have worked on the film and given it a soul."[37] Presumably large parts of our environment, natural or man-made, resist duplication.

The formative tendency

The film maker's formative faculties are offered opportunities far exceeding those offered the photographer. The reason is that film extends into dimensions which photography does not cover. These differ from each other according to area and composition. With respect to areas, film makers have never confined themselves to exploring only physical reality in front of the camera but, from the outset, persistently tried to penetrate the realms of history and fantasy. Remember Méliès. Even the realistic-minded Lumière yielded to the popular demand for historical scenes. As for composition, the two most general types are the story film and the non-story film. The latter can be broken down into the experimental film and the film of fact, which on its part comprises, partially or totally, such subgenres as the film on art, the newsreel, and the documentary proper.

It is easy to see that some of these dimensions are more likely than others to prompt the film maker to express his formative aspirations at the expense of the realistic tendency. As for areas, consider that of fantasy: movie directors have at all times rendered dreams or visions with the aid of settings which are anything but realistic. Thus in RED SHOES Moira Shearer dances, in a somnambulistic trance, through fantastic worlds avowedly intended to project her unconscious mind—agglomerates of landscape-like forms, near-abstract shapes, and luscious color schemes which have all the traits of stage imagery. [Illus. 8] Disengaged creativity thus drifts away from the basic concerns of the medium. Several dimensions of composition favor the same preferences. Most experimental films are not even designed to focus on physical existence; and practically all films following the lines of a theatrical story evolve narratives whose significance overshadows that of the raw material of nature used for their implementation. For the rest, the film maker's formative endeavors may also impinge on his realistic loyalties in dimensions which, because of their emphasis on physical reality, do not normally invite such encroachments; there are enough documentaries with real-life shots which merely serve to illustrate some self-contained oral commentary.

Clashes between the two tendencies

Films which combine two or more dimensions are very frequent; for instance, many a movie featuring an everyday-life incident includes a dream sequence or a documentary passage. Some such combinations may lead to overt clashes between the realistic and formative tendencies. This happens whenever a film maker bent on creating an imaginary universe from freely staged material also feels under an obligation to draw on camera-reality. In his HAMLET Laurence Olivier has the cast move about in a studio-built, conspicuously stagy Elsinore, whose labyrinthine architecture seems calculated to reflect Hamlet's unfathomable being. Shut off from our real-life environment, this bizarre structure would spread over the whole of the film were it not for a small, otherwise insignificant scene in which the real ocean outside that dream orbit is shown. But no sooner does the photographed ocean appear than the spectator experiences something like a shock. He cannot help recognizing that this little scene is an outright intrusion; that it abruptly introduces an element incompatible with the rest of the imagery. How he then reacts to it depends upon his sensibilities. Those indifferent to the peculiarities of the medium, and therefore unquestioningly accepting the staged Elsinore, are likely to resent the unexpected emergence of crude nature as a letdown, while those more sensitive to the properties of film will in a flash realize the make-believe character of the castle's mythical splendor. Another case in point is Renato Castellani's ROMEO AND JULIET. This attempt to stage Shakespeare in natural surroundings obviously rests upon the belief that camera-reality and the poetic reality of Shakespeare verse can be made to fuse into each other. Yet the dialogue as well as the intrigue establish a universe so remote from the chance world of real Verona streets and ramparts that all the scenes in which the two disparate worlds are seen merging tend to affect one as an unnatural alliance between conflicting forces.

Actually collisions of this kind are by no means the rule. Rather, there is ample evidence to suggest that the two tendencies which sway the medium may be interrelated in various other ways. Since some of these relationships between realistic and formative efforts can be assumed to be aesthetically more gratifying than the rest, the next step is to try to define them.

THE CINEMATIC APPROACH

It follows from what has been said in the preceding chapter that films may claim aesthetic validity if they build from their basic properties; like photographs, that is, they must record and reveal physical reality. I have already dealt with the possible counterargument that media peculiarities are in general too elusive to serve as a criterion;* for obvious reasons it does not apply to the cinematic medium either. Yet another objection suggests itself. One might argue that too exclusive an emphasis on the medium's primary relation to physical reality tends to put film in a strait jacket. This objection finds support in the many existing films which are completely unconcerned about the representation of nature. There is the abstract experimental film. There is an unending succession of "photoplays" or theatrical films which do not picture real-life material for its own sake but use it to build up action after the manner of the stage. And there are the many films of fantasy which neglect the external world in freely composed dreams or visions. The old German expressionist films went far in this direction; one of their champions, the German art critic Herman G. Scheffauer, even eulogizes expressionism on the screen for its remoteness from photographic life.[38]

Why, then, should these genres be called less "cinematic" than films concentrating on physical existence? The answer is of course that it is the latter alone which afford insight and enjoyment otherwise unattainable. True, in view of all the genres which do not cultivate outer reality and yet are here to stay, this answer sounds somewhat dogmatic. But perhaps it will be found more justifiable in the light of the following two considerations.

* See pp. 12–13.

First, favorable response to a genre need not depend upon its adequacy to the medium from which it issues. As a matter of fact, many a genre has a hold on the audience because it caters to widespread social and cultural demands; it is and remains popular for reasons which do not involve questions of aesthetic legitimacy. Thus the photoplay has succeeded in perpetuating itself even though most responsible critics are agreed that it goes against the grain of film. Yet the public which feels attracted, for instance, by the screen version of *Death of a Salesman*, likes this version for the very virtues which made the Broadway play a hit and does not in the least care whether or not it has any specifically cinematic merits.

Second, let us for the sake of argument assume that my definition of aesthetic validity is actually one-sided; that it results from a bias for one particular, if important, type of cinematic activities and hence is unlikely to take into account, say, the possibility of hybrid genres or the influence of the medium's nonphotographic components. But this does not necessarily speak against the propriety of that definition. In a strategic interest it is often more advisable to loosen up initial one-sidedness—provided it is well founded—than to start from all too catholic premises and then try to make them specific. The latter alternative runs the risk of blurring differences between the media because it rarely leads far enough away from the generalities postulated at the outset; its danger is that it tends to entail a confusion of the arts. When Eisenstein, the theoretician, began to stress the similarities between the cinema and the traditional art media, identifying film as their ultimate fulfillment, Eisenstein, the artist, increasingly trespassed the boundaries that separate film from elaborate theatrical spectacles: think of his ALEXANDER NEVSKY and the operatic aspects of his IVAN THE TERRIBLE.[39]

In strict analogy to the term "photographic approach" the film maker's approach is called "cinematic" if it acknowledges the basic aesthetic principle. It is evident that the cinematic approach materializes in all films which follow the realistic tendency. This implies that even films almost devoid of creative aspirations, such as newsreels, scientific or educational films, artless documentaries, etc., are tenable propositions from an aesthetic point of view—presumably more so than films which for all their artistry pay little attention to the given outer world. But as with photographic reportage, newsreels and the like meet only the minimum requirement.

What is of the essence in film no less than photography is the intervention of the film maker's formative energies in all the dimensions which the medium has come to cover. He may feature his impressions of this or that segment of physical existence in documentary fashion, transfer hallucinations and mental images to the screen, indulge in the rendering of rhythmical patterns, narrate a human-interest story, etc. All these creative efforts are in keeping with the cinematic approach as long as they benefit, in some way or other, the medium's substantive concern with our visible world. As in photography, everything depends on the "right" balance between the realistic tendency and the formative tendency; and the two tendencies are well balanced if the latter does not try to overwhelm the former but eventually follows its lead.

THE ISSUE OF ART

When calling the cinema an art medium, people usually think of films which resemble the traditional works of art in that they are free creations rather than explorations of nature. These films organize the raw material to which they resort into some self-sufficient composition instead of accepting it as an element in its own right. In other words, their underlying formative impulses are so strong that they defeat the cinematic approach with its concern for camera-reality. Among the film types customarily considered art are, for instance, the above-mentioned German expressionist films of the years after World War I; conceived in a painterly spirit, they seem to implement the formula of Hermann Warm, one of the designers of THE CABINET OF DR. CALIGARI settings, who claimed that "films must be drawings brought to life."[40] Here also belongs many an experimental film; all in all, films of this type are not only intended as autonomous wholes but frequently ignore physical reality or exploit it for purposes alien to photographic veracity.* By the same token, there is an inclination to classify as works of art feature films which combine forceful artistic composition with devotion to significant subjects and values. This would apply to a number of adaptations of great stage plays and other literary works.

Yet such a usage of the term "art" in the traditional sense is misleading. It lends support to the belief that artistic qualities must be attributed precisely to films which neglect the medium's recording obligations in an attempt to rival achievements in the fields of the fine arts, the theater, or literature. In consequence, this usage tends to obscure the aesthetic value of films which are really true to the medium. If the term "art" is reserved for productions like HAMLET or DEATH OF A SALESMAN, one will find it difficult indeed to appreciate properly the large amount of creativity that goes into many a documentary capturing material phenomena for their own sake. Take Ivens's RAIN or Flaherty's NANOOK, docu-

* For the experimental film, see chapter 10.

mentaries saturated with formative intentions: like any selective photographer, their creators have all the traits of the imaginative reader and curious explorer; and their readings and discoveries result from full absorption in the given material and significant choices. Add to this that some of the crafts needed in the cinematic process—especially editing—represent tasks with which the photographer is not confronted. And they too lay claim to the film maker's creative powers.

This leads straight to a terminological dilemma. Due to its fixed meaning, the concept of art does not, and cannot, cover truly "cinematic" films—films, that is, which incorporate aspects of physical reality with a view to making us experience them. And yet it is they, not the films reminiscent of traditional art works, which are valid aesthetically. If film is an art at all, it certainly should not be confused with the established arts.* There may be some justification in loosely applying this fragile concept to such films as NANOOK, or PAISAN, or POTEMKIN which are deeply steeped in camera-life. But in defining them as art, it must always be kept in mind that even the most creative film maker is much less independent of nature in the raw than the painter or poet; that his creativity manifests itself in letting nature in and penetrating it.

* Arnold Hauser belongs among the few who have seen this. In his *The Philosophy of Art History*, p. 363, he says: "The film is the only art that takes over considerable pieces of reality unaltered; it interprets them, of course, but the interpretation remains a photographic one." His insight notwithstanding, however, Hauser seems to be unaware of the implications of this basic fact.

The Establishment of Physical Existence

"The task I'm trying to achieve is above all to make you see."
(D. W. Griffith to an interviewer in 1913)[1]

IN ESTABLISHING physical existence, films differ from photographs in two respects: they represent reality as it evolves in time; and they do so with the aid of cinematic techniques and devices.

Consequently, the recording and revealing duties of the two kindred media coincide only in part. And what do they imply for film in particular? The hunting ground of the motion picture camera is in principle unlimited; it is the external world expanding in all directions. Yet there are certain subjects within that world which may be termed "cinematic" because they seem to exert a peculiar attraction on the medium. It is as if the medium were predestined (and eager) to exhibit them. The following pages are devoted to a close examination of these cinematic subjects. Several lie, so to speak, on the surface; they will be dealt with under the title "recording functions." Others would hardly come to our attention or be perceptible were it not for the film camera and/or the intervention of cinematic techniques; they will be discussed in the subsequent section "revealing functions." To be sure, any camera revelation involves recording, but recording on its part need not be revealing.

RECORDING FUNCTIONS

Movement

At least two groups of quite common external phenomena are naturals for the screen. As might be expected, one is made up of all kinds of movements, these being cinematic because only the motion picture camera is able to record them. Among them are three types which can be considered cinematic subjects par excellence.

THE CHASE

"The chase," says Hitchcock, "seems to me the final expression of the motion picture medium."[2] This complex of interrelated movements is motion at its extreme, one might almost say, motion as such—and of course it is immensely serviceable for establishing a continuity of suspenseful physical action. Hence the fascination the chase has held since the beginning of the century.[3] The primitive French comedies availed themselves of it to frame their space-devouring adventures. Gendarmes pursued a dog who eventually turned the tables on them (*Course des sergeants de ville*); pumpkins gliding from a cart were chased by the grocer, his donkey, and passers-by through sewers and over roofs (*La Course des potirons*, 1907; English title: THE PUMPKIN RACE). For any Keystone comedy to forgo the chase would have been an unpardonable crime. It was the climax of the whole, its orgiastic finale—a pandemonium, with onrushing trains telescoping into automobiles and narrow escapes down ropes that dangled above a lion's den.

But perhaps nothing reveals the cinematic significance of this reveling in speed more drastically than D. W. Griffith's determination to transfer, at the end of all his great films, the action from the ideological plane to that of his famous "last-minute rescue," which was a chase pure and simple. Or should one say, a race? In any case, the rescuers rush ahead to overwhelm the villains or free their victims at the very last moment, while simultaneously the inner emotion which the dramatic conflict has aroused yields to a state of acute physiological suspense called forth by exuberant physical motion and its immediate implications. Nor is a genuine Western imaginable without a pursuit or a race on horseback. As Flaherty put it, Westerns are popular "because people never get tired of seeing a horse gallop across the plains."[4] Its gallop seems still to gain momentum by contrast with the immense tranquility of the faraway horizon.

DANCING

The second type of specifically cinematic movement is dancing. This does not apply, of course, to the stage ballet which evolves in a space-time outside actuality proper. Interestingly enough, all attempts at "canning" it adequately have so far failed. Screen reproductions of theatrical dancing either indulge in a completeness which is boring or offer a selection of attractive details which confuse in that they dismember rather than preserve the original. Dancing attains to cinematic eminence only if it is part and parcel of physical reality. René Clair's early sound films have judiciously been called ballets. True, they are, but the performers are real-life Parisians who just cannot help executing dance movements when going about their love adventures and minor quarrels. With infinite subtlety Clair guides them along the divide between the real and unreal. Sometimes it appears as though these delivery boys, taxi drivers, girls, clerks, shopkeepers, and nondescript figures are marionettes banding together and parting from each other according to designs as delicate as lacework; and then again they are made to look and behave like ordinary people in Paris streets and bistros. And the latter impression prevails. For, even granted that they are drawn into an imaginary universe, this universe itself reflects throughout our real world in stylizing it. What dancing there is, seems to occur on the spur of the moment; it is the vicissitudes of life from which these ballets issue.

Fred Astaire too prefers apparent impromptu performances to stage choreography; he is quite aware that this type of performance is appropriate to the medium. "Each dance," says he, "ought to spring somehow out of character or situation, otherwise it is simply a vaudeville act."[5] This does not mean that he would dispense with theatrical production numbers. But no sooner does he perform in vaudeville fashion than he breaks out of the prison of prearranged stage patterns and, with a genius for improvisation, dances over tables and gravel paths into the everyday world. It is a one-way route which invariably leads from the footlights to the heart of camera-reality. Astaire's consummate dancing is meant to belong among the real-life events with which he toys in his musicals; and it is so organized that it imperceptibly emerges from, and disappears, in the flow of these happenings.

But what could be more inseparable from that flow than "natural" dancing? Time and again film makers have trained their cameras on dancing couples and scenes of social dancing, as if irresistibly attracted by the cinematic nature of movements which grow out of life itself. Think of the beautiful ballroom episodes in JEZEBEL and PYGMALION or the elaborate cancan sequence in MOULIN ROUGE. And there is Roger Tilton's documentary JAZZ DANCE, an apt montage of candid shots conveying the collective ecstasy of jazz addicts. Every moviegoer will recall no end of examples. Records of dancing sometimes amount to an intrusion into the dancer's intimate privacy. His self-forgetting rapture may show in queer gestures and distorted facial expressions which are not intended to be watched, save by those who cannot watch them because they themselves participate in the dancing. Looking at such secret displays is like spying; you feel ashamed for entering a forbidden realm where things are going on which must be experienced, not witnessed. However, the supreme virtue of the camera consists precisely in acting the voyeur.

The third type of motion which offers special interest cinematically is not just another group of interrelated movements but movement as contrasted with motionlessness. In focusing upon this contrast, films strikingly demonstrate that objective movement—any movement, for that matter—is one of their choice subjects. Alexander Dovzhenko in both ARSENAL and EARTH frequently ,stops the action to resume it after a short lull. The first phase of this procedure—characters or parts of them abruptly ceasing to move—produces a shock effect, as if all of a sudden we found ourselves in a vacuum. The immediate consequence is that we acutely realize the significance of movement as an integral element of the external world as well as film.

But this is only part of the story. Even though the moving images on the screen come to a standstill, the thrust of their movement is too powerful to be discontinued simultaneously. Accordingly, when the people in ARSENAL or EARTH are shown in the form of stills, the suspended movement nevertheless perpetuates itself by changing from outer motion into inner motion. [Illus. 9] Dovzhenko has known how to make this metamorphosis benefit his penetrations of reality. The immobile lovers in EARTH become transparent; the deep happiness which is moving them turns inside out. And the spectator on his part grasps their inward agitation because the cessation of external motion moves him all the more intensely to commune with them.[6] Yet despite these rewarding experiences he cannot help feeling a certain relief when eventually the characters take on life again— an event which marks the second and final phase of the procedure. It is a return to the world of film, whose inherent motion alone renders possible such excursions into the whirlpool of the motionless.

Instead of transforming, Dovzhenko-fashion, moving life into live immobility, the film maker may also contrast movement with any of the innumerable phases comprising it. In the beach episode of the silent German film MENSCHEN AM SONNTAG, a remarkable semi-documentary of 1929, snapshots of the bathers, taken by a photographer on the spot, are inserted in different places; and the snapshots snatch from the flow of movement precisely such bodily postures as are bizarre and in a sense unnatural.[7] The contrast between the bustling bodies and the poses they assume in the cuts-in could not be stronger. At the sight of these rigid and ludicrous poses the spectator cannot help identifying motionlessness with lifelessness and, accordingly, life with movement; and still under the impact of the preceding commotion, he is at the same time likely to react to the sudden change from meaningful *temps durée* into mechanical *temps espace* with spontaneous laughter. Unlike the Dovzhenko stills which draw him deeper and deeper into their orbit, the snapshots on the beach strike him as funny for freezing life into an absurd standstill. It is worth mentioning that they had also the sociological function of exposing the ideological emptiness of lower middle-class people of the period.[8]

Inanimate objects

Since the inanimate is featured in many paintings, one might question the legitimacy of characterizing it as a cinematic subject. Yet it is a painter —Fernand Léger—who judiciously insists that only film is equipped to sensitize us, by way of big close-ups, to the possibilities that lie dormant in a hat, a chair, a hand, and a foot.[9] Similarly Cohen-Séat: "And I? says the leaf which is falling.–And we? say the orange peel, the gust of wind. . . . Film, whether intentionally or not, is their mouthpiece."[10] Nor should it be forgotten that the camera's ability to single out and record the orange peel or the hand marks a decisive difference between screen and stage, so close to each other in some respects. Stage imagery inevitably centers on the actor, whereas film is free to dwell on parts of his appearance and detail the objects about him. In using its freedom to bring the inanimate to the fore and make it a carrier of action, film only protests its peculiar requirement to explore all of physical existence, human or nonhuman. Within this context it is of interest that in the early 'twenties, when the French cinema was swamped with theatrical adaptations and stage-minded dramas, Louis Delluc tried to put the medium on its own feet by stressing the tremendous importance of objects. If they are assigned the role due to them, he argued, the actor too "is no more than a detail, a fragment of the matter of the world."[11]*

Actually, the urge to raise hats and chairs to the status of full-fledged actors has never completely atrophied. From the malicious escalators, the unruly Murphy beds, and the mad automobiles in silent comedy to the cruiser Potemkin, the oil derrick in Louisiana Story and the dilapidated kitchen in Umberto D., a long procession of unforgettable objects has passed across the screen—objects which stand out as protagonists and all but overshadow the rest of the cast. [Illus. 10] Or remember the powerful presence of environmental influences in The Grapes of Wrath; the part played by nocturnal Coney Island in Little Fugitive; the interaction between the marshland and the guerrilla fighters in the last episode of

* See p. 97.

PAISAN. Of course, the reverse holds true also: films in which the inanimate merely serves as a background to self-contained dialogue and the closed circuit of human relationships are essentially uncinematic.

REVEALING FUNCTIONS

"I ask that a film *discover* something for me," declares Luis Buñuel, who is himself a fiery pathfinder of the screen.[12] And what are films likely to discover? The evidence available suggests that they assume three kinds of revealing functions. They tend to reveal things normally unseen; phenomena overwhelming consciousness; and certain aspects of the outer world which may be called "special modes of reality."

Things normally unseen

The many material phenomena which elude observation under normal circumstances can be divided into three groups. The first includes objects too small to be readily noticed or even perceived by the naked eye and objects so big that they will not be fully taken in either.

THE SMALL AND THE BIG

The small   The small is conveyed in the form of close-ups. D. W. Griffith was among the first to realize that they are indispensable for cinematic narration. He initiated their use, as we now know it, in AFTER MANY YEARS (1908), an adaptation of Tennyson's *Enoch Arden*. There his memorable first close-up appeared within contexts which Lewis Jacobs describes as follows: "Going further than he had ventured before, in a scene showing Annie Lee brooding and waiting for her husband's return, Griffith daringly used a large close-up of her face. . . . He had another surprise, even more radical, to offer. Immediately following the close-up of Annie, he inserted a picture of the object of her thoughts—her husband cast away on a desert isle."[13]

On the surface, this succession of shots seems simply designed to lure the spectator into the dimension of her intimate preoccupations. He first watches Annie from a distance and then approaches her so closely that he sees only her face; if he moves on in the same direction, as the film invites him to do, it is logical that he should penetrate Annie's appearance and land inside her mind. Granting the validity of this interpretation, the close-up of her face is not an end in itself; rather, along with the subsequent shots, it serves to suggest what is going on behind that face—

Annie's longing for reunion with her husband. A knowingly chosen detail of her physique thus would help establish the whole of her being in a dramatic interest.

The same obviously holds true of another famous Griffith close-up: Mae Marsh's clasped hands in the trial episode of INTOLERANCE. It almost looks as if her huge hands with the convulsively moving fingers were inserted for the sole purpose of illustrating eloquently her anguish at the most crucial moment of the trial; as if, generally speaking, the function of any such detail exhausted itself in intensifying our participation in the total situation.[14] This is how Eisenstein conceives of the close-up. Its main function, says he, is "not so much to *show* or to *present* as to *signify*, to *give meaning*, to *designate*." To designate what? Evidently something of importance to the narrative. And montage-minded as he is, he immediately adds that the significance of the close-up for the plot accrues to it less from its own content than from the manner in which it is juxtaposed with the surrounding shots.[15] According to him, the close-up is primarily a montage unit.

But is this really its only function? Consider again the combination of shots with the close-up of Annie's face: the place assigned to the latter in the sequence intimates that Griffith wanted us also to absorb the face for its own sake instead of just passing through and beyond it; the face appears before the desires and emotions to which it refers have been completely defined, thus tempting us to get lost in its puzzling indeterminacy. Annie's face is also an end in itself. And so is the image of Mae Marsh's hands. [Illus. 11] No doubt it is to impress upon us her inner condition, but besides making us experience what we would in a measure have experienced anyway because of our familiarity with the characters involved, this close-up contributes something momentous and unique—it reveals how her hands behave under the impact of utter despair.*

Eisenstein criticizes the close-ups in Griffith films precisely for their relative independence of the contexts in which they occur. He calls them isolated units which tend "to show or to present"; and he insists that to the extent that they indulge in isolation they fail to yield the meanings which the interweaving processes of montage may elicit from them.[16] Had Eisenstein been less possessed with the magic powers of montage he

---

* Balázs, *Der sichtbare Mensch*, p. 73, defines the meaning of the close-up in a similar way. In his review of George Stevens's A PLACE IN THE SUN, Mr. Bosley Crowther says of the typical close-up in this film that it is "contrived to catch the heartbeat of agitated blood in youthful veins, the heat of flesh released from pressure, the flash of fear or desperation in troubled eyes." (Crowther, "Seen in Close-up," *The New York Times*, Sept. 23, 1951.)

would certainly have acknowledged the cinematic superiority of the Griffith close-up. To Griffith such huge images of small material phenomena are not only integral components of the narrative but disclosures of new aspects of physical reality. In representing them the way he does, he seems to have been guided by the conviction that the cinema is all the more cinematic if it acquaints us with the physical origins, ramifications, and connotations of all the emotional and intellectual events which comprise the plot; that it cannot adequately account for these inner developments unless it leads us through the thicket of material life from which they emerge and in which they are embedded.

Now suppose we look at a big close-up—say, Mae Marsh's hands. As we are watching them, something strange is bound to happen: we will forget that they are just ordinary hands. Isolated from the rest of the body and greatly enlarged, the hands we know will change into unknown organisms quivering with a life of their own. Big close-ups metamorphose their objects by magnifying them. Proust's narrator anticipates this metamorphosis in his description of an enterprise which, though it is not precisely a lover's performance, yet turns out to be a kiss—a kiss he eventually places on Albertine's cheek: "As my mouth was gradually to approach the cheeks which my eyes had suggested to it that it should kiss, my eyes, changing their position, saw a different pair of cheeks; the throat, studied at closer range and as though through a magnifying glass, shewed in its coarse grain a robustness which modified the character of the face."[17] Any huge close-up reveals new and unsuspected formations of matter; skin textures are reminiscent of aerial photographs, eyes turn into lakes or volcanic craters. Such images blow up our environment in a double sense: they enlarge it literally; and in doing so, they blast the prison of conventional reality, opening up expanses which we have explored at best in dreams before.[18]

It is not the big close-up alone which changes familiar sights into unusual patterns. Like it, diverse cinematic techniques and devices draw on shots of physical reality to evolve pictures or combinations of pictures which deviate from the conventional image of that reality. An interesting case in point is Kuleshov's "creative geography," a device which dissolves given spatial interrelationships.[19] Pictures of material phenomena taken in different places are juxtaposed in such a way that their combination evokes the illusion of a spatial continuity which of course is found nowhere in nature. The artificial space thus created is mostly intended as an excursion into the realm of fantasy (which does not imply that it might not as well be made to bring out inherent potentialities of physical reality itself). In René Clair's ENTR'ACTE, for instance, the camera tilts from the lower half of the ballerina up to the head of a bearded male so as to suggest, playfully, an impossible figure composed of these disparate pieces. And in Maya Deren's STUDY IN CHOREOGRAPHY FOR CAMERA a dancer lifts his leg in the woods and puts it down in a private room, thereby becoming part of a scenery whose unreal changes recall the intangible transitions of dream images.[20] Or think of the insertion of negatives and the reversal of time: they certainly go far in defying our habits of seeing. Other types of this bizarre imagery will be discussed later. Together they occupy an area which may be called "reality of another dimension" or "contrived reality."

Now these deviant images raise a fascinating problem: what exactly is their relation to physical existence proper? Critics ranking the cinema on a level with the traditional arts refer to instances of reality of another dimension in support of their opinion that films are not, or at least need not be, primarily concerned with the rendering of the given outer world; and that, accordingly, the film maker is at liberty to neglect its representation in favor of whatever visions or fantasies he wants to convey.

But this is a crude approach to the problem. Actually, contrived-reality pictures, such as the big close-up of Mae Marsh's hands, are ambiguous; they may or may not bear on physical reality as commonly perceived. If they form part of an otherwise realistic film, they are likely to affect us as an outgrowth of the same realism which animates the rest of the picture; they will be conceived, that is, as disclosures of hidden aspects of the world about us. Thus Mae Marsh's hands deepen our insight into the bodily components of the whole of her existence. Similarly, certain shots in JAZZ DANCE which, taken out of the context, would hardly resemble any known real-life objects, initiate us into the secrets of a material universe set afire by the dancers' frenzy. [Illus. 12] If, on the other hand, pictures constituting reality of another dimension are used as elements of creative compositions unconcerned about physical reality, they lose their reality character and often impress one as freely invented shapes. Many an experimental film plays upon the ambiguity of these deviant pictures by transforming them, before our eyes, from representations of reality into patterns completely disengaged from the latter. In LA MARCHE DES MACHINES, for instance, big close-ups of machine parts, still recognizable as such, turn into rhythmically moving forms which no longer refer back to their origins.

Yet the fact that these close-ups of machine parts readily lend themselves to substituting for free-floating abstractions should not make one forget that they are essentially derivatives of camera-reality. And of course, what applies to them holds true of all types of images belonging to reality of another dimension. In consequence, these deviant images will be all the more significant if they keep close to the real-life material from which they stem; only then can they be expected to assume the revealing functions peculiar to the medium.

In its preoccupation with the small the cinema is comparable to science. Like science, it breaks down material phenomena into tiny particles, thereby sensitizing us to the tremendous energies accumulated in the microscopic configurations of matter. These analogies may well be related to the nature of film. It is quite possible indeed that the construction of the film image from shots of minute phases of movement favors the reverse tendency toward decomposing given wholes. Is it really surprising that a medium so greatly indebted to nineteenth-century concern for science should show characteristics inherent in the scientific approach? Incidentally, the very ideas and impulses responsible for the rise of film have also left their imprint on Proust's novel. This would account for its parallels with film—especially the sustained use Proust makes in it of the close-up. In truly cinematic fashion he magnifies throughout the smallest elements or cells of reality, as if prompted by a desire to identify them as the source and seat of the explosive forces which make up life.

The big   Among the large objects, such as vast plains or panoramas of any kind, one deserves special attention: the masses. No doubt imperial Rome already teemed with them. But masses of people in the modern sense entered the historical scene only in the wake of the industrial revolution. Then they became a social force of first magnitude. Warring nations resorted to levies on an unheard-of scale and identifiable groups yielded to the anonymous multitude which filled the big cities in the form of amorphous crowds. Walter Benjamin observes that in the period marked by the rise of photography the daily sight of moving crowds was still a spectacle to which eyes and nerves had to get adjusted. The testimony of sensitive contemporaries would seem to corroborate this sagacious observation: The Paris crowds omnipresent in Baudelaire's *Les Fleurs du mal* function as stimuli which call forth irritating kaleidoscopic sensations; the jostling and shoving passers-by who, in Poe's *Man of the Crowd*, throng gas-lit London provoke a succession of electric shocks.[21]

At the time of its emergence the mass, this giant animal, was a new and upsetting experience. As might be expected, the traditional arts proved unable to encompass and render it. Where they failed, photography easily succeeded; it was technically equipped to portray crowds as the accidental agglomerations they are. Yet only film, the fulfillment of photography in a sense, was equal to the task of capturing them in motion. In this case the instrument of reproduction came into being almost simultaneously with one of its main subjects. Hence the attraction which masses exerted on still and motion picture cameras from the outset.[22] It is certainly more than sheer coincidence that the very first Lumière films featured a crowd of workers and the confusion of arrival and departure at a railway station. Early Italian films elaborated upon the theme;[23] and D. W. Griffith, inspired by them, showed how masses can be represented cinematically. The Russians absorbed his lesson, applying it in ways of their own.

The fact that big objects are as inaccessible to the stage as small ones suffices to range them among the cinematic subjects. Any such object—say, a wide landscape—may be recorded by a long distance shot; but, despite their significance in Griffith films, shots of this type are seldom enough to establish a large phenomenon to the full.[24] There is something to reveal about it which is not given away in the total picture of it. The big differs from the small in that it can be exhausted only by a combination of pictures taken from different distances. Faced with the task of capturing the substance of a large-scale landscape, film ought to proceed like a tourist who, in strolling through that landscape, lets his eyes wander about so that his ultimate image of it will be composed of sundry details and vistas.[25] Consider a street demonstration. "In order to receive a clear and definite impression of the demonstration," says Pudovkin, "the observer must perform certain actions. First he must climb upon the roof of a house to get a view from above of the procession as a whole and measure its dimension; next he must come down and look out through the first-floor window at the inscriptions carried by the demonstrators; finally, he must mingle with the crowd to gain an idea of the outward appearance of the participants."[26]

All these obligations may be taken care of by a single traveling shot which successively shows the ensemble and diverse elements of it. But the most primitive, most common procedure is a juxtaposition of long shots and close shots. Whether such a combination of pictures begins with a long shot or a close shot is as immaterial as is the number of shots used in the process. What does matter is that the alternating shots launch the spectator on a movement enabling him really to grasp the street demonstration or whatever tends to overwhelm him through its oversized proportions. Even though this editing unit assumes a particularly incisive function when applied to big objects, it is also needed for penetrations of normal-sized phenomena—descriptions, that is, which do not confine themselves to duplicating conventional reality. Griffith closes in on Annie's face only after having presented her whole figure, and it is in effect the combination of these two or more shots out of which her image arises.

The sequence long shot——close shot——long shot, etc., is a basic editing sequence.

The general use made of this sequence points to another resemblance between cinematic and scientific procedures. Science postulates principles bearing on the nature of the universe or some dimension of it, deduces their implications, and tries to verify them by experiment and observation. The physical universe being indefinable, this is an endless process, involving ever new hypotheses, ever new verifications. Facts emerge which do not conform to the original propositions; consequently, more fitting propositions must be evolved and again tested, and so on. It is a process which can also be described as a continuous to-and-fro movement between the hypothesized qualities of complex entities and the observed qualities of their elements (which partly elude direct observation, though). The similarity between this movement and the editing sequence long shot ——close shot——long shot, etc., consists precisely in their common aspiration to comprehend, each in its way, large ensembles and eventually nature itself.[27]

THE TRANSIENT

The second group of things normally unseen comprises the transient. Here belong, first, fleeting impressions—"the shadow of a cloud passing across the plain, a leaf which yields to the wind."[28] Evanescent, like dream elements, such impressions may haunt the moviegoer long after the story they are called upon to implement has sunk into oblivion. The manes of the galloping horses—flying threads or streamers rather than manes—in the chariot race episode of Fred Niblo's BEN HUR are as unforgettable as the fiery traces of the projectiles that tear the night in DESERT VICTORY. [Illus. 13] The motion picture camera seems to be partial to the least permanent components of our environment. It may be anticipated that the street in the broadest sense of the word is a place where impressions of this kind are bound to occur. "The cinema," says Aragon, delighting in its snapshot-like predilection for the ephemeral, "has taught us more about man in a few years than centuries of painting have taught: fugitive expressions, attitudes scarcely credible yet real, charm and hideousness."[29]

Second, there are movements of so transitory a nature that they would be imperceptible were it not for two cinematic techniques: accelerated-motion, which condenses extremely slow and, hence, unobservable developments, such as the growth of plants, and slow-motion, which expands movements too fast to be registered. Like the big close-up, these correlated techniques lead straight into "reality of another dimension." Pictures of stalks piercing the soil in the process of growing open up imaginary areas; and racing legs shown in slow-motion do not just slow down but change in appearance and perform bizarre evolutions—patterns remote from reality as we know it. Slow-motion shots parallel the regular close-ups; they are, so to speak, temporal close-ups achieving in time what the close-up proper is achieving in space. That, unlike the latter, they are used rather infrequently, may be traced to the fact that the enlargement of spatial phenomena, as effected by the close-up, seems more "natural" to us than the expansion of a given time interval. (On the other hand, it appears that film makers draw more readily on slow-motion than on the reverse technique—perhaps simply because it does not require so lengthy preparations.)

As contrived-reality pictures, the deviant images gained by both techniques, especially slow-motion, may well figure in nonrealistic experimental films. Yet they live up to the cinematic approach only if they are made to fulfill a revealing function within contexts focusing on physical existence. The late Jean Epstein, who felt so immensely attracted by "reality of another dimension," considered this their true destination. Referring to waves in slow-motion and clouds in accelerated-motion, he declared that for all their "startling physics and strange mechanics" they "are but a portrait—seen in a certain perspective—of the world in which we live."[30]

BLIND SPOTS OF THE MIND

The third and last group of things normally unseen consists of phenomena which figure among the blind spots of the mind; habit and prejudice prevent us from noticing them.[31]* The role which cultural standards and traditions may play in these processes of elimination is drastically illustrated by a report on the reactions of African natives to a film made on the spot. After the screening the spectators, all of them still unacquainted with the medium, talked volubly about a chicken they allegedly had seen picking food in the mud. The film maker himself, entirely unaware of its presence, attended several performances without being able to detect it. Had it been dreamed up by the natives? Only by scanning his film foot by foot did he eventually succeed in tracing the chicken: it appeared for a fleeting moment somewhere in a corner of a picture and then vanished forever.[32]

The following types of objects are cinematic because they stubbornly escape our attention in everyday life.

Unconventional complexes   Film may bare real-life complexes which the conventional figure-ground patterns usually conceal from view. Imagine

* Cf. also the Proust quote, p. 14.

a man in a room: accustomed as we are to visualize the human figure as a whole, it would take us an enormous effort to perceive instead of the whole man a pictorial unit consisting, say, of his right shoulder and arm, fragments of furniture and a section of the wall. But this is exactly what photography and, more powerfully, film may make us see. The motion picture camera has a way of disintegrating familiar objects and bringing to the fore—often just in moving about—previously invisible interrelationships between parts of them. These newly arising complexes lurk behind the things known and cut across their easily identifiable contexts. Jazz Dance, for instance, abounds with shots of ensembles built from human torsos, clothes, scattered legs, and what not—shapes which are almost anonymous. In rendering physical existence, film tends to reveal configurations of semi-abstract phenomena. Sometimes these textures take on an ornamental character. In the Nazi propaganda film Triumph of the Will moving banners fuse into a very beautiful pattern at the moment when they begin to fill the screen.

The refuse Many objects remain unnoticed simply because it never occurs to us to look their way. Most people turn their backs on garbage cans, the dirt underfoot, the waste they leave behind. Films have no such inhibitions; on the contrary, what we ordinarily prefer to ignore proves attractive to them precisely because of this common neglect. Ruttmann's Berlin includes a wealth of sewer grates, gutters, and streets littered with rubbish; and Cavalcanti in his Rien que les heures is hardly less garbage-minded. To be sure, shots in this vein may be required by the action, but intrigues inspired by a sense of the medium are often so devised that they offer the camera ample opportunity to satisfy its inborn curiosity and function as a rag-picker; think of the old silent comedies—e.g. Chaplin's A Dog's Life—or pictures which involve crime, war, or misery. Since sights of refuse are particularly impressive after spectacles extolling the joy of living, film makers have repeatedly capitalized on the contrast between glamorous festivities and their dreary aftermath. You see a banquet on the screen and then, when everybody has gone, you are made to linger for a moment and stare at the crumpled tablecloth, the half-emptied glasses, and the unappetizing dishes. The classical American gangster films indulged in this effect. Scarface opens on a restaurant at dawn, with the remnants of the nocturnal orgy strewn over floors and tables; and after the gangsters' ball in Sternberg's Underworld Bancroft totters through a maze of confetti and streamers left over from the feast. [Illus. 14]

The familiar Nor do we perceive the familiar. It is not as if we shrank from it, as we do in the case of refuse; we just take it for granted without giving it a thought. Intimate faces, streets we walk day by day, the house we live in—all these things are part of us like our skin, and because we know them by heart we do not know them with the eye. Once integrated into our existence, they cease to be objects of perception, goals to be attained. In fact, we would be immobilized if we focused on them. This is confirmed by a common experience. A man entering his room will immediately feel disturbed if during his absence something has been changed in it. But in order to find out about the cause of his uneasiness he must discontinue his routine occupations; only in deliberately scrutinizing, and thus estranging, the room will he be able to discover what it actually is that has been changed. Proust's narrator is acutely aware of this very estrangement when he suddenly sees his grandmother not as he always believed her to be but as she really is or at least as she would appear to a stranger—a snapshot likeness severed from his dreams and memories.

Films make us undergo similar experiences a thousand times. They alienate our environment in exposing it. One ever-recurrent film scene runs as follows: Two or more people are conversing with each other. In the middle of their talk the camera, as if entirely indifferent to it, slowly pans through the room, inviting us to watch the faces of the listeners and various furniture pieces in a detached spirit. Whatever this may mean within the given context, it invariably dissolves a well-known total situation and thereby confronts the spectator with isolated phenomena which he previously neglected or overlooked as matter-of-course components of that situation. As the camera pans, curtains become eloquent and eyes tell a story of their own. The way leads toward the unfamiliar in the familiar. How often do we not come across shots of street corners, buildings, and landscapes with which we were acquainted all our life; we naturally recognize them and yet it is as if they were virgin impressions emerging from the abyss of nearness. The opening sequence of Vigo's ZERO DE CONDUITE shows two boys traveling back to school by train. Is it just an ordinary night trip? Vigo manages to transform a familiar railway compartment into a magic wigwam in which the two, drunk from their boasts and pranks, are floating through the air.[33]

This transformation is partly achieved with the aid of a device, both photographic and cinematic, which deserves some attention—the use of uncommon camera angles. Vigo occasionally represents the railway compartment slantwise and from below so that the whole room seems to drift along in the haze from the cigars which the high-strung schoolboys are smoking, while little toy balloons hover to and fro before their pale faces. Proust knew about the alienating effect of this device. After having mentioned that certain photographs of scenery and towns are called "admirable," he continues: "If we press for a definition of what their admirers mean by that epithet, we shall find that it is generally applied to some unusual picture of a familar object, a picture different from those that we are accustomed to see, unusual and yet true to nature, and for that reason doubly impressive because it startles us, makes us emerge from our habits, and at the same time brings us back to ourselves by recalling to us an earlier impression." And to concretize this definition, he refers to the picture of a cathedral which does not render it as it is normally seen—namely, in the middle of the town—but is taken from a point of view from which the building "will appear thirty times the height of the houses."[34] It has been observed that a little change in make-up suffices to alter the appearance of a man completely; slight deviations from the conventional perspective are likely to be of similar consequence. In a review of Jean Epstein's COEUR FIDELE, which indulges in unusual camera angles, René Clair therefore wonders why so many film directors resort to all kinds of photographic tricks when they "might arouse so much curiosity by a simple inclination of their camera."[35] Because of their metamorphosing power, shots from unusual angles are frequently exploited for propaganda purposes. There is always the possibility that such shots may turn into contrived-reality pictures.

The confrontation with objects which are familiar to us for having been part and parcel of our early life is particularly stirring. Hence the peculiar, often traumatic effect of films resuscitating that period. It need not be the period of our own childhood, for in the child real experiences mingle indiscriminately with imagined ones based on picture books and grandmother tales. Such retrospects as THE GOLDEN 'TWENTIES, 50 YEARS BEFORE YOUR EYES, and PARIS 1900—documentaries of 1950 assembled from authentic newsreels, contemporary feature films, and photographs—explore patterns of custom and fashion which we once accepted unquestioningly. Now that they resume life on the screen, the spectator cannot help laughing at the ridiculous hats, overstuffed rooms, and obtrusive gestures impressed upon him by the veracious camera. As he laughs at them, however, he is bound to realize, shudderingly, that he has been spirited away into the lumber room of his private self. He himself has dwelt, without knowing it, in those interiors; he himself has blindly adopted conventions which now seem naïve or cramped to him. In a flash the camera exposes the paraphernalia of our former existence, stripping them of the significance which originally transfigured them so that they changed from things in their own right into invisible conduits.

Unlike paintings, film images encourage such a decomposition because of their emphatic concern with raw material not yet consumed. The thrill of these old films is that they bring us face to face with the inchoate, cocoon-like world whence we come—all the objects, or rather sediments of objects, that were our companions in a pupa state. The most familiar, that which continues to condition our involuntary reactions and spontaneous impulses, is thus made to appear as the most alien. If we find these obsolete sights funny, we respond to them also with emotions which range from fright at the sudden emergence of our intimate being to nostalgic melancholy over the inexorable passing of time. Numerous films—among them Clair's THE ITALIAN STRAW HAT and LES DEUX TIMIDES, and many a mystery drama laid in the Victorian era—draw on the incomparable spell of those near and faraway days which mark the border region between the present and the past. Beyond it the realm of history begins.

Phenomena overwhelming consciousness

Elemental catastrophes, the atrocities of war, acts of violence and terror, sexual debauchery, and death are events which tend to overwhelm consciousness. In any case, they call forth excitements and agonies bound to thwart detached observation. No one witnessing such an event, let alone playing an active part in it, should therefore be expected accurately to account for what he has seen.[36] Since these manifestations of crude nature, human or otherwise, fall into the area of physical reality, they range all the more among the cinematic subjects. Only the camera is able to represent them without distortion.

Actually the medium has always shown a predilection for events of this type. There is practically no newsreel that would not indulge in the ravages of an inundation, a hurricane, an airplane crash, or whatever catastrophe happens to be at hand. The same applies to feature films. One of the first film strips ever made was THE EXECUTION OF MARY QUEEN OF SCOTS (1895); the executioner cuts off her head and then holds it in his uplifted hand so that no spectator can possibly avoid looking at the frightful exhibit. Pornographic motifs also emerged at a very early date. The path of the cinema is beset with films reveling in disasters and nightmarish incidents. Suffice it to pick out, at random, the war horrors in Dovzhenko's ARSENAL and Pabst's WESTFRONT 1918; the terrible execution sequence at the end of THUNDER OVER MEXICO, a film based on Eisenstein's Mexican material; the earthquake in SAN FRANCISCO; the torture episode in Rossellini's OPEN CITY [Illus. 15]; the depiction of a Polish Nazi concentration camp in THE LAST STOP; the scene with the young hoodlums wantonly mistreating a blind man in Buñuel's LOS OLVIDADOS. [Illus. 25]

Because of its sustained concern with all that is dreadful and off limits, the medium has frequently been accused of a penchant for cheap sensationalism. What lends support to this verdict is the indisputable fact that films have a habit of dwelling on the sensational much longer than any moral purpose would seem to justify; it often is as if that purpose served merely as a pretext for rendering a savage murder or the like.

In defense of the medium one might argue that it would not be the mass medium it is if it failed to provide stunning sensations; and that, in offering them, it only follows a venerable tradition. Since time immemorial, people have craved spectacles permitting them vicariously to experience the fury of conflagrations, the excesses of cruelty and suffering, and unspeakable lusts—spectacles which shock the shuddering and delighted onlooker into unseeing participation.

Yet this argument misses the point. The point is, rather, that the cinema does not simply imitate and continue the ancient gladiator fights or the *Grand Guignol* but adds something new and momentous: it insists on rendering visible what is commonly drowned in inner agitation. Of course, such revelations conform all the more to the cinematic approach if they bear on actual catastrophes and horrors. In deliberately detailing feats of sadism in their films, Rossellini and Buñuel force the spectator to take in these appalling sights and at the same time impress them on him as real-life events recorded by the imperturbable camera.[37] Similarly, besides trying to put across their propaganda messages, the Russian films of the 'twenties convey to us the paroxysmal upheavals of real masses which, because of their emotional *and* spatial enormity, depend doubly upon cinematic treatment to be perceptible.

The cinema, then, aims at transforming the agitated witness into a conscious observer. Nothing could be more legitimate than its lack of inhibitions in picturing spectacles which upset the mind. Thus it keeps us from shutting our eyes to the "blind drive of things."[38]

Special modes of reality

Finally films may expose physical reality as it appears to individuals in extreme states of mind generated by such events as we have mentioned, mental disturbances, or any other external or internal causes. Supposing such a state of mind is provoked by an act of violence, then the camera often aspires to render the images which an emotionally upset witness or participant will form of it. These images also belong among the cinematic subjects. They are distorted from the viewpoint of a detached observer; and they differ from each other according to the varying states of mind in which they originate.

In his TEN DAYS THAT SHOOK THE WORLD, for instance, Eisenstein composes a physical universe reflecting exultation. This episode runs as follows: At the beginning of the October Revolution, worker delegates succeed in bringing a contingent of Cossacks over to their side; the Cossacks put their half-drawn swords with the ornamented pommels back into their sheaths, and then the two groups boisterously fraternize in a state of euphoria. The ensuing dance scene is represented in the form of an accelerated montage sequence which pictures the world as experienced by the overjoyed. In their great joy, dancers and onlookers who constantly mingle cannot help perceiving incoherent pieces of their immediate environment in motion. It is a whirling agglomerate of fragments that surrounds them. And Eisenstein captures this jumble to perfection by having follow each other—in a succession which becomes ever faster with the growing ecstasy —shots of Cossack boots executing the *krakoviak*, worker legs dancing through a puddle, clapping hands, and faces inordinately broadened by laughter.

In the world of a panic-stricken individual laughter yields to grimacing and dazzling confusion to fearful rigidity. At any rate, this is how Ernö Metzner conceived of that world in his UEBERFALL. Its "hero" is a wretched little fellow who gets a lucky break thanks to a coin he furtively picks up in the street and then stakes in a crap game. As he walks away with his wallet stuffed, a thug follows him at a steadily diminishing distance. [Illus. 16] The man is scared. No sooner does he take to his heels than all the objects about him make common cause with his pursuer. The dark railway underpass turns into a sinister trap; frozen threats, the dilapidated slum houses close ranks and stare at him. (It is noteworthy that these effects are largely due to accomplished photography.) Temporarily saved by a streetwalker, who puts him up in her room, the man knows that the thug continues to lie in wait for him down in the street. The curtain moves, and he feels that the room itself harbors dangers. There is no escape wherever he looks. He looks into the mirror: what shines out of it are distorted reflections of his mask-like features.[39]

Inherent Affinities

IF PHOTOGRAPHY survives in film, film must share the same affinities. Accordingly, four of the five affinities which seem to be characteristic of film should be identical with those of photography. Nevertheless they call for renewed discussion because of their extended scope and their specifically cinematic implications. The last affinity to be examined—for the "flow of life"—is peculiar to film alone, since photography cannot picture life in motion.

THE UNSTAGED

As has been pointed out, everything reproducible in terms of the camera may be represented on the screen—which means that, for instance, the "canning" of a theatrical performance is in principle unobjectionable. Yet I have stressed that films conform to the cinematic approach only if they acknowledge the realistic tendency by concentrating on actual physical existence—"the beauty of moving wind in the trees," as D. W. Griffith expressed it in a 1947 interview in which he voiced his bitterness at contemporary Hollywood and its unawareness of that beauty.[1] In other words, film, notwithstanding its ability to reproduce, indiscriminately, all kinds of visible data, gravitates toward unstaged reality. And this in turn has given rise to two interrelated propositions regarding staging: First, staging is aesthetically legitimate to the extent that it evokes the illusion of actuality. Second, by the same token anything stagy is uncinematic if it passes over the basic properties of the medium.

There would be nothing to be added were it not for the last proposition about staginess. Although the general statement that the artificiality of stagy settings or compositions runs counter to the medium's declared preference for nature in the raw is certainly to the point, it nevertheless requires qualification. Experience shows that the uncinematic effect of staginess is mitigated in at least two cases.

For one thing, take all the films which, from THE CABINET OF DR. CALIGARI to the Japanese GATE OF HELL, are palpably patterned on paintings: it is true that they ignore unadulterated reality, reality not yet subjected to painterly treatment, but at the same time they meet Hermann Warm's request that films should be "drawings brought to life."* Now their compliance with his request is of consequence cinematically. One will remember that in the preceding chapter movement as contrasted with motionlessness has been identified as a subject of cinematic interest. Films bringing "drawings . . . to life" may be considered an annex to this group; if they do not contrast motion with a state of rest, yet they picture the birth of motion out of that state. In fact, we experience the sensation of nascent movement whenever seemingly painted figures and objects take on life in spite of their inherent immobility. The experience is all the more stirring since they cannot help preserving the character of drawings. As the protagonists of CALIGARI—Dr. Caligari himself and the medium Cesare—move through expressionist settings, they continue to fuse with the motionless shadows and bizarre designs about them.[2] And some scenes of GATE OF HELL are nothing but scrolls set moving as if by a magic wand. What attracts us in these films is the miracle of movement as such. It adds a touch of cinema to them.

As for the other case, a similar effect may be produced with the aid of specifically cinematic techniques and devices. This is in keeping with what has been said about the relationships between the basic and technical properties of film in the second chapter. According to the rule advanced there, even a film with stagy settings—to mention only this one aspect of staginess—may acquire a cinematic quality provided its technical execution testifies to a sense of the medium; whereby it is understood, though, that such a film is under all circumstances less cinematic than a film devoted to camera-reality. In Olivier's HAMLET the camera is continually on the move, thus making the spectator almost forget that the interiors through which it travels and pans are intended to externalize the mood of the play rather than impart that of anything external; or to be more precise, he must divide his attention between two conflicting worlds which are supposed to merge into a whole but actually do not blend well: the cinematic world suggested by camera movement and the deliberately unreal world established by the stage designer. In the same way Fritz Lang manages to imbue the flood episode of his METROPOLIS, a film of unsurpassable staginess in many respects, with a semblance of cinematic life. The fleeing crowds in that episode are staged veraciously and rendered

* See p. 39.

through a combination of long shots and close shots which provide exactly the kind of random impressions we would receive were we to witness this spectacle in reality. Yet the cinematic impact of the crowd images somewhat suffers from the fact that the scene is laid in architectural surroundings which could not be more stylized.*

THE FORTUITOUS

The fortuitous being a characteristic of camera-reality, film no less than photography is attracted by it. Hence the major role assigned to it in a truly cinematic genre, the American silent film comedy. To be sure, the minor triumphs of Buster Keaton or Chaplin's Tramp over destructive natural forces, hostile objects, and human brutes were sometimes due to feats of acrobatic skill. Yet unlike most circus productions, film comedy did not highlight the performer's proficiency in braving death and surmounting impossible difficulties; rather, it minimized his accomplishments in a constant effort to present successful rescues as the outcome of sheer chance. Accidents superseded destiny; unpredictable circumstances now foreshadowed doom, now jelled into propitious constellations for no visible reason. Take Harold Lloyd on the skyscraper: what protected him from falling to death was not his prowess but a random combination of external and completely incoherent events which, without being intended to come to his help, dovetailed so perfectly that he could not have fallen even had he wanted to. Accidents were the very soul of slapstick.[3]

The affinity of film for haphazard contingencies is most strikingly demonstrated by its unwavering susceptibility to the "street"—a term designed to cover not only the street, particularly the city street, in the literal sense, but also its various extensions, such as railway stations, dance and assembly halls, bars, hotel lobbies, airports, etc. If the medium's descent from, and kinship with, photography needed additional confirmation, this very specific preference, common to both of them, would supply it. Within the present context the street, which has already been characterized as a center of fleeting impressions, is of interest as a region where the accidental prevails over the providential, and happenings in the nature of unexpected incidents are all but the rule. Startling as it may sound, since the days of Lumière there have been only few cinematic films that would not include glimpses of a street, not to mention the many films in which some street figures among the protagonists.

It was D. W. Griffith who initiated this tradition. For prototypes of cinematically significant imagery one will always have to revert to him. He

* Cf. pp. 36–7.

featured the street as an area dominated by chance in a manner reminiscent of Lumière's shots of crowded public places. In one of his early films, which bears the suggestive title THE MUSKETEERS OF PIG ALLEY, much of the action is laid in dingy houses, a New York East Side street teeming with nondescript passers-by, a low dive, and a small yard between cheap tenement houses where teenagers forever loiter about. [Illus. 17] More important, the action itself, which revolves around a thievery and ends on a pursuit, grows out of these locales. They offer opportunities to the criminal gang to which the thief is committed; and they provide the adventitious encounters and promiscuous gatherings which are an essential element of the intrigue. All this is resumed on a broader scale in the "modern story" of Griffith's INTOLERANCE. There the street takes on an additional function reserved for it: it turns into the scene of bloody clashes between striking workers and soldiers sent out against them. (The sights of the crowds of fleeing workers and the corpses left behind foreshadow the Russian films of the Revolution.)

Yet if the street episodes of the "modern story" involve the depiction of mass violence, they do by no means exhaust themselves in it. Eisenstein praises them for something less glaring—the way in which they impress upon the spectator the fortuitous appearances and occurrences inseparable from the street as such. In 1944, all that he remembered of these episodes was an ephemeral passer-by. After having described him, Eisenstein continues: "As he passes he interrupts the most pathetic moment in the conversation of the suffering boy and girl. I can remember next to nothing of the couple, but this passer-by who is visible in the shot only for a flashing glimpse stands alive before me now—and I haven't seen the film for twenty years! Occasionally," he adds, "these unforgettable figures actually walked into Griffith's films almost directly from the street: a bit-player developed in Griffith's hands to stardom; the passer-by who may never again have been filmed."[4]

ENDLESSNESS

Like photography, film tends to cover all material phenomena virtually within reach of the camera. To express the same otherwise, it is as if the medium were animated by the chimerical desire to establish the continuum of physical existence.

24 consecutive hours

This desire is drastically illustrated by a film idea of Fernand Léger's. Léger dreamed of a monster film which would have to record painstakingly the life of a man and a woman during twenty-four consecutive hours: their work, their silence, their intimacy. Nothing should be omitted; nor should they ever be aware of the presence of the camera. "I think," he observed, "this would be so terrible a thing that people would run away horrified, calling for help as if caught in a world catastrophe."[5] Léger is right. Such a film would not just portray a sample of everyday life but, in portraying it, dissolve the familiar contours of that life and expose what our conventional notions of it conceal from view—its widely ramified roots in crude existence. We might well shrink, panic-stricken, from these alien patterns which would denote our ties with nature and claim recognition as part of the world we live in and are.

Routes of passage

In passing through the continuum of physical existence, the film maker may choose different routes. (Since the continuum is endless, his urge to render it completely, if only in one single direction, is of course unrealizable. So he will have to use certain devices, such as the fade-in, the fade-out, the lap-dissolve, etc., in order to mark the necessary breaks in the representation of the continuum and/or smoothly to connect different sections of it.)

Five routes of passage are discernible.

First, films may cover vast expanses of physical reality. Think of travelogues or feature films involving travel: they have certainly a cinematic flavor, provided they sustain the impression of traveling and show real concern for the far-distant places they picture in the process. Also chases belong here in a sense. Laffay, who extols the "pure poetry of deplacement" manifest in cinematic travel films, says of chases that they "open up the universe on all sides and make us gauge its infinite solidarity."[6]

The solidarity of the universe can be demonstrated either by showing phenomena in different places successively in a time sequence, as is the case with chases, or by creating the impression that these phenomena offer themselves to view at one and the same moment. The latter alternative, which stresses their co-existence, represents an instance of "reality of another dimension," in as much as it amounts to a cinematic interference with conventional time; by dint of sheer editing the spectator is led to witness widely scattered events simultaneously so that he gets the feeling of being omnipresent. Of course, the assemblage of such events serves the purpose only if the film maker succeeds in suggesting a spatial continuum with their aid. Ruttmann in his BERLIN, a cross section of

Berlin everyday life in documentary style, tries to accomplish this task by capturing simultaneous phenomena which, owing to certain analogies and contrasts between them, form comprehensible patterns. Much like Vertov, he cuts from human legs walking the street to the legs of a cow and juxtaposes the luscious dishes in a deluxe restaurant with the appalling food of the very poor.[7]

Yet these linkages are purely decorative and rather obvious. More meaningful is the dense fabric into which various sections of space are woven in Room's remarkably mature BED AND SOFA, a 1926 Soviet film which dramatizes the bad housing conditions in contemporary Moscow. Its sustained emphasis on ubiquity enables the spectator to encompass, as if in one glance, overcrowded lodgings and wide city prospects, thus stirring him to wonder at their unaccountable togetherness.[8] Another significant example of simultaneity, pointed out by Laffay,[9] is A NIGHT AT THE OPERA. In this film, the Marx Brothers confirm the solidarity of a given universe by violently destroying it; the whole universe seems to collapse when all the objects filling it are removed from their set locales and forced to mingle, hodge-podge fashion.*

Second, films may follow the chain of causes and effects responsible for some event. This route, too, marks an attempt to suggest the continuum of physical reality or at least a continuum largely involving it. The attempt is all the more true to the medium since it is bound to drive home the impact which, as Cohen-Séat puts it, "the most minute incidental circumstances [exert] on the unfolding of destinies."[10] His statement implies that the affinity for the fortuitous goes well together with the concern for causal interrelationships. Leaving aside the many science films whose job it is to trace, one by one, the reasons behind some physical or psychological phenomenon, there are enough feature films in which the same inquisitiveness asserts itself. D. W. Griffith insists on detailing, in his last-minute-rescue episodes, all the factors which obstruct or facilitate the rescuers' heroic enterprise. Collisions and interventions, trains missed or jumped, horses on highways and legs negotiating floes—everything that contributes, in one sense or another, toward the final result is exposed to scrutiny.

Even assuming that Griffith delays the inevitable happy ending as long as possible for the purpose of increasing audience suspense, he implements this intention in a manner which testifies to his genuine concern with establishing the connecting links between the initial stage of the action

---

* Note that the representation of spatial simultaneity on the screen has struck the imagination of writers and artists. When John Dos Passos in some of his novels juxtaposes simultaneous events at different points of the globe, he clearly follows the lead of the cinema.

and its accomplishment. There is something of the explorer's curiosity about the eagerness with which he exhibits minor motivations and accessory moments. And being contagious, this curiosity itself creates suspense—the kind of suspense aroused, for instance, by Pabst's silent film, THE SECRETS OF A SOUL. In it the dramatic interest lies with the psychoanalytical investigation of the causes that have produced the hero's phobia toward knives. Part science, part fiction, this pictorial analysis leads into the thicket of a bygone psychophysical world, implicating a succession of affect-laden surroundings and objects. Emphasis on the unfolding of causal interrelationships seems to call for a reversal of the course which narratives devoted to the "unfolding of destinies" are usually taking. They move forward with Time, while THE SECRETS OF A SOUL travels from the present into the past. More outspoken than this Pabst film, both CITIZEN KANE and RASHOMON start with a *fait accompli* and from there wander back to shed light on its trail. In the latter film three or four people in a position to know how the murder stated at the outset was committed relate the relevant facts as they allegedly perceive them. Each account recovers the chain of events but not even two of them actually coincide. RASHOMON represents, among other things, a cinematic effort to impress upon us the inexhaustibility of the causal continuum.

Third, films may, so to speak, caress one single object long enough to make us imagine its unlimited aspects. Since this route offers less opportunity for dramatic action than the routes suggesting geographical and causal endlessness, it has scarcely been followed so far. Oertel avails himself of it in those parts of his THE TITAN which are consecrated to the depiction of Michelangelo's sculptures. Under constantly changing light conditions the camera repeatedly pans or travels at close range over the limbs and the torso of some statue, deriving from the identical original an abundance of two-dimensional patterns. No matter to what extent these patterns still bear on the statue they explore, they are cinematic in as much as they tend to immerse us in the infinity of shapes that lie dormant in any given one.[11] Robert Bresson in his DIARY OF A COUNTRY PRIEST seems to aspire to the same kind of infinity. The face of the young priest looks different each time you look at him; ever-new facets of his face thread this film.

Fourth, films may evoke the innumerable experiences which an individual is likely to undergo in a single crucial moment of his life. As in many cases of causal interrelationships, this possibility involves material reality without being confined to it. It was envisaged by Eisenstein in the *monologue intérieur* which he planned to incorporate into his treatment of AN AMERICAN TRAGEDY. The monologue is to take place at the dramatic moment when Clyde is prepared to drown Roberta and make it look like an accident. It is evident that for an understanding of the ensuing trial much depends on what is going on in Clyde's mind at this juncture. Eisenstein therefore resolved to film the inner workings of his hero's mind—an idea which, as he relates in an essay of 1932, interested Joyce intensely. In the same essay Eisenstein also recalls his "montage lists," preliminary notes in which he tried to frame this inner monologue; they provided that the sequence should project not only Clyde's thought processes but the whole interaction, causative or not, between them and the external events of the moment:

> What wonderful sketches those montage lists were!
> Like thought, they would sometimes proceed with visual images. . .
> Then suddenly, definite intellectually formulated words—as "intellectual" and dispassionate as pronounced words. With a black screen, a rushing image-less visuality.
> Then in passionate disconnected speech. Nothing but nouns. Or nothing but verbs. Then interjections. With zigzags of aimless shapes, whirling along with these in synchronization.
> Then racing visual images over complete silence.
> Then linked with polyphonic sounds. Then polyphonic images. Then both at once.
> Then interpolated into the outer course of action, then interpolating elements of the outer action into the inner monologue.

Eisenstein may have been convinced that the narrative had reached a point where full insight into Clyde's psychological condition was indispensable; but he could not possibly believe, even if he refused to admit it, that the inner monologue he planned was nothing more than an adequate implementation of story requirements. Actually these "montage lists" are "wonderful" because their rapturous wording testifies to an intoxication with the flux of images and sounds which defies any boundaries, any restrictions arising from outside considerations. The monologue, as Eisenstein outlined it, clearly exceeds the framework of the story, however generous the allowance made for it; it even exceeds Clyde's own being; what it tends to convey instead is the endless series of circumstances and sensations which close in on Clyde at this particular moment.

In listing them, Eisenstein, so his words suggest, not only cared little about story necessities but took positive delight in being released from them, in being for once permitted to record, or rather seem to record, a plethora of sense data without too much regard for their contribution to the total effect of the story itself. This is confirmed by his conclusion: "the material of the sound-film is not dialogue. *The true material of the sound-film is, of course, the monologue.*"[12] The true material, that is, is not merely life in the dimension of articulate meanings but life underneath—

a texture of impressions and expressions which reaches deep into physical existence.

Fifth and finally, films may represent an indefinite number of material phenomena—e.g. waves, machine parts, trees, and what not—in such a way that their forms, movements, and light values jell into comprehensible rhythmical patterns. The tendency thus to defy content in favor of rhythm will be examined in chapter 10.* Suffice it here to mention that this route of passage has been initiated in the days of the French *avant-garde,* when Germaine Dulac and others were championing the *cinéma pur*—a cinema aspiring to compositions intended as the equivalent of a symphony.

THE INDETERMINATE

Psychophysical correspondences

As an extension of photography, film shares the latter's concern for nature in the raw. Though natural objects are relatively unstructured and, hence, indeterminate as to meaning, there are varying degrees of indeterminacy. Notwithstanding their relative lack of structure, a somber landscape and a laughing face seem to have a definite significance in any given culture; and the same holds true of certain colors and light effects. Yet even these more outspoken phenomena are still essentially indefinable, as can be inferred from the readiness with which they change their apparently fixed meaning within changing contexts. To take an example from the screen, in ALEXANDER NEVSKY the Teutonic knights are clothed in white hoods; the white usually suggestive of innocence here is made to signify scheming ruthlessness. In the same way, dependent on the context, the somber landscape may connote defiant intrepidity and the laughing face hysterical fear.

Natural objects, then, are surrounded with a fringe of meanings liable to touch off various moods, emotions, runs of inarticulate thoughts; in other words, they have a theoretically unlimited number of psychological and mental correspondences. Some such correspondences may have a real foundation in the traces which the life of the mind often leaves in material phenomena; human faces are molded by inner experiences, and the patina of old houses is a residue of what has happened in them. This points to a two-way process. It is not only the given objects which function as stimuli; psychological events also form nuclei, and of course they on their part have physical correspondences. Under the influence of the shock he

* See especially pp. 183–7.

suffers when dipping a madeleine into his tea, Proust's narrator is, body
and soul, transported back to places, scenes, and the core of names many
of which amount to overpowering images of things external. The generic
term "psychophysical correspondences" covers all these more or less fluid
interrelations between the physical world and the psychological dimension
in the broadest sense of the word—a dimension which borders on that
physical universe and is still intimately connected with it.

For reasons discussed in earlier pages, screen images tend to reflect the
indeterminacy of natural objects. However selective, a film shot does not
come into its own unless it incorporates raw material with its multiple
meanings or what Lucien Sève calls the "anonymous state of reality." Incidentally, Sève, a brilliant young French critic, is quite aware of this characteristic of the cinematic shot. He judiciously remarks that the shot "de-
limits without defining" and that it has the quality, "unique among the
arts, of offering not much more explanations than reality" itself.[13]

But this raises a vitally important problem of editing.

A basic editing principle

Any film maker evolving a narrative is faced with the task of simultaneously living up to two obligations which seem to be difficult to reconcile.

On the one hand, he will have to advance the action by assigning to
each shot a meaning relevant to the plot. That this reduction of meanings
falls to editing was demonstrated by Kuleshov in the experiment he conducted together with Pudovkin. In order to prove the impact of editing on
the significance of shots, he inserted one and the same shot of Mosjukhin's
otherwise noncommittal face in different story contexts; the result was
that the actor's face appeared to express grief on a sad occasion and smiling
satisfaction in a pleasant environment.[14] In terms of the Kuleshov experiment, the film maker must therefore insert Mosjukhin's face in such a way
that it assumes the significance required by the story at this particular
place. (As will be seen later,* some story types depend for implementation
to a larger extent than others on the removal of all meanings which do not
"belong.")

On the other hand, the film maker will wish to exhibit and penetrate
physical reality for its own sake. And this calls for shots not yet stripped
of their multiple meanings, shots still able to release their psychological
correspondences. Accordingly, he must see to it that Mosjukhin's face retains, somehow, its virgin indeterminacy.

* See especially pp. 221–2.

But how can one meet this last requirement within the framework of an exacting narrative? Jean Epstein once protested his weakness for the standardized pistol scene in American films of the mid-'twenties—the pistol would be slowly removed from a half-open drawer and would then be enlarged to fill the screen, an enormous menace vaguely foreshadowing the crucial moment: "I loved this pistol. It appeared as a symbol of a thousand possibilities. The desires and disappointments it represented; the mass of combinations to which it offered a clue."[15] What distinguishes this pistol scene is obviously the way it is edited. The shots comprising it are so juxtaposed that at least one of them—that of the pistol—preserves a certain independence of the intrigue. And Epstein revels in it because it does not just point forward to something that will subsequently happen but stands out as an image iridescent with multiple meanings. Nevertheless this shot may well benefit the action. It is possible, then, to integrate shots of indistinct meaningfulness into a narrative.

This possibility should not come as a surprise to the reader, for he is already familiar with it from the analysis of the first Griffith close-up in AFTER MANY YEARS. Griffith, it could be shown there, manages to sustain the indeterminacy of Annie's face by provisionally withholding its specific significance. It all is a matter of editing.

Examples of this editing procedure are fairly frequent. When in THE THIRD MAN the evil-minded boy appears for the first time he is a nondescript figure stirring our imagination; only on the occasion of his later re-emergence is he made to play a well-defined role which automatically curtails previous speculations on his potentialities. In the opening sequence of THE END OF ST. PETERSBURG the image of a windmill seems to be inserted gratuitously while the young peasant is seen leaving his homestead for the big city. The windmill means nothing in particular and therefore means everything. But no sooner does the peasant approach the giant industrial plant where he will try to find a job than the image of the windmill is cut in again and now of course signifies his nostalgia for the countryside. Or think of those pictures in POTEMKIN which, for being only loosely connected with the unfolding story, invite the audience to absorb their manifold connotations—the silhouettes of ships in the harbor; the shadows of the sailors who carry the body of their dead comrade up the iron steps, etc.[16]*

---

* In 1929, Eisenstein, the theoretician, differentiated between the prevalent meaning of a film shot—its "dominant"—and its multiple other meanings, which, in analogy to music, he called the "overtones" of the shot. And he declared himself determined not to neglect the latter in the dominant. But as so often with Eisenstein, this gain in theoretical insight tended to make him self-conscious as an artist. His

Notwithstanding their latent or ultimately even manifest bearing on the narrative to which they belong, all these shots are more or less free-hovering images of material reality. And as such they also allude to contexts unrelated to the events which they are called upon to establish. Their cinematic quality lies precisely in their allusiveness, which enables them to yield all their psychological correspondences. Hence the infatuation of sensitive film makers or critics with pictorial material of a purely allusive character. "The frown of a tower," says Herman G. Scheffauer, "the scowl of a sinister alley, . . . the hypnotic draught of a straight road vanishing to a point—these exert their influences and express their natures; their essences flow over the scene and blend with the action. A symphony arises between the organic and the inorganic worlds and the lens peers behind inscrutable veils."[17]

This leads to the formulation of a basic editing principle: any film narrative should be edited in such a manner that it does not simply confine itself to implementing the intrigue but also turns away from it toward the objects represented so that they may appear in their suggestive indeterminacy.

THE "FLOW OF LIFE"

It follows from what has just been said that cinematic films evoke a reality more inclusive than the one they actually picture. They point beyond the physical world to the extent that the shots or combinations of shots from which they are built carry multiple meanings. Due to the continuous influx of the psychophysical correspondences thus aroused, they suggest a reality which may fittingly be called "life." This term as used here denotes a kind of life which is still intimately connected, as if by an umbilical cord, with the material phenomena from which its emotional and intellectual contents emerge. Now films tend to capture physical existence in its endlessness. Accordingly, one may also say that they have an affinity, evidently denied to photography, for the continuum of life or the "flow of life," which of course is identical with open-ended life. The concept "flow of life," then, covers the stream of material situations and happenings with all that they intimate in terms of emotions, values, thoughts. The implication is that the flow of life is predominantly a material rather than a mental continuum, even though, by definition, it extends into the mental dimension. (It might tentatively be said that films favor life in the form of

---

deliberate montage on overtones in later films yields scenes and episodes which strike one as labored; they are far less convincing than the really indeterminate shots which he spontaneously inserted in POTEMKIN and TEN DAYS.

everyday life—an assumption which finds some support in the medium's primordial concern for actuality.)

Once again the street

Eisenstein has been quoted as saying that the "unforgettable figures" in Griffith's films occasionally walked into them "almost directly from the street." Within the same context Eisenstein also remarks that "Griffith's inimitable bit-characters . . . seem to have run straight from life onto the screen."[18]* Inadvertently he thus equates life with the street. The street in the extended sense of the word is not only the arena of fleeting impressions and chance encounters but a place where the flow of life is bound to assert itself. Again one will have to think mainly of the city street with its ever-moving anonymous crowds. The kaleidoscopic sights mingle with unidentified shapes and fragmentary visual complexes and cancel each other out, thereby preventing the onlooker from following up any of the innumerable suggestions they offer. What appears to him are not so much sharp-contoured individuals engaged in this or that definable pursuit as loose throngs of sketchy, completely indeterminate figures. Each has a story, yet the story is not given. Instead, an incessant flow of possibilities and near-intangible meanings appears. This flow casts its spell over the *flâneur* or even creates him. The *flâneur* is intoxicated with life in the street—life eternally dissolving the patterns which it is about to form.[19]

The medium's affinity for the flow of life would be enough to explain the attraction which the street has ever since exerted on the screen. Perhaps the first deliberately to feature the street as the scene of life was Karl Grune in a half-expressionist, half-realistic film which significantly bears the title THE STREET (*Die Strasse*). Its hero is a middle-aged *petit bourgeois* possessed with the desire to escape from the care of his lifeless wife and the prison of a home where intimacy has become deadening routine. The Street calls him. There life surges high and adventures are waiting for him. He looks out of the window and sees—not the street itself but a hallucinated street. "Shots of rushing cars, fireworks, and crowds form, along with shots taken from a roller coaster, a confusing whole made still more confusing by the use of multiple exposures and the insertion of transparent close-ups of a circus clown, a woman, and an organ-grinder."[20] One evening he walks out into the real street—studio-built, for that matter—and gets more than his fill of sensations, what with card sharpers, prostitutes, and a murder to boot. Life, an agitated sea, threatens to drown him. There is

* Cf. p. 63.

no end of films in this vein. If it is not a street proper they picture, it is one of its extensions, such as a bar, a railway station, or the like. Also, life may change its character; it need not be wild and anarchical as with Grune. In Delluc's FIEVRE or Cavalcanti's EN RADE a mood of *fin-de-siècle* disenchantment and nostalgic longing for faraway countries lingers in crowded sailor hangouts. And in Vittorio De Sica's THE BICYCLE THIEF and UMBERTO D. the omnipresent streets breathe a tristesse which is palpably the outcome of unfortunate social conditions. [Illus. 18] But whatever its dominant characteristics, street life in all these films is not fully determined by them. It remains an unfixable flow which carries fearful uncertainties and alluring excitements.

Stage interludes

Stage episodes not only occur in numerous regular feature films, such as THE BIRTH OF A NATION or LA GRANDE ILLUSION, but form the backbone of most run-of-the-mill musicals. Chaplin as the Tramp has occasionally been fond of disrupting theatrical performances; and E. A. Dupont in his VARIETY has effectively contrasted dependable on-stage perfection with unpredictable off-stage passion.

Stage interludes within otherwise realistic films assume a cinematic function to the extent that they throw into relief the flow of life from which they detach themselves. Paradoxical as it may seem, the stagy, normally against the grain of the medium, assumes a positive aesthetic function if it is made to enhance the unstaged. Accordingly, the more stylized a cut-in theatrical production number, the better does it lend itself to serving as a foil to camera-reality. Many a film affording glimpses of opera scenes actually exaggerates their artificiality so as to sensitize us, by way of contrast, to the flow of haphazard events surging around that opera isle. In Germaine Dulac's THE SMILING MADAME BEUDET, a French *avant-garde* film of 1922, the superimposed images of singers in the roles of Faust and Mephistopheles are visibly intended to ridicule operas for their glamorous aloofness from the boredom of small-town streets, unloved people, and vain daydreams—all those corrosive influences which compose and decompose Madame Beudet's drab existence. Perhaps the best opera satire ever made is that incomparable stage sequence in René Clair's LE MILLION in which two corpulent singers deliver a love duet, while behind them two young lovers, hidden from the theater audience by the sets, are so profoundly enamored of each other that they seem unaware of being in a place where they do not belong. [Illus. 19] They are strangers there; and their genuineness as real-life characters is highlighted by the constant parallels which the camera draws between them and the performers whose every move is carefully planned.*

Yet this is not all. Clair manages to confer upon the loving couple and their world the very magic which the stage is supposed to radiate. When looking at the fat singers from the angle of the man in the pit, we see them in a setting which, however enchanting, is unaffected by their voices and incapable of stirring any illusions. It remains what it is—painted canvas. But no sooner are the lovers brought into focus than this very scenery undergoes a miraculous change, even though the close shots used in presenting it infallibly reveal it to be sheer pretense. A piece of paste-board drifting past sham blossoms becomes a frail white cloud; the scraps of paper released from the flies turn into fragrant rose petals. Thus stage illusion is debunked and at the same time called upon to convey the glow and glory of unadulterated life.

Despite its unique attractiveness for film, the visible world as it surrounds us here and now is only one of the areas which film makers have explored since the archaic days of the medium. Films or film sequences invading other areas, especially the realms of history and fantasy, are quite common. They raise aesthetic problems of interest.

* See pp. 151–2.

II. AREAS AND ELEMENTS

History and Fantasy

ONE THING IS EVIDENT: whenever a film maker turns the spotlight on a historical subject or ventures into the realm of fantasy, he runs the risk of defying the basic properties of his medium. Roughly speaking, he seems no longer concerned with physical reality but bent on incorporating worlds which to all appearances lie outside the orbit of actuality.

The following pages deal with some major difficulties arising from such an annexation to the screen of the past or an "unreal" universe, and with significant attempts at a reconciliation between these pictorial ventures and the demands of the cinematic approach.

HISTORY

Difficulties

Unlike the immediate past, the historical past must be staged in terms of costumes and settings completely estranged from present-day life. Consequently, it is inevitable that any moviegoer susceptible to the medium should feel uneasy about their irrevocable staginess. The cinema's preference for the unstaged may even condition his sensibilities to such an extent that, deaf to the promptings of the action, he involuntarily substitutes untampered-with nature for the make-believe world on the screen. Identifying himself with the camera, that is, he does not naïvely succumb to the magic of the allegedly recaptured past but remains conscious of the efforts going into its construction. "The camera," says Cavalcanti, "is so literal-minded that if you show it actors dressed up, it *sees* actors-dressed-up, not characters."[1] Period costumes recall the theater or a masquerade.

Aside from their staginess, historical films have another characteristic difficult to bear with: they are finite; they obstruct the affinity of the medium for endlessness. As the reproduction of a bygone era, the world they show is an artificial creation radically shut off from the space-time continuum of the living, a closed cosmos which does not admit of extensions. Looking at such a film, the spectator is likely to suffer from claustrophobia. He realizes that his potential field of vision strictly coincides with the actual one and that, accordingly, he cannot by a hair's breadth transcend the confines of the latter. True, films dealing with current subjects may also unfold in staged locales, but since these locales duplicate real-life surroundings, the audience is free to imagine that the camera roams reality itself without being hampered in exploring it. Historical films preclude the notion of endlessness because the past they try to resurrect no longer exists. This is what Laffay objects to in them: "Take, for instance, a picture of the siege of Paris in '71. Excellent composition, impeccable taste. . . . The *gardes mobiles* do not in the least look as if they came from the costumier. All is perfect. What prevents me from admiring? . . . One cannot help feeling that, if the camera were displaced, however slightly, to the right or the left, it would only chance upon the void or the bizarre paraphernalia of a studio. . . . Now the cinema must, on the contrary, feature the inexhaustible by sustaining the impression that the place photographed is a random place, that one might have selected another as well, and that the camera eye might, with no damage done, move about in all directions."[2]

At this point a science-fiction fantasy of Elie Faure's comes to mind. He dreams of a documentary film made *now* of the Passion of Christ from a far-distant star and sent to the earth by a projectile or rendered accessible to us by means of interplanetary projection.[3] If this dream materialized, we would be eye-witnesses to the Last Supper, the Crucifixion, the agony in Gethsemane. Film being film, we would moreover be in a position to take in all the seemingly insignificant happenings incidental to those momentous events—the soldiers shuffling cards, the clouds of dust whirled up by the horses, the moving crowds, the lights and shadows in an abandoned street. Faure's fascinating proposal helps to corroborate the observation just made. Let us for the sake of argument assume that a historical film about the Passion has been staged which matches his imaginary documentary in every respect. Obviously this ideal production will nevertheless differ from the latter in that it does not convey the impression of probing a universe at the film maker's free disposal. There is no potential endlessness in it. The spectator will admire it for showing things as they *could* have happened, but he will not be convinced, as he would be when watching Faure's documentary, that things actually happened this way. And his admiration is bound to mingle with a feeling of constraint provoked by his implicit awareness that all that he sees—the clouds of dust, the crowds, and the lights and shadows—has been deliberately inserted and that the margin of the pictures once and for all marks the edge of the world before his eyes. As compared with the miraculous documentary which suggests infinite reality, this supposedly perfect historical film reveals itself to be no more than a lively reconstruction which, as such, lacks cinematic life.

But can a historical film really be as perfect as that? What obstructs complete authenticity is the near-impossibility of making present-day actors fit into the costumes they wear. Conditioned by long-term environmental influences, their more subtle facial expressions and gestures are all but unadaptable. The costumes fully belong to the past, while the actors are still half in the present. This inevitably leads to conventions hardly compatible with a medium which gravitates toward the veracious representation of the external world.

Compromises

Like films with contemporary subjects, historical films may narrate stories which do not lend themselves to being related in cinematic terms and therefore oblige the sensitive film maker to try as best he can to adjust, somehow, his narrative to the screen. A conspicuous story type in this vein will be treated in chapter 12; and so will the adjustments to which it gives rise. For the present, only such compromises claim attention as tend to mitigate the inherently uncinematic character of films that resuscitate the past.

SHIFT TO CAMERA-REALITY

One way out is to shift the emphasis from history proper to camera-reality. The most resolute attempt at a solution along these lines is Carl Dreyer's The Passion of Joan of Arc, a film which has been called an "exploration of the human face" in documentary fashion.[4] [Illus. 20] Dreyer narrates, or tries to narrate, the life story of Joan through an unending series of densely interwoven close-ups of faces, thus largely eliminating the effects of staginess and finiteness which as a rule are inseparable from historical films. Of course, he cannot completely avoid ensemble scenes, and whenever they are inserted it is inevitable that the marked contrast between these scenes with their stylized accessories and the live texture of close-ups should make them appear all the more as lifeless constructions. Yet this is beside the point. The cinematic quality of the physiognomic documentary itself is bought at a price. True, Dreyer succeeds in distilling camera-reality out of a historical theme, but this very reality proves to be unreal. Isolated entities, the faces he lavishly displays resist being localized in time so stubbornly that they do not even raise the issue of whether or not they are authentic; and his unrelenting concern with them more likely than not entails the suppression of a great deal of material phenomena which are no less contingent on the drama than the faces themselves. JOAN OF ARC evades the difficulties bound up with historical films only because it neglects history—a neglect sustained by the photographic beauty of its close-ups.[5] It unfolds in a no-man's land which is neither the past nor the present.

Dreyer in his JOAN OF ARC aims at transforming the whole of past reality into camera-reality. His film is the only known instance of a radical "solution" in this direction. But does it also mark the only way of attaining the goal Dreyer envisions? A possibility as radical as this one would be the following: one might think of a film which suggests the infinite chain of causes and effects interlinking the historical events as we know them. Such an effort toward establishing a causal continuum—an effort in keeping with the cinematic approach, for reasons indicated in the preceding chapter—would bring to the fore numerous incidents instrumental in the "unfolding of destinies" and thus lure the spectator out of the closed cosmos of poster-like *tableaux vivants* into an open universe. However, this possibility, which involves critical probing into sanctioned legends, has not yet come true on a noticeable scale.* Conceivably enough: it breeds nonconformity and threatens to substitute enlightenment for entertainment. As matters stand, the historian's quest and history on the screen are at cross-purposes.

Yet if Dreyer's sweeping experiment has not been repeated, there has been no lack of attempts to follow the realistic tendency at least within the given framework of otherwise conventional historical pageants. Many of them include episodes which almost look like camera penetrations of present-day reality (which in part they are, of course). They feature cinematic subjects, such as crowds, acts of violence, chases, treat them or whatever they focus upon in a manner which does justice to the affinities of the medium, and unsparingly avail themselves of specifically cinematic techniques. Think of the mass movements and chases in the historical parts

---

* In Paris, shortly before the outbreak of World War II, the film director Slatan Dudow told me of a project of his: he planned to make a historical film on wars, tracing the changes in warfare to technological changes and changing economic conditions. Significantly, this film, which conforms to the possibility suggested in the text, would have resulted in a documentary.

of INTOLERANCE or the superb chariot-race sequence in Fred Niblo's BEN HUR. The spectator may be so thrilled by the chariot race that he forgets history in his actual sensations. All these episodes are plainly intended to overshadow the artificiality of the pictorial reconstructions and re-establish a maximum of immediate physical existence.

CONCERN WITH AUTHENTICITY

Instead of imbuing history with camera-life, the film maker may also move in the opposite direction in order to mediate between the past and the cinema; he may go the limit, that is, in portraying the modes of being peculiar to some historical era. To be sure, such an objective calls for complete immersion in that era and consequently interferes with the cinematic approach at the outset. But if films in this line draw on the pictorial material of the period to be resurrected, they are nevertheless apt to show characteristics which are in a measure cinematic.

Take again a Dreyer film—his DAY OF WRATH. [Illus. 21] This remarkable film obviously rests upon the sensible premise that the experience of spatial and temporal endlessness is a relatively modern experience and that therefore the attempt to reproduce the declining Middle Ages in terms of a nineteenth-century medium constitutes a violation of historical truth. When the Inquisition tried and burned witches, the world was stationary rather than dynamic, thinly populated rather than crowded; there was not yet the sensation of dizzying physical movement and the amorphous masses were still to come. It was essentially a finite cosmos, not the infinite world of ours.

Dreyer, apparently determined to convey late medieval mentality in all its dimensions, does not even try to instill cinematic life into his film, except for what may have been a slip on his part—the episode of the lovers strolling through the woods. This episode, with its problematic mixture of real trees and period costumes, perfectly illustrates the clash between the realistic and formative tendencies discussed in chapter 2. The trees form part of endless reality which the camera might picture on and on, while the lovers belong to the orbit of an intrinsically artificial universe. No sooner do the lovers leave it and collide with nature in the raw than the presence of the trees retransforms them into costumed actors. But on the whole Dreyer fashions his imagery after paintings of the period and indeed succeeds in keeping out crude actuality. (The touches of modern psychology he adds to the plot are quite another thing.) It is as if old Dutch masters had come to life. And in accordance with their appearance, the characters are like monads; they move slowly about, and there is a spatial distance between them which reflects their resistance to promiscuous mingling.

Granted that DAY OF WRATH runs counter to the declared preferences of the medium, it is of a certain interest cinematically in two respects. First, by breathing life into counterparts of paintings this film creates the illusion of nascent movement, which after all is a cinematic subject. Second, DAY OF WRATH definitely exerts the appeal of authenticity, and the cinematic effect thus produced is sufficiently intense to divert attention from the fact that it has been obtained in the uncinematic area of history. The film might almost be called a dramatized pictorial record, even though it bears on a universe which can only be constructed, not recorded. Both JOAN OF ARC and DAY OF WRATH, then, have traits of a documentary—the former because it breaks away from the past, the latter because it is faithful to it.

Examples of the second alternative are not infrequent. Feyder in his CARNIVAL IN FLANDERS also takes his cue from the art of the historical period he depicts. Parts of Castellani's ROMEO AND JULIET and of GATE OF HELL follow the very same pattern. Of the Czech film THE EMPEROR AND THE GOLEM a 1955 New York review says that "nearly every scene suggests a period painting come to life."[6]

FANTASY

From the cinematic viewpoint it is perhaps best to term "fantasy" all predominantly visual experiences, avowedly imagined or believed to be true to fact, which belong to worlds beyond camera-reality proper—the supernatural, visions of any kind, poetic imagery, hallucinations, dreams, etc. Unlike history, which is problematic cinematically because it lacks the character of present-day actuality, the fantastic may manifest itself here and now and fuse with real-life impressions. But since it lies outside the area of physical existence, it seems to be as unmanageable as the past in terms of the cinematic approach.

And yet, throughout the history of the medium, fantasy has been a much-coveted theme. Prompted by their formative urges, film makers have tried since the days of Méliès to annex to the screen this realm, with its apparitions, angels, demons and kaleidoscopic dream images, as is illustrated by an unending series of films, such as NOSFERATU, THE FOUR HORSEMEN OF THE APOCALYPSE, THE THIEF OF BAGDAD, LA FILLE D'EAU, LA PETITE MARCHANDE D'ALLUMETTES, VAMPYR, PETER PAN, PETER IBBETSON, DEAD OF NIGHT, etc., etc.

Common practice is backed up by theory. Most writers on film see no reason for differentiating between the unreal and the real and, accordingly, refuse to consider camera-reality a privileged area. René Clair, for instance, rejects realism as an unfounded limitation of the medium's potentialities: "The flexibility of cinematic expression which in a flash passes from the objective to the subjective and simultaneously evokes the abstract and the concrete does not justify [the assumption] that film confines itself to [following] an aesthetics as narrow as that of realism."[7] A number of critics even go so far as to contend that "the true import of the cinema is the realm of dreams."[8] The opinion of these extremists finds some support in the undeniable fact that, due to its specific techniques, film is better equipped than the other representational media to render visible things that have been imagined. Add to this the belief in the overwhelming significance of inner life and the widespread confusion of film with the traditional arts. Also, many a film maker's insistence on his freedom as a creative artist may blind him to the restrictions imposed on the formative tendency by the peculiarities of the medium.

Scheme of analysis

The representation of fantasy on the screen may or may not conform to the cinematic approach. To find out about the possibilities involved and evaluate them correctly, we will have to examine two factors which play a major part in the rendering of the fantastic. One concerns the ways in which fantasy is established: whether in a stagy manner; with the aid of specifically cinematic devices; or in the material of physical reality itself. Since this factor raises problems of technique, it will be called the "technical" factor.

The other factor concerns the relations of fantasy to physical reality within a given work on the screen. It is evident that the relations between them must vary with the weights allotted to each. Two alternatives claim attention. Fantasy may or may not be allowed the same relevance to the medium as visible actuality. Take a supernatural event: in the first case it may be assigned a role which suggests that it is at least as amenable to cinematic treatment as a real-life event; in the second, it may be made to appear as belonging to a realm less adequate to the cinema than nature in the raw. This factor will be called "relational."

The cinematic or uncinematic quality of screen fantasies obviously results from the interplay of both factors. For example, the uncinematic effect of a stagy hallucination may well lose its sting if the hallucination emerges from, and remains subordinated to, contexts devoted to physical existence. This example also illustrates the analytical procedures to be followed. It would seem advisable to inquire into the three ways in which fantasy may be established technically and to determine, in each stage of this inquiry, the influence of the two "relational" alternatives.*

Fantasy established in a stagy manner

The first stage of the inquiry into the "technical" factor centers on films which represent the fantastic by way of bizarre settings, contrived accessories, unusual make-up, and the like. Whether or not their outspoken staginess marks such creations as uncinematic depends on the manner in which the "relational" factor asserts itself in their representation.

FIRST ALTERNATIVE (Fantasy pretends to the same aesthetic legitimacy as actuality)

From THE CABINET OF DR. CALIGARI on, films or film sequences forgo the natural world in favor of an imagined one which cannot deny its origin in the studio. True, in some such films—e.g. Fritz Lang's old DESTINY or RED SHOES—spectacles of stagy fantasy mingle with renderings of real-life material, but the mixture is effected in a way which clearly points to the film makers' underlying belief that nature has no title to preferential treatment and that theatricality is as valid as is camera-realism. Incidentally, even D. W. Griffith occasionally turns into a naïve visionary: one of the final shots of his INTOLERANCE unabashedly portrays the heavens, with a chorus of veiled angels intervening in an earthly prison riot.[9]

Obviously screen fantasies which rely on staginess and at the same time claim to be valid manifestations of the medium run counter to the basic aesthetic principle; they pass over the specific potentialities of the medium for the sake of objectives which the cinema is not particularly fit to fulfill. Griffith's veiled angels would be a natural for religious painting; and the fantastic worlds in DESTINY or STAIRWAY TO HEAVEN are efforts to expand and cinematize what is essentially stage illusion. Small wonder that this strikes a responsive chord in all those who yearn for Art on the screen. CALIGARI is the prototype of films of fantasy which are a "leap into the world of art," to use a phrase coined by Monk Gibbon in his eulogy of the RED SHOES ballet.[10]

Yet if CALIGARI is an admirable achievement in more than one respect,[11] it is so not because of its aspiration to art in the traditional sense.

---

* The subsequent inquiry covers, on principle, fantasy in all types of film. Yet it should be noted that the dream-like imagery of many experimental films requires special comment. This imagery which often serves to project inner-life processes, especially the contents of the subconscious, will be dealt with in chapter 10.

Rather, as a "leap into the world of art" this unique film is a retrogression, for all the fascination its recourse to expressionist painting may exert. The controversy it has aroused conceivably revolves around its radical negation of camera-realism. In the early 'twenties, René Clair praised CALIGARI and DESTINY precisely for driving home the share of subjectivity that should go into film making; the very artificiality of their settings, lighting, and acting seemed to him a triumph of the intellect over the given raw material. But it appears that Clair was then so disturbed by a contemporary trend in favor of too mechanical a conception of the "realistic dogma" that he overstated his case; he failed to envisage the possibility of films which, like his later Paris comedies, would give subjectivity, including the intellect, its due and yet acknowledge the supremacy of physical reality.[12]

The crude tenor of Eisenstein's verdict on CALIGARI—he called it a "barbaric carnival of the destruction of the healthy human infancy of our art"[13]—may be traced to the fact that he passed judgment on it toward the end of the war against Nazi Germany. Other relevant comments on Caligarism fall into line with the proposition of this book. The German expressionist films, says Cavalcanti, "went out of fashion because the directors were attempting to use the camera in a way which is not proper to it. At this time the pictures got farther and farther away from reality."[14] Neergaard confronts Carl Dreyer's handling of fantasy in VAMPYR with the procedures applied in CALIGARI and arrives at the conclusion that the latter is nothing but "photographed theater."[15] Probably influenced by French *avant-garde* moods, even Jean Cocteau condemned CALIGARI, in 1923 or 1924, for deriving its macabre effects from eccentric settings rather than the activities of the camera[16]—Cocteau, who later was to make films extremely vulnerable to similar objections.

Since sustained stagy fantasy is a special case of staginess in general, its uncinematic character naturally admits of the same alleviations as the latter's.* In addition, if fantasy of the type under consideration appears within otherwise realistic-minded feature films, in the form of a dream or the like, it is surrounded by real-life events which inevitably claim predominance, thereby subduing the insert's uncinematic quality. However, this does not always work with dreams built from conspicuously theatrical material; for instance, the theatricality of the dream sequences in LADY IN THE DARK is too penetrating to be toned down by the realistic character of the rest of the film.

* See pp. 60–62. For instance, even though the Jack-the-Ripper episode of the old German film WAXWORKS is a fantasy laid in expressionist settings, it nevertheless has a semblance of cinematic life because of the admirable skill with which it is implemented technically. The "montage" of this fantasy makes you forget its remoteness from camera-reality. (Cf. Kracauer, *From Caligari to Hitler*, pp. 86–7.)

SECOND ALTERNATIVE (Fantasy is assigned a role of lesser validity than physical reality)

Stagy fantasy supports rather than obstructs the cinematic approach under two conditions. First, it does so whenever it takes on the function of a stage interlude in realistic films. In this case, it becomes acceptable cinematically for making, by way of contrast, the spectator more sensitive to the camera-reality surrounding it, a reality with which it is not intended to compete. Numbers of films involving backstage life, among them the first part of RED SHOES, thus afford glimpses of theatrical performances in a fantastic vein. And these interludes invariably benefit the naturalness of the adjacent scenes.

Second, fantasy, however stagy, conforms to the spirit of the medium if it is treated in a playful manner which invalidates the aspirations bound up with it in the first alternative. Chaplin has repeatedly explored this avenue. In his SUNNYSIDE he ridicules the Ballet Russe in a dance performance with wood nymphs—phantom girls in Greek costumes from a never-never land.[17] [Illus. 22] And there is the burlesque heaven in THE KID: the grimy slum court is transformed into a place of celestial bliss, with its inhabitants posing as white-clad angels; even the little dog grows wings, and the bully plays a harp as he flies about with the others between the flower-decorated façades.[18] To be sure, both episodes are dreams and as such not intended to match in significance the real-life action from which they digress and to which they lead back again. But they are also cinematic for a reason which has nothing to do with their function as dreams. Far from trying to conceal their staginess, Chaplin exaggerates it overtly and thus suggests that they should not be taken seriously. They are fantasies in a playful or ironical mood; and this precludes the impression that they have been devised to picture an imaginary world as real as the world about us. Their very staginess denotes that they spring from a primary concern for physical reality. Unlike Griffith's veiled angels, Chaplin's are parodies. This need not be done through dreams. Many a musical—for instance, THE BAND WAGON—indulges in fantasies whose deliberate extravagance in terms of settings and *décor* disavows their claim to credibility. Of course, everything depends upon the ratio between theatricality and playfulness. In STAIRWAY TO HEAVEN the stagy scenery is so obtrusive and elaborate that it neutralizes not only the amusing intentions behind it (which are thin indeed) but also the dream character of the whole film.

Fantastic monsters in films attempting to pass them off as realistic figures—think of the Frankenstein monster, King Kong, the Wolf Man, etc.—raise a moot problem. Introduced as a valid film theme, they plainly fall under the first alternative which covers uncinematic staginess. Yet they may be staged and manipulated so skillfully that they merge with their real-life environment and evoke the illusion of being virtually real. Is nature not capable of spawning monsters? Their possible verisimilitude, which is a tribute paid to camera-realism, after all brings them back into the orbit of the cinema. Nor should it be forgotten that at least some monsters are represented with a condoning twinkle in the eye.

Fantasy established by means of cinematic devices

Of interest here is only the application of such devices to material which renders reality as we commonly perceive it. From Nosferatu to The Ghost Goes West or Moulin Rouge innumerable films rely on the metamorphosing power of cinematic (and photographic) techniques to develop the fantastic from real-life shots. In Nosferatu it is negatives and the one-turn-one-picture technique which serve the purpose; in other films multiple exposures, superimpositions, distorting mirrors, special editing devices and what not are summoned to conjure up the supernatural, the unreal. It should be noted that not all fantasies can be produced this way. Winged angels, for instance, must be staged; and they inevitably look stagy because of the wings added to their natural appearance.

For the adequacy to the medium of this type of fantasy one will again have to consider the "relational" factor with its two alternatives. The question is whether or not the otherworldly is credited with the same validity as physical reality.

FIRST ALTERNATIVE

Take Nosferatu, the first and still representative instance of this rare subgenre: its protagonist is a bloodsucking vampire who wreaks havoc on all the people and places he haunts.[19] The whole film is a device-created horror fantasy which postulates the existence of specters and their intervention in the course of everyday life. [Illus. 23] Yet in constructing supernatural mysteries from real-life material and insisting on their reality, Nosferatu neglects those mysteries inherent in the material itself. Nevertheless films or film episodes in this vein—think, for instance, of certain device-fraught scenes of The Fall of the House of Usher—are in a measure cinematic because they lean on the technical properties of the medium for the creation of their demons and apparitions. One might properly call them a *tour de force*. It is not accidental that they occur only sporadically. Their magic wears off all the more easily since it results from devices which, it is true, are peculiar to the cinema but are used here for purposes outside its main concerns. The spectator soon recognizes them as tricks pure and simple and disparages them accordingly.[20]

SECOND ALTERNATIVE

Device-created fantasies confirm the superior validity of physical reality and, hence, acquire a cinematic quality if they are either treated in a playful manner or assigned the role of dreams. In the former case, the emphasis may first of all be on toying with physical existence. The prototype of this variety of the fantastic is the old silent film comedy, which derives additional fun from exaggerating natural movements through slow motion, fast motion, and other technical tricks. Chases proceed with astronomical speed; jumps come to a standstill in mid-air; collisions are avoided miraculously in the last split-second. All this happens, though it cannot happen, in normal everyday surroundings. The people on the screen are plain people; the highways and bars look familiar. Fictional reality in the old comedies has a pronounced factual character, sustained by visuals which are artless records rather than expressive photographs,[21] visuals forever concentrating on the turmoil of physical clashes and coincidences. It is crude material life dear to the instantaneous camera. The contrast between these real-life incidents and the interspersed trick scenes could not be stronger. And since the latter flagrantly defy all the laws of nature, they deepen the impression that real-life moments enhance the comic aspects of nature—nature filled with goblins and guardian angels. Outright illusion thus points up cinematic life. It should be added that the illusion itself, this toying with the known conditions of our physical world, is a delightful experience in its own right. Chaplin's dream interludes not only accentuate the actual misery of the Tramp but anticipate freedom from strictures and positive happiness. There is a touch of utopia about these challenges to space, time, and gravitation.

Or the emphasis can be on toying with fantasy itself. In this case fantastic events are made to appear as real. The phantoms and revenants in Le Voyage imaginaire, The Invisible Man, The Ghost Goes West, Topper, Here Comes Mr. Jordan, Blithe Spirit, The Ghost and Mrs. Muir, and It's a Wonderful Life behave just like the rest of us mortals. They muddle in human affairs as would a neighbor, and achieve their miracles in a matter-of-course way which soothes the suspicions plain common sense might otherwise entertain. All devices used tend to assimilate other-worldly activities to the ordinary run of things. Speaking of The Ghost Goes West, Allardyce Nicoll points to this realism in the fantastic: "Everything introduced there was possible in the sense that, although we might rationally decide that these events could not actually have taken place, we recognized that, granted the conditions which might make them achievable, they would have assumed just such forms as were cast on the screen. The ghost was thus a 'realistic' one."[22] Films in this line, then, adjust the supernatural to the natural instead of alienating the latter. Their spooky ingredients seem well-nigh indistinguishable from those "small moments of material life"[23] which Lumière was the first to capture. Significantly, Capra's IT's A WONDERFUL LIFE is crowded with quasi-documentary shots which refer to real and unreal happenings alike.

Even though in the long run the spectator will also tire of devices introducing fantasy playfully, he may nevertheless accept them more readily than tricks which establish it as a valid film theme. Presumably the former arouse less inner resistance because of their greater adequacy to the medium.

Device-created dreams in realistic films go beyond stagy ones in that they not only acknowledge the ascendancy of the real world in their capacity of dreams but are actually derived from shots rendering that world. Instead of culminating in nonrealistic imagery, they feature images, however manipulated, of given material phenomena. Most objects and characters in the dreams of THE SECRETS OF A SOUL have already appeared in the real-life episodes of this film and do not deny their origin in them. Or take the dying Toulouse-Lautrec's dream-like vision in MOULIN ROUGE: Chocolat, La Goulue, and the others who now hover, aerial spirits, before his inner eye, radiantly emerging from the dark wall and dancing into nothingness to the muted sounds of Offenbach, are essentially the same figures he so often saw perform when he was still very much alive. To be sure, all these images are processed and/or edited in a manner designed to enhance their dream character, but they practically never transgress camera-reality to such an extent that they would not be identifiable as derived from it. The many ambiguous shots among them which represent "reality of another dimension"—slow-motion pictures, shots from unusual angles, etc.—are as a rule so handled that they recall the natural data from which they are won rather than develop into detached shapes. It is as if the impact of the realistic tendency kept them in the fold.

What holds true of photographic film does of course not apply to animated cartoons. Unlike the former, they are called upon to picture the unreal—that which never happens. In the light of this assumption, Walt Disney's increasing attempts to express fantasy in realistic terms are aesthetically questionable precisely because they comply with the cinematic approach. From his first MICKEY MOUSE films to CINDERELLA and beyond it, Disney has drawn the impossible with a draftsman's imagination, but the draftsman in him has become more and more camera-conscious. There is a growing tendency toward camera-reality in his later full-length films. Peopled with the counterparts of real landscapes and real human beings, they are not so much "drawings brought to life"* as life reproduced in drawings. Physical detail, which was visibly pencil-born in Disney's early cartoons, merely duplicates life in his later ones. The impossible, once the *raison d'être* of his craft, now looks like any natural object. It is nature once again which appears in Snow White, Bambi, and Cinderella. To intensify this impression Disney shoots his sham nature as he would the real one, with the camera now panning over a huge crowd, now swooping down on a single face in it. The effects thus produced make us time and again forget that the crowd and the face in it have been devised on a drawing board. They might have been photographed as well. In these cartoons false devotion to the cinematic approach inexorably stifles the draftsman's imagination.

Fantasy established in terms of physical reality

The third and last stage of the inquiry into the technical factor bears on a type of fantasy which cannot be better defined than by a statement Carl Dreyer made while working on his Vampyr: "Imagine that we are sitting in an ordinary room. Suddenly we are told that there is a corpse behind the door. In an instant the room we are sitting in is completely altered: everything in it has taken on another look; the light, the atmosphere have changed, though they are physically the same. This is because *we* have changed, and the objects *are* as we conceive them. That is the effect I want to get in my film."[24] Dreyer tried hard to get it. Vampyr with its cast of partly nonprofessional actors is shot in natural surroundings and relies only to a limited extent on tricks[25] to put across its "vague hints of the supernatural."[26] "The strangest thing about this extremely fantastic film," remarks Neergaard, "is that Dreyer has never worked with more realistic material."[27] [Illus. 24]

Yet if the fantastic is mainly built from "realistic material," the "relational" factor ceases to be a decisive issue. In other words, it no longer matters much whether or not fantasies lay claim to the same validity as physical reality; provided they concentrate on real-life shots, they conform to the basic properties of the medium.

However, they may do so in different degrees, dependent on the ex-

* See p. 39.

tent to which they involve natural causes. The more they pretend to otherworldliness, the less will their underlying intention be in keeping with their truth to camera-reality. Assuming that fantasies established with the aid of real-life material are supernatural events palpably intended as such, their representation is therefore liable to produce an equivocal effect. This applies, for instance, to Dreyer's VAMPYR as well as Epstein's THE FALL OF THE HOUSE OF USHER, with its shots of fanciful tree trunks, floating mists, and weird toads. Epstein proceeds like Dreyer; despite his intermittent recourse to devices, especially slow-motion, he too makes an effort to suggest the presence of supernatural influences through visuals which are straight records of material phenomena.

But since the plots of both films take the existence of the supernatural more or less for granted, its presence does not simply follow from these visuals. Rather, the latter serve as corroborative evidence; they are selected and edited with a view to bearing out what has already been insinuated independently—the realistic character of otherworldly powers. Consequently, the cinematic quality of both films suffers from the fact that they picture physical data for a purpose reducing the data's significance. Instead of being free to get immersed in the images of the tree trunks, the mists, and the toads, the spectator must from the outset conceive of them as tokens of the supernatural. The task, imposed upon these realistic images, of making the unreal seem real, gives them actually the appearance of something unreal. Hence the impression of stagnant artificiality these films arouse.

An interesting case in point is also the finale of Dovzhenko's ARSENAL, as described by Sadoul: "The film concluded on a metaphoric soaring [envolée]. The worker insurgents were fusilladed. But the hero, pierced by bullets, continued to march even though he was evidently dead."[28] From a purely visual angle the shot of the marching worker is cinematic for portraying untampered-with reality. Since we know, however, that the worker is dead and that dead workers cannot march, we immediately realize that the marching hero is a mirage. That he lives on as if nothing had happened transforms him from a real being into a symbol with a propaganda message; he now signifies the ongoing revolution. So the shot of him is drained of its realistic character while still being realistic. Its symbolic function, which makes it illustrate a meaning conferred on it from without, interferes with its cinematic function of revealing an aspect of physical existence.

By the same token, fantasies of the type under consideration are completely in accordance with the cinematic approach if they are not only pictured in terms of camera-reality but characterized as phenomena somehow contingent on it. Then the meaning bound up with them bears out the realistic quality of the shots through which they materialize. DEAD OF NIGHT includes episodes along these lines. In one of them a sleepless patient in a private hospital room looks out of the window in the middle of the night and sees a sunlit street with a black hearse in it whose coachman invites him to get in: "There is just place for one inside." After his dismissal from the hospital the cured patient wants to board a bus and suddenly recoils because the driver is the double of that ghostly coachman and addresses the very same words to him. The bus crashes, of course. Another episode of this film clearly features a split-personality case: assuming all the traits of an independent individual, the dummy of a ventriloquist rebels against his master, who is defined throughout as a mentally sick person. Both fantasies are cinematic for two reasons. First, they are established by means of shots indistinguishable from shots of common everyday life; were it not for the particular place assigned to it within the film, the sunlit street that appears in the middle of the night would just be a real sunlit street. Second, both fantasies are cast in the role of hallucinations originating in strange or morbid states of mind. Accordingly, they can be interpreted as representing what in earlier contexts has been called "special modes of reality." The ghostly coachman and the rebellious dummy are reality as it appears to a man with the gift of second sight and a schizophrenic respectively.

And how does reality appear to a madman? Luis Buñuel in the superb church episode of his EL supplies an ingenious answer. Possessed with insane jealousy, Francisco, the film's protagonist, follows a couple whom he believes to be his wife and her alleged lover into the cathedral and there is just about to shoot them when he discovers that he mistook strangers for his prospective victims. He sits down; the service has begun and people are praying. As he looks up, he experiences the shock of his life: ever more people gaze at him, greatly amused by his foolishness. Even the priest discontinues the ritual and, looking in Francisco's direction, laughingly taps his forehead with his finger. The whole cathedral reverberates with laughter and he, Francisco, is the butt of it. But then again a pious humming sets in, while people are bent over their prayer books. So it goes on, scenes of devotion alternating with outbursts of hilarity. It should be noted that the churchgoers both laugh and pray in reality and that, accordingly, the shots of the madman's hallucination also picture reality without any artifice—his particular reality. A bit of editing does the trick. This extreme realism in the fantastic is of course possible only because it is common knowledge that no one laughs during religious services.

Remarks on the Actor

THE FILM ACTOR occupies a unique position at the junction of staged and unstaged life. That he differs considerably from the stage actor was already recognized in the primitive days when Réjane and Sarah Bernhardt played theater before the camera; the camera let them down pitilessly. What was wrong with their acting, the very acting which all theatergoers raved about?

Stage actor and screen actor differ from each other in two ways. The first difference concerns the qualities they must possess to meet the demands of their media. The second difference bears on the functions they must assume in theatrical plays and film narratives respectively.

QUALITIES

How can the stage actor's contribution to his role be defined in terms of the cinema? To be sure, like the film actor, he must draw on his nature in the widest sense of the word to render the character he is supposed to represent; and since his projective powers are rarely unlimited, a measure of type-casting is indispensable for the stage also. But here the similarities end. Due to the conditions of the theater, the stage actor is not in a position directly to convey to the audience the many, often imperceptible details that make up the physical side of his impersonation; these details cannot cross the unbridgeable distance between stage and spectator. The physical existence of the stage performer is incommunicable. Hence the necessity for the stage actor to evoke in the audience a mental image of his character. This he achieves by means of the theatrical devices at his disposal—a fitting make-up, appropriate gestures and voice inflections, etc.

Significantly, when film critics compare the screen actor with the stage actor they usually speak of the latter's exaggerations, overstatements, amplifications.[1] In fact, his mask is as "unnatural" as his behavior, for otherwise he would not be able to create the illusion of naturalness. Instead of drawing a true-to-life portrait which would be ineffective on the stage, he works with suggestions calculated to make the spectators believe that they are in the presence of his character. Under the impact of these suggestions they visualize what is actually not given them. Of course, the play itself supports the actor's conjurer efforts. The situations in which he appears and the verbal references to his motives and fears and desires help the audience to complement his own definitions so that the image he projects gains in scope and depth. Thus he may attain a magic semblance of life. Yet life itself, this flow of subtle modes of being, eludes the stage. Is it even aspired to in genuine theater?

Emphasis on being

Leonard Lyons reports the following studio incident in his newspaper column: Fredric March, the well-known screen and stage actor, was making a movie scene and the director interrupted him. "Sorry, I did it again," the star apologized. "I keep forgetting—this is a movie and I mustn't act."[2]

If this is not the whole truth about film acting it is at least an essential part of it. Whenever old films are shown at the New York Museum of Modern Art, the spectators invariably feel exhilarated over expressions and poses which strike them as being theatrical. Their laughter indicates that they expect film characters to behave in a natural way. Audience sensibilities have long since been conditioned to the motion picture camera's preference for nature in the raw. And since the regular use of close-ups invites the spectator to look for minute changes of a character's appearance and bearing, the actor is all the more obliged to relinquish those "unnatural" surplus movements and stylizations he would need on the stage to externalize his impersonation. "The slightest exaggeration of gesture and manner of speaking," says René Clair, "is captured by the merciless mechanism and amplified by the projection of the film."[3] What the actor tries to impart—the physical existence of a character—is overwhelmingly present on the screen. The camera really isolates a fleeting glance, an inadvertent shrug of the shoulder. This accounts for Hitchcock's insistence on "negative acting, the ability to express words by doing nothing."[4] "I mustn't act," as Fredric March put it. To be more precise, the film actor must act as if he did not act at all but were a real-life person caught in the act by the camera. He must seem to *be* his character.[5] He is in a sense a photographer's model.

Casualness

This implies something infinitely subtle. Any genuinely photographic portrait tends to sustain the impression of unstaged reality; and much as it concentrates on the typical features of a face, these features still affect us as being elicited from spontaneous self-revelations. There is, and should be, something fragmentary and fortuitous about photographic portraits. Accordingly, the film actor must seem to be his character in such a way that all his expressions, gestures, and poses point beyond themselves to the diffuse contexts out of which they arise. They must breathe a certain casualness marking them as fragments of an inexhaustible texture.

Many a great film maker has been aware that this texture reaches into the deep layers of the mind. René Clair observes that with screen actors spontaneity counts all the more, since they have to atomize their role in the process of acting;[6] and Pudovkin says that, when working with them, he "looked for those small details and shades of expression which . . . reflect the inner psychology of man."[7] Both value projections of the unconscious. What they want to get at, Hanns Sachs, a film-minded disciple of Freud's, spells out in psychoanalytical terms: he requests the film actor to advance the narrative by embodying "such psychic events as are before or beyond speech . . . above all those . . . unnoticed ineptitudes of behavior described by Freud as symptomatic actions."[8]

The film actor's performance, then, is true to the medium only if it does not assume the airs of a self-sufficient achievement but impresses us as an incident—one of many possible incidents—of his character's unstaged material existence. Only then is the life he renders truly cinematic. When movie critics sometimes blame an actor for overacting his part, they do not necessarily mean that he acts theatrically; rather, they wish to express the feeling that his acting is, somehow, too purposeful, that it lacks that fringe of indeterminacy or indefiniteness which is characteristic of photography.

Physique

For this reason the film actor is less independent of his physique than the stage actor, whose face never fills the whole field of vision. The camera not only bares theatrical make-up but reveals the delicate inter-play between physical and psychological traits, outer movements and inner changes. Since most of these correspondences materialize unconsciously, it is very difficult for the actor to stage them to the satisfaction of an au-dience which, being in a position to check all pertinent visual data, is wary of anything that interferes with a character's naturalness. Eisenstein's 1939 claim that film actors should exert "self-control . . . to the millimeter of movement"[9] sounds chimerical; it testifies to his ever-increasing and rather uncinematic concern for art in the traditional sense, art which completely consumes the given raw material. Possessed with formative aspirations, he forgot that even the most arduous "self-control" cannot produce the effect of involuntary reflex actions. Hence the common recourse to actors whose physical appearance, as it presents itself on the screen, fits into the plot —whereby it is understood that their appearance is in a measure sympto-matic of their nature, their whole way of being. "I choose actors exclusively for their physique," declares Rossellini.[10] His dictum makes it quite clear that, because of their indebtedness to photography, film productions de-pend much more than theatrical productions on casting according to physi-cal aspects.

FUNCTIONS

From the viewpoint of cinema the functions of the stage actor are determined by the fact that the theater exhausts itself in representing inter-human relations. The action of the stage play flows through its characters; what they are saying and doing makes up the content of the play—in fact, it is the play itself. Stage characters are the carriers of all the meanings a theatrical plot involves. This is confirmed by the world about them: even realistic settings must be adjusted to stage conditions and, hence, are limited in their illusionary power. It may be doubted whether they are intended at all to evoke reality as something imbued with meanings of its own. As a rule, the theater acknowledges the need for stylization.* Realistic or not, stage settings are primarily designed to bear out the characters and their interplay; the idea behind them is not to achieve full authenticity— unattainable anyway on the stage—but to echo and enhance the human entanglements conveyed to us by acting and dialogue. Stage imagery serves as a foil for stage acting. Man is indeed the absolute measure of this

---

* In his *Stage to Screen*, Vardac submits that the realistic excesses of the nine-teenth-century theater anticipated the cinema. To the extent that the theater then tried to defy stage conditions, he argues, it was already pregnant with the new, still unborn medium.

universe, which hinges on him. And he is its smallest unit. Each character represents an insoluble entity on the stage; you cannot watch his face or his hands without relating them to his whole appearance, physically and psychologically.

Object among objects

The cinema in this sense is not exclusively human.* Its subject matter is the infinite flux of visible phenomena—those ever-changing patterns of physical existence whose flow may include human manifestations but need not climax in them.

In consequence, the film actor is not necessarily the hub of the narrative, the carrier of all its meanings. Cinematic action is always likely to pass through regions which, should they contain human beings at all, yet involve them only in an accessory, unspecified way. Many a film summons the weird presence of furniture in an abandoned apartment; when you then see or hear someone enter, it is for a transient moment the sensation of human interference in general that strikes you most. In such cases the actor represents the species rather than a well-defined individual. Nor is the whole of his being any longer sacrosanct. Parts of his body may fuse with parts of his environment into a significant configuration which suddenly stands out among the passing images of physical life. Who would not remember shots picturing an ensemble of neon lights, lingering shadows, and some human face?

This decomposition of the actor's wholeness corresponds to the piecemeal manner in which he supplies the elements from which eventually his role is built. "The film actor," says Pudovkin, "is deprived of a consciousness of the uninterrupted development of the action in his work. The organic connection between the consecutive parts of his work, as a result of which the distinct whole image is created, is not for him. The whole image of the actor is only to be conceived as a future appearance on the screen, subsequent to the editing of the director."[11]

"I mustn't act"—Fredric March is right in a sense he himself may not have envisaged. Screen actors are raw material;[12] and they are often made to appear within contexts discounting them as personalities, as actors. Whenever they are utilized this way, utter restraint is their main virtue. Objects among objects, they must not even exhibit their nature but, as Barjavel remarks, "remain, as much as possible, below the natural."[13]

* See pp. 45–6.

TYPES

The non-actor

Considering the significance of the screen character's unstaged nature and his function as raw material, it is understandable that many film makers have felt tempted to rely on non-actors for their narrative. Flaherty calls children and animals the finest of all film material because of their spontaneous actions.[14] And Epstein says: "No set, no costume can have the aspect, the cast of truth. No professional faking can produce the admirable technical gestures of a topman or a fisherman. A smile of kindness, a cry of rage are as difficult to imitate as a rainbow in the sky or the turbulent ocean."[15] Eager for genuine smiles and cries, G. W. Pabst created them artificially when shooting a carousal of anti-Bolshevist soldiery for his silent film, THE LOVE OF JEANNE NEY: he herded together a hundred-odd Russian ex-officers, provided them with vodka and women, and then photographed the ensuing orgy.[16]

There are periods in which non-actors seem to be the last word of a national cinema. The Russians cultivated them in their revolutionary era, and so did the Italians after their escape from Fascist domination. Tracing the origins of Italian neorealism to the immediate postwar period, Chiaromonte observes: "Movie directors lived in the streets and on the roads then, like everybody else. They saw what everybody else saw. They had no studios and big installations with which to fake what they had seen, and they had little money. Hence they had to improvise, using real streets for their exteriors, and real people in the way of stars."[17] When history is made in the streets, the streets tend to move onto the screen.* For all their differences in ideology and technique, POTEMKIN and PAISAN have this "street" quality in common; they feature environmental situations rather than private affairs, episodes involving society at large rather than stories centering upon an individual conflict. In other words, they show a tendency toward documentary.

Practically all story films availing themselves of non-actors follow this pattern. Without exception they have a documentary touch. Think of such story films as THE QUIET ONE, LOS OLVIDADOS, or the De Sica films, THE BICYCLE THIEF and UMBERTO D.: in all of them the emphasis is on the world about us; their protagonists are not so much particular in-

---

* A notable exception was the German cinema after World War I: it shunned outer reality, withdrawing into a shell. See Kracauer, *From Caligari to Hitler*, pp. 58–60.

dividuals as types representative of whole groups of people. These narratives serve to dramatize social conditions in general. The preference for real people on the screen and the documentary approach seem to be closely interrelated.

The reason is this: it is precisely the task of portraying wide areas of actual reality, social or otherwise, which calls for "typage"—the recourse to people who are part and parcel of that reality and can be considered typical of it. As Rotha puts it: " 'Typage' . . . represents the least artificial organisation of reality."[18] It is not accidental that film directors devoted to the rendering of larger segments of actual life are inclined to condemn the professional actor for "faking." Like Epstein, who turns against "professional faking," Rossellini is said to believe that actors "fake emotions."[19] This predilection for non-actors goes hand in hand with a vital interest in social patterns rather than individual destinies. Buñuel's Los Olvidados highlights the incredible callousness of despondent juveniles; the great De Sica films focus on the plight of the unemployed and the misery of old age insufficiently provided for. [Illus. 25 and 54] Non-actors are chosen because of their authentic looks and behavior. Their major virtue is to figure in a narrative which explores the reality they help constitute but does not culminate in their lives themselves.

The Hollywood star

In institutionalizing stars, Hollywood has found a way of tapping natural attractiveness as if it were oil. Aside from economic expediency, though, the star system may well cater to inner needs common to many people in this country. This system provides variegated models of conduct, thus helping, however obliquely, pattern human relationships in a culture not yet old enough to have peopled its firmament with stars that offer comfort or threaten the trespasser—stars not to be mistaken for Hollywood's.

The typical Hollywood star resembles the non-actor in that he acts out a standing character identical with his own or at least developed from it, frequently with the aid of make-up and publicity experts. As with any real-life figure on the screen, his presence in a film points beyond the film. He affects the audience not just because of his fitness for this or that role but for being, or seeming to be, a particular kind of person—a person who exists independently of any part he enacts in a universe outside the cinema which the audience believes to be reality or wishfully substitutes for it. The Hollywood star imposes the screen image of his physique, the real or a stylized one, and all that this physique implies and connotes on every role he creates. And he uses his acting talent, if any, exclusively to feature the individual he is or appears to be, no matter for the rest whether his self-portrayal exhausts itself in a few stereotyped characteristics or brings out various potentialities of his underlying nature. The late Humphrey Bogart invariably drew on Humphrey Bogart whether he impersonated a sailor, a private "eye," or a night club owner.

But why is any one chosen for stardom while others are not? Evidently, something about the gait of the star, the form of his face, his manner of reacting and speaking, ingratiates itself so deeply with the masses of moviegoers that they want to see him again and again, often for a considerable stretch of time. It is logical that the roles of a star should be made to order. The spell he casts over the audience cannot be explained unless one assumes that his screen appearance satisfies widespread desires of the moment—desires connected, somehow, with the patterns of living he represents or suggests.*

The professional actor

Discussing the uses of professional actors and non-actors, Mr. Bernard Miles, himself an English actor, declares that the latter prove satisfactory only in documentary films. In them, says he, "non-actors achieve all, or at any rate most, that the very best professional actors could achieve in the same circumstances. But this is only because most of these pictures avoid the implications of human action, or, where they do present it, present it in such a fragmentary way as never to put to the test the training and natural qualities which differentiate an actor from a non-actor." Documentary, he concludes, "has never faced up to the problem of sustained characterization."[20]

Be this as it may, the majority of feature films does raise this problem. And challenged to help solve it, the non-actor is likely to forfeit his naturalness. He becomes paralyzed before the camera, as Rossellini observes;[21] and the task of restoring him to his true nature is often impossible to fulfill. There are exceptions, of course. In both his BICYCLE THIEF and UMBERTO D., Vittorio De Sica—of whom they say in Italy that he "could lure even a sack of potatoes into acting"[22]—succeeds in making people who never acted before portray coherent human beings. Old Umberto D., a rounded-out character with a wide range of emotions and reactions, is all the more memorable since his whole past seems to come alive in his intensely touching presence. But one should keep in mind that the

* See pp. 163–4.

Italians are blessed with mimetic gifts and have a knack of expressive gestures. Incidentally, while producing THE MEN, a film about paraplegic veterans, director Fred Zinnemann found that people who have undergone a powerful emotional experience are particularly fit to re-enact themselves.[23]

As a rule, however, sustained characterization calls for professional actors. Indeed many stars are. Paradoxically enough, the over-strained non-actor tends to behave like a bad actor, whereas an actor who capitalizes on his given being may manage to appear as a candid non-actor, thus achieving a second state of innocence. He is both the player and the instrument; and the quality of this instrument—his natural self as it has grown in real life—counts as much as his talent in playing it. Think of Raimu. Aware that the screen actor depends upon the non-actor in him, a discerning film critic once said of James Cagney that he "can coax or shove a director until a scene from a dreamy script becomes a scene from life as Cagney remembered it."[24]

Only few actors are able to metamorphose their own nature, including those incidental fluctuations which are the essence of cinematic life. Here Paul Muni comes to mind—not to forget Lon Chaney and Walter Huston. When watching Charles Laughton or Werner Krauss in different roles, one gets the feeling that they even change their height along with their parts. Instead of appearing as they are on the screen, such protean actors actually disappear in screen characters who seem to have no common denominator.

Dialogue and Sound

THE TERM "sound" is commonly used in two senses. Strictly speaking, it refers to sound proper—all kinds of noises, that is. And in a loose way it designates not only sound proper but the spoken word or dialogue as well. Since its meaning can always be inferred from the contexts in which it appears, there is no need for abandoning this traditional, if illogical, usage.

INTRODUCTION

Early misgivings

When sound arrived, perceptive film makers and critics were full of misgivings, in particular about the addition of the spoken word, this "ancient human bondage," as one of them called it.[1] They feared, for instance, that speech might put an end to camera movement—one fear at least which soon turned out to be unfounded.[2] To Chaplin a talking Tramp was so utterly unconceivable that he satirized conventional dialogue in both CITY LIGHTS and MODERN TIMES. As far back as 1928—the Russian studios had not yet introduced sound apparatus—Eisenstein, Pudovkin, and Alexandrov issued a joint Statement on sound film in which dim apprehensions alternated with constructive suggestions. This Statement, still of the highest interest, was probably inspired and edited by Eisenstein. A student of materialistic dialectics, he acknowledged sound as a historic necessity because of its emergence at a moment when the further evolution of the medium depended on it. For with the plots becoming ever more ambitious and intricate, only the spoken word would be able to relieve the silent film from the increasing number of cumbersome captions and explanatory visual inserts needed for the exposition of the intrigue. On the other hand, Eisenstein and his co-signers were convinced that the inclusion of dialogue would stir up an overwhelming desire for stage illusion. Their Statement predicted a flood of sound films indulging in "'highly cultured dramas' and other photographed performances of a theatrical sort."[3] Eisenstein did not seem to realize that what he considered a consequence of dialogue actually existed long before its innovation. The silent screen was crammed with "highly cultured dramas." "Misled by the fatal vogue of 'adaptations,'" said Clair in 1927, "the dramatic film is built on the model of theatrical or literary works by minds accustomed to verbal expression alone."[4] It might be added that all these film makers and critics accepted sound later on, though not unconditionally.

Basic requirement

The pronounced misgivings in the period of transition to sound can be traced to the rising awareness that films with sound live up to the spirit of the medium only if the visuals take the lead in them. Film is a visual medium.[5] To cite René Clair again, he says he knows of people less familiar with the history of the movies who stubbornly believe some otherwise well-remembered silent film to have been a talkie; and he shrewdly reasons that their slip of memory should give pause to all those reluctant to endorse the supremacy of the image.[6] The legitimacy of this requirement follows straight from the irrevocable fact that it is the motion picture camera, not the sound camera, which accounts for the most specific contributions of the cinema; neither noises nor dialogue are exclusively peculiar to film. One might argue that the addition of speech would seem to justify attempts at an equilibrium between word and image, but it will be seen shortly that such attempts are doomed to failure. For sound films to be true to the basic aesthetic principle, their significant communications must originate with their pictures.

In dealing with sound, it is best to treat dialogue—or speech, for that matter—and sound proper separately. Especially in the case of speech, two kinds of relationships between sound and image should be considered. The first concerns the role they are assigned—i.e., whether the messages of a film are primarily passed on through the sound track or the imagery. The second concerns the manner in which sound and image are synchronized at any given moment. There are various possibilities of synchronization. All of them have a bearing on the adequacy of the spoken word to the medium.

DIALOGUE

The role of the spoken word

PROBLEMATIC USES

What caused Eisenstein's gloom when he anticipated that the arrival of sound would generate a flood of "highly cultured dramas"? No doubt he feared lest the spoken word might be used as the carrier of all significant statements and thus become the major means of propelling the action. His fears were all too well-founded. At the beginning of sound the screen went "speech-mad," with many film makers starting from the "absurd assumption that in order to make a sound film it is only necessary to photograph a play."[7] And this was more than a passing vogue. The bulk of existing talkies continues to center on dialogue.

Dialogue in the lead The reliance on verbal statements increases, as a matter of course, the medum's affinity for the theater. Dialogue films either reproduce theatrical plays or convey plots in theatrical fashion. This implies that they automatically turn the spotlight on the actor, featuring him as an insoluble entity, and by the same token exile inanimate nature to the background.[8] Most important, emphasis on speech not only strengthens this tendency away from camera-life but adds something new and extremely dangerous. It opens up the region of discursive reasoning, enabling the medium to impart the turns and twists of sophisticated thought, all those rational or poetic communications which do not depend upon pictorialization to be grasped and appreciated. What even the most theatrical-minded silent film could not incorporate—pointed controversies, Shavian witticisms, Hamlet's soliloquies—has now been annexed to the screen.

But when this course is followed, it is inevitable that out of the spoken words definite patterns of meanings and images should arise. They are much in the nature of the loving memories which Proust's narrator retains of his grandmother and which prevent him from realizing her crude physique as it appears in a photograph. Evoked through language, these patterns assume a reality of their own, a self-sufficient mental reality which, once established in the film, interferes with the photographic reality to which the camera aspires.* The significance of verbal argumen-

* Borderline cases are the comedies by Frank Capra and Preston Sturges which just manage to counterbalance their sophisticated dialogue by visuals of independent interest—fresh slapstick incidents that complement, and compensate for, the witty repartee.

tation, verbal poetry, threatens to drown the significance of the accompanying pictures, reducing them to shadowy illustrations.[9] Erwin Panofsky makes this very point in his trenchant attack on a literary approach to the medium: "I cannot remember a more misleading statement about the movies than Mr. Eric Russell Bentley's in the Spring Number of the *Kenyon Review*, 1945: 'The potentialities of the talking screen differ from those of the silent screen in adding the dimension of dialogue—which could be poetry.' I would suggest: 'The potentialities of the talking screen differ from those of the silent screen in integrating visible movement with dialogue which, therefore, had better not be poetry.' "[10]

Equilibrium   Those aware of the theatrical effects of dialogue film and yet adverse to reducing the role of verbal communications tend to envisage the above-mentioned possibility of an equilibrium between word and image as a workable solution. Allardyce Nicholl considers Max Reinhardt's film A MIDSUMMER NIGHT'S DREAM a case in point, and defends the latter's equal concern for "visual symbols" and "language" on the strength of an interesting argument. Shakespeare's dialogue, says he, addressed itself to an audience which, confronted with a growing language and still unaccustomed to acquiring knowledge through reading, was much more acutely alert to the spoken word than is the modern audience. Our grasp of spoken words is no longer what it was in Shakespeare's times. Reinhardt is therefore justified in trying to enliven the dialogue by supplementing it with an opulent imagery. This imagery, Nicholl reasons, mobilizes our visual imagination, thus benefiting the verbal communications whose stimulating power has long since subsided.[11]

The fallacy of Nicholl's argument is obvious. In fact, he himself seems to doubt its conclusiveness; before advancing it, he admits that one might as well condemn A MIDSUMMER NIGHT'S DREAM for assigning to the pictures on the screen a role apt to divert the audience from the appeal of Shakespeare's language. Well, exactly this is bound to happen. Because of their obtrusive presence the luxuriant images summoned by Reinhardt cannot be expected to revitalize the dialogue by stimulating the spectator's allegedly atrophied sensitivity to it; instead of transforming the spectator into a listener, they claim his attention in their own right. So the word meanings are all the more lost on him. The balance to which the film aspires turns out to be unachievable. (For the rest, A MIDSUMMER NIGHT'S DREAM, with its stagy settings and lack of camera movement, is nothing but a lifeless accumulation of splendors which cancel one another out.)

Perhaps the most noteworthy attempt at an equilibrium between verbal and pictorial statements is Laurence Olivier's HAMLET, a film which breathes a disquiet that is much to the credit of its director. Olivier wants to transfer, undamaged, all the beauties of Shakespeare's dialogue to the screen. Yet endowed with a keen film sense, he also wants to avoid photographed theater and therefore plays up the role of the visuals and the significance of cinematic devices. The result is a *tour de force* as fascinating as it is exasperating. On the one hand, Olivier emphasizes the dialogue, inviting us to revel in its suggestive poetry; on the other, he incorporates the dialogue into a texture of meaningful shots whose impact prevents us from taking in the spoken lines. [Illus. 26]

During Hamlet's great soliloquy the camera, as if immune to its magic, explores his physique with an abandon which would be very rewarding indeed were we not at the same time requested to absorb the soliloquy itself, this unique fabric of language and thought. The spectator's capacity being limited, the photographic images and the language images inevitably neutralize each other;[12] like Buridan's ass, he does not know what to feed upon and eventually gets starved. HAMLET is a remarkable, if quixotic, effort to instill cinematic life into an outspoken dialogue film. But you cannot eat your cake and have it.

CINEMATIC USES

All the successful attempts at an integration of the spoken word have one characteristic in common: they play down dialogue with a view to reinstating the visuals. This may be done in various ways.

Speech de-emphasized   Practically all responsible critics agree that it heightens cinematic interest to reduce the weight and volume of the spoken word so that dialogue after the manner of the stage yields to natural, life-like speech.[13] This postulate is in keeping with the "basic requirement"; it rests upon the conviction that the medium calls for verbal statements which grow out of the flow of pictorial communications instead of determining their course. Many film makers have accordingly de-emphasized speech. Cavalcanti remarked in 1939: "Film producers have learned in the course of the last ten years that use of speech must be economical, and be balanced with the other elements in the film, that the style employed by the dialogue writers must be literal, conversational, non-literary: that the delivery must be light, rapid and offhand, to match the quick movements of the action, and the cuts from speaker to speaker."[14]

René Clair's Paris comedies, for instance, meet these requests to the letter; the dialogue in them is casual, so casual in fact that their characters sometimes continue to converse while disappearing in a bar. For a moment you may still see them linger behind the window and move their lips with appropriate gestures—an ingenious device which repudiates drastically the goals and claims of dialogue film proper. It is as if Clair wanted to demonstrate *ad oculos* that the spoken word is most cinematic if the messages it conveys elude our grasp; if all that actually can be grasped is the sight of the speakers.

The tendency toward embedding dialogue in visual contexts is perhaps nowhere illustrated so strikingly as in that episode of RUGGLES OF RED GAP in which Charles Laughton as Ruggles recites Lincoln's Gettysburg Address. At first glance, this episode would seem to be about the opposite of a fitting example, for, in delivering the speech, Ruggles is not only fully conscious of its significance but eager to impress it upon his listeners in the bar. His recital, however, also serves another purpose, a purpose of such an immediate urgency that it outweighs the impact of Lincoln's words themselves. The fact, established by their rendering, that Ruggles knows them by heart reveals to the audience his inner metamorphosis from an English gentleman's gentleman into a self-reliant American.

In complete accordance with this major objective, the camera closes in on Ruggles's face when he, still talking to himself, mumbles the first sentences of the speech, and then shows him again as he stands up and confidently raises his voice. The camera thus anticipates our foremost desire. Indeed, concerned with the change Ruggles has undergone rather than the text he declaims, we want nothing more than to scan his every facial expression and his whole demeanor for outward signs of that change. The episode is a rare achievement in that it features a speech which so little interferes with the visuals that, on the contrary, it makes them stand out glaringly. Things are arranged in such a manner that our awareness of the speech's content kindles our interest in the meanings of the speaker's appearance. Of course, this is possible only in case of a speech which, like Lincoln's, is familiar to the audience. Since the listeners need not really pay attention to it to recall what belongs among their cherished memories, they may take in the words and yet be free to concentrate on the accompanying pictures. Imagine Ruggles advancing a dramatically important new thought instead of reciting the Gettysburg speech: then the audience would hardly be in a position to assimilate the simultaneous verbal and pictorial statements with equal intensity.

Speech undermined from within When first incorporating the spoken word, Chaplin aimed at corroding it. He ridiculed speeches which, had they been normally rendered, would infallibly have conveyed patterns of language-bound meanings. The point is that he did not render them normally. In the opening sequence of CITY LIGHTS the orators celebrating the unveiling of a statue utter inarticulate sounds with the grandiloquent intonations required by the occasion. This sequence not only makes fun of the inanity of ceremonious speeches but effectively forestalls their absorption, thus inviting the audience all the more intensely to look at the pictures. In the feeding machine episode of MODERN TIMES Chaplin attains about the same ends with the aid of a gag which works like a delayed-time bomb. When the inventor of the machine begins to explain it, his whole performance is calculated to trap us into believing that he himself does the talking; then a slight movement of the camera makes us abruptly realize that his sales talk comes from a record player. As a joke on our gullibility this belated revelation is doubly exhilarating. And naturally, now that the man whom we believed to be the speaker is exposed as a dummy, a leftover from mechanization, we no longer pay attention to what the phonograph is pouring forth but turn from naïve listeners into dedicated spectators. (In two of his more recent films, MONSIEUR VERDOUX and LIMELIGHT, Chaplin has reverted to dialogue in theatrical fashion. From the angle of the cinema this is undeniably a retrogression. Yet Chaplin is not the only great artist to have suffered from the limitations of his medium. One grows older, and the urge to communicate pent-up insight precariously acquired sweeps away all other considerations. Perhaps Chaplin's desire to speak his mind has also something to do with his lifelong silence as a pantomime.)

Groucho Marx too undermines the spoken word from within. True, he is given to talking, but his impossible delivery, both glib like water flowing down tiles and cataclysmic like a deluge, tends to obstruct the sanctioned functions of speech. Add to this that he contributes to the running dialogue without really participating in it. Silly and shrewd, scatterbrained and subversive, his repartees are bubbling self-assertions rather than answers or injunctions. Groucho is a lusty, irresponsible extrovert out of tune with his partners. Hence the obliqueness of his utterances. They disrupt the ongoing conversation so radically that no message or opinion voiced reaches its destination. Whatever Groucho is saying disintegrates speech all around him. He is an eruptive monad in the middle of self-created anarchy. Accordingly, his verbal discharges go well with Harpo's slapstick pranks, which survive from the silent era. Like the gods of antiquity who after their downfall lived on as puppets, bugbears, and other minor ghosts, haunting centuries which no longer believed in them, Harpo is a residue of the past, an exiled comedy god condemned or permitted to act the part of a mischievous hobgoblin. Yet the world in which he appears is so crowded with dialogue that he would long since have vanished were it not for Groucho, who supports the spectre's destructive designs. As dizzying as any silent collision, Groucho's word cascades wreak havoc on language, and among the resultant debris Harpo continues to feel at ease.

Shift of emphasis from the meanings of speech to its material qualities
Film makers may also turn the spotlight from speech as a means of communication to speech as a manifestation of nature. In PYGMALION, for instance, we are enjoined to focus on Eliza's Cockney idiom rather than the content of what she is saying. This shift of emphasis is cinematic because it alienates the words, thereby exposing their material characteristics.[15] Within the world of sound the effect thus produced parallels that of photography in the visible world. Remember the Proust passage in which the narrator looks at his grandmother with the eyes of a stranger: estranged from her, he sees her, roughly speaking, as she really is, not as he imagines her to be. Similarly, whenever dialogue is diverted from its conventional purpose of conveying some message or other, we are, like Proust's narrator, confronted with the alienated voices which, now that they have been stripped of all the connotations and meanings normally overlaying their given nature, appear to us for the first time in a relatively pure state. Words presented this way lie in the same dimension as the visible phenomena which the motion picture camera captures. They are sound phenomena which affect the moviegoer through their physical qualities. Consequently, they do not provoke him, as would obtrusive dialogue, to neglect the accompanying visuals but, conversely, stir him to keep close to the latter, which they supplement in a sense.

Examples are not infrequent. To revert to PYGMALION, it is the type of Eliza's speech which counts. Her manner of expressing herself, as recorded by the sound camera, represents a peculiar mode of being which claims our attention for its own sake. The same holds true of those parts of the dialogue in MARTY which help characterize the Italian-American environment; the bass voice in the coronation episode of IVAN THE TERRIBLE; the echo scene in Buñuel's ROBINSON CRUSOE; and the lumps of conversation tossed to and fro in MR. HULOT's HOLIDAY. When in Tati's admirable comedy, one of the most original since the days of silent slapstick, Hulot checks in at the reception desk of the resort hotel, the pipe in his mouth prevents him from pronouncing his name clearly. Upon request, he politely repeats the performance and, this time without pipe, enunciates the two syllables "Hulot" with so overwhelming a distinctness that, as in the case of his initial mutter, you are again thrust back on the physical side of his speech; the utterance "Hulot" stays with you not as a communication but as a specific configuration of sounds.

"There is something peculiarly delightful," says Ruskin, ". . . in passing through the streets of a foreign city without understanding a word that anybody says! One's ear for all sound of voices then becomes entirely impartial; one is not diverted by the meaning of syllables from recognizing the absolute guttural, liquid, or honeyed quality of them: while the gesture of the body and the expression of the face have the same value for you that they have in a pantomime; every scene becomes a melodious opera to you, or a picturesquely inarticulate Punch."[16] This is, for instance, confirmed by the song which Chaplin as a dancing waiter improvises in his MODERN TIMES: a hodge-podge of melodious, if incomprehensible, word formations, it is both an attractive sound composition in its own right and an ingenious device for attuning the spectator perfectly to the pantomime which the involuntary rhapsodist is meanwhile performing.

And of course, Ruskin's observation accounts for the cinematic effect of multilingual films. A number of them, partly semi-documentaries, were produced after World War II. G. W. Pabst's KAMERADSCHAFT and Jean Renoir's LA GRANDE ILLUSION, both bilingual, anticipated this trend which grew out of the tribulations of the war when millions of ordinary people, cut off from their native countries, intermingled all over Europe. In the Rossellini film PAISAN, which reflects most impressively the ensuing confusion of mother tongues, an American G.I. tries to converse with a Sicilian peasant girl; he soon supplements unintelligible words with drastic gestures and thus arrives at an understanding of a sort. But since this primitive approach is not achieved through the dialogue itself, the sounds that compose it take on a life of their own. And along with the dumb show, their conspicuous presence as sounds challenges the spectator empathically to sense what the two characters may sense and to respond to undercurrents within them and between them which would, perhaps, be lost on him were the words just carriers of meanings. The theater which hinges on dialogue shuns foreign languages, while the cinema admits and even favors them for benefiting speechless action.

Emphasis on voices as sounds may also serve to open up the material regions of the speech world for their own sake. What is thought of here is a sort of word carpet which, woven from scraps of dialogue or other kinds of communications, impresses the audience mainly as a coherent sound pattern. Grierson coins the term "chorus" to define such patterns and mentions two instances of them: the film THREE-CORNERED MOON, in which the chorus or carpet consists of bits of conversation between unemployed people queueing up in bread lines; and BEAST OF THE CITY, a Hollywood film about the Chicago underworld, with an episode which features the monotonous wireless messages from police headquarters. "It went something like this: 'Calling Car 324 324 Calling Car 528 528

Calling Car 18 18,' etc., etc. . . ."[17] Now these "choruses" may be inserted in such a way that it is they rather than the synchronized visuals which captivate the spectator—or should one say, listener? Being all ear, he will not care much about what the pictures try to impart.

On the surface, this use of speech seems to go against the grain of the medium by disregarding the visual contributions. And yet it is cinematic by extension. The voice patterns brought into focus belong to the physical world about us no less than its visible components; and they are so elusive that they would hardly be noticed were it not for the sound camera which records them faithfully. Only in photographing them like any visible phenomenon—not to mention mechanical reproduction processes outside the cinema—are we able to lay hold on these transitory verbal conglomerates. The fact that they palpably form part of the accidental flow of life still increases their affiliations with the medium. An excellent case in point is JUNGLE PATROL, a Hollywood B picture about American combat fliers in New Guinea. This film culminates in a sequence of terrific air fights which, however, are not seen at all. What we do see instead is a loudspeaker in the operations hut hooked in to the planes' inter-coms. As the ill-fated fights take their course, different voices which seem to come from nowhere flow out of the radio set, forming an endless sound strip.[18] To be sure, we grasp the tragic implications of their blurred messages. But this is not the whole story they are telling us. Rather, the gist of it is the constant mutter itself, the fabric woven by voice after voice. In the process of unfolding, it sensitizes us to the influences of space and matter and their share in the individual destinies.

Manner of synchronization

RELEVANT CONCEPTS

A. *Synchronism—asynchronism* Sound may or may not be synchronized with images of its natural source.

Example of the first alternative:
1. We listen to a speaking person while simultaneously looking at him.

Examples of the second alternative:
2. We turn our eyes away from the speaker to whom we listen, the result being that his words will now be synchronized with, say, a shot of another person in the room or some piece of furniture.
3. We hear a cry for help from the street, look out of the window, and see the moving cars and buses without, however, taking in the traffic noises,

because we still hear only the cry that first startled us. (This example originates with Pudovkin.[19])

4. While watching, for instance, a documentary, we listen to the voice of a narrator who never appears on the screen.

Before I go further, several technical terms must be explained. One commonly speaks of "synchronism" when the sounds and images coinciding on the screen are also synchronous in real life, so that they can in principle be photographed by the synchronized sound and motion picture cameras.* And one speaks of "asynchronism" when sounds and images which do *not* occur simultaneously in reality are nevertheless made to coincide on the screen. But how do these concepts relate to the two alternatives under discussion? The first alternative—sound synchronized with images of its natural source—evidently represents the most outspoken and perhaps the most frequent instance of *synchronism* and may therefore be termed accordingly. The second alternative—sound synchronized with images other than those of its source—includes, it is true, the cases illustrated by example 2—cases, that is, which under certain conditions come under the heading of synchronism. But change the conditions and they exemplify asynchronism. They are ambiguous borderline cases. Except for them, the second alternative covers exclusively unequivocal instances of asynchronous sound, as can easily be inferred from examples 3 and 4. It is therefore permissible to identify this alternative as *asynchronism*.

For the purposes of analysis one will in addition have to differentiate between sound which, actually or virtually, belongs to the world presented on the screen (examples 1-3) and sound which does not (example 4). Following Karel Reisz's suggestion, these two possibilities may be labeled *actual* sound and *commentative* sound respectively.[20] Synchronism inevitably involves the former, whereas asynchronism admits of both varieties.

B. Parallelism—counterpoint Let us now temporarily disregard these alternatives and inquire instead into what sound on the one hand and the images synchronized with it on the other try to impart. Words and visuals may be so combined that the burden of communication falls to either alone, a case in which they can, loosely speaking, be said to express parallel meanings. Or of course, they may carry different meanings, in

---

* To avoid confusion between the term "synchronization," which is used in a purely formal sense, and the term "synchronism," the latter will be put in quotation marks wherever a misunderstanding might arise.

which case both of them contribute to the message issuing from their synchronization.

Example of the first alternative:

5. Take example 1—some verbal communication synchronized with shots of the speaker. Assuming that the content of his words is all that counts at the moment, the accompanying shots do not add anything that would have to be considered. They are all but unnecessary. It is obvious that the reverse might happen as well: the speaker's gestures or features, impressed upon us by eloquent images, bring out his intentions so drastically that the words he simultaneously utters amount to a sheer repetition of what these images are telling us anyway.

Arrangements of this kind are usually termed *parallelism*.

Example of the second alternative:

6. The same example of synchronous sound may also serve to elucidate the second alternative—sounds and visuals denoting different things. In this case the pictures do not parallel the speaker's verbal statements but bear on matters not included in them. Perhaps a close-up of his face reveals him to be a hypocrite who does not really mean what he says. Or his appearance, as rendered on the screen, complements his words, stimulating us to elaborate on their inherent significance in this or that direction. For the rest, the extent to which the synchronized pictorial and verbal statements differ from each other is of little interest. The main thing is that they do differ and that the meaning of the scene which they establish results from their co-operation.

In the literature on film this kind of relationship between sound and visuals is called *counterpoint*.

There are, then, two pairs of alternatives: synchronism–asynchronism; parallelism–counterpoint. Yet these two pairs do not assert themselves independently of each other. Rather, they are invariably interlinked in such a way that one alternative of either pair fuses with one of the other. A table may help clarify the characteristics of the resultant four types of synchronization.

THE FOUR TYPES OF SYNCHRONIZATION

Legend

SYNCHRONISM

TYPE I: *Parallelism* (speech and image carrying parallel meanings). See example 5.

TYPE II: *Counterpoint* (speech and image carrying different meanings). See example 6.

TYPE III: *Parallelism* (IIIa involves *actual* sound; IIIb *commentative* sound). Examples will follow.

TYPE IV: *Counterpoint* (for IVa and IVb, see just above). Examples will follow.

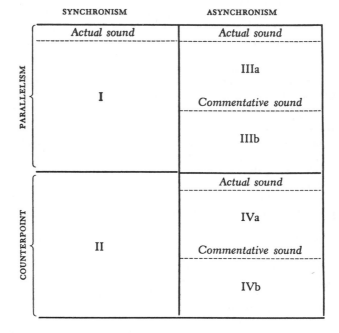

EXISTING THEORIES

Only now that all relevant concepts have been defined is it possible to resume the main line of thought with a chance of success. The problem is: what do the varying relationships between image and speech imply for the latter's inadequacy or adequacy to the medium?

It might be best to take a look at the existing theories first. Most critics hold that, for an integration of sound into film, much, if not all, depends upon the methods of synchronization. This is not to say that they would ignore the significance of the role assigned to speech; as has been pointed out above, they usually repudiate the ascendancy of dialogue in favor of films in which speech is kept subdued. But they practically never think of establishing a meaningful connection between that role and the manner in which words and visuals are synchronized. And their emphasis on synchronization techniques indicates that they take them to be the decisive factor.

This bias goes hand in hand with the tendency, equally widespread in theoretical writings, to follow the example of the Russians, who not only championed counterpoint and asynchronism when sound arrived but plainly assumed that both procedures are inseparable from each other. In their joint Statement of 1928 Eisenstein, Pudovkin, and Alexandrov declare: "*Only a contrapuntal use* of sound in relation to the visual montage piece will afford a new potentiality of montage development and perfection."[21] And somewhat later Pudovkin remarks: "It is not generally recognized that the principal elements in sound film are the asynchronous and not the synchronous."[22] He and Eisenstein took it for granted that asynchronism inevitably calls for a contrapuntal handling of sound and, conversely, the latter for asynchronism. Presumably it was their obsession with the montage principle which made them believe in the supreme virtues of this particular combination, blinding them to other, equally rewarding possibilities. The reader need hardly be told that the Russian doctrine entails, or at least encourages, the no less untenable identification of parallelism with "synchronism."[23]

Even though, thanks to three decades of talkies, modern writers in the field are more discerning than the authors of this oversimplified doctrine,[24] they continue in a measure to endorse the latters' insistence on the cinematic merits of asynchronous sound and its contrapuntal use. And Pudovkin's main argument in support of his proposition is still fully upheld. He defends asynchronism—or counterpoint, for that matter —on the ground that it conforms best to real-life conditions, whereas cases of parallelism, says he, materialize much less frequently than we are inclined to think. To prove his thesis he constructs the above-mentioned example of a cry for help from the street which stays with us as we look out of the window, drowning the noises of the moving cars and buses now before our eyes (example 3). And what about our natural behavior as listeners? Pudovkin describes some of the ways in which our eyes happen to wander while we are following a conversation. We may go on watching a man who has just finished talking and now listens to a member of the party; or we may prematurely look at a person all set to answer the actual speaker; or we may satisfy our curiosity about the effects of a speech by scanning, one by one, the faces of the listeners and studying their reactions.[25] All three alternatives—it is easy to see that they fall into line with our example 2—are drawn from everyday life; and all of them represent at least borderline cases of asynchronism, with word and image being interrelated in contrapuntal fashion. The gist of Pudovkin's argument is that this type of synchronization is cinematic because it corresponds to our habits of perception and, hence, renders reality as we actually experience it.

No doubt the theories presented here carry much weight. Yet from the angle of this book they suffer from two shortcomings. First, they attribute to the methods of synchronization independent significance, even though these methods are only techniques which may serve any purpose, cinematic or not. Second, they plead for contrapuntal asynchronism on the ground that it reflects faithfully the manner in which we perceive reality. What accounts for the cinematic quality of films, however, is not so much their truth to our experience of reality or even to reality in a general sense as their absorption in camera-reality—visible physical existence.

How dispose of these shortcomings? Let us proceed from the following observation: Any film maker wants to canalize audience attention and create dramatic suspense as a matter of course. Accordingly, he will in each particular case resort to such methods of synchronization as he believes to be the most fitting ones. Supposing further he is a skilled artist, his choices are certainly "good" in the sense that they establish the narrative as effectively as is possible under the given circumstances.

But are they for that reason also necessarily "good" in a cinematic sense? Their adequacy to the medium obviously depends upon the "goodness" of the narrative which they help implement. Does the narrative grow out of verbal or visual contributions?—this is the question. The decisive factor, then, is the role which speech plays within the contexts under consideration. If speech is in the lead, even the most knowing film maker cannot avoid synchronizing it with the images in ways which disqualify the latter as a source of communication. Conversely, if the visuals predominate, he is free to avail himself of modes of synchronization which, in keeping with the cinematic approach, advance the action through pictorial statements.

An interesting fact emerges at this point. As I have emphasized, the existing theories usually recommend a contrapuntal treatment of asynchronous sound, while cautioning against parallel synchronization. Now it can easily be shown that my new proposition corroborates these theories up to a point. In case verbal communications prevail, the odds are that the imagery will parallel them. The reverse alternative—speech being deemphasized—greatly favors counterpoint, which stirs the visuals to become eloquent. Eisenstein and Pudovkin were of course not wrong in advocating a contrapuntal use of sound. But from the present viewpoint they did so for the wrong reasons.

To sum up, in the light of our proposition the ascendancy of dialogue entails problematic methods of synchronization, whereas the dominance of pictorial communications brings cinematic methods within the accomplished film director's reach. But what methods of synchronization are actually at his disposal? Evidently the four types represented in our table. The task is now to ascertain the uses he must or may make of them in either of the two possible total situations. Let us again take a look at that table, this time with a view to inquiring into what happens to the four types of synchronization (1) when word meanings carry the day, and (2) when the pictures retain full significance.

THE DOMINANCE OF SPEECH ENTAILING PROBLEMATIC USES

Synchronism

Type I: Parallelism   This commonplace manner of synchronization—the sight of a speaker adding nothing to what he is saying—has already been discussed above (example 5). In any such case the pictures are degraded to pointless illustrations. Moreover, absorbed as we are in the speaker's communication, we will not even care to watch them closely. Visible material reality, the camera's major concern, thus evaporates before the spectator's unseeing eyes.

Type II: Sham counterpoint   Scenes with the emphasis on speech occasionally include a shot of the speaker which seems intended to add something of its own to the synchronized words; perhaps the film maker has inserted a close-up of the speaker's face for the purpose of tacitly qualifying through it the manifest content of his utterances. However, since, according to premise, these utterances themselves are all that matters at the moment, we will naturally try to take them in as best we can, and therefore we will hardly be able simultaneously to grasp such implications of the face as point in another direction. More likely than not we will not notice the speaker's face at all. Or if we do notice it, we will at most be surprised at the way he looks without giving further thought to it. In this case, it is true, parallelism yields to an attempt at counterpoint, but the attempt is abortive because the undiminished impact of the words emasculates the accompanying images, blurring their divergent meanings.

Asynchronism

Notwithstanding the wide response which the Russian directors' preference for asynchronous sound has found in the literature on film, there is actually not the slightest difference between asynchronism and parallelism with respect to their cinematic potentialities. It will presently be seen that the former may be as "bad" as the latter (or of course, the latter as "good" as the former).

Type III: Parallelism   To begin with *actual* sound (IIIa), think of the numerous films in which one of the actors mentions the war; no sooner does he mention it than the image of him gives way to a battlefield scene, an airfight, or the like—some short cut-in plainly designed to lend color to his portentous reference. Or another instance: often a film director sees fit to insert shots of the Eiffel Tower or Big Ben at the very moment the speaker on the screen, perhaps a traveler back home from abroad, pronounces the magic words Paris or London. With some benevolence one might interpret these inserts as an attempt, on the part of the film director, to make up for the ascendancy of speech, as a tribute he is paying to the medium's affinity for visual communications. Yet these efforts are wasted, for the asynchronous images of the battlefield and the Eiffel Tower just duplicate the verbal statements with which they are juxtaposed. Even worse, in unnecessarily illustrating the juxtaposed words they narrow down their possible meanings. In combination with the shot of the Eiffel Tower the word Paris no longer invites us to indulge in enchanting memories but, due to the presence of that shot, calls forth stereotyped notions which now hem in our imagination. Nor are we free to perceive the Eiffel Tower picture for its own sake; within the given context it is nothing but a token, a sign.

Considering the frequency of such pictorial adornments, Fellini's reserve in his LA STRADA is all the more remarkable. The roving circus people are seen camping on the dreary outskirts of a city and one of them says something to the effect that they have now reached Rome. At this point a shot of a Roman landmark would have not merely paralleled the place-name but assumed the legitimate function of rendering visible the larger environment. Nothing of the kind happens, however; we just hear the word Rome and that is that. It is as if Fellini, wary of pictorial diversions, has found this value-laden word sufficiently suggestive to drive home to us, by way of contrast, the itinerants' pitiful existence and indifference.

Commentative sound (IIIb)—the speaker not belonging to the world presented—lends itself to two kinds of parallelism, both common in American documentaries. First, the imagery amounts to a halfway comprehensible continuity: then the commentator, as if jealous of the pictures' ability to make themselves understood without his assistance, may nevertheless overwhelm them with explanations and elaborations. Newsreel and sport film commentators are prone to drowning even self-evident visual contexts in a veritable deluge of words. Pare Lorentz's THE RIVER, which tells the story of the Mississippi basin from the disastrous exploitation of its soil in the past to the successful rehabilitation efforts of the Tennessee Valley

Authority, is so vivid a pictorial narrative that only a minimum of speech would be needed to fill the few gaps left. Yet Lorentz finds its necessary to superimpose upon this narrative endless lyrical tirades. They largely duplicate the imagery; and the spoken place-names, especially, evoke associations and poetic images which remove the visuals still further from the center of attention.

Second, all important communications are entrusted to the commentator from the outset so that his verbal statements jell into a coherent and intelligible whole: then it is inevitable that the synchronized pictures should be cast in a subsidiary role. Instead of being interrelated in an organic manner, they succeed each other jerkily, supplementing, somehow, the speaker's self-sufficient recital. Documentaries in this vein are very frequent indeed. Their prototype was, perhaps, the MARCH OF TIME series, which included many films that were just spoken editorials, with the visuals thrown into the bargain.[26] And what about the residual functions of the visuals themselves? But this matter will be taken up later on.

Type IV: Sham counterpoint It has already been shown (under the heading Type II) that, as long as speech prevails, attempts at a contrapuntal handling of synchronous sound are doomed to failure. Of course, in case of asynchronism such attempts stand no greater chance of being successful. To illustrate, first, *actual* asynchronous sound (IVa), consider the above-cited Pudovkin example of the three ways in which we may follow a conversation. Of interest here is especially the last alternative—the so-called "reaction shots" which focus on the faces of listeners for the obvious purpose of making us aware of their reactions to the speaker. Well, under the given conditions these images will beckon us vainly. Drawn into the orbit of the words that fall on our ears, we cannot help losing sight of what hovers before our eyes. The sway of speech voids the listeners' faces, to the detriment of their contrapuntal effects.

A nice example of sham counterpoint involving *commentative* sound (IVb) is Hamlet's great soliloquy in Laurence Olivier's adaptation of the play. This sequence has on an earlier occasion served to demonstrate that an equilibrium between words and images of approximately equal weight, if possible at all, is likely to result in their mutual neutralization rather than a reinforcement of either. Two points remain to be added. First, the soliloquy must be characterized as commentative speech because Olivier, by means of the echo-chamber device, conveys the impression that it is not so much Hamlet as his incorporeal soul which does the talking. The Hamlet we see is, himself, a listener, not a speaker; he listens, and reacts, to his own "inner" voice which rises from depths beyond the world presented.

Second, in emphasizing Hamlet's features throughout the soliloquy and thus imbuing them with meanings of their own, Olivier obviously wants to establish contrapuntal relations between the words and the synchronized images. But here too applies what has been said above: the contrapuntal influences from Hamlet's outward appearance will be lost on those immersed in the monologue's word imagery.

THE DOMINANCE OF THE VISUALS FAVORING CINEMATIC USES

Synchronism

Type I: Parallelism Imagine again that we are watching a speaking character; this time, however, the visuals, not the words, are the main source of communication. Imagine further that the speaker's words do not add anything to the synchronized pictures of him but just parallel them, thus duplicating their messages (see last part of example 5). Were there no words at all, we would still understand what his looks are meant to express. This type of parallelism vividly illustrates the tremendous significance of the role in which speech is cast. The reader will remember that, if speech prevails, the duplicative imagery is reduced to an unseen accompaniment—a state of things which obstructs the cinematic approach. Now that the visuals prevail, the passage with the image of the speaker retains its cinematic quality despite the presence of duplicative words. Supposing these words are really superfluous, they will at worst amount to a minor nuisance. Yet are they under all circumstances sheer ballast? Unnecessary as a duplication, they may nevertheless increase the realistic effect of a scene. And this would largely compensate for their otherwise gratuitous insertion.

Type II: Counterpoint As has already been shown in example 6, the face of a speaking person may carry meanings which conflict with, or complement, those of his synchronized verbal statements. This is clearly a case of "synchronism," with images and words relating to each other contrapuntally. Note that they can be interlinked in such a way only because speech no longer claims undivided attention—an alternative which, other conditions being equal, entails sham counterpoint—but is sufficiently deemphasized to let the images have their say. Genuine counterpoint on the screen is bound up with the predominance of the visuals; at any rate, it is their contributions which account for the cinematic character of this particular linkage.

Laughton's delivery of the Gettysburg Address in Ruggles of Red Gap illustrates this point to perfection.* Throughout the recital, close-ups and

* See p. 107.

medium shots of Laughton-Ruggles alternate with "reaction shots" featuring the increasingly attentive customers in the bar. As the familiar Lincoln words drop in on us, we experience something intimately related to their flow but not implied by them—Ruggles' happiness about his integration into the community and the customers' recognition that he now "belongs." This story is told by the pictures alone. To be sure, they cannot possibly tell it without the synchronized speech which touches off their contrapuntal suggestions, but the speech itself recedes, assuming the modest role of a catalytic accompaniment.

Orson Welles's OTHELLO includes an example of synchronous counterpoint which is noteworthy for being contrived against heavy odds. Pictured at close range, Othello and Iago walk atop the ramparts, the upper part of their figures being silhouetted against the sky and the sea. As they move on, the well-known dialogue develops, with Iago sowing the seeds of suspicion and Othello gradually succumbing to the poison. At first glance this sequence does not seem to offer the slightest opportunity for counterpoint to assert itself. The whole dramatic interest lies in the dialogue, which therefore should be expected to take the life out of the accompanying pictures. Yet Orson Welles manages to resuscitate them by disintegrating the dense verbal fabric. It takes time for Iago's insinuations to sink into the Moor's mind, and when the latter finally reacts, Iago resumes his offensive only after having pondered the victim's reply. The dialogue is thus interspersed with stretches of silence, a silence which would be complete were it not punctuated by rhythmic footfalls. But instead of referring back to the verbal argument, these sounds all the more sensitize us to the physical appearance of the two walking men from whom they issue. So their images which fuse with the sea and the sky about them regain momentum and intimate much of what is left unsaid. Along with the footfalls, they make us privy to processes which the words conceal rather than expose. By means of these intervals, then, Welles succeeds in removing the dialogue from its vantage position and imbuing the visuals with contrapuntal meanings.

Asynchronism

Type III: Parallelism There is no need for elaborating on this type because it resembles type I in every respect. If the screen shows snow-covered mountain peaks and we hear a temporarily invisible tourist (IIIa: *actual* sound) or a commentator (IIIb: *commentative* sound) remark that the mountains now on view are covered with snow, we may find such a duplicative statement unnecessary, but provided it is made in a casual way, it will certainly not detract attention from the pictures. At least with actual sound, incidental parallelism of this kind is perhaps even required, say, to help characterize a verbose speaker, keep up dramatic suspense, maintain continuity in the dimension of language, etc.

Type IV: Counterpoint   No sooner is the emphasis on the visuals than this type of sychronization displays all the cinematic virtues ascribed to it in the literature. In the case of *actual* sound (IVa) the source of speech rarely remains invisible throughout. For any number of compositional reasons the image of a speaking person may appear only after his voice has already been heard or emerge when he starts talking and then yield to other images equally synchronized with his voice. The first alternative comes true, for instance, in that episode of Jean Epstein's TEMPESTAIRE in which we see the wild ocean, to the accompaniment of a song which might as well be identified as commentative sound; but as the song continues, we are eventually brought face to face with the girl who does the singing. Typical of the more common second alternative are reaction shots, which of course acquire full revealing power once speech has ceased to play a major role. The peculiar effects produced by either alternative are negligible here in view of the fact that both of them challenge the spectator to explore an essentially cinematic universe.

Take the Elsie episode of M, in which Fritz Lang features the despair of a mother whose little girl does not come home from school. She looks out of the window and, at the end of her tether, shouts the name of her girl. The air is filled with her shout. Then she disappears and we see instead, still reverberating with her "Elsie," the empty stairwell of the house and its empty attic—images followed by Elsie's unused plate on the kitchen table, the ball she was playing with, and the balloon with which the murderer won the confidence of the child.[27] Now the juxtaposition of the asynchronous shout "Elsie" with the shots of the stairwell and the attic is likely to affect us in two ways: it sensitizes us to the indescribable sadness of these shots; and it causes us to relate their sadness to the despair behind that shout. In other words, the stairwell and the attic do not just serve to illustrate the state of mind of Elsie's mother; rather, they impress themselves upon us for their own sake so that, in looking at the screen, we cannot help being aware of some of their properties, innate or not; hence, what we actually experience is the interplay between them and the moods or drives responsible for the mother's outcry. The Elsie episode lures the responsive spectator deep into the dimension of psychophysical correspondences.

Another example: after having killed her assailant with a knife, the young heroine of Alfred Hitchcock's BLACKMAIL finally returns to her parents' shop and there overhears the chatter of a gossipy woman customer. The camera is just focusing on the listening girl, as the woman suddenly drops the word "knife." At this moment time seems to come to a stop: the word "knife" lingers on, an ever-repeated threat, and so does the face of the girl—a drawn-out interlude filled exclusively with her close-up and the ominous word. Then the spell subsides. The woman resumes her prattle and we realize that she actually never discontinued it.[28] In pointing to the impenetrable contexts of physical and psychological influences, both this famous "knife" scene and the Elsie episode confirm the medium's affinity for a causal continuum. They arrest the course of action to probe into the twilight regions from which it arises. Instead of advancing the intrigue, they proceed in the reverse direction—away from its denouement toward its premises and origins. Thus they complement the story proper, offering glimpses of the endless trail it leaves behind.

"Let us imagine a film in which the spoken text would substitute for the written text of the captions, remain the servant of the image, and intervene only as an 'auxiliary' means of expression—a brief, neutral text to which the pursuit of visual expression would in no way be sacrificed. A bit of intelligence and good will would suffice to reach an agreement about this compromise."[29]

René Clair published these lines, which concern *commentative* sound (IVb) as early as 1929, when he was groping for possibilities of putting speech to good cinematic use. The gist of his proposition is that sparse verbal commentary which confines itself to providing indispensable information does not, or need not, interfere with the pictures on which it bears counterpointwise. Others soon experimented in this direction. In Lang's *M* the police commissioner talks with his superior over the phone, and while he explains to him the difficulties with which police investigations are faced, one sees cops and plain-clothes men proceeding along the lines of his verbal report.[30] Sacha Guitry in his THE STORY OF A CHEAT has set a less mechanical, better integrated pattern: the old "cheat" in the role of the narrator cynically reminisces about his youthful exploits; yet instead of covering the ground exhaustively, he just advances a few caption-like hints, leaving it to the visuals to take their cue from them. In consequence, the narrative proper consists of long stretches of largely silent film touched off and framed by his expository words.[31]

The same type of contrapuntal relation between subdued commentary and a veritable flow of visuals materializes in a limited number of documentaries, mainly from England and Nazi Germany. In these films, which, perhaps, owe something to the English bent for understatement and/or the German sense of polyphonic instrumentation, the narrator does not simply introduce or complement the visuals but comments upon them obliquely. It is as if he himself sat in the audience and occasionally felt prompted to voice an aside—some slant on the pictures he watches. Far from disrupting the pictorial continuity, his casual remarks open up avenues of thought which, for being unsuspected, may well increase our sensitivity to the multiple meanings of the imagery.

SOUND PROPER

About the nature of sounds

Sounds—this term meaning exclusively noises here—can be arranged along a continuum which extends from unidentifiable to recognizable noises. As for the former, think of certain noises in the night: they are, so to speak, anonymous; you have no idea where they come from.[32] At the opposite pole are sounds whose source is known to us, whether we see it or not. In everyday life, when we hear barking, we immediately realize that a dog must be around; and as a rule we do not go wrong in associating church bells with the sound of chimes.

Those puzzling noises which the night is apt to produce attune the listener primarily to his physical environment because of their origin in some ungiven region of it. But what about the many identifiable noises at the other end of the continuum? Take again chimes: no sooner does one hear them than he tends to visualize, however vaguely, the church or the clock tower from which they issue; and from there his mind may leisurely drift on until it happens upon the memory of a village square filled with churchgoers who stream to the service in their Sunday best. Generally speaking, any familiar noise calls forth inner images of its source as well as images of activities, modes of behavior, etc., which are either customarily connected with that noise or at least related to it in the listener's recollection. In other words, localizable sounds do not as a rule touch off conceptual reasoning, language-bound thought; rather, they share with unidentifiable noises the quality of bringing the material aspects of reality into focus. This comes out very clearly in scenes where they are combined with speech. It could be shown above that in the great dialogue scene of Orson Welles's OTHELLO the intermittent footfalls of Iago and the Moor, far from increasing the impact of the dialogue, help shift audience attention to the protagonists' bodily presence.

In sum, as Cavalcanti once put it, "noise seems to by-pass the intelligence and speak to something very deep and inborn."[33] This explains why, in the era of transition to sound, those addicted to the silent staked their last hopes on films that would feature noises rather than words.[34] So Eisenstein in a 1930 talk at the Sorbonne: "I think the '100% all-talking film' is silly. . . . But the sound film is something more interesting. The future belongs to it."[35] According to René Clair (who, incidentally, did not share Eisenstein's illusions about the future), the connoisseurs' preference for noises then rested upon the belief that, as material phenomena, they evoke a reality less dangerous to the images on the screen than the kind of reality conveyed by the all-out talkie.[36] Nothing would seem to be more justified than this belief. Sounds whose material properties are featured belong to the same world as the visuals and, hence, will hardly interfere with the spectator's concern for the latter.

Yet is the film maker really obliged under all circumstances to emphasize the material characteristics of the sounds he inserts? Actually, he is free to divest certain sounds of their natural substance, so that they no longer refer to the physical universe from which they flow; disembodied entities, they then assume other functions. As a matter of course, this possibility involves exclusively localizable noises.

Reliance on symbolic meanings

Indeed, localizable noises often carry familiar symbolic meanings. And if the film maker capitalizes on these meanings in the interest of his narrative, the noises yielding them turn from material phenomena into units which, much like verbal statements, serve as components of mental processes.

René Clair playfully uses sound this way when he shows the main characters of his LE MILLION scrambling for the jacket which they believe to harbor the coveted lottery ticket. Instead of resorting to "synchronous" sound, he synchronizes the scramble with noises from a Rugby game. These commentative noises virtually parallel the actual fight and at the same time relate contrapuntally to it. Evidently they are intended to establish an analogy between the visible fight and an imaginary game; their purpose is to ridicule the seriousness of the scramble by making the participants look like Rugby players who toss the jacket about as if it were a ball. Assuming the asynchronous ball noises really implement Clair's intentions, they affect us not so much through their material qualities as through their function of signifying a Rugby game—any Rugby game, for that matter. It is their symbolic value which counts. In consequence, they do not induce the spectator closely to watch the pictures but invite him to enjoy an amusing analogy which has all the traits of a literary aperçu. In fact, what the sounds try to suggest might have been imparted by words as well. The whole scene is problematic cinematically because it culminates in a jocular comparison which, being imposed from without on the images of the scramble, inevitably obscures their inherent meanings. Add to this that the commentative noises may not even fulfill the function which Clair assigns to them; it is doubtful indeed whether they are specific enough to be necessarily associated with the idea of a ball game. Not all identifiable sounds are familiar to all the people; nor can all such sounds be localized with absolute certainty. Perhaps, many a spectator, unable to grasp the significance of the Rugby noises, will find them merely bizarre.*

Parenthetically, analogies of this type may also be staged with the aid of images rather than sounds. In the opening scene of Chaplin's MODERN TIMES a shot of rushing sheep is followed by a shot of fast-moving workers. Within the given context the image of the sheep assumes exactly the same function as the ball game noises in LE MILLION: it is not shown for its own sake but serves to intimate, in juxtaposition with the subsequent shot, the similarity between workers and sheep. Are the workers not equally gullible? When they appear we cannot help laughing at the surprising rise of this lofty simile out of two unsuspicious matter-of-fact shots. The simile itself carries ideological implications which automatically consume the material substance of its pictorial constituents. Significantly, Chaplin relates that his MODERN TIMES developed from an "abstract idea"—the idea of commenting on our mechanized way of life.[37]

Sometimes, especially in theatrical adaptations of stage dramas, the symbolic potentialities of familiar sounds are exploited in a crude manner palpably inspired by venerable stage traditions. As the tragic conflict approaches its climax, the surge of human passions is synchronized with the sinister noises of a storm outdoors. Raging nature, suggested by these asynchronous actual sounds, is thus made to parallel the impending catastrophe in gloomy interiors for the purpose of intensifying audience participation. Such a use of sound will hardly ingratiate itself with the sensitive moviegoer. It rests upon the premise of a closed universe in which natural events correspond to human destinies—a notion incompatible with camera-realism, which presupposes the endless continuum of physical existence. Moreover, the attention which the spectator must pay to the symbolic meaning of the storm noises preempts his concern for the meanings of their material characteristics. Because of its emphasis on mental reality the whole arrangement is not likely to benefit the pictures.**

---

* Old slapstick comedies have frequently been post-synchronized with noises in ways reminiscent of this sound gag of Clair's. We see, for instance, a silent character talking, but what we hear is the blasts of a motor car horn. The effect is funny, if gross.

** This kind of symbolic parallelism seems to prove attractive to minds conceiving of the cinema in terms of the established arts. In 1930, speculating on the possibility of using sound artistically, Fondane, "Du muet au parlant . . ." in L'Herbier, ed., *Intelligence du cinématographe*, p. 157, proposed to synchronize "the noise of a

Another possibility in a similar vein is the following: the howling storm denoting an upheaval of nature may be synchronized, counterpointwise, with shots of peaceful family life in order to forewarn the audience that malevolent forces are about to invade that world of peace. Yet while in the example discussed just above, the storm noises convey a meaning which can easily be grasped, paralleling the obvious meaning of the soaring human passions, these very same noises are well-nigh unintelligible when they relate contrapuntally to pictures whose significance strongly differs from theirs. The reason is that the symbolic content of identifiable sounds is too vague to serve, by itself alone, as a basis for the construction of analogies or similes. It is highly improbable that a spectator immersed in the peaceful images on the screen will conceive of the howling storm as an ominous portent. Perhaps he will believe the discordant storm noises to be sheer coincidence—an explanation, by the way, which would at least do justice to the preferences of the medium. But be this as it may, one thing is sure: the symbolic counterpoint aspired to falls flat. Sound used contrapuntally must relate to the synchronized images in an understandable way to signify something comprehensible.

So much for sound symbolism. Film makers have resorted to it only sporadically. What they usually feature is not so much the symbolic meanings of recognizable noises as the material properties of sounds, identifiable or not. The subsequent analysis bears exclusively on sounds in the latter sense.

Role

Sounds in their capacity as material phenomena do not weaken the impact of the juxtaposed pictures. This all but self-evident assumption implies that the role which sounds are made to play in a film is a negligible factor. Speech and sound proper differ radically in that the former's dominance blurs the visuals, whereas the occasional dominance of noises is of little consequence. Supposing shrill screams or the blasts of an explosion are synchronized with images of their source and/or its environment: much as they will leave their imprint on the spectator's mind, it is unlikely that they will prevent him from taking in the images; rather, they may prompt him to scrutinize the latter in a mood which increases his susceptibility to

---

shattering glass with the image of a man who has forfeited his happiness and reminisces about it." But this proposition defeats its purpose inasmuch as no spectator can be expected to derive so recherché an analogy from a juxtaposition of ill-defined sounds and pictures.

their multiple meanings—are not the screams and the blasts indeterminate also?

One might even go further. Sounds share with visible phenomena two characteristics: they are recorded by a camera; and they belong to material reality in a general sense. This being so, camera explorations of the sound world itself can be said to lie, by extension, in a cinematic interest. Flaherty, who was loath to entrust the spoken word with any important message, extolled the contributions of "characteristic" sounds: "I wish I could have had sound for NANOOK. . . . It takes the hiss of the wind in the North and the howls of the dogs to get the whole feeling of that country."[38] Now, film makers have at all times used close-ups and other devices to exhibit the innumerable phenomena which comprise camera-reality. So the late Jean Epstein's proposal to penetrate the universe of natural sounds in a similar manner would seem to be quite logical.

Epstein's general idea was to break down, by means of sonic slow motion, complex sound patterns into their elements. In his LE TEMPESTAIRE he thus details the various noises of which a violent storm consists, synchronizing them with remarkable shots of the ocean. The film, an experiment as ingenious as it is fascinating, extends the cinematic approach into the region of sound in such a way that the acoustic revelations and the pictorial communications reinforce rather than neutralize each other. Epstein himself accounts for his procedures in this film as follows: "Like the eye, the ear has only a very limited power of separation. The eye must have recourse to a slowing down. . . . Similarly, the ear needs sound to be enlarged in time, i.e., sonic slow motion, in order to discover, for instance, that the confused howling of a tempest is, in a subtler reality, a manifold of distinct noises hitherto alien to the human ear, an apocalypse of shouts, coos, gurgles, squalls, detonations, timbres and accents for the most part as yet unnamed." In analogy to slow-motion movements these unnamed noises might be called "sound reality of another dimension."[39]

Manner of synchronization

PARALLELISM

All the notions a noise is apt to evoke more or less revolve around its source. This makes for another difference between speech and sound. While both "synchronous" and asynchronous speech may carry meanings which parallel those of the synchronized images, sound admits of such meanings only in case of "synchronism" (see type I in table, p. 114). There are seeming exceptions; remember the examples which illustrate parallelism between the symbolic meanings of asynchronous sounds and the meanings of the simultaneous images (type III, a and b). Yet these examples confirm the rule because they involve sound merely as a symbolic entity designed to transmit near-verbal communications. Sound there substitutes for language, up to a point. (Incidentally, commentative noises may, for comic effect, parallel verbal statements referring to them. For instance, a screen character mentions a storm and at this very moment you hear a storm howling. In this case the storm noises function like duplicative images; they illustrate the verbal reference to the storm in exactly the same manner as does a shot of the Eiffel Tower the word Paris.)

With noises, then, "synchronism" is a prerequisite of parallelism. We see a dog and hear it barking. For reasons of artistic economy Clair objects to parallelism to the extent that it entails a duplication of effects: "It is of little importance to *hear* the noise of applause if one *sees* the hands which applaud."[40] Nor is parallelism always in accordance with the way in which we actually perceive sounds. The range of an individual's acoustic impressions is a variable of his psychological condition. Here belongs Pudovkin's observation that a cry for help in the street will keep us from registering the noises of the cars and buses before our eyes. But what if the traffic noises are nevertheless inserted? Such excess sounds occur in many a film. Parallelism handled mechanically runs the risk of falsifying reality as we experience it.

On the whole, however, parallel synchronous sound is as acceptable aesthetically as is parallel synchronous speech in films in which the visuals set the tune. Clair's criticism of duplicative parallelism is not entirely fair. For one, he endorses sound film and yet fails to indicate that duplicative noises are unavoidable in it. In addition, his objection to them is over-scrupulous, as can be inferred from his own example: the noise of applause may be unimportant, but it does certainly not lessen the spectator's interest in the applauding hands. Duplicative sounds might even work like an appropriate musical accompaniment, causing us to commune more intensely with the pictures.

COUNTERPOINT

Synchronism "Synchronous" sounds relating contrapuntally to the images of their source (type II) open up aspects of material reality not implied by the images themselves. In the dialogue scene of OTHELLO the footfalls of Iago and the Moor do not just duplicate what we see anyway but markedly contribute to make us really see it. Similarly, in the last episode of PAISAN the cry of the forlorn infant tottering among the corpses adds something to the image of him. A crude utterance of helpless dread and extreme despair, it belongs among those "characteristic" sounds which Flaherty meant when he spoke of "the hiss of the wind in the North." In addition, as a straight expression of the infant's inmost nature, this terrific cry sheds new light on his outer appearance. The image we watch thus gains in depth. And the spectator will all the more readily respond to it since the cry itself is so upsetting emotionally that it brings his whole being into play.

Asynchronism   In 1929, after having taken a look at the first American talkies in London, René Clair singled out for praise the following scene of BROADWAY MELODY: we hear the noise of a car door slammed shut, while we see the anguished face of Bessie Love watching from the window an event in the street which we do not see but which the noise enables us to identify as the departure of a car. The beauty of this short scene, says Clair, is that it concentrates on the face of the actress and simultaneously tells a story which the silent cinema would have had to convey through several images. And he concludes: "Sound has replaced the image at an opportune moment. It seems to be in this economy of its means of expression that sound film has a chance of finding its original effects."[41] What Clair endorses is asynchronous actual sound issuing from an identifiable source and relating contrapuntally to the synchronized images (type IVa). To generalize and complement his argument, this mode of synchronization is significant cinematically for three reasons:

(1) It permits, if not invites, us to absorb the given visuals.

(2) It enables us to dispose of images with extrinsic functions—the kind of images, that is, which in earlier contexts have been called "explanatory visual inserts."* The noise of the car door slammed shut thus stands for cumbersome cut-ins which would have just served to keep us posted on the departure of the car. His infatuation with camera-reality notwithstanding, Flaherty, exactly like Clair, welcomed the possibility of superseding such pictures by sounds suggesting them: "Sounds are pictures in themselves; you can use them without the supporting visual image—once the sound has been identified—to recall things without having to show them."[42]

(3) Finally, sound in the form of asynchronous counterpoint stirs our imagination to explore reality in accordance with the affinities of the medium. One of the routes we then follow leads into the wider material environment, as is illustrated by Clair's own example from BROADWAY MELODY. The noise of the departing car not only benefits our involvement in Bessie Love's face—this is the point made by Clair himself—but draws us away from it to the street in which cars and people are carrying on as usual. Passages in a similar vein are fairly frequent. The wonderful swamp sequence of King Vidor's HALLELUJAH reverberates with confused sound patterns which impress upon the audience the invisible presence of life in the swamp—an effect resembling, somehow, that of the flow of messages

* See pp. 102–3.

from the planes' intercoms in JUNGLE PATROL. Or think of the Marseille episode in UN CARNET DE BAL: summoned by the persistent crane noises, the whole harbor invades the shabby room in which the action takes place. In BACK STREET much the same device is applied. And there is the incomparable Apache episode in Clair's SOUS LES TOITS DE PARIS. As the Apaches hold up their prospective victim in a gas-lit suburban street, plain railway noises—the whistle of a locomotive, the clatter of rolling cars—unexpectedly pierce the night. They seem entirely unmotivated; and yet, in registering them, we feel they contribute something essential. Their irrational presence brings the whole environment to the fore, enforcing its full participation; and their palpably accidental nature sensitizes us to the fragmentary character of the contexts of which the holdup itself is only a part. Those railway sounds enhance camera-reality at large.

Sometimes asynchronous noises used this way lure us into the sphere of psychophysical correspondences. In PAISAN we hear the infant's cry before seeing him; it is synchronized with shots of the guerrilla fighters stealthily advancing through the marshes. To be sure, the cry is to make us anticipate the horrors that have caused it. But since its source is yet ill-defined, we spontaneously relate it to the landscape, engulfing friends and enemies alike. The sky is leaden; the marshes smell of death. It is as if nature itself gave vent to its indescribable sadness, as if these shapeless wails came from the depths of its soul. In Renoir's THE HUMAN BEAST the song from a nearby dance hall, which functions as a noise in this case, fills Séverine's room. Stillness sets in as Jacques is murdering the girl; then, after all is over and done with, the dance hall sounds become again audible.[43] Through their disappearance and resurgence Renoir subtly denotes the murderer's changing states of mind in the dimension of involuntary sense reactions—a dimension characterized by its osmotic affiliations with the material surroundings. Hence the cinematic flavor of the allusive alternations between sound and silence.

To conclude with a very complex example of this type of synchronization, Elia Kazan's ON THE WATERFRONT contains a scene in which Marlon Brando confesses to the girl he loves that he participated in the murder of her brother. The scene is shot outdoors, with a view of the harbor. Now the salient point is that we do not hear Brando tell the story of the murder which we have witnessed anyway: the piercing sound of a ship's siren drowns both his confession and the girl's answer. The ship being visible in the background, this sound falls certainly under the title of synchronous parallelism. Yet since our eyes are riveted not so much on the ship as the figures of Brando and the girl, the tooting of the siren also represents an instance of asynchronous counterpoint with respect to the latter. And in this capacity the drawn-out sound assumes two cinematic functions: it plays up environmental influences; and it sustains audience concern for the images. Needless to add that they fully reveal what is going on between and in the lovers.

Commentative counterpoint (type IVb) is practically nonexistent, except for cases in which the symbolic meanings of sounds are featured at the expense of their material properties.*

* See example, p. 127.

Music

BEFORE DEALING with the aesthetic aspects of film music, its physiological functions must be considered. It is they which account for the otherwise inexplicable fact that films are practically never shown without music.

PHYSIOLOGICAL FUNCTIONS

The archaic era

Even in the primitive days sustained efforts were made to redeem the cinema from its inherent silence.[1] A "narrator" in the flesh tried to humor the audience; phonograph records were more or less successfully synchronized with corresponding images so that the benevolent spectator might nurture the illusion of listening to a cock crow, an aria, or even bits of conversation; and of course, musical accompaniment emerged at the outset. Those premature attempts at sound and speech were abortive; the narrator yielded to captions, and the phonograph records disappeared after a while.[2] The time for sound film had not yet come. What survived was music—some mechanical contrivance or a pianist. It has been suggested that the early film exhibitors availed themselves of music to drown the disturbing noises of the projector.[3] But this explanation is untenable; as a matter of fact, the noisy projector was soon removed from the auditorium proper, whereas music stubbornly persisted. There must have been a more compelling reason for its rise. That this reason was not identical with a specifically aesthetic urge follows from the initial indifference to the content and meaning of the tunes selected—any music would do if it were only music and fairly popular at that. The important thing was musical accompaniment as such. From the very beginning people seem to have felt that the sheer presence of music considerably increases the impact of the silent images. Film music was originally an ingredient of film performances rather than an element of film itself. Its vital function was to adjust the spectator physiologically to the flow of images on the screen.

Music, imagery, and spectator

THE SILENT ERA

Soundless reality   This adjustment is needed because our real-life environment is filled with sounds. Even though we may for long stretches be unaware of their presence, yet our eyes cannot register a single object without our ears participating in the process. Everyday reality arises out of a constant mingling of visual and aural impressions. There is practically no silence. The dead of night is alive with a thousand noises, and were even all of them suppressed, still we could not avoid breathing. Life is inseparable from sound. Accordingly, the extinction of sound transforms the world into limbo—a common sensation of people abruptly stricken with deafness. "The palpable reality of life," as one of them puts it, "was suddenly void— its elemental phenomena suspended. Silence fell upon the world like a hush of death."[4] This perfectly applies to the silent screen, with its characters who act as real persons would without ever emitting a sound, and its trees and waves which ripple noiselessly in an inaudible wind. Inveterate moviegoers will remember having come, occasionally, across old silent pictures unaccompanied by music or films whose sound track suddenly failed. It is a frightening experience; shadows aspire to corporeal life, and life dissolves into intangible shadows.

Film shots being photographs by extension, one should expect the latter to produce the same effect. Yet photographs are essentially self-contained. The reason is our awareness of their limited potentialities. Since we know that they can record only such configurations of visible reality as appear in a tiny fraction of time, it just does not occur to us to mistake them for a counterpart of the whole of reality and feel disturbed by their partiality to purely visual impressions. Things change when they yield to film shots which indeed render the world in motion. Although film shots are also photographs, they portray reality with an inclusiveness denied to stills. So we succumb to the illusion they arouse in us: we believe them to be not so much photographs as reproductions of life in its fullness.

Or rather, we would believe this were it not for the fact that they pass across the screen in complete silence. However, the illusion of full-fledged reality they evoke is so powerful that we nevertheless try to perpetuate it by substituting for it the reverse illusion—exactly as love may turn into hatred and thus manage to survive. Instead of acknowledging the photographic qualities of the silent film shots, we involuntarily conceive of them, with a distinct feeling of unpleasantness, as pale apparitions haunting the very places where the equivalents of real objects, real persons, should have appeared.[5] These images affect us as a ghost-like replica of the world we live in—the limbo through which the deaf are moving. And once we have identified them as phantoms, they tend to disintegrate before our eyes, like all apparitions.

Visuals restored to photographic life Here is where music comes in. Like sound proper, or even more so, it has a tendency to stimulate the listener's receptiveness in general. Experiments have shown that a light seems to shine brighter when a buzzer is sounded;[6] capitalizing on this "intersensory" effect, music lights up the pale silent images on the screen so that they will stay with us. Of course, music is not just sound; it is rhythmical and melodious movement—a meaningful continuity in time. Now this movement not only acts upon our sense organs, causing them to participate in it, but communicates itself to all our simultaneous impressions.[7] Hence, no sooner does music intervene than we perceive structured patterns where there were none before. Confused shifts of positions reveal themselves to be comprehensible gestures; scattered visual data coalesce and follow a definite course. Music makes the silent images partake of its continuity. Besides creating that brightness which keeps them close to us, it incorporates them into the inner time in which we grasp significant contexts. Ghostly shadows, as volatile as clouds, thus become trustworthy shapes.

No doubt musical accompaniment breathes life into the silent pictures. But it resuscitates them only to make them appear as what they are—photographs. This is a point of great importance. Contrary to what one would be inclined to think, music is not intended to restore mute spectacles to full reality by adding sound to them. Exactly the reverse holds true: it is added to draw the spectator into the very center of the silent images and have him experience their photographic life. Its function is to remove the need for sound, not to satisfy it. Music affirms and legitimates the silence instead of putting an end to it. And it fulfills itself if it is not heard at all[8] but gears our senses so completely to the film shots that they impress us as self-contained entities in the manner of photographs.

Suspense-laden silence Surprisingly, this effect is intensified when in moments of extreme suspense music suddenly stops, leaving us alone with the silent pictures. It is a device used in the circus to enhance sensational stunts. One should expect the abandoned pictures to fall flat; what actually happens, however, is that they attract us more vigorously than the music-supported images preceding them. Take THE FROGMEN, a semi-documentary about one of the U.S. Navy's underwater demolition teams during World War II: the film culminates in several episodes depicting the team's amazing submarine exploits—episodes conspicuous for their lack of musical accompaniment. Yet the silence which envelops these human amphibians does not transform them into apparitions floating through a void; on the contrary, it increases the spectator's confidence in their reality, his concern for their underwater evolutions.

How can one explain the fascination such images exert? Even granted that the spell they cast over us owes something to the breathtaking adventures they picture, we would nevertheless find them disquieting rather than inspiring were it not for the music prior to the lull. That we accept them so unreservedly must be laid to the fact that the music has loaded our sensorium with sympathetic energies. Even though it withdraws before the decisive moment is reached, still its afterglow illumines the silent climax more effectively than would its continued presence. In a similar way do the stills in Dovzhenko's ARSENAL and EARTH benefit by the external motion around them.*—Incidentally, images unaccompanied by sound may also be impressive when they feature a scene or event which imposes silence on all those witnessing it. Walter Ruttmann in his MELODY OF THE WORLD, says Cavalcanti, "built up a big climax of guns in a war sequence, worked it up to a close-up of a woman emitting a piercing shriek, and cut at once to rows of white crosses—in silence." Cavalcanti adds: "In the hands of an artist of Ruttmann's calibre, silence can be the loudest of noises."[9]

Excursion: Tinting   As if music did not suffice to bring out the essence of film shots, the silent era supplemented it by a device intended to invigorate them on the visual plane also—the tinting of whole film passages. Shades of red helped amplify a conflagration or the outbreak of elemental passions, while blue tints were considered a natural for nocturnal scenes involving the secret activities of criminals and lovers. The different hues plainly served to establish audience moods in keeping with the subject and the action. But besides canalizing the spectator's emotions, they also produced an effect which, for being less noticeable, was actually more important; it resulted from the use of color as such rather than a specific color.

Any color suggests dimensions of total reality ungiven in black-and-white representations. The addition of color was therefore bound further to enliven images which, victimized by silence, all too easily assumed a ghostlike character. Tinting was a ghost-laying device. Moreover, the application

* See p. 44.

of one and the same color to larger units of successive shots counteracted the latter's lack of coherence in the wake of complete silence. (However, this proved to be a blessing only if the uniform red or blue was sufficiently discreet to let transpire the various meanings of the shots it overlaid.) For the rest, much as color parallels music, it cannot possibly substitute for it. There is enough evidence that all-color films depend no less than ordinary ones on musical support. The tints echoed music in the dimension of the visuals themselves.

The drunken pianist I still remember, as if it were yesterday, an old moviehouse which was my favorite haunt in faraway days. Originally an elegant revue theater, it boasted rows of richly decorated boxes which radiated a glamour at variance with the theater's later purpose. The music there was supplied by a gray-haired pianist as decrepit as the faded plush seats and the gilded plaster cupids. He too had seen better days. In his youth he had been a gifted artist with a brilliant future ahead of him, but then he had taken to the bottle, and all that now reminded one of those promising beginnings was his fluttering *lavallière*, a leftover from student life with its dream of glory. He was rarely what you would call sober. And whenever he performed, he was so completely immersed in himself that he did not waste a single glance on the screen. His music followed an unpredictable course of its own.

Sometimes, perhaps under the spell of a pleasant intoxication, he improvised freely, as if prompted by a desire to express the vague memories and ever-changing moods which the alcohol stirred in him; on other occasions he was in such a stupor that he played a few popular melodies over and over again, mechanically adorning them with glittering runs and quavers. So it was by no means uncommon that gay tunes would sound when, in a film I watched, the indignant Count turned his adulterous wife out of the house, and that a funeral march would accompany the blue-tinted scene of their ultimate reconcilation. This lack of relation between the musical themes and the action they were supposed to sustain seemed very delightful indeed to me, for it made me see the story in a new and unexpected light or, more important, challenged me to lose myself in an uncharted wilderness opened up by allusive shots.

Precisely by disregarding the images on the screen, the old pianist caused them to yield many a secret. Yet his unawareness of their presence did not preclude improbable parallels: once in a while his music conformed to the dramatic events with an accuracy which struck me all the more as miraculous since it was entirely unintended. It was the same kind of sensation which I experienced when, walking the streets, I discovered that some painted clock dial outside a watchmaker's shop marked the exact hour as I was passing by. And these random coincidences, along with the stimulating effects of the normal discrepancies, gave me the impression that there existed after all a relationship, however elusive, between the drunken pianist's soliloquies and the dramas before my eyes—a relationship which I considered perfect because of its accidental nature and its indeterminacy. I never heard more fitting accompaniment.

SOUND ERA

When sound arrived, the musicians disappeared from the moviehouses, but the type of music they had contributed survived as part of the sound track. In fact, the talkies too resort to music which, as Aaron Copland puts it, "one isn't supposed to hear, the sort that helps to fill the empty spots between pauses in a conversation."[10] It need not fill the pauses only. Stravinsky observes that it has "the same relationship to the drama that restaurant music has to the conversation at the individual restaurant table." ("I cannot accept it as music," he acidly concludes.)[11]

Be this as it may, musical accompaniment—"commentative" music, that is—has become institutionalized in sound film also. Does it retain a vital function there, or is it just a leftover from the days of the silent? In support of the latter alternative one might argue that commentative music, once a much-needed antidote against enforced silence, ceases to be legitimate now that we are in a position to substitute real-life sounds for it. Since these sounds are actually omnipresent, there is little danger that the pictures will ever be deserted by them. Why then introduce outside music at all? As an artificial ingredient it is inconsistent with natural noises anyway; and it certainly interferes with the naturalness of films in which full advantage is taken of the plethora of existing sounds. The upshot is that musical accompaniment is a thing of the past which had better be completely omitted.[12]

It all sounds logical. And yet this proposition must be rejected, for it rests on a premise at variance with the theoretical conceptions we have hitherto been employing. Its premise is that films aspire to full naturalness; that they come into their own only if they render the whole of reality, with equal emphasis on both sound and image.* But precisely this is doubtful. Let us imagine a film replacing commentative music throughout by the texture of actual noises. Such a film aims at recording total reality; and the naturalness it thus achieves may well impress us so strongly that we every now and then neglect the visible phenomena proper. As a matter of fact, when we are confronted with reality as a whole we do not always pay special attention to its visual aspects. (This does not contradict the experi-

* In ANATOMY OF A MURDER, for instance, full naturalness seems to be mistaken for camera-reality.

ence that noises in films often increase rather than lessen the spectator's concern for the synchronized pictures. The point at issue here is not so much the effect of specific noises as that of a film's naturalness.) How then are the pictures brought into focus again? It is of course commentative music which does the job.

Add to this the following two considerations. First, in spite of their omnipresence, natural sounds are perceived only intermittently.* Films intended to reproduce reality as we experience it are therefore likely to include stretches without sound; or if they do insist on rendering all existing noises, we just will be impervious to them on various occasions. Consequently, musical accompaniment is needed to keep the pictures close to us during the intervals in which sounds are not recorded or remain inaudible for psychological reasons. Second, music might sustain images on the point of being submerged by words. For instance, A HATFUL OF RAIN loses in cinematic impact by ascetically abstaining from commentative music in its many dialogue scenes. (Of course, what is wrong with this film in the first place is precisely its overemphasis on dialogue.) In such cases, however, musical accompaniment is hardly more than an expedient.

AESTHETIC FUNCTIONS

The drunken pianist in the old moviehouse seems to have been an anachronism, for even in his days "the incongruity of playing lively music to a solemn film became apparent."[13] Generally speaking, it was early felt that in an aesthetic interest pictorial and musical communications would have to be interrelated, somehow. Or as Hanns Eisler formulates it: "Picture and music, however indirectly or even antithetically, must correspond to each other."[14] And in what ways are they made to correspond? Besides serving as *commentative* music or accompaniment, music is being used as *actual* music and as the *nucleus* of films.

Commentative music

PARALLELISM

Parallel commentative music restates, in a language of its own, certain moods, tendencies, or meanings of the pictures it accompanies. Thus a speedy gallop illustrates a chase, while a powerful *rinforzando* reflects the imminent climax, as it unfolds on the screen.[15] In addition to conditioning the spectator physiologically to the photographic nature of the film shots,

* See Pudovkin's example, pp. 111–12.

music in this vein may also assume the cinematic function of underscoring discreetly some of their implications.

Now it is possible to differentiate between various types of accompaniment and arrange them along a continuum, the one pole of which is marked by music which aims at conveying the peculiar mood of a whole narrative rather than corroborating any specific sequence of it. This applies, for instance, to the melodies which, in the form of a leitmotif, thread Carol Reed's THE THIRD MAN and Chaplin's LIMELIGHT respectively. It should be added that they not only epitomize the emotional content of the films to which they belong but remain throughout what Copland calls a "background filler."[16] If tinting echoes music in the dimension of the visuals, these ever-recurrent tunes amount to a sort of local color in the dimension of music itself. So it happens, of course, that the zither melody parallels some scenes of THE THIRD MAN—among them those of nocturnal Vienna, with its statues and squares—while relating obliquely, or even contrapuntally, to others. [Illus. 27] The zither player recalls the drunken pianist.

There is, in LIMELIGHT as well as THE THIRD MAN, a fluctuating relationship between the stable background music and the changing visuals which throws into relief the latter's significance for the story without unduly restricting their indeterminacy. In other words, either leitmotif challenges us to penetrate the imagery. And yet it does not disappear behind the pictorial messages. All eyes that we are, we also bend our ears to the zither melody and the Chaplin tune. Paradoxically, these two pieces are both sheer accompaniment and independent contributions. They function as a background noise like any "restaurant music," and they claim our attention for being beautiful in their own right.

But how can they be one thing and its opposite at the same time? The solution is perhaps that they play the two conflicting roles alternately. We ignore them as long as they attune us to the spectacles on the screen; yet no sooner do we get immersed in the moods of decaying and aging inherent in the latter than we cannot help realizing that the very music which we have not heard before admirably evokes these moods by itself alone. And the surprising discovery that it has been present all the time further adds to the attraction which it now exerts on us. Then the process begins again: the tunes become inaudible once more, sending us back into the pictures.

The opposite pole of the continuum is occupied by music which illustrates not a general mood but a particular visual theme—mostly one featured in this or that film episode. A case in point is the speedy gallop synchronized with images of a chase. Provided they are confined to the role of "background fillers," such accompaniments serve at least as physiological stimuli. And they are desirable cinematically if they duplicate, and thereby reinforce, the material side of the pictorial themes which they accompany.

Think again of the gallop: more likely than not it suggests not so much the goal of the chase as its turbulence.

However, to sustain a visual theme and to overemphasize it is two different things. Parallel commentative music may be so outspoken or obtrusive that it no longer functions as an accompaniment but assumes a leading position.[17] In this case it overreaches itself and tends to blind one to the less obvious traits of the episode whose major theme it duplicates. Especially scores arranged from melodies with fixed meanings are apt to produce a blinding effect. There are popular tunes which we traditionally associate with circus performances, funerals, and other recurrent real-life events; whenever these tunes, which long since have become clichés, are synchronized with corresponding images, they automatically call forth stereotyped reactions to them. A few bars of Mendelssohn's *Wedding March* suffice to inform the spectator that he is watching a wedding and to remove from his consciousness all visual data which do not directly bear on that ceremony or conflict with his preconceived notions of it.

In his nature films Disney even goes so far as to edit realistic shots of animal life in such a manner that, against all probability, the resultant scenes live up to the expectations which the accompanying familiar melodies arouse in us. Animals dance or glide down a slope like sportsmen, in full accordance with strains intimating precisely these activities. It is fun contrived with the aid of musical clichés and cinematic devices. Yet, of course, once this clever falsification of nature in the material of camera-reality itself becomes a standing procedure, the trickery is recognized as such and ceases to be amusing. By the way, visual clichés are at least as common as musical ones. The drawn-out kiss at the end of many Hollywood films is a standardized portent of happiness rather than a noteworthy kiss.[18]

COUNTERPOINT

Much of what has been said about parallel commentative music also holds true of contrapuntal accompaniment. If the latter tends to remain in the background it can be expected to bolster up the visuals. Imagine the close-up of a sleeping face which appears to the rhythms of nightmarish music:[19] it is all but inevitable that the intriguing discrepancy between these sounds and so peaceful a picture should puzzle us. And in quest of a solution we may feel urged to probe into the face—its psychological correspondences, its potential changes. If, on the other hand, contrapuntal music usurps the leading role, it functions like any verbal communication determining the course of action. "A well-placed dissonant chord," says Copland, "can stop an audience cold in the middle of a sentimental scene, or a calculated wood-wind passage can turn what appears to be a solemn moment into a belly-laugh."[20] In both instances the impact of the musical motif is likely to reduce that of the imagery.

Their similarities notwithstanding, however, parallel and contrapuntal accompaniment differ in one important respect. In case of parallelism the film maker is bound to have the music duplicate what the pictures impart, while in the case of counterpoint he is at liberty to assign to it all possible functions and tasks. He may, for instance, entrust it with symbolic meanings. For Pudovkin to do precisely this was the straight consequence of his prejudice in favor of asynchronous counterpoint, which in turn led him to insist that music "must retain its own line." In the second part of his first sound film, DESERTER, he used it as the carrier of a message entirely unrelated to the actual situation. Gloomy pictures of a demonstration of defeated workers are there synchronized with an uplifting music which he inserted in the firm conviction that it would drive home the unbroken fighting spirit of the defeated and moreover make the audience anticipate their ultimate triumph.[21]

Actually it is hard to believe that even a sympathetic Communist audience will readily grasp this message. The uplifting music might as well express the feelings of the temporary victors. Here you have again the case of the howling storm intended to foreshadow the breakup of the juxtaposed family idyl.* Like sound proper, music is quite able to help characterize such concepts and notions as are already given us; but it cannot define or symbolize them by itself alone. The DESERTER music misses its purpose—not to mention that it is also problematic in as much as this particular purpose involves the dimension of ideology rather than material reality and its extensions.

RELATION TO THE NARRATIVE

Yet what matters cinematically is not only the relation of commentative music to the synchronized visuals—which alone has been examined so far—but its relation to the narrative as well. At first glance, the assumption that musical accompaniment must be geared to the action would seem to be self-evident. Is it not obvious that especially contrapuntal music will have to meet this requirement? Its alien motifs—alien to what the images themselves convey—appear to be pointless if they do not contribute to the unfolding of the plot.

Considerations such as these form the backbone of the ruling theory. As early as 1936 Kurt London submitted that music in sound films has to serve the "psychological advancement of the action." He continues as follows: "It [music] has to connect dialogue sections without friction; it has to establish association of ideas and carry on developments of

* See p. 127.

thought; and, over and above all this, it has to intensify the incidence of climax and prepare for further dramatic action."[22] Ernest Lindgren, who adopts London's proposition wholesale, enlarges it by the request that music should occasionally "provide emotional relief."[23] Eisler chimes in, expressly including contrapuntal accompaniment: "Even in marginal cases —for instance, when the scene of a murder in a horror picture is accompanied by deliberately unconcerned music—the unrelatedness of the accompaniment must be justified by the meaning of the whole as a special kind of relationship. Structural unity must be preserved even when the music is used as a contrast."[24] Nor is Copland indifferent to the structural functions of music; were it otherwise he would not enhance its usefulness as a means of "tying together a visual medium which is, by its very nature, continually in danger of falling apart."[25]

Music which thus assists in building up the narrative is surely in a dramaturgical interest. But this does not mean that it is also necessarily "good" in a cinematic sense. Rather, it may greatly benefit the narration and yet run counter to the affinities of film. As with the modes of synchronization in case of speech, its adequacy to the medium depends upon the "goodness" of the narrative which it supports.* The fact that practically all critics confuse the dramaturgic quality of film music with its cinematic quality must be laid to the failure of the traditional theory to differentiate between cinematic and uncinematic types of narratives. Once you ignore these differences, you are naturally obliged to assume that musical accompaniment is all the better if it sustains dramatic continuity and/or helps create suspense.

The ruling theory is too formal. Its fallacy is to take it for granted that all kinds of stories are equally fit to be represented on the screen. They are not. It may be anticipated here what will be discussed in more detail in chapter 12—that at least one common type of plot stubbornly resists cinematic treatment: the "theatrical" story. One of the reasons why this story form does not lend itself to the cinematic approach is that it has, so to speak, an ideological center; whenever it materializes, mental reality takes precedence over physical reality. Supposing now a film narrating such a story has a musical score which complies with its structural obligations to the full, thereby enhancing the theatrical character of that story; then this score is precisely because of its dramaturgic perfection as inadequate to the medium as is the story itself. In giving the latter its due, it inevitably highlights contents and meanings remote from camera-life. The character of the story form determines that of the music implementing it loyally. Hence the necessity of putting in brackets what has been said above about the parallel and contrapuntal uses of musical accompani-

* See p. 116.

ment. The nightmarish music need not invite us to probe into the sleeping face with which it is synchronized;* if it serves to prop up a theatrical narrative, it will draw us away from the face into dimensions in which physical existence is of little consequence.

The all-important thing is, of course, that musical accompaniment enlivens the pictures by evoking the more material aspects of reality. Narratives which live up to the spirit of the medium enable structurally integrated music to achieve this objective, whereas theatrical plots prevent it from doing so. Accordingly, music designed to service the latter is the more cinematic the less smoothly it fits them. In other words, within uncinematic narratives its dramaturgic maladjustment may easily turn out to be a virtue. There it stands a good chance of acquiring a cinematic quality, if it points up not the given story intentions but material phenomena passed over by them. Its merit there consists in neglecting rather than advancing the action. The drunken pianist who performed without looking at the screen was not far wrong after all.

Actual music

INCIDENTAL MUSIC

Think of a fiddling beggar or an errand-boy whistling a tune.[26] These random instances show that incidental music is essentially a casual performance embedded in the flow of life. Hence its cinematic character. Far from calling attention to itself for its own sake, it is, as its name says, incidental to some total situation of interest. Like inobtrusive accompaniment, incidental music plays a background role. This implies that it can be made to support the visuals, no matter how it is synchronized with them. Much of what has been said about the modes of synchronization in case of sound proper also holds true of incidental music. The reason is that the latter resembles natural sound in its strong affiliations with the environment. The whistling of the errand-boy belongs among the many noises which fall upon our ear wherever we go; a hurdy-gurdy melody enlivens the street in which it lingers. It is the location of the melody, not its content, which counts.

Suffice it here to illustrate the similarities between incidental music and noises by an example which has already been introduced to clarify one of the cinematic functions of asynchronous contrapuntal sound—the song from the nearby dance hall in THE HUMAN BEAST.** This song, which was then identified as a noise, serves yet another purpose than the one dis-

* See p. 141.
** See p. 131.

cussed before: exactly as the swamp noises in HALLELUJAH, it summons the wider material environment from which it issues. To be more precise, besides projecting, through its intermittent emergence, the murderer's inner condition, the song conjures up the crowded dance hall ablaze with light reflections and, beyond it, regions ruled by chance encounters and ephemeral contacts. Séverine's room widens to include these regions in which the murder ranges among the contingencies of life. (Winthrop Sargeant points out that the "trick of depicting murder to the accompaniment of trivial music is also to be found now and then in opera." And referring to *Rigoletto* and *Carmen*, he observes: "The very triviality of the music . . . indicates that the death is not a heroic one but merely the extinction of a rather pathetic human being who asked little more of life than the shimmering and inexpensive dream of happiness evoked by the melody."[27])

For the rest, it is understood that, like speech and noise, incidental music may be alternately synchronized with images of its source and other images. This alternation of synchronism and asynchronism has been repeatedly put to good use. In René Clair's SOUS LES TOITS DE PARIS, for instance, several tenants of an apartment house sing, hum, or play one and the same popular song which is audible throughout, whereas the tenants themselves are seen only when the panning and tilting camera somewhere in front of the house comes to focus on the rooms they occupy. [Illus. 28] The tune, whose musical quality is irrelevant within this context, not only motivates the camera movement but prompts us, through its very uniformity, to watch closely the differential behavior of the performers which adds to the comic effect of the tune's pervasiveness. Lang in his M avails himself of the same device. He first establishes the child-murderer's compulsive habit of whistling a popular theme from Grieg's *Peer Gynt* music[28] and then capitalizes on our familiarity with this habit to insert the Grieg motif without showing the whistler. What we see instead are shop windows and crowded streets and a blind beggar who clearly recalls having ·heard the ominous whistle. And we participate all the more intensely in the street life before our eyes since we now know, as does the beggar, that the murderer is again prowling the town.

MUSIC AS PRODUCTION NUMBER: PROBLEMATIC USES

Since the arrival of sound the screen has been flooded with opera scenes, concert pieces, solo recitals, songs, etc., in a continuous attempt to combine the pleasures of the ear with those of the eye. Here again the issue at stake is the adequacy to film of such renderings. They may be problematic or cinematic, according to the use made of them.

It need hardly be stressed that films featuring music for its own sake are inconsistent with the medium. As we listen to a musical production number on the screen, we cannot help exchanging the dimension of outer impressions for that of inner sensations aroused by the inflowing rhythms and sound patterns—a shift of emphasis which evidently goes against the grain of film. We might as well sit in a concert hall. But are we really transformed into concertgoers? Interestingly, it is as if the spirit of the cinema interfered with this transformation. Imagine a film devoted to the reproduction of a concerto; imagine further that everything has been done to increase the impact of its rendition—camera activities are reduced to a minimum and the visuals never try to create diversions. Under these favorable circumstances we should, in principle, be in a position to enjoy undisturbedly the beauty of the concert and its peculiar significance. Yet this is not what actually happens.

When during a musical performance in a film the camera ceases to move—like a concertgoer who forgets to breathe because of his involvement in the score—the ensuing loss of pictorial life does not as a rule benefit our responsiveness as listeners but, on the contrary, makes us feel uneasy about the design behind the whole performance; it is as though life had gone out of the music also. With camera-reality being subdued, music, however perfectly executed, affects us as something that does not "belong"—a protracted intrusion rather than a crowning achievement. The result is ennui, provided the moviegoer in us does not deliberately surrender to the concertgoer. But this would be an act of resignation.

MUSIC AS PRODUCTION NUMBER: CINEMATIC USES

Despite their incompatibility with the cinema, musical production numbers may be put to good use. One possibility is the *musical*; it features songs and the like in a manner which acknowledges, somehow, the peculiarities of the medium. Another possibility is for the film maker to try to *integrate* music for its own sake into the flow of cinematic life.

The musical

Reminiscent of vaudeville, the musical is an improbable composite of songs in operetta fashion, colorful ballets borrowed from the music hall, bits of comedy dialogue, stage interludes, and any kind of solo performances. It pretends to unity and threatens to fall into pieces. No one could honestly say that a musical makes sense. Yet it may be great entertainment—even cinematic entertainment at that.

The genre took shape early in the sound era when the initial bondage to the theater was overcome. In Europe Thiele's DREI VON DER TANKSTELLE (1930) and the first René Clair talkies, those marvelous blends of comedy and musical, were signal events. Hollywood seized upon the musical as an antidote against Depression moods and a contribution to New Deal optimism. Ernst Lubitsch prepared the ground with his LOVE PARADE (1929), MONTE CARLO (1930), and THE SMILING LIEUTENANT (1931), object lessons in the fine art of planting lyrics inconspicuously. FORTY-SECOND STREET (1933) revived the backstage intrigue whose cast of entertainers offers a welcome pretext for onstage acts. The annual BROADWAY MELODIES and BIG BROADCASTS outrivaled all stage revues in sumptuous displays of legs, settings, and individual talents. Veritable landmarks were Fred Astaire's dance films in which he performed with Ginger Rogers; they combined feats of skill with charming designs in ways which benefited the cinema.[29] And so it goes on.[30] The musical has become a well-established genre.

At first glance its over-all pattern is extremely simple. Musicals develop along the lines of a story which is sufficiently outspoken to preclude their dissolution into a revue or variety show and not outspoken enough to endow them with the coherence of a comedy or operetta indulging in sundry digressions. And this story—some flirtation or a love conflict spiced with jealousy—is usually a real-life story of a sort. The New York street scenes in George Stevens's SWING TIME or Vincente Minelli's THE BAND WAGON come as near to ordinary life as does the Paris of René Clair. [Illus. 29] In addition, the songs of a musical are as a rule contingent on the intrigue threading it. Clair's SOUS LES TOITS DE PARIS revolves around a song of this title which could not be introduced more naturally; the camera travels from a chimney landscape down to street level, and we see Albert, the street singer, recite his newest ditty amidst a crowd of neighbors and passers-by. In musicals proper the songs frequently take off from a casual word or elaborate upon action in progress.

Yet can the action itself be said to be real? As a matter of fact, musicals lack the serious-mindedness of regular films, and whenever they picture everyday life they do so with a twinkle. Their tenuous intrigue sometimes turns out to be as contrived as their dances and lyrics. The delivery boys in LE MILLION now behave like plain humans, now engage in a pursuit which has all the traits of a ballet; it would be difficult indeed to make out where they belong.* Similarly, the songs tend to invade the reality intimated by the narrative, so that an episode which aims at giving the impression of life as it is at the same time partakes of the artificial nature of the songs. Most musicals abound in such dizzying overlaps.

* See p. 43.

Add to this a predilection for conspicuous staginess. Musicals care so little about photographic veracity that they often present scenes of everyday life in theatrical terms. And of course, each production number serves them as a pretext to excel in spectacular sights. Ballets proceed from sparkling interiors to implausible locales, and songs are heard in a studio-made never-never land. THE BAND WAGON is replete with fanciful scenery built from stylized canvases which do not even pretend to spatial depth. Altogether the genre gravitates toward stagy fantasy, not camera-realism.

With this in mind, it is hard to understand why musicals should prove attractive as films. Their unrealistic settings and self-contained songs would seem to be germane to the stage rather than the screen. To be sure, both songs and settings are offered in a playful mood which somewhat mitigates their inherent theatricality,* but this does not by itself suffice to explain the genre's affiliations with the cinema. And yet it is in a measure a screen genre for the following reasons:

First, musicals invariably capitalize on everyday incidents to launch their diverse production numbers. It is as if purposeful composition yielded to improvisation in them. In the Astaire musicals, as a critic puts it, "the discovery was made that the happiest screen dances were not those that pretend to be part of a stage show, but rather the intimate, seemingly impromptu affairs that spring from the action of the moment, offering as their only excuse for being the fact that the dancer simply can not keep his feet still."[31] The same holds true of the musical renditions as a matter of course. But nothing could be more characteristic of camera-reality than the fortuity of the phenomena and events comprising it. Accordingly, in making its songs appear as an outgrowth of life's contingencies, the genre shows an affinity, however mediated, for the cinematic medium.

Second, musicals reflect tensions at the core of the cinema—tensions arising from the always possible conflict between the realistic and the formative tendency. The former manifests itself in the musical's stubborn, if halfhearted, insistence on a plot of a sort which loosely interlinks real-life happenings, while the latter accounts for the continual emergence of songs and other production numbers. What I have called the "cinematic approach" results from the "right" balance between these tendencies. Now it is true that the musical does not attempt to establish that balance, yet it achieves something else which is hardly less important. Through its very structure it illustrates the eternal struggle for supremacy between the realistic tendency, suggested by the threadbare intrigue, and the formative tendency, which finds its natural outlet in the songs. But is it not biased in favor of autonomous production numbers? Much as it concentrates on

* Cf. p. 86.

musical performances for their own sake, the genre does not permit them to take the lead and submerge the real-life happenings. Rather, it keeps these performances apart as isolated entities, thus avoiding uncinematic fusions of music and film—fusions, that is, in which free creativity wins out over the concern for our visible world. Unlike films rendering operas, musicals prefer a fragmentized whole to a false unity. This is why Eisler endorses the genre: "The topical songs and production numbers in a musical comedy . . . have never served to create the illusion of a unity of the two media . . . but functioned as stimulants, because they were foreign elements which interrupted the dramatic context."[32]

In sum, the musical playfully affirms cinematic values in the dimension of sheer divertissement. It rejects, by implication, the claim to dominance of the songs and ballets in which it indulges; and all its staginess does not prevent it from paying tribute to camera-life.

Integration

There has been no lack of successful attempts to integrate musical performances into otherwise realistic contexts. All of them have one thing in common: instead of isolating music in the interest of its purity, they remove it from the center of attention so that it comes as near as possible to being an element of film.

Part of the environment or an interlude A perfect example is Hitchcock's 1956 version of his old thriller, THE MAN WHO KNEW TOO MUCH. The film culminates in a drawn-out sequence laid in London's Albert Hall during the performance of a cantata. Yet the performance itself serves only as a foil to the suspense-laden action. We know that arrangements have been made to murder the foreign diplomat in the audience at the very moment when the music reaches its climax; we watch the professional killer in his box train his gun on the prospective victim; and we tremble lest the heroine, who forces her way through the crowded house with its many staircases and corridors, might come too late to prevent the crime. Note that the murder is to coincide with a previously specified phase of the score—a clever trick which seems to bring the performance into focus; but since we listen to the music for a purpose alien to it, its intrinsic meanings are likely to be lost on us. Here you have a musical production number which conforms to the medium by functioning as part of the environment—a temporarily important requisite.

At the same time, however, the concert continues to impress us as a performance attractive in its own right. Does this obstruct the effect of its subordination to real-life events? On the contrary, in the capacity of an autonomous performance the cantata works like any stage interlude: precisely because of its being a self-contained composition it strengthens the impact of accidental life about it, making the incidents appear as even more incidental. The cantata in the Hitchcock film may be conceived of as both part of the environment and a musical interlude. For the rest, no matter to what extent such interludes—flashes of a performing orchestra or a solo recital—are interwoven with their surroundings, they are enjoyable cinematically in as much as they enhance the reality character of the sequence that encompasses them.*

A component of the narrative   A common procedure is to embed musical production numbers in plots designed to explain and justify their emergence realistically. Following the pattern of THE JAZZ SINGER, the memorable predecessor of the talkies proper, numerous films narrate the life of some virtuoso, composer or showman whose whole career is dedicated to music. Consequently, any musical contribution is not so much an end in itself as a means of building up that life; it owes at least part of its significance to the story it implements. In Henry Koster's charming ONE HUNDRED MEN AND A GIRL, a film about an unemployed orchestra and Deanna Durbin's arduous fight for its rehabilitation, every musical insert advances, corroborates, or extends real-life events so that their flow persists during its execution. As we listen to the songs Deanna sings and the concert pieces Stokowski conducts, we never cease to be concerned with the girl's attempts to win the conductor over to her cause, and the suspense in which we are thus kept limits, if not exceeds, the purely aesthetic gratifications. [Illus. 30] This is all the more legitimate since the action consists largely of everyday incidents benefiting the cinematic approach; much is related through gentle gags reminiscent of silent comedy.

The urge to incorporate what music a film includes into cinematic reality is so strong that it even shows in pictures which serve the express purpose of rendering musical works. OF MEN AND MUSIC, a documentary which presents such star performers as Artur Rubinstein, Jascha Heifetz, and Dimitri Mitropoulos, fully lives up to its title; not content with simply conveying their performances—which is what it has been produced for after all—it also affords glimpses of their private existence, their more intimate moments. The Rubinstein solos, for instance, are wrapped in an interview with the artist; he volunteers autobiographical details, sits down and plays, and then goes on conversing. A CONVERSATION WITH PABLO CASALS, originally produced for TV, is in exactly the same vein; whatever the master plays, grows out of the interview situation, illustrating his

* See p. 73.

views or demonstrating his Centaur-like oneness with his instrument. Music in film, it appears, must be an accessory in order to be bearable.

A product of real-life processes To divest music of its autonomy, some films dwell on the creative processes preceding its birth so as to drag the finished work back into the vicissitudes of life from which it is wrested. Julien Duvivier in his Johann Strauss film, THE GREAT WALTZ, pictures the rise of *Tales from the Vienna Woods* out of impressions that close in on Strauss during his drive through these very woods—the coachman whistles while the birds are twittering and, *voilà*, the waltz takes shape. Similarly, WALZERKRIEG features the creation of the Radetzky March. Here also belongs the Mitropoulos episode in OF MEN AND MUSIC. The bulk of it consists of a rehearsal, with the conductor time and again interrupting the orchestra; and only after having eavesdropped on the musicians' shirt-sleeved efforts to render the opus—efforts suggestive of the possibilities that lie dormant in it—are we eventually permitted to get a taste of its full-dress performance. The promise is preferred to the fulfillment, the act of choosing to the definite choice.

This leads to another alternative much along the same lines—the concern with the execution of music rather than music proper. We hardly ever listen to a musical performance in films partial to camera-life without being challenged to divide our attention between its revelations and the executants—their hands, their faces. As if determined to ignore the performance as a musical event, the camera now moves along the rows of the brasses and violoncellos, now singles out the soloist or conductor for closer inspection. (Or like a boy playing truant, it deserts the orchestra altogether and settles on the enraptured features of a woman in the audience.) And we naturally follow its course. What seems to be idle curiosity, an unwarranted preoccupation with the nonessential, thus gets the better of intense listening—a shift of balance required by a medium in which nothing is more essential than the transitory.

Music recaptured This loyalty to the medium might prove singularly rewarding. Precisely because it launches the spectator on visual pursuits, it might lead him to the kernel of the music he unavoidably neglects, so that he resembles the fairy-tale prince who, after a series of trials testing his devotion and steadfastness, ultimately finds his beloved at the most unexpected place. In the opera episode of LE MILLION the camera does not pay much attention to the fat singers and their love duet but literally turns its back on them, meandering through the painted stage world and focusing on the quarreling lovers gone astray in it. We watch the reconciliation between the two, a pantomime to the sounds of the duet which ends with a fiery embrace; and we realize that the lovers are transported and driven into each other's arms by the enchanting voices and harmonies. And then something miraculous happens: absorbed in the sight of the lovers, we enter so completely into them that we are no longer aware of their presence but, as if we were they, yield to the impact of the duet. Having penetrated the images, we find at their core, waiting for us, the very music we were forced to abandon.*

Music as the nucleus of film

VISUALIZED MUSIC

The term "visualized music" applies to films in which the music, commentative or actual, determines the selection and the rhythmic configurations of visuals that are intended to reflect the music's moods and meanings in one way or another.

Some such films draw on nature in the raw. A portion of Alexandrov-Eisenstein's ROMANCE SENTIMENTALE consists of real-life shots expressive of autumnal sadness and springtime exuberance. And the documentary, SONGS WITHOUT WORDS, offers impressions of Venice—ranging from water reflections to church windows, shadows to stone masks—in an attempt to pass them off as projections of Mendelssohn music. If it is not reality itself, it may be a semblance of it; think of Cavalcanti's P'TITE LILI, a highly stylized affair coming straight out of the French popular song, La Barrière. Or real-life shots mingle with abstract forms, as in Germaine Dulac's DISQUE No. 957. And there are the animated cartoons; numbers of them utilize a mixture of imitations of reality and abstractions, or perferably abstractions alone, to translate music into visual terms. This trend, if trend it is, comes to full bloom in Oskar Fischinger's creations. His obstinate pursuits involve a whole geometry in motion whose contractions and expansions, ritardandos and accelerations strictly correspond to the synchronized Liszt or Brahms. As a specialist in the field, Fischinger collaborated briefly with Disney on the latter's FANTASIA.

Practically all these compositions are in the nature of experimental film, a cluster of types which will be discussed in chapter 10. But the following observation would seem to be relevant here; it bears on the role of music in the films under consideration. Entirely in keeping with the basic requirement that the imagery should take precedence over sound, music tends to surrender its leading position in them, slipping back into the role

* See pp. 73–4.

of an accompaniment. This is, for instance, what occurs in FANTASIA, with its "illustrations" of Beethoven's Pastoral Symphony, Schubert's Ave Maria, etc. Even though the music fathers the images, it is invariably overpowered by them; and instead of seeming to set the tune, as it actually does, it affects us as an accompaniment in the usual sense of the word. It is as if the medium could not assimilate music in a major role and therefore automatically rejected its priority claims. Of course, Fischinger or Disney are fully entitled to make their animated cartoons convey the spirit of music. It is just that as a rule music will relinquish its ascendancy.

So a puzzling situation arises. According to premise, the visuals, whatever their own appeal, serve to externalize or at least parallel the synchronized musical work. Yet the music responsible for their appearance and arrangement is relegated to the background so that the images implement something that is well-nigh nonexistent. With films of this kind the spectator is in a predicament. The shots he would like to take in refer him to the music inspiring them, but the music itself also withdraws from the scene.

OPERATIC PERFORMANCES

When attending an opera, we are prepared to take the stark improbabilities of this monstrous amalgam in our stride. They belong to its essence. Without them, the music could not possibly breathe. However changing it is in style, opera as an art form opens up a world bathed in music and sometimes even rising out of this music—a world more irrevocably remote from common reality than any other stage world.

The operatic world is, whatever else, a world of magic invocations. Its arias stop time; its landscapes are grounded in melodies; its sung passions transfigure physical life instead of penetrating it. The world of opera is built upon premises which radically defy those of the cinematic approach.

In an article praising Reinhardt's MIDSUMMER NIGHT'S DREAM (which has all the traits of an opera film), the late Franz Werfel contended that "it is undoubtedly the sterile reproduction of the external world with its streets, interiors, railway stations, restaurants, cars and beaches that has so far impeded the rise of film to the realm of art."[33] One could not state the reverse of truth with more precision. Film will come close to art—or perhaps be art—only if it does not deny its origin in photography but, on the contrary, affirms it by probing the external dimension which Werfel despised. One of the screen's more nearly justifiable preoccupations is to dissolve stage magic and trace the physical aspects of the realms which opera invokes. It is also natural for film—and therefore artistically promising—to prefer the enchantments of an obscure railway station to the painted splendor of enchanted woods.

Opera on the screen is a collision of two worlds detrimental to both. This does not invalidate the relative usefulness of films which merely aim at reproducing some opera performance as faithfully as possible. These "canned" operas have no other ambition than to record such performances and give people unacquainted with them at least a vague idea of what the real thing is like. But there are also more ambitious films which, in the name of Art, try to fuse the two conflicting worlds into a new and superior whole. As should be expected, this allegedly superior whole invariably reveals itself as an eclectic compromise between irreconcilable entities—a sham whole distorting either the opera or the film or both.

Abel Gance in Louise, a film version of the Charpentier opera, goes the limit in attempting to adapt the original to the requirements of the cinema. One of the masters of his métier, he converts the recitatives into dialogue and tries to counterbalance such operatic elements as he does preserve by significant camera work.[34] He even succeeds in establishing a precarious equilibrium between music and imagery in the scene in which Louise's father sings *Je suis ton père* and dandles the heroine on his knees as if she were still a little child. During this song the camera approaches the two closely, isolates their faces, and then glides down to exhibit the texture of their clothes and the life of their hands in big close-ups which draw us into the very vortex of inarticulate childhood, whose memory the song itself evokes. For the rest, however, the opera is mutilated by Gance's insistence on cinematic narration, while the latter suffers from the constant interference of opera music (and of Grace Moore).

Gian-Carlo Menotti's THE MEDIUM is even more of a fragile hybrid, for, unlike Gance, who simply wanted to make an opera into a film, this composer-director aspires to the perfect union of the two media, a union without concessions and sacrifices. His MEDIUM is meant to be both genuine opera and genuine film—a veritable screen opera. On the one hand, his camera explores street scenes, furniture pieces, and facial expressions with an inquisitiveness which sends the spectator's imagination rambling through the expanses of material reality; on the other, he has his characters deliver even their most banal communications in the form of recitatives, so that the spectator turns into a listener who would like to shut his eyes. [Illus. 31] The medium's three clients walk silently upstairs to her room—a real-life action captured with photographic accuracy. Then clients and medium engage in a sung conversation—an opera scene which continues to be defined by purely cinematic sights.

It is not as if we were disturbed merely by the strange artificiality of these recitatives or their paralyzing effect on the pictures. Rather, what actually happens to us is that we are caught in a terrifying clash between cinematic realism and operatic magic. Menotti's film is an abortive attempt to integrate two modes of approach which exclude each other for historical, social, and aesthetic reasons. And the spectacle of their enforced fusion may so affect a sensitive spectator or listener that he feels he is being torn asunder.

In TALES OF HOFFMANN no such overt clash occurs. Yet Michael Powell and Emeric Pressburger, the art-happy creators of this extravaganza, offer the most problematic "solution" of all: instead of adjusting their opera to the screen after the manner of Gance, or concocting, with Menotti's daring, some indigestible mixture of the two media, they completely suppress photographic life for the sake of operatic mood. Their film is, in a measure, nothing but photographed theater. The students behave as they would on the stage, the Greek landscapes smell of paint, and the close-ups wasted on Rounseville's Hoffmann make it overwhelmingly clear that he is an opera singer rather than a film character. This would be defensible, however tedious, if it were inspired by a desire to render just a model performance of the work. Powell and Pressburger, however, are out for more—except perhaps in the last episode, which comes closest to canned-opera and for this very reason is despairingly arid as film. Not content with giving us a taste of the original, they avail themselves of all the cinematic tricks and illusions at their disposal to trim and enrich the original. TALES OF HOFFMANN unfolds on a sort of superstage crammed with ballets, color, costumes, and ornamental forms.

There is something to be said in favor of this fantastic pageant, though. Much as it is impaired by bombast and an irritating confusion of styles, it is nevertheless a spectacle which transcends the possibilities of the stage and has its moments of fascination—especially when Moira Shearer floats through iridescent space. No doubt it is cinema. But it is cinema estranged from itself because of its surrender to operatic values and meanings. The whole pageant is contrived to exalt the magic of the Offenbach opera. Having thrown out the cinema as a means of capturing real life, Powell and Pressburger reintroduce it to evolve an imagery which is essentially stage imagery, even though it could not be staged in a theater. They retrogress from all that is fresh in Lumière to Méliès's theatrical *féeries*. Their presumable objective is a *Gesamtkunstwerk*, with the opera as its nucleus—a screen work answering Werfel's deceptive dream of the rise of film to the realm of art.

Yet the cinema takes revenge upon those who desert it. Exactly like Disney's animations in FANTASIA, these visual orgies consume the music on which they feed. The opera atrophies, and what remains is a parasitic *mise-en-scène* which stuns the mind by dazzling the eyes. Built from miraculous studio effects, it shuts out any miracle which the camera might reveal. The ripple of a single leaf suffices to denounce its treacherous glamour.

The Spectator

EFFECTS

DURING THE SILENT ERA practically all critics were agreed that films affect the spectator in specific ways. In 1926, for instance, René Clair likened the images on the screen to visions such as invade our sleep and the spectator himself to a dreamer under the spell of their suggestive power.[1] Working through images, silent films most certainly produced effects peculiar to the cinema. (To be sure, there were then enough "photoplays" and theatrical adaptations which merely illustrated plots detachable from the medium, but even they often included shots or scenes whose singular impact did not simply result from the significance of the intrigue they had to sustain.)

One might argue that what holds true of the silent film no longer applies to the talkies. Audience-reaction research in this field having only begun, we will have to rely on more or less impressionistic observations for relevant information. The literature of the past decades is rich in them. For the most part they concur in suggesting that the arrival of sound has not noticeably altered the picture: that actually the present-day moviegoer undergoes much the same experiences as the moviegoer in the days of the silent.[2] René Clair in 1950, it is true, remarks that speech and sound add an element of reality to the cinema which prevents it from setting the spectator dreaming—the very effect he himself had attributed to it in 1926.[3] Yet more likely than not his 1950 remark bears on films overburdened with dialogue rather than talkies which, like his own Paris comedies, continue to emphasize the visuals and therefore may well conform to the cinematic approach. Silent or not, film—cinematic film, that is—can be expected to influence the spectator in a manner denied to other media.

Impact on the senses

Different kinds of pictures call forth different reactions; some address themselves directly to the intellect, some function merely as symbols or such. Let us assume that, unlike the other types of pictures, film images affect primarily the spectator's senses, engaging him physiologically before he is in a position to respond intellectually. This assumption finds support in the following arguments:

First, film records physical reality for its own sake. Struck by the reality character of the resultant images, the spectator cannot help reacting to them as he would to the material aspects of nature in the raw which these photographic images reproduce. Hence their appeal to his sensitivity. It is as if they urged him through their sheer presence unthinkingly to assimilate their indeterminate and often amorphous patterns.

Second, in keeping with its recording obligations, film renders the world in motion. Take any film you can think of: by dint of its very nature it is a succession of ever-changing images which altogether give the impression of a flow, a constant movement. And there is of course no film that would not represent—or, rather, feature—things moving. Movement is the alpha and omega of the medium. Now the sight of it seems to have a "resonance effect," provoking in the spectator such kinesthetic responses as muscular reflexes, motor impulses, or the like. In any case, objective movement acts as a physiological stimulus. Henri Wallon describes the kind of fascination it exerts on us: "We cannot turn our eyes away from the film whose images supersede each other—not only because we would then drop the thread of the story and no longer understand what will follow but also because there is in the flow of the successive images a sort of attraction, a sort of inducement [*induction*] enjoining us, our attention, our senses, our vision, not to lose anything [of that flow]. The movement, then, is in itself something attractive and captivating."[4] And how can we explain its compulsory attractiveness? Copei, for instance, traces it to our biological heritage by saying that many animals do not notice an object of interest to them—their prey, their enemy—unless it is moving about.[5] Be this as it may, the effect itself appears to be well-established: representations of movement do cause a stir in deep bodily layers. It is our sense organs which are called into play.

Third, film not only records physical reality but reveals otherwise hidden provinces of it, including such spatial and temporal configurations as may be derived from the given data with the aid of cinematic techniques and devices. The salient point here is that these discoveries (which have been exhaustively treated in earlier contexts) mean an increased demand on the spectator's physiological make-up. The unknown shapes he encounters involve not so much his power of reasoning as his visceral faculties. Arousing his innate curiosity, they lure him into dimensions where sense impressions are all-important.

Lowered consciousness

All this favors organic tensions, nameless excitements. "It is not mainly a more or less marked complacency," says Cohen-Séat about the spectator's condition, "which makes one renounce the effort to use his mental and superior capacities; rather, even a mind most capable of reflective thought will find out that this thought remains powerless in a turmoil of shock-like emotions." Within the same context Cohen-Séat also speaks of the "mental vertigo" which befalls the spectator and the "physiological tempests" raging in him.[6]

With the moviegoer, the self as the mainspring of thoughts and decisions relinquishes its power of control. This accounts for a striking difference between him and the theatergoer, which has been repeatedly pointed out by European observers and critics. "In the theater I am always I," a perceptive French woman once told this writer, "but in the cinema I dissolve into all things and beings."[7] Wallon elaborates on the process of dissolution to which she refers: "If the cinema produces its effect, it does so because I identify myself with its images, because I more or less forget myself in what is being displayed on the screen. I am no longer in my own life, I am in the film projected in front of me."[8]

Films, then, tend to weaken the spectator's consciousness. Its withdrawal from the scene may be furthered by the darkness in moviehouses. Darkness automatically reduces our contacts with actuality, depriving us of many environmental data needed for adequate judgments and other mental activities. It lulls the mind.[9] This explains why, from the 'twenties to the present day, the devotees of film and its opponents alike have compared the medium to a sort of drug and have drawn attention to its stupefying effects[10]—incidentally, a sure sign that the spoken word has not changed much. Doping creates dope addicts. It would seem a sound proposition that the cinema has its habitués who frequent it out of an all but physiological urge.[11] They are not prompted by a desire to look at a specific film or to be pleasantly entertained; what they really crave is for once to be released from the grip of consciousness, lose their identity in the dark, and let sink in, with their senses ready to absorb them, the images as they happen to follow each other on the screen.*

Excursion: Propaganda and film

The moviegoer is much in the position of a hypnotized person. Spellbound by the luminous rectangle before his eyes—which resembles the glittering object in the hand of a hypnotist—he cannot help succumbing to the suggestions that invade the blank of his mind.[12] Film is an incomparable instrument of propaganda.[13] Hence Lenin's dictum: "The cinema is for us the most important instrument of all the arts."[14]

Grierson, who considered documentary film a godsend for propaganda messages, once said that "in documentary you do not shoot with your head only but also with your stomach muscles."[15] And when asked whether in his opinion the illiterate peasants in India might profit by films popularizing reforms, Pudovkin used surprisingly similar terms: "The film is the greatest teacher because it teaches not only through the brain but through the whole body."[16]

For an idea to be sold it must captivate not only the intellect but the senses as well. Any idea carries a host of implications, and many of them—especially the latent ones, relatively remote from the idea itself—are likely to provoke reactions in deep psychological layers comprising behavior habits, psychosomatic preferences, and what not. The prospective believer may reject an idea intellectually and yet accept it emotionally under the pressure of unconscious drives (which he usually rationalizes in an effort to pay tribute to reason). Or the reverse may happen: he repudiates an idea because his emotional resistance to it proves stronger than the attraction it exerts on his intellect. To be effective, propaganda must supplement its reasoning power with insinuations and incentives apt to influence the "stomach muscles" rather than the "head."

Films do precisely this—provided of course they are not just illustrated sales talk but, as both Grierson and Pudovkin imply, genuine films, with the emphasis on pictorial communications. Since film images lower the spectator's critical faculties, it is always possible to select and arrange them in such a way that they adjust his senses to the idea advertised. They need not refer directly to it; on the contrary, the more they proceed by

* David Low, the famous English caricaturist, once told Mr. Paul Rotha—who kindly passed this on to me—that he has the habit of going to a moviehouse and just enjoys letting the movement from the images flow over him. He never knows what film he sees but gets tremendous relaxation from his work by such immersion in the screen.

indirection—showing events and situations seemingly unconnected with the message they impart—the greater the chance that they reach unconscious fixations and bodily tendencies which might have a bearing, however distant, on the championed cause.

Many propaganda films, documentaries or not, try to canalize inner dispositions. Having learned from the Russians of the 'twenties,* the Nazi film makers, with their reliance on instincts, were masters in the art of mobilizing the twilight regions of the mind. Take that flashback scene in their triumphant war documentary, VICTORY IN THE WEST, in which French soldiers are seen mingling with Negroes and dancing in the Maginot Line: these excerpts, which the Nazis put together from French film material they had captured, were obviously calculated to make the spectator infer that the French are flippant and degenerate and thus to lure him spontaneously—by means of psychological mechanisms of which he would hardly be aware—into the camp of the wholesome and dynamic victors.[17] It was debunking in a way, or rather, sham-debunking; and the recourse to it most certainly played a role in manipulating the spectator's mind. The complete absence of verbal comment further increased the challenging power of the images, which made them all the more able to stir up in him organic dislikes and sympathies, confused fears, and dim expectations. And his knowledge that they were well-authenticated disposed of any scruples he might initially have entertained about their validity.

This leads to another reason for the effectiveness of film propaganda, a reason, though, which applies exclusively to documentary films. They are supposed to be true to fact; and is not truth the best propaganda weapon? Whenever a documentary succeeds in swaying the minds, part of its success is due to the spectator's conviction that he is in the presence of irrefutable evidence. Everybody tends to believe that pictures taken on the spot cannot lie. Obviously they can. Assuming a film passed off as a neutral documentary does not include scenes staged for the purpose in mind but confines itself, as it should, to rendering reality pure and simple—there is, however, no way for the spectator to make sure whether he is getting his money's worth—yet it may feature certain aspects of a given object at the expense of others and thus influence our approach to it. The actual shots are of necessity a selection from among possible shots.

Other factors are operative also. A change in lighting, and one and the same face appears in a new guise. (This is confirmed by a fascinating experiment which the German photographer Helmar Lerski made in

---

* It was Goebbels who praised POTEMKIN as a model and told the German film makers that they should glorify the Nazi "revolution" by similar films. See Kracauer, *From Caligari to Hitler,* p. 289.

Palestine during the 'thirties. His model, he told me in Paris, was a young man with a nondescript face who posed on the roof of a house. Lerski took over a hundred pictures of that face from a very short distance, each time subtly changing the lights with the aid of screens. Big close-ups, these pictures detailed the texture of the skin so that cheeks and brows turned into a maze of inscrutable runes reminiscent of soil formations, as they appear from an airplane. The result was amazing. None of the photographs recalled the model; and all of them differed from each other. Out of the original face there arose, evoked by the varying lights, a hundred different faces, among them those of a hero, a prophet, a peasant, a dying soldier, an old woman, a monk. Did these portraits, if portraits they were, anticipate the metamorphoses which the young man would undergo in the future? Or were they just plays of light whimsically projecting on his face dreams and experiences forever alien to him? Proust would have delighted in Lerski's experiment with its unfathomable implications.)

Variations of camera angles are of similar consequence. In their screen apotheoses of the Russian Revolution, Eisenstein and Pudovkin availed themselves of unusual angles to magnify the class struggle and enforce audience participation with the workers. Some Czarist henchman or member of the bourgeoisie was focused upon from a point near to his feet so that he seemed to rise to towering heights—a foreshortening suggesting his arrogance and ruthlessness. [Illus. 32] (In other contexts, the same procedure might suggest the hero.)

Sometimes music is called in to confer upon the synchronized shots and scenes a significance we would otherwise not attribute to them. In VICTORY IN THE WEST, for instance, musical themes with stereotyped meanings rekindle weary soldier faces, transform an English tank into a toy, and conversely, assign to a few moving Nazi tanks the major task of intimating the irresistible advance of the German army.[18] In his nature films Disney goes the limit in exploiting this procedure which uses, or misuses, the plain emotional appeals of certain tunes as leading stimuli.*

Yet were a documentary maker to refrain from coloring the images themselves and instead attempt to give an unbiased account of real-life facts—think of the English documentary HOUSING PROBLEMS which is a model case of objective reporting[19]—he still would be able to convey his propaganda messages through sheer editing. Kuleshov's famous experiment once and for all demonstrates this possibility.** A classic example is the leftist newsreel which scandalized Berlin in 1928. Issued by an association of red-tinged German intellectuals, it was composed exclusively

* See p. 141.
** See p. 69.

of indifferent shots from UFA newsreels which had been exhibited before without annoying anyone. Only the arrangement of the shots was altered.[20] All of which proves that our confidence in the veracity of documentary films rests on uncertain ground. But why, then, do we so easily surrender to the kind of evidence they offer? Our reliance on it is not entirely unjustified since documentaries do picture real things and happenings after all; and it is upheld and strengthened by the trance-like condition in which we find ourselves when looking at the screen.

For the sake of completeness it might finally be mentioned that the effectiveness of screen propaganda must also be laid to the reproducibility of film. The cinema, says Rotha, possesses the "virtues of mechanized performances to a million persons, not once but countless times a day, tomorrow, and, if the quality is good enough, ten years hence."[21]

Dreaming

Lowered consciousness invites dreaming. Gabriel Marcel, for instance, has it that the moviegoer finds himself in a state between waking and sleeping which favors hypnagogic fantasies.[22] Now it is fairly evident that the spectator's condition has something to do with the kind of spectacle he watches. In Lebovici's words: "Film is a dream . . . which makes [one] dream."[23] This immediately raises the question as to what elements of film may be sufficiently dream-like to launch the audience into reveries and perhaps even influence their course.

ABOUT THE DREAM CHARACTER OF FILMS

Manufactured dreams To the extent that films are mass entertainment they are bound to cater to the alleged desires and daydreams of the public at large.[24] Significantly, Hollywood has been called a "dream factory."[25] Since most commercial films are produced for mass consumption, we are indeed entitled to assume that there exists a certain relationship between their intrigues and such daydreams as seem to be widespread among their patrons; otherwise expressed, the events on the screen can be supposed to bear, somehow, on actual dream patterns, thereby encouraging identifications.

It should be noted in passing that this relationship is necessarily elusive. Because of their vagueness mass dispositions usually admit of diverse interpretations. People are quick to reject things that they do not agree with, while they feel much less sure about the true objects of their leanings and longings. There is, accordingly, a margin left for film producers who aim at satisfying existing mass desires. Pent-up escapist needs, for instance, may be relieved in many different ways. Hence the permanent interaction between mass dreams and film content. Each popular film conforms to popular wants; yet in conforming to them it inevitably does away with their inherent ambiguity. Any such film evolves these wants in a specific direction, confronts them with one among several meanings. Through their very definiteness films thus define the nature of the inarticulate from which they emerge.[26]

However, the daydreams which Hollywood—of course, not Hollywood alone—concocts and markets are beside the point within this particular context. They come true mainly in the intrigue, not in the whole of the film; and more often than not they are imposed upon the medium from without. Much as they may be relevant as indices of subterranean social trends, they offer little interest aesthetically. What matters here is not the sociological functions and implications of the medium as a vehicle of mass entertainment; rather, the problem is whether film as film contains dream-like elements which on their part send the audience dreaming.

Stark reality   Cinematic films may indeed be said to resemble dreams at intervals—a quality so completely independent of their recurrent excursions into the realms of fantasy and mental imagery that it shows most distinctly in places where they concentrate on real-life phenomena. The documentary shots of Harlem houses and streets in Sidney Meyers's THE QUIET ONE, especially its last section, would seem to possess this quality. [Illus. 33] Women are standing, all but motionless, in house doors, and nondescript characters are seen loitering about. Along with the dingy façades, they might as well be products of our imagination, as kindled by the narrative. To be sure, this is an intended effect, but it is brought about by a clear-cut recording of stark reality. Perhaps films look most like dreams when they overwhelm us with the crude and un-negotiated presence of natural objects—as if the camera had just now ex-tricated them from the womb of physical existence and as if the umbilical cord between image and actuality had not yet been severed. There is something in the abrupt immediacy and shocking veracity of such pictures that justifies their identification as dream images. Certain other communi-cations peculiar to the medium have about the same effect; suffice it to mention the dream-like impressions conveyed by sudden displacements in time and space, shots comprising "reality of another dimension," and passages which render special modes of reality.

THE TWO DIRECTIONS OF DREAMING

Toward the object   Released from the control of consciousness, the spectator cannot help feeling attracted by the phenomena in front of him. They beckon him to come nearer. They arouse, as Sève puts it, disquiet rather than certainty in the spectator and thus prompt him to embark on an inquiry into the being of the objects they record, an inquiry which does not aim at explaining them but tries to elucidate their secrets.[27] So he drifts toward and into the objects—much like the legendary Chinese painter who, longing for the peace of the landscape he had created, moved into it, walked toward the faraway mountains suggested by his brush strokes, and disappeared in them never to be seen again.

Yet the spectator cannot hope to apprehend, however incompletely, the being of any object that draws him into its orbit unless he meanders, dreamingly, through the maze of its multiple meanings and psychological correspondences. Material existence, as it manifests itself in film, launches the moviegoer into unending pursuits. His is a peculiar brand of sensibility which the Frenchman Michel Dard was perhaps the first to notice. In 1928, when the silents were at the peak, Dard found new sensibility in young people who were haunting the moviehouses; he characterized it in terms which, though exuberant, have all the earmarks of genuine first-hand experience: "Never, in effect, has one seen in France a sensibility of this kind: passive, personal, as little humanistic or humanitarian as possible; diffuse, unorganized, and self-unconscious like an amoeba; deprived of an object or rather, attached to all [of them] like fog, [and] penetrant like rain; heavy to bear, easy to satisfy, impossible to restrain; displaying everywhere, like a roused dream, that contemplation of which Dostoevski speaks and which incessantly hoards without rendering anything."[28] Does the spectator ever succeed in exhausting the objects he contemplates? There is no end to his wanderings. Sometimes, though, it may seem to him that, after having probed a thousand possibilities, he is listening, with all his senses strained, to a confused murmur. Images begin to sound, and the sounds are again images. When this indeterminate murmur—the murmur of existence—reaches him, he may be nearest to the unattainable goal.

The cap resembling a leopard Dreaming processes in the other direction are a product of psychological influences. Once the spectator's organized self has surrendered, his subconscious or unconscious experiences, apprehensions and hopes tend to come out and take over. Owing to their indeterminacy, film shots are particularly fit to function as an ignition spark. Any such shot may touch off chain reactions in the moviegoer—a flight of associations which no longer revolve around their original source but arise from his agitated inner environment. This movement leads the spectator away from the given image into subjective reveries; the image itself recedes after it has mobilized his previously repressed fears or induced him to revel in a prospective wish-fulfillment. Reminiscing about an old film, Blaise Cendrars relates: "The screen showed a crowd, and in this crowd there was a lad with his cap under his arm: suddenly this cap which was like all other caps began, without moving, to assume intense life; you felt it was all set to jump, like a leopard! Why? I don't know."[29] Perhaps the cap transformed itself into a leopard because the sight of it stirred involuntary memories in the narrator (as did the madeleine in Proust)—memories of the senses resuscitating inarticulate childhood days when the little cap under his arms was the carrier of tremendous emotions, which in a mysterious way involved the spotted beast of prey in his picture book.[30]

Interrelation between the two movements   These apparently opposite movements of dreaming are in practice well-nigh inseparable from each other. Trance-like immersion in a shot or a succession of shots may at any moment yield to daydreaming which increasingly disengages itself from the imagery occasioning it. Whenever this happens, the dreaming spectator, who originally concentrated on the psychological correspondences of an image striking his imagination more or less imperceptibly, moves on from them to notions beyond the orbit of that image—notions so remote from what the image itself implies that there would be no meaning in still counting them among its correspondences proper. Conversely, because of his continued exposure to the radiations from the screen, the absentee dreamer can be expected again and again to succumb to the spell of the images he left behind and to persevere in their exploration. He is wavering between self-absorption and self-abandonment.

Together the two intertwined dream processes constitute a veritable stream of consciousness whose contents—cataracts of indistinct fantasies and inchoate thoughts—still bear the imprint of the bodily sensations from which they issue. This stream of consciousness in a measure parallels the "flow of life," one of the main concerns of the medium. Consequently, films featuring that flow are most likely to initiate both movements of dreaming.

GRATIFICATIONS

Film and television

At this point the issue of audience gratifications comes into view. It might be objected that the concern with them is rather immaterial at a time when, due to the popularity of television, movie attendance has been steadily dropping. Yet this objection is untenable for several reasons. First, the fact that the two media share certain essential characteristics would seem to justify the conclusion that television affords at least some of the satisfactions which make, or made, so many people crave the movies. Accordingly, even assuming for the sake of argument that the cinema is definitely waning, an inquiry into the onetime moviegoer's delights would offer a much-needed frame of reference for any attempt to explain the mass appeal of television itself. Second, actually films are by no means a thing of the past. Along with their audience, flocks of them have immigrated to the television sets. And like the conqueror who surrenders to the culture of the conquered, television increasingly feeds on the fare of the moviehouses; indeed, it may be in part the continued impact of the old medium which accounts for the attractiveness of the new one. Third, judging from precedents, the belief that the current trend in favor of television bespeaks the decline of the traditional cinema is entirely unwarranted. The theater was said to be dead when the movies became fashionable; however, it has not only resisted, unscathed, the onslaught of the cinema but has profited by it in many ways. Similarly, recent developments in this country tend to show that the misgivings of the big radio networks about the repercussions of television are exaggerated. The latter's ascent, it appears, leads to a cleavage of functions between the two media which is advantageous to radio also. So the cinema may well weather the crisis. Its potentialities are far from being exhausted, and the social conditions which favored its rise have not yet changed substantially. (Incidentally, it is certainly not the wide screen which strengthens the medium's chances for survival.)

Hunger for life

In 1921, Hugo von Hofmannsthal published an article, *Der Ersatz fuer Traeume* [*The Substitute for Dreams*], in which he identified the crowds of moviegoers as the masses that people the big industrial centers and cities—factory workers, lesser employees, and the like. Their minds are empty, says he, because of the kind of life which society enjoins on them. These people suspect language of being an instrument of society's control over them and fear it accordingly; and they are afraid lest the knowledge transmitted by newspapers or at party meetings might lead ever farther away from what, their senses tell them, is life itself. So they escape to the cinema with its silent films, which prove all the more attractive since they are silent. There the moviegoer finds the fuller life which society denies to him. He has dreamed of it in his childhood days, and the cinema is a substitute for those dreams.[31]

It almost sounds as if Hofmannsthal is hinting at the imaginary pleasures which the working masses may derive from the many films that feature success stories or afford glimpses of the idle rich.[32] As a matter of fact, however, he does not in the least care about the economic and social needs of the worker and lower middle classes; nor is he interested in the stereotyped story patterns which serve as a safety valve for these needs. Rather, what does concern him is the ability of film to gratify a deep-rooted, all but metaphysical desire which he attributes to the working classes for reasons connected with his own class status and the environmental influences working on him at the time. For the masses to sit in the moviehouses and watch the screen, Hofmannsthal has it, is like "the ride through the air with the devil Asmodi who strips off all roofs, bares all secrets." In other words, it is life in its inexhaustibility which the cinema offers to masses in want of it. Hofmannsthal says so explicitly. He speaks of the "life essence" condensed in the pictures which fill the dreaming spectator's imagination. And he poignantly compares the dreams that pass across the screen with the "glistening wheel of life which spins around eternally."

Statements in keeping with the two assumptions that there is a widespread hunger for "life" and that film is uniquely equipped to satisfy it thread the history of the medium. As early as 1919, a Viennese author declares that in the cinema we feel "the pulse of life itself . . . and give ourselves up to its overwhelming abundance so immeasurably superior to our imagination."[33] In 1930, Beucler, the French writer, after having praised film for bringing, like a dream, the universe within our reach, mentions that once a stranger accosted him in a moviehouse, saying: "To me the cinema is as precious as life."[34] This word might have been used as a motto to a German audience survey conducted by Wolfgang Wilhelm and incorporated in his 1940 doctoral dissertation, *Die Auftriebswirkung des Films* [*The Uplifting Effect of Film*]. His survey is based on data from a questionnaire administered to twenty university students and teachers, plus twenty-three intensive interviews with subjects of different occupations and age groups.[35] Although this random sample is far too small in scope to be conclusive, it is of interest in as much as it bears out some major points made by Hofmannsthal. Here are a few responses:

"The film is more life than the theater. In the theater I watch a work of art which, somehow, appears to be elaborated. After a film performance I feel as if I had been in the middle of life." (a housewife)*
"One would like to get something out of life after all." (a young worker)
"A good film helps me to get in touch with people and with 'life.'" (a nurse)

* This statement parallels that of the French woman, quoted p. 159.

"The less interesting the people I know the more frequently do I go to the movies." (a businessman)

"Some days a sort of 'hunger for people' (*Menschenhunger*) drives me into the cinema." (a student)

"What drives me to the movies is hunger for sensation, a tickling of the nerves (aroused) by unusual situations, fight, impassioned clashes, love scenes, crowd pictures, unknown worlds, underworld . . . war, society." Interestingly, this respondent adds: "The film as a whole may be bad, but given the right mood, I am on the whole satisfied if details of the kind mentioned meet my expectations." (a student)[36]

The survey shows that, contrary to what Hofmannsthal assumes, the conditions prevailing among the working masses are not, or at least not alone, responsible for the urge to frequent the moviehouses. The masses of film addicts include people of other walks of life as well. Regarding their inner motivations, all that the above statements and responses suggest is that the inveterate moviegoer seems to suffer from alienation, from loneliness. There is, in addition, evidence that he does not feel he is being suppressed or rejected by society. Rather, he traces his suffering to an isolation due not only to his lack of sufficient and satisfactory human relationships but to his being out of touch with the breathing world about him, that stream of things and events which, were it flowing through him, would render his existence more exciting and significant. He misses "life." And he is attracted by the cinema because it gives him the illusion of vicariously partaking of life in its fullness.

The concept of life as such

Life as a powerful entity—as it asserts itself, for instance, in the poems of Walt Whitman and, perhaps, Emile Verhaeren—is a concept of relatively recent origin. It would be tempting to try to follow the evolution of this concept, say, from the time of the Romantics via Nietzsche and Bergson up to our days, but such a study goes beyond the scope of the present book, being a large-scale proposition in its own right. Suffice it to mention two developments which perhaps have helped to generate the nostalgia for life as such. First, there is the rise of modern mass society and the concomitant disintegration of beliefs and cultural traditions which had established a set of norms, affinities, and values for the individual to live by. It is possible that the corrosion of normative incentives makes us focus on life as their matrix, their underlying substratum.

Second, we live in an "age of analysis," which means among other things that with modern man abstract thought tends to get the better of concrete experience. Whitehead for one was deeply aware that scientific knowledge is much less inclusive than aesthetic insight, and that the world we master technologically is only part of the reality accessible to the senses, the heart. The concept of life may also designate this reality which transcends the anemic space-time world of science. Significantly, Wilhelm concludes from his interview material that one of the uplifting effects of film consists in enabling those whose sensibilities have been blunted by the predominance of technology and analytical thinking to resume "sensuous and immediate" contact with "life."[37] What is thus embraced, is precisely the kind of reality which eludes measurement.

Film—the "glistening wheel of life"

And how do films gratify the isolated individual's longings? He recalls the nineteenth-century *flâneur* (with whom he has otherwise little in common) in his susceptibility to the transient real-life phenomena that crowd the screen. According to the testimony available, it is their flux which affects him most strongly. Along with the fragmentary happenings incidental to them, these phenomena—taxi cabs, buildings, passers-by, inanimate objects, faces—presumably stimulate his senses and provide him with stuff for dreaming. Bar interiors suggest strange adventures; improvised gatherings hold out the promise of fresh human contacts; sudden shifts of scene are pregnant with unforeseeable possibilities. Through its very concern for camera-reality, film thus permits especially the lonely spectator to fill his shrinking self—shrinking in an environment where the bare schemata of things threaten to supersede the things themselves—with images of life as such—glittering, allusive, infinite life. Evidently, these loosely connected images, which he may of course interweave in many ways, are so profoundly satisfactory to the dreamer because they offer him routes of escape into the mirage-like world of concrete objects, striking sensations, and unusual opportunities. All that has been said so far indicates that the delight he takes in films does not, or need not, stem from their intrigue proper. To quote Chaperot, "sometimes right in the middle of a film whose whole intrigue we know and whose lamentable threads we even anticipate, do we not suddenly have the feeling that the image rises to a superior plane and that the 'story' is not more than of secondary importance?"[38] * What redeems the film addict from his isolation is not so much the spectacle of an individual destiny which might again isolate him as the sight of people mingling and communing with each other

* See p. 72.

according to ever-changing patterns. He seeks the opportunity of drama rather than drama itself.

Child-like omnipotence

In availing himself of this opportunity he gratifies still another desire. As has been mentioned above, Hofmannsthal assumes that the spectator's dreams revive those of his childhood days which have sunk into his unconscious. "This whole subterranean vegetation," he remarks, "trembles down to its darkest roots, while the eyes elicit the thousandfold image of life from the glittering screen."[39] If Hofmannsthal is right, the moviegoer again becomes a child in the sense that he magically rules the world by dint of dreams which overgrow stubborn reality. This proposition is also echoed in the German audience survey. "I can be everywhere, standing above as the god of this world," says a student of psychology. And a woman teacher: "One is, so to speak, like God who sees everything and one has the feeling that nothing eludes you and that one grasps all of it."[40]

The satisfaction which both respondents derive from their imaginary omnipotence is perhaps symptomatic of our current situation. This situation is not only characterized by the waning of binding norms and beliefs and a loss of concreteness—the two developments which help explain the hunger for life—but by a third factor as well: the increasing difficulty for the individual to account for the forces, mechanisms, and processes that shape the modern world, including his own destiny. The world has grown so complex, politically and otherwise, that it can no longer be simplified. Any effect seems separated from its manifold possible causes; any attempt at a synthesis, a unifying image, falls short. Hence a widespread feeling of impotence in the face of influences become uncontrollable for eluding definition. No doubt many among us suffer, consciously or not, from being exposed, helplessly, to these influences. So we look for compensations. And film, it appears, is apt to afford temporary relief. In the cinema "one grasps all of it," as the woman teacher puts it. There the frustrated may turn into the kings of creation.

Return from the dreamland

Yet the spectator is not dreaming all the time. Every moviegoer will have observed that spells of trance-like absorption alternate with moments in which the drugging effect of the medium seems to wear off. Now he gets lost in the flow of images and intimate reveries, now he feels he is drifting ashore again. And no sooner does he recover a measure of consciousness than he is quite naturally eager to try to draw the balance of what he experiences under the impact of the sense impressions that close in on him. Here the momentous issue of the significance of film experience arises, an issue which must for the time being be left unresolved.*

* See p. 285.

ILLUSTRATIONS

1
Eugene Atget: Paris Street

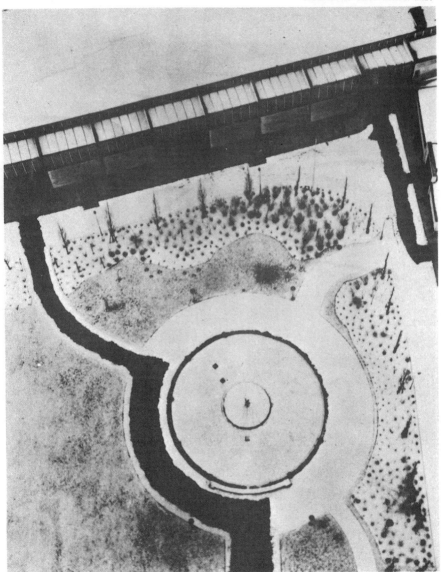

2
László Moholy-Nagy: From Berlin Wireless Tower, 1928

William A. Garnett: Nude Dune, 1953

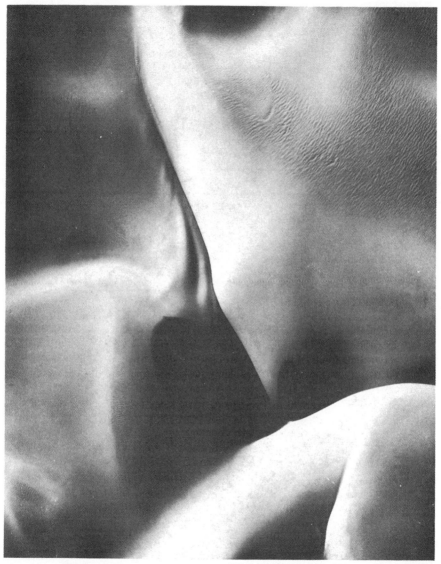

AERIAL PHOTOGRAPH OF A SAND DUNE IN DEATH VALLEY
COURTESY OF WILLIAM A. GARNETT

4
Mary Ann Dorr: Chairs in the Sunlight

5
Henri Cartier-Bresson: Children in Ruins, Spain, 1933

6
Arrival of a Train
Lumière, France

7
AN IMPOSSIBLE VOYAGE
Georges Méliès, France

8
THE RED SHOES
Michael Powell and Emeric Pressburger, Great Britain

9
EARTH
Alexander Dovzhenko, U.S.S.R.

10
Louisiana Story
Robert J. Flaherty, U.S.A.

11
INTOLERANCE
D. W. Griffith, U.S.A.

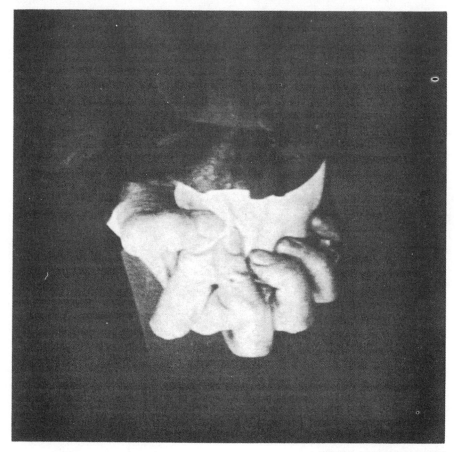

12
Jazz Dance
Roger Tilton, U.S.A.

13
DESERT VICTORY
Army Film and Photographic Unit and the
Royal Air Force Film Production Unit, Great Britain

14
UNDERWORLD
Josef von Sternberg, U.S.A.

15
OPEN CITY
Roberto Rossellini, Italy

16
UEBERFALL
Ernö Metzner, Germany

17
THE MUSKETEERS OF PIG ALLEY
D. W. Griffith, U.S.A.

18
THE BICYCLE THIEF
Vittorio De Sica, Italy

19
LE MILLION
René Clair, France

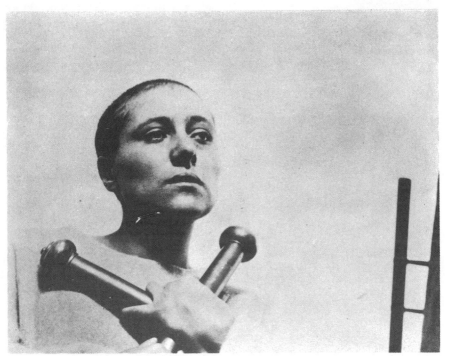

20
JOAN OF ARC
Carl Dreyer, France

21
DAY OF WRATH
Carl Dreyer, Denmark

22
Sunnyside
Charles Chaplin, U.S.A.

23
NOSFERATU
F. W. Murnau, Germany

24
VAMPYR
Carl Dreyer, France

25
LOS OLVIDADOS
Luis Buñuel, Mexico

27
THE THIRD MAN
Sir Carol Reed, Great Britain

28
Sous les toits de Paris
René Clair, France

29
THE BAND WAGON
Vincente Minelli, U.S.A.

ONE HUNDRED MEN AND A GIRL
Henry Koster, U.S.A.

31
THE MEDIUM
Gian-Carlo Menotti, U.S.A.

32
THE END OF ST. PETERSBURG
V. I. Pudovkin, U.S.S.R.

33
The Quiet One
Sidney Meyers, U.S.A.

34
ENTR'ACTE
René Clair, France

35
Ballet mecanique
Fernand Léger, France

36
Un Chien Andalou
Luis Buñuel and Salvador Dali, France

37
THE MYSTERY OF PICASSO
Henri-Georges Clouzot, France

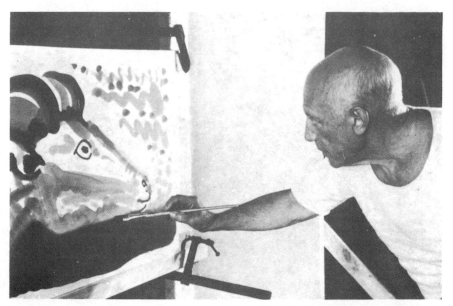

38
HOUSING PROBLEMS
Edgar Anstey and Sir Arthur Elton, Great Britain

39
BORINAGE
Joris Ivens and Henri Storck, Belgium

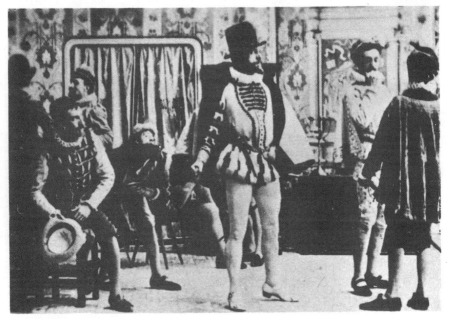

40
Assassination of the Duc de Guise
Film d'Art, France

41
IVAN THE TERRIBLE
Sergei M. Eisenstein, U.S.S.R.

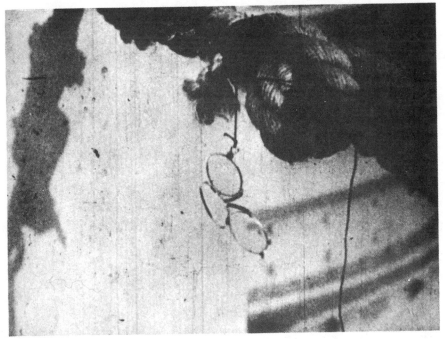

42
POTEMKIN
Sergei M. Eisenstein, U.S.S.R.

WILD STRAWBERRIES
Ingmar Bergman, Sweden

44
GERVAISE
René Clément, France

45
DIARY OF A COUNTRY PRIEST
Robert Bresson, France

46
Le Rouge et le Noir
Claude Autant-Lara, France

47

PEOPLE IN THE CITY
Arne Sucksdorff, Sweden

NATIONAL FILM ARCHIVE, LONDON

48
MOANA
Robert J. Flaherty, U.S.A.

49
ON THE BOWERY
Lionel Rogosin, U.S.A.

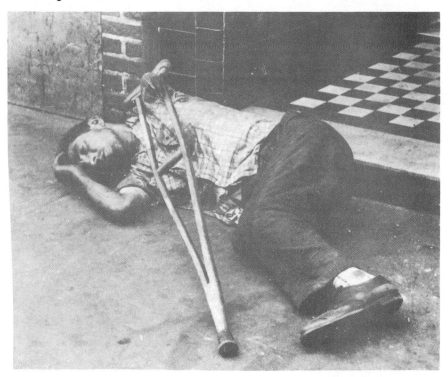

50
TOGETHER
Lorenza Mazzetti, Great Britain

51
LITTLE FUGITIVE
Morris Engel, Ruth Orkin, and Ray Ashley, U.S.A.

52
PAISAN: Roman Episode
Roberto Rossellini, Italy

53
SIDE STREET STORY
Eduardo De Filippo, Italy

54
UMBERTO D.
Vittorio De Sica, Italy

55
La Strada
Federico Fellini, Italy

56
CABIRIA
Federico Fellini, Italy

57
RASHOMON
Akira Kurosawa, Japan

58
THE PILGRIM
Charles Chaplin, U.S.A.

59
LE SANG DES BETES
Georges Franju, France

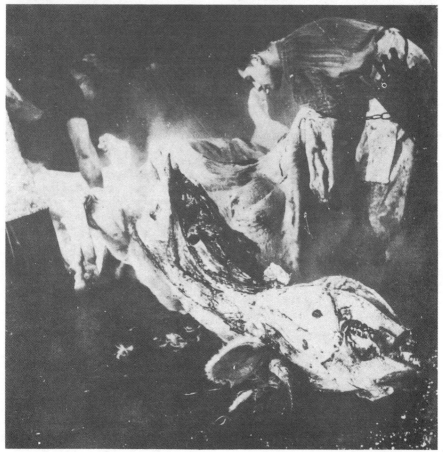

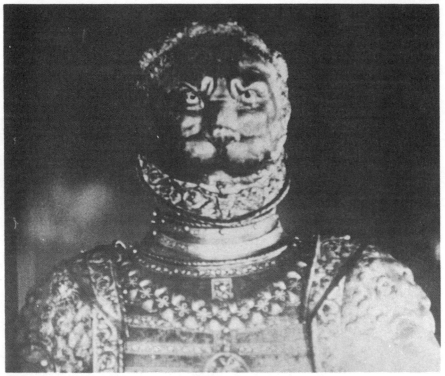

60
L'Hotel des Invalides
Georges Franju, France

61

Aparajito
Satyajit Ray, India

III. COMPOSITION

Experimental Film

INTRODUCTION: THE TWO MAIN FILM TYPES

THE TWO MOST GENERAL FILM TYPES are the story film and the non-story film, the latter comprising the bulk of *experimental* films and all the varieties of the *film of fact*. Supposing now a film maker susceptible to the peculiarities of his medium is free to choose between the story and non-story film. Will he spontaneously prefer one of them or will he dismiss the whole idea of such a choice in the belief that both admit of equally satisfactory solutions?

Gross as this issue may seem, it has been much-debated in the literature, especially by those favoring the first alternative. They usually hold that story-telling interferes with the cinematic approach. Before looking into the *avant-garde*'s revolt against the story film, we might well ponder two comments in the same vein from other quarters, completely independent of each other, which point up the significance of the issue.

There is, first, an observation by André Maurois, which is all the more poignant since it stems from a genuine experience of this sensitive writer: "In a moviehouse I visited they advertised *Larmes de clown* [TEARS OF A CLOWN] and showed a series of quite beautiful pictures which presented a circus ring, clowns rolling a big ball, a lion threatening a dancer; all this was beautiful, obscure, and suggestive like certain poems by Saint-John Perse. Next week I went to see the film. It was an honest, coherent, sentimental, and flat story. Its whole poetic charm was due to the fact that the film had been cut arbitrarily. In stripping the events of their excess of common sense, one relieves the spectator from the necessity of judging, bringing him closer to poetic emotion. In consequence, there is a conflict in film between intrigue and poetry. If the intrigue is too interesting, everything passes as in a novel; one would like to jump the description. If the film is designed to teach us a moral truth, it becomes as bad as a didactic poem." Maurois goes on to suggest that, to maintain the "poetic" element in a feature film its action proper should be preceded by pictures creating atmosphere after the manner of Balzac and also of Chaplin in his A WOMAN OF PARIS. For the rest, Maurois envisages as an alternative a more radical solution of the conflict—the *cinéma pur* which "would be composed of pictures arranged according to a rhythm, without any intrigue."[1] Small wonder, incidentally, that he conceives of the possibility of "pure cinema"; the French *avant-garde* film had its heyday in 1927 when he published these remarks.

Second, twenty years later Lucien Sève developed a theory which centers on the very same theme. With Sève the discrepancy between "poetry" and "intrigue" hinted at by Maurois turns into a conflict between the properties of the "shot" [*plan*] and those of the "sequence." "The cinema is ambiguous," says he. "It is based on the shot—which tends to isolate itself and attract an attention of the inquiring variety*—as well as on the sequence which creates a definite unity of meaning between the shots and arouses in the spectator an intense desire for continuation. From the spectator's point of view one might call this the law of double interest; he usually finds the film too long and the shots too short because he has, spontaneously, the two contrary tendencies to retain the shot in order to exhaust its riches and to relinquish it as soon as he has decoded it sufficiently to satisfy his curiosity and his taste for drama." (It need hardly be pointed out that this terminology is misleading. What Sève calls a "shot" may well amount to a "montage" of shots, as, for instance, in the classic Eisenstein films; and what he calls a "sequence" is plainly an episode in some feature film edited in such a way that its over-all meaning obscures the multiple meanings of the shots or shot units comprising it.)

Sève then proceeds to illustrate his thesis that concern with the sequence weakens the power of the shot; that a screen aspiring to story-telling automatically forfeits the chance of conveying specifically cinematic messages: "I follow an American gangster film, and the screen tells me that the bank employee gets in his car to return home in a hurry. From the moment at which I see him pull up before his house I know in advance that I may as well pay less attention: he'll pass the lobby, walk upstairs, get out his key, switch on the indirect light. At this moment I shall again watch closely, for he might find someone sitting in his armchair. . . . While a gesture of Chaplin calls for my extreme attention because it may any time stray in an unexpected direction, here I know

---

* Cf. reference to Sève, p. 165.

the gesture before seeing it and, already anticipating its future, care little about its evolution."

And what does this imply for the cinematic narrative? It "enriches the eye less than it does the conceptualizing and verbalizing mind. Accordingly," Sève continues, "the spectator is like a reader of novels and can be defined in terms of a similar activity—a quest for intentions rather than shapes, an intense desire for drama, not gestures. . . . Whether the film amounts to a drama, a detective story, a myth, an everyday incident [fait divers], or a tract, the result is invariably the same." It might be added that, exactly as Maurois, Sève points to the possibility of cinéma pur— films which do not tell stories but are based on the shot instead of the sequence. He holds, however, that pure cinema remains more or less an ideal because it repudiates the aesthetics of literature and therefore has not been able to "solve the problem of establishing a work."[2]

ORIGINS

The avant-garde movement

Historically, experimental film originates in the European avant-garde movement of the 'twenties, which in turn took much of its inspiration from contemporary art. Over half of the avant-garde were writers and painters,* with the latter forming the main contingent. In 1921, Viking Eggeling and Hans Richter, two painter-friends working in Germany, redeemed the geometrical compositions they had evolved on scrolls from their stationary existence. The former composed his DIAGONAL SYMPHONY of spirals and comb-like shapes, while Richter in his RHYTHM 21 coaxed black, gray, and white squares into charming rhythmical exercises.[3] It was painting in motion, "drawings brought to life."** But Richter-Eggeling's abstractions initiated only one of the trends which make up the avant-garde. With headquarters in Paris, this very complex movement was also strongly influenced by surrealism in literature and painting; and of course, it let itself be stimulated by various fresh approaches within the national cinemas at large, such as the German expressionist film, American film comedy, the Swedish film with its dreams and superimpositions, and the ingenious "montage" methods of the Russians.

---

* This does not hold true of the modern experimenters, most of whom have chosen film directly as their art medium.
** See p. 39.

Paradigmatic character of the avant-garde

After a temporary lull, experimental film has made a comeback since World War II. In this country, there is presently a marked concern for it on the part of young artists—think of the films of the Whitney brothers, Maya Deren, Sidney Peterson, Curtis Harrington, etc. And it is not the artists alone who cultivate the genre. Perhaps even more symptomatic of its revival, if revival it is, is an increasing consumer demand, as evidenced by the steady growth of film societies.[4] Now the salient point here is that, all in all, the current output sticks to the patterns developed in the 'twenties; that, except for minor adjustments to the contemporary scene and the incorporation of films on art, not much has changed in terms of motivations, preferences, and objectives. As of old, some experimenters specialize in the animation of abstract forms; and the others strictly follow the surrealist tradition in projecting their poetic visions, yearnings, frustrations.

Hence the possibility of studying experimental film at its source. This is all the more fortunate, since the artists of the 'twenties rarely missed an opportunity to spell out their ideas and aspirations. It should be noted, though, that only such *avant-garde intentions* and *film trends* will be considered as seem to be characteristic of the whole of experimental film.

AVANT-GARDE INTENTIONS

The controversial story

"PURE CINEMA"

The *avant-garde* artists broke away from the commercialized cinema not only because of the inferior quality of the many adaptations from plays and novels that swamped the screen but, more important, out of the conviction that the story as the main element of feature films is something alien to the medium, an imposition from without. It was a revolt against the story film as such, a concerted effort to shake off the fetters of the intrigue in favor of a purified cinema. The literature of the time abounds with protestations to this effect. In 1921, Jean Epstein called the story a "lie" and declared categorically: "There are no stories. There have never been stories. There are only situations without tail or head; without beginning, center, and end."[5] A 1927 statement by Germaine Dulac, one of the leading *avant-garde* artists, is particularly noteworthy for tracing pure cinema to Lumière and elaborating upon the sad fact that the lessons of his "unnarratable" ARRIVAL OF A TRAIN had not been heeded. Instead of recognizing the new aesthetics inherent in the Lumière brothers' camera, she argues, one was content with subordinating it to traditional aesthetics: "One set out to group animated photographs around an external action . . . rather than studying, for its own sake, the conception of movement in its brutal and mechanical visual continuity . . . one assimilated the cinema to the theater." In conclusion, Mme Dulac accuses those who imprison cinematic action in a narrative of a "criminal error."[6] It was logical that ASSASSINATION OF THE DUC DE GUISE, the first *film d'art* and the archetype of all theatrical films to come, should be rediscovered by the *avant-garde* and exhibited in their moviehouses to the accompaniment of music ridiculing it.[7]

LIMITED RECOGNITION OF THE STORY

Despite the deprecation of the story film, however, many *avant-garde* film directors refused to dispense with a story—partly for the simple reason that the industry insisted on it as a prerequisite of appreciable box-office returns.* Abel Gance, Marcel L'Herbier, and Jean Epstein experimented within the framework of commercial films. Of special interest is a group of *avant-garde* story films which includes, for instance, Delluc's FIEVRE, Germaine Dulac's THE SMILING MADAME BEUDET, Cavalcanti's EN RADE, and Kirsanov's MENILMONTANT. These films had a characteristic in common which sets them apart: unlike the contrived plots of the contemporary screen, their tenuous intrigues were in the nature of real-life episodes. That dedicated representatives of the movement thus endorsed the episode, clearly suggests that they believed it least to interfere with what they considered pure cinema.** Yet it will suffice here to mention these excursions into story-telling in passing. Within the present context the emphasis is not so much on them as on the non-story film which was the *avant-garde*'s chief concern after all.

Cinematic language

Determined to strip film of all theatrical and literary elements that threatened to overlay its substance, the artists of the 'twenties conceivably

---

* In 1925, René Clair, who never fully endorsed *cinéma pur* anyway, expressed himself in favor of compromises with the commercial cinema. He jesuitically suggested that the *avant-garde* film director should introduce, "by a sort of ruse, the greatest number of purely visual themes into a scenario made to satisfy everyone." (Clair, *Réflexion faite*, p. 104. See also Brunius, "Experimental Film in France," in Manvell, ed., *Experiment in the Film*, pp. 89–90.)

** For the episode film, see chapter 14.

felt the urge to build from the ingrained properties of their medium. They aimed at telling whatever they wanted to tell in a language peculiar to the cinema. This explains their intense preoccupation with cinematic techniques and devices, such as close-ups, tracking shots, unusual camera angles, quick cutting, slow motion, distortions, soft-focus photography, gauzes.[8] Not all contents are equally fit to be conveyed by the same modes of expression. So the artists used the language they developed for the representation of specifically cinematic subjects; it was as if this language by itself alone attracted themes more or less inaccessible to the traditional arts. Thus the *avant-garde* screen did not confine itself to human interaction in the manner of the commercial cinema but abounded with close-ups of inanimate objects; and it showed a marked preference for unfamiliar sights and for the very small.[9]

Physical reality

As might be expected, both the *avant-garde*'s aversion to story-telling and its concomitant indulgence in cinematic devices and subjects benefited the realistic tendency up to a point. The film camera and the techniques at his disposal permitted the artist to get the most out of physical reality; and like the creative photographer he derived a certain satisfaction from detecting, in the given material, forms and movements which seemed to be completely unreal. There was a turn to documentary—pictorial accounts that would bring to the fore otherwise hidden aspects of nature. In his 1923 review of Gance's LA ROUE, this grandiose drama of the road whose foolish sentimentality is fortunately somewhat compensated for by marvelous cinematic penetrations of the railway world, René Clair exclaims: "Ah! If Mr. Abel Gance would give up having locomotives say 'yes' and 'no,' attributing to an engine-driver the thoughts of an ancient hero . . . ! If he would create a pure documentary, he who knows how to bring to life the detail of a machine, a hand, a branch, smoke."[10] (Later on, Clair would renege his youthful rebellion against films with a story.) And Germaine Dulac observes in retrospect: "One could find the very subjects of pure cinema in certain scientific documentaries . . . dealing, for example, with the formation of crystals, the trajectory of a bullet . . . the evolution of microbes, of insects in their expressions and their life."[11]

More than one *avant-garde* documentary reveled in the expressions and the life of Paris streets, Paris people; Lacombe in his LA ZONE pictured states of "suburban sadness," to use, or rather misuse, a term of David Riesman's; Clair assembled impressions of the Eiffel Tower in LA TOUR; and Cavalcanti with his RIEN QUE LES HEURES initiated the series of city "symphonies," ranging from Ruttmann's BERLIN to Sucksdorff's postwar film on Stockholm, PEOPLE IN THE CITY. Or remember such imaginative readings as Ivens's RAIN, which unfolds the magnificent spectrum of a drab rainfall; Vigo's brilliant, if immature, A PROPOS DE NICE, so expressive of revolutionary ardor and a constant awareness of death; and, of course, Buñuel's LAND WITHOUT BREAD, in which he reverted from his surrealist ventures to the monstrous core of reality itself. Released in the early 'thirties after the *avant-garde* movement had come to an end, this terrifying documentary bared the depths of human misery, prefiguring the near future with its unspeakable horrors and sufferings.

"The least realistic of arts"

Yet the documentary was hardly less of a side line than the episode film. Associated with the Dadaists, cubists, and surrealists, the *avant-garde* film makers did not repudiate the hegemony of the story to exchange it for another restrictive imposition—that of the raw material of nature. Rather, they conceived of film as an art medium in the established sense and consequently rejected the jurisdiction of external reality as an unjustified limitation of the artist's creativity, his formative urges. True, they upheld the predominance of the imagery against those who subordinated it to the requirements of an intrigue, recognized visible movement as something essential to film, and indeed deigned incorporating existing physical phenomena, but all this did not prevent them from aspiring to complete independence of outer restraints and identifying pure cinema as a vehicle of autonomous artistic expression. Brunius, himself a onetime *avant-garde* artist, poignantly epitomizes their outlook in saying: "A new claim was advanced now for the right of film, as of poetry or painting, to break away from both realism and didacticism, from documentary and fiction, in order to refuse to tell a story . . . and even to create forms and movements instead of copying them from nature."[12] Endorsing this claim, Brunius calls the cinema "the *least realistic* of arts."[13]

The *avant-garde* film maker, then, was guided by intentions which may be described as follows:

(1) He wished to organize whatever material he chose to work on according to rhythms which were a product of his inner impulses, rather than an imitation of patterns found in nature.

(2) He wished to invent shapes rather than record or discover them.

(3) He wished to convey, through his images, contents which were an outward projection of his visions, rather than an implication of those images themselves.

AVANT-GARDE TRENDS

What kind of experimental film did grow out of intentions such as these? Some are highly individual productions. Alexandrov's ROMANCE SENTIMENTALE, for instance, defies classification by being a crude mixture, or rather, inventory, of all imaginable *avant-garde* innovations and aspirations. Nor would it be easy to pigeonhole, say, Hans Richter's GHOSTS BEFORE BREAKFAST, in which he employs trick after trick to picture the shenanigans of hats and dishes in full rebellion against their everyday chores. And of course, ENTR'ACTE by René Clair holds a place of its own.

Entr'acte

This "classic of absurdity"[14] deserves special comment as the only non-story, nondocumentary *avant-garde* experiment which suggests a definite attachment to camera-reality. ENTR'ACTE can roughly be divided into two parts, the first of which features not so much rhythmical movement as the content of a dream (supposedly dreamt by a person who visited a fair the evening before). The dream images—among them a fragile paper boat floating through the sky above a Paris roof landscape—are loosely connected in the manner of free associations, drawing on analogies, contrasts, or no recognizable principle at all. Cigarettes standing on end become the columns of a Greek temple; the skirt of a dancing ballerina turns into an opening flower; and when the camera tilts up from her skirt to show us the rest of the ballerina we see instead of her head that of a bearded male. It is like a performance of Méliès's magician. Incidentally, the resemblance to Méliès is reinforced by the fact that some scenes are unashamedly stagy. The salient point is that all this is not meant to carry a message. The transformation of the cigarettes into Greek columns is nothing but a toying with remote similarities; the imaginary body composed of the ballerina's lower half and the bearded head is an outright Dadaist effrontery. In short, fantasy is treated playfully and, hence, confirms rather than obstructs the spirit of the medium.*

There is internal evidence to the effect that Clair did not think of placing fantasy above camera-reality; that his playfulness in handling the dream images sprang from his loyalty to the cinematic approach. Consider the second part of the film which, unlike the first, features rhythm. In it the dream continues in a sense; but from a delicate fabric of incoherent contents it changes into a straight burlesque centering, Dada fashion,

* Cf. pp. 86–7.

upon a funeral procession. The procession moves first through an amusement park in slow motion, then gathers momentum, and eventually races after the hearse, which, now entirely on its own, rushes headlong through the streets and down a country road. [Illus. 34] The impression of dizzying speed results from an ingenious "montage" which combines cuts-in of a roller coaster ride with a mingling of treetops and bits of the road —a sequence matched only by the "beautiful visual frenzy"[15] of the merry-go-round episode in Epstein's CŒUR FIDELE (released shortly before ENTR'ACTE). Once again, the interest here lies with the creation, through cinematic devices, of slow and fast movements and the rhythmical sensations they provide.

And how does Clair proceed to convey these rhythms? The important thing is that, in order to represent them, he does not use abstract forms in obedience to then common *avant-garde* demands but actually avails himself of real-life material; in other words, he subordinates his formative urges to the exigencies of the realistic tendency. Reminiscent of the chases in French and American silent film comedies, the sequence of the racing funeral procession acknowledges physical reality in toying with it. One might also say of this sequence that it depicts a special mode of reality—reality as perceived by those who are moving at extreme speed. The playfulness of the film's first part, then, is of a piece with the realism of the second.

For the rest, ENTR'ACTE has all the traits of an exercise. It almost looks as if in this film Clair had deliberately tried out everything that can be done within the medium in terms of fantasy and technique. He would later greatly profit by the experience thus gained.

Emphasis on rhythm

VISUAL MUSIC

The fact that Eggeling, Richter, and Ruttmann called their first abstract productions DIAGONAL SYMPHONY, RHYTHM 21, and OPUS 1 respectively intimates that they aspired to a sort of visual music. It was an aspiration common to many French *avant-garde* artists. As early as 1920, even before the Eggeling-Richter films had appeared, Louis Delluc exclaimed: "I have . . . seen an admirable technical phenomenon. I have seen cadence."[16] Henri Chomette on his part spoke of a new film genre the images of which "follow each other in the manner not of phrases of a narrative but phrases of a musical suite."[17] "There is the symphony, pure music," asserted Germaine Dulac and then asked: "Why should the cinema not also have its symphony?"[18] A declared partisan of *cinéma pur*, she insisted on the correspondence between visual and musical rhythms.[19]

The visual "symphonies" of the period had two organizational characteristics. First, at least some of the artists producing these films found it convenient to follow the lead of a musical piece in evolving their pictorial sequences. Madame Dulac in her DISQUE 957 translated, or believed to translate, the Chopin Prelude no. 6 into a continuity for the eyes; and Oskar Fischinger was fond of patterning his rhythmical abstractions on given music, classical or otherwise. Suffice it to mention the actual occurrence of such fusions between music and film; the aesthetic problem they raise has already been dealt with in previous contexts.*

The second characteristic has to do with the material rhythmicized. Germaine Dulac pointed to it when she defined cinema as "the art of the movement and the visual rhythms of life and the imagination."[20] Her definition sanctioned what was then customary practice; the visual rhythms were imparted through both things imagined and real-life phenomena. The penchant for invented shapes resulted in a number of films confining themselves to sheer abstractions; Marcel Duchamp's ANAEMIC CINEMA with its concentric circles and rotating spirals goes far in this direction. Other rhythmical films were less puristic. Take DISQUE 957 or Richter's FILM STUDY 1926: the movements contrived in them involve not only abstract patterns but natural objects as well. Some such composite creations even show a marked concern for physical reality; Léger's BALLET MECANIQUE, for instance, includes only a minimum of drawn or painted geometrical forms.[21]

ENCROACHMENT ON CAMERA-REALITY

What exactly is the function of the real-life inserts in *avant-garde* films featuring visual music? On the one hand, their authors were keen on capturing, with the aid of genuinely cinematic techniques, interesting details and unusual sights fit to stimulate audience sensitivity to the world about us; in DISQUE 957 water drops trickle down a window pane and floating mists make an alley look mysterious. On the other hand, the same artists recorded such material phenomena not to establish physical reality but for a compositional purpose: they wanted to build from them a self-sufficient sequence of rhythmical movements.

This is strikingly illustrated by that quasi-realistic episode of BALLET MECANIQUE, in which a washerwoman climbs a flight of stairs without ever safely arriving at the top; no sooner is she about to reach it than she finds herself back again at the bottom and resumes her ascent. [Illus. 35] By means of a simple editing trick she is thus made to trudge up and up an

* See pp. 152–3. Cf. also p. 149.

endless number of times. Now the stubborn reiteration of her performance is palpably not meant to impress upon us this particular woman in the act of climbing; were it otherwise, she would not invariably behave in the same way but slow down after a while and show the usual symptoms of weariness. And since the shots of the woman fail to account of her presence, we do not experience their possible meanings either; looking at the repetitious woman, it never occurs to us that her vain climb might reflect the toils of Sisyphus. Actually, what we are watching is not so much a real-life figure mounting a nightmarish flight of stairs as the movement of climbing itself. The emphasis on its rhythm obliterates the reality of the woman executing it so that she turns from a concrete person into the pale carrier of a specific kind of motion.* Due to the obtrusiveness of the movements they perform, the saucepan lids and egg beaters with which she is mingling[22] are likewise reduced to near-abstract shapes. They vanish from sight, so to speak, and what remains of them is as immaterial as the grin of the Cheshire cat. Léger himself traced his BALLET MECANIQUE to his desire "to create the rhythm of common objects in space and time, to present them in their plastic beauty."[23] Does he not misinterpret his film? Such "plastic beauty" as he, perhaps, presents in it is inherent in the rhythms rather than the objects overshadowed by them. If the intrinsic beauty of objects is found anywhere, it is in Dovzhenko's EARTH, not in the Léger film; and Dovzhenko reveals that beauty not by having his objects achieve impressive movements but, conversely, by showing them in a state of complete motionlessness.

All this amounts to saying that the real-life shots in the rhythmical *avant-garde* films suffer from emasculation. Instead of suggesting the continuum of physical existence from which they are elicited, they function as elements of compositions which, almost by definition, shut out nature in the raw. True, the devotees of visual music trained their camera on natural objects, but their formative aspirations, manifest in a permanent preoccupation with formal values and sundry movements, blunted their sense of the medium's affinity for the unstaged, the incidental, the not yet shaped. The "artist" in them won out over the "reader."

In their films the flow of rhythms—if it is a flow—continually disrupts the flow of life, and once they are isolated from the latter, the phenomena belonging to it cannot become eloquent. The images of the falling water drops and the mysterious alley in DISQUE 957 hold out a promise which, by no fault of theirs, is revoked instantly.

---

* Hans Richter in his GHOSTS BEFORE BREAKFAST borrowed this motif from the Léger film, the only difference being that he featured a man climbing a ladder instead of a woman trying to negotiate a flight of stairs.

There is reason to assume that exclusive concern with rhythmical editing not only proves a drain on the real-life material rendered but entails a tendency to move still further away from it in the direction of the abstract. This assumption is borne out by the frequent use made in pertinent *avant-garde* films of shots which picture "reality of another dimension" in such a manner that the real objects they represent change into abstract patterns. It has been pointed out in chapter 3 that images involving this border region are essentially ambiguous; depending on the contexts within which they appear, they may be identified as genuine abstractions or continue to impress us as real-life images.* And it has equally been drawn attention there to Deslav's 1928 experiment, LA MARCHE DES MACHINES, in which big close-ups of machine parts indulge in rhythmical evolutions, thereby completely renouncing their original realistic character. If it is not machine parts which serve as a starting-point for unreal forms, it is light reflections or growing crystals. Wherever rhythm is the *raison d'être* of films, one is justified in speaking of an irreversible movement from natural objects to nonobjective shapes. (Incidentally, this tendency seems to be on the increase: most rhythmic-minded contemporary experimenters in America—e.g., the Whitney brothers, Douglas Crockwell, Francis Lee, James E. Davis, etc.—try to steer clear of given nature altogether.[24])

It appears, then, that the trend in favor of rhythm reaches its climax with films which, like RHYTHM 21, the Fischinger studies, or to name a more modern example, Crockwell's GLENS FALLS SEQUENCE, feature autonomous abstractions. Technically, they are not infrequently animated cartoons or at least resemble them by reproducing shapes and movements created in specially prepared materials. If they attain to "plastic beauty," these creations are certainly enjoyable in their own right. Some amount to gay and amusing statements; others, alas, are rather boring. (Yet boredom and purely formal beauty need not be mutually exclusive.)

The question is whether rhythmical "symphonies," fully abstract or not, should be considered cinema at all. To the extent that they are animated cartoons they constitute a genre outside the photographic film proper and can therefore be disregarded at once. As for the rest of them, it is fairly obvious that their creators resort to film not as a photographic medium but as a means of setting imaginative designs, preferably nonobjective ones, in motion. On the whole, these films are not even intended as

* See pp. 49–50.

films; rather, they are intended as an extension of contemporary art into the dimension of movement and time. One might still argue that they are cinematic in as much as they implement their underlying intentions with the aid of techniques peculiar to film. But in doing so, they neglect the basic properties of the medium, which definitely take precedence over its technical properties. It is not by accident that such compositions give the impression of photographed paintings, with the time dimension added —especially in case they prefer abstractions to camera explorations. BALLET MECANIQUE with its tinge of cubism seems to come straight out of Léger's canvases. Like the prints of the experimental photographers, films emphasizing rhythm had better be classified as a new branch of the established arts.

Emphasis on content

SURREALISTIC FILMS

In the second half of the 'twenties the emphasis increasingly shifted from rhythm to content. The surrealistic movement then gathered momentum, and under its impact the *avant-garde* endeavored to transfer to the screen dream sequences, psychological developments, unconscious or subconscious processes, and the like—much of it inspired by Freud and to a lesser extent Marxism. Germaine Dulac's THE SEASHELL AND THE CLERGYMAN, which centered on a priest in the throes of forbidden sex desires, and Man Ray's L'ETOILE DE MER, which illustrated a love poem of Robert Desnos by means of distorted and artificially blurred images, marked a transition between rhythmical *cinéma pur*, with its indulgence in abstractions and cinematic language, and what may be called the "surrealistic" trend. The most original and representative surrealistic work of the period was Buñuel-Dali's UN CHIEN ANDALOU; its erratic and irrational imagery, which was plainly intended to subject the audience to a shock treatment à la Dada, seemed to spring from, and refer back to, a play of varied impulses in deep psychological layers. Cocteau's THE BLOOD OF A POET, a literary fantasy in pictures, also belongs to this group, his assertion to the contrary notwithstanding.* The trend is so little passé that it has been vigorously revived in America since World War II. Recent experimental films by Maya Deren, Curtis Harrington, Kenneth Anger, Gregory Marko-

---

* At the beginning of 1939, I attended a meeting of the Paris circle of the *Amis des Soules*, in which, prior to a screening of THE BLOOD OF A POET, a letter by Cocteau was read. Among other things, he declared in it that this film had nothing whatsoever to do with surrealism.

poulos, and others externalize sundry frustrations, inhibitions, and longings, with a certain predilection for the oblique emotional experiences of
adolescents, homosexual or not.[25] As compared with the old *avant-garde*
output, this new crop stresses more intensely feelings of alienation, while
being poorer in social and political overtones. It might be mentioned in
passing that Richter too has gone surrealist with his DREAMS THAT MONEY
CAN BUY.

Much as it would be tempting to comment on some important films
in the surrealistic vein, the task here is, rather, to ascertain the common
characteristics of the whole genre; only then will it be possible to appraise
its adequacy to the medium in the light of our basic assumptions. In the
case of the surrealistic trend it is perhaps indicated to state expressly what
is implied throughout—that such an appraisal need not have a direct
bearing on the value of films as human documents and manifestations of
collective fears or desires.

COMMON CHARACTERISTICS

Surrealism vs. abstraction   The surrealists of the late 'twenties were
quite aware that they dealt in content rather than form; that much can
be inferred from the insistence with which they repudiated one-sided
emphasis on rhythm and the concomitant use of nonobjective material.
Michel Dard, for instance, declared that films which confine themselves to
displaying "several geometrical lines painstakingly varied by [way of] all
tricks of the trade" were undeniably pure but that the term "pure," as
applied to them, "was synonymous with something congealed, short of
breath, and barren."[26] And according to the *avant-garde* poet Antonin
Artaud, who wrote the script of THE SEASHELL AND THE CLERGYMAN, we
just "remain insensible to pure geometrical shapes which in themselves
mean nothing."[27] Modern film artists in quest of self-expression do not
hesitate either to denounce abstract formalism. As Maya Deren puts it:
"My main criticism of the concept behind the usual abstract film is that
it denies the special capacity of film to manipulate real elements as
realities, and substitutes, exclusively, the elements of artifice (the method
of painting)."[28] Side by side with the abstract trend there existed, and
still exists, an urge for statements rich in meaningful content.

Prevalence of inner reality   The content itself evidently falls into the
area of fantasy. To be precise, it is fantasy which, by implication, claims to
be more real and weighty than the world of our senses. Add to this the
surrealists' understandable insouciance regarding staginess, as illustrated
by the donkey carcasses on the grand pianos in UN CHIEN ANDALOU or the
snow-covered court yard in THE BLOOD OF A POET. Yet we have already seen

in chapter 5 that such a film type—stagy fantasy of uncontested validity—
cannot help producing an uncinematic effect.*

And there the matter might rest were it not for the fact that surrealistic films have a trait in common which distinguishes them from the
rest of the films of fantasy. Unlike the bulk of the latter, they are based
on the belief that inner reality is infinitely superior to outer reality. In
consequence, their foremost objective is to render visible, without the aid
of a story or any other rational device, the stream of inner life and all that
it carries along in terms of instincts, dreams, visions, etc. It is not as if
the surrealists denied that the "outer skin of things, the epidermis of
reality . . . are the raw material of the cinema,"[29] but they unanimously
hold that this shadowy and ephemeral material gains significance only if
it is made to convey man's inward drives and concerns down to their unconscious roots.

Dali rejoices—he would—in the possibility for the artist "to systematize confusion and thus to help to discredit completely the world of
reality."[30] And of course, those film fans of the 'twenties who took their
cue from psychoanalysis were confident that the cinema was predestined
to "express the most profound mechanisms of our soul"[31] ** and "penetrate the caverns of the unconscious where the images perceived, with all
their associations of ideas, classify themselves."[32] (In the days of the
avant-garde these ideas ranged from Dada's attack against ingrained
conventions to anarchistic outbursts and revolutionary protests.) To the
surrealistic film makers, then, camera-reality is a sort of limbo; and they
seize on external phenomena for the sole purpose of representing the inner
world in its continuity. It is the only reality that matters to them.

PROBLEMATIC SYMBOLISM

But if shots of natural objects or stagy arrangements of them are to
denote the inner-life events around which any surrealistic film revolves,
they necessarily assume the function of signs, of symbols. And the burden
of signifying these events falls to them alone—except for the rare cases
in which they are given something to lean on in the form of a poem designed to serve as an intermediary between the imagery and the dreams or
visions which that imagery is supposed to make transparent. (Whenever
this happens—think of L'ETOILE DE MER with its captions of the Desnos
poem—the poem is likely to defeat its purpose in two alternative ways:
either it shares the fate of visualized music and turns into an unheeded
accompaniment;† or it retains the lead, which means the images will be

* See pp. 84–5.
** Cf. p. 66.
† See pp. 152–3.

degraded to sheer illustrations.) Whether or not the visuals in surrealistic films are always intended as symbols, it is inevitable that they should be conceived as such by the spectator.

The extant literature is crowded with interpretations along these lines. Commenting on UN CHIEN ANDALOU, Jacques Brunius observes that "in the scene where the young man is prepared to take the girl by erotic assault, what he drags behind him . . . at the end of two ropes . . . —corks, melons, priests, pianos filled with donkey-carrion—are the memories of his childhood and upbringing."[33] [Illus. 36] As might be expected, THE BLOOD OF A POET touched off exegesis in grand style. George Morrison, for instance, revels in decoding the film's pictorial ciphers: "The mirror through which the poet escapes from his prison is Truth, the mouth which comes alive is Illusion, the false suicide is a false ideal, not worth dying for, etc."[34] A litterateur rather than a film maker, Cocteau himself encouraged such high-flown conjectures. According to his own testimony, "the poet's solitude is so great, he so lives what he creates, that the mouth of one of his creations lives in his hand like a wound, and that he loves this mouth, that he loves himself, in short, that he wakes up in the morning with this mouth against him like a pick-up, that he tries to get rid of it, and that he gets rid of it on a dead statue."[35]

Hans Richter also feels called upon to act as self-interpreter; he has it that the "Narcissus" episode of his DREAMS THAT MONEY CAN BUY "follows Jung rather than Freud when Narcissus falls suddenly out of love with Narcissus and has to face his true self."[36] Sometimes authoritative explanations are not needed at all because of the clarity with which the manifest pictorial content projects the inner situation envisaged by the film maker at this particular point. When we see, with the eyes of the dreaming heroine of Maya Deren's MESHES OF THE AFTERNOON, a black-clad woman whose face is a mirror instead of a face, we immediately realize that the woman—she may be the dreamer herself—is a symbol, not an apparition, and that she symbolizes the dreamer's self-reflection in the wake of her compulsory isolation from her fellow-beings.

For obvious reasons surrealistic films as a rule draw more heavily than rhythmical compositions on real-life material. One familiar example is the fascinating and truly realistic shot of a small street crowd seen from far above in UN CHIEN ANDALOU. If this shot were integrated into contexts suggestive of camera-reality and the flow of life, it would invite us dreamily to probe into its indeterminate meanings. Yet actually we are not permitted to absorb it, for the symbolic function assigned to surrealistic images automatically prevents them from unfolding their inherent potentialities. Convinced of the immense significance of inner reality, the *avant-garde* surrealists—to speak only of the initiators of the trend—enhanced it in a medium with a natural affinity for external reality; they availed themselves of the camera in a literary rather than genuinely cinematic interest. The word-image of the mouth of a poet's creation living in his hand like a wound may be very poetic; from the angle of the cinema, however, the photographic picture of this strange hand signifies nothing but a real hand with a real, mouth-like wound in it—a natural, if inexplicable, phenomenon which does not possess the poetic quality of the word-image.* As early as 1925, René Clair, who, with his keen sense of the métier, could not help being aware of the strained meaningfulness and enforced staginess of surrealistic imagery, explicitly refused to believe "that the cinema is the best means of surrealistic expression." He cautiously added, though, that film "nevertheless remains a field of incomparable surrealistic activity for the mind of the spectator."[37]

In thus transferring surrealism from the screen to the spectator, Clair presumably wanted to hint at the manner in which films devoted to physical reality—cinematic films, that is—represent inner-life configurations. They are no less capable than surrealistic films of doing so, but they leave it to the spectator to apprehend their possible references to inward reality. With cinematic films symbols are not, surrealistic fashion, imposed from without on visuals selected or manufactured for the sole purpose of illustrating them; rather, they are a by-product—or an outgrowth, if you wish—of pictures whose main function it is to penetrate the external world. This differential treatment of symbols must be traced to the fact that, unlike cinematic films, surrealistic ones are intended as art in the traditional sense. Accordingly, they are more or less in the nature of a closed composition. And this in turn entails an imagery which exhausts itself in trying to project what its creator believes to have put into it. Since cinematic films on their part explore physical reality without ever completely consuming it, they will not so much feature as release symbolic meanings. Symbols true to the medium are invariably implied. Take the sled with the painted rosebud on it which, for a transient moment, emerges amidst the heap of junk at the end of CITIZEN KANE; the allusive long-distance shot of Rome after the execution scene in OPEN CITY; the lone horse at dawn in LA STRADA; the beautiful finale of CABIRIA with its enchanted woods in which tears and music, grief and the joy of living fuse into each other: to be sure, all these pictures admit of symbolic interpretation, but so does life which they faithfully portray, life whose every aspect points beyond itself.

---

* Similarly, Sève, "Cinéma et méthode," *Revue internationale de filmologie*, July-Aug. 1947, vol. I, no. 1: 45, says that "unlike a painted door, or a door on the stage, a door in the cinema has not the function of balancing, separating, or symbolizing, but merely [serves] to open and shut itself."

Conclusions

It appears, then, that the experimental film makers, whether favoring rhythmical abstractions or surrealistic projections of inner reality, approach the cinema with conceptions which alienate it from nature in the raw, the fountainhead of its peculiar power. Their formative aspirations gravitate toward achievements in the spirit of modern painting or literature—a preference for independent creativity which smothers their concern with camera explorations, their curiosity about reality at large. Liberating film from the tyranny of the story, they subject it to that of traditional art. In fact, they extend art into the cinema. "Help the development of film as a fine art form . . . ," reads a 1957 leaflet of the New York Creative Film Foundation. But the artist's freedom is the film maker's constraint.

One does well to remember, though, that the *avant-garde*'s experiments in cinematic language, rhythmical editing, and the representation of near-unconscious processes greatly benefited film in general. Nor should it be forgotten that, like Buñuel, many an *avant-garde* artist became realistic-minded and outward-bound; Joris Ivens and Cavalcanti, for instance, turned to social documentary.[38]

The Film of Fact

INTRODUCTION

Genres

THE OTHER TYPE of non-story film is the film of fact, so called because it shuns fiction in favor of unmanipulated material. In order to avoid dealing at length with classification problems insoluble anyway it is perhaps best to enter under this title the following three genres which may be supposed to cover all relevant variants: (1) the newsreel; (2) the documentary, including such subgenres as the travelogue, scientific films, instructional films, etc.; and (3) the relatively new species of the film on art. True, this last genre comprises a group of productions which have all the traits of experimental films, but the balance amounts exactly to the kind of films which John Read, a young art film maker, has in mind when he says that "one makes films about art and artists for the same reasons that one makes films about ships and shipbuilders or savage tribes in remote parts of the world."[1] * Otherwise expressed, many of these films have a documentary quality. It would therefore seem justified to treat the whole genre within the present chapter.

Characteristics

Except for those sequences of art films which picture works of art—works, that is, which reach into the dimension of unstaged reality without

---

* Read directed a film about Henry Moore. The films on Walter Sickert, John Piper, and Stanley Spencer he made at the B.B.C. Television Service were supervised by Paul Rotha who headed B.B.C.'s TV Documentary Department in 1953–5. (Personal communication by Mr. Rotha.) This may account for Read's insistence that art films should be documentary films about art and artists.

completely belonging to it*—factual films concentrate on actual physical existence. Of course this does not exclude staging and re-enacting, should the need arise, or the occasional use of charts and diagrams. Although both documentary and the newsreel reflect the real world, they differ in their approach to it. The latter shows, in a brief and neutral manner, current events of allegedly general interest, whereas documentaries elaborate on natural material for a variety of purposes, with the result that they may range from detached pictorial reports to glowing social messages.[2] These two genres date as far back as the childhood days of the medium; and they conform in varying degrees to what Mesguich once said about the cinema, meaning Lumière's: "Its lens opens on the world."**

Yet in the case of the film of fact it opens only on part of the world. Newsreels as well as documentaries feature not so much the individual and his inner conflicts as the world he lives in. In Rotha's words, documentary "depends on the individual's interest in the world around him." Anxious to drive home this point, Rotha continues: "If there are human beings, they are secondary to the main theme. Their private passions and petulances are of little interest."[3] This is of tremendous importance, the implication being that factual films do not explore all aspects of physical reality; they omit, for instance, those contingent on "private passions," as related by an intrigue. "Special modes of reality" seem to lie outside their possibilities. The consequences of this limitation in range will become apparent at the end of the chapter.

Scope of investigation

The newsreel does not pose problems that would invite comment within these contexts. It meets the minimum requirements of the cinematic approach as a matter of course, with the realistic tendency prevailing over the tendency toward form construction.† Actually, pronounced formative efforts would even interfere with the recording job assigned to the genre. Newsreel shots are all the more true to type if they retain the character of straightforward snapshots, testifying to on-the-spot improvisation rather than a concern for rounded-out composition. This is naturally not meant to minimize the significance of discerning selectivity in the shooting and editing of newsreel material.[4]

Nor need the instructional film be considered. Its objective is to transmit useful knowledge and special skills, and there is no definite correlation between cinematic treatment and the attainment of this goal.

* See p. 29.
** See p. 31.
† Cf. p. 38.

Some of the psychological films released by the National Film Board of Canada with a view to spreading awareness of mental disorders are bad cinema and good object lessons. It happens, of course, that perfect indoctrination goes together with high cinematic quality; for instance, the pictures which Sir Arthur Elton produced for the Shell Film Unit—think of his TRANSFER OF POWER—are both admirable pieces of education and excellent films. Yet in many a case the issue at stake precludes regard for the affinities of the medium. Occupational training films have often to rely predominantly on verbal explanations to deliver their particular message. One may even venture the assumption that cinematic penetrance is apt to divert audience attention from the learning process proper. Formally a subgenre of documentary, the instructional film more or less belongs to the family of audio-visual aids.

THE FILM ON ART

Art films have come into prominence since the last war. Before examining them, I should like to mention a phenomenon which seems to materialize whenever halfway realistic paintings and drawings, or rather, details of them, are being transferred to the screen. Provided it is really the moving camera, not the still camera, which records these landscapes or portraits, their screen reproductions evoke three-dimensional life more vividly than do the originals themselves.

Gain in three-dimensional naturalness

This easily observable effect may be tentatively traced to the following three factors. First, the moviegoer expects to be confronted with images of given reality. And due to this expectation, he will spontaneously be inclined to think of shots detailing a realistic canvas as photographic records of the three-dimensional objects represented on it. He might feel tempted, for instance, to identify the image of a woman's head in a Rubens portrait with a shot of the living model herself. In consequence, the pictures seem to gain in spatial depth.

Second, the practice, customary especially with experimental art film makers, of compartmentalizing a painting without showing the whole of it—a practice which no art critic will readily endorse*—is likely to sustain

* Bolen, "Films and the Visual Arts," in Bolen, ed., *Films on Art: Panorama 1953* (French edition: p. 7 n.), mentions that at the Amsterdam Congress of the International Art Film Federation an art critic requested the directors of art films to reproduce, in each film on a work of art, that work in its entirety at the beginning of the film.

this illusion. If the spectator does not learn what a painting in its frame looks like, he lacks a frame of reference which would tell him where the close-ups of that painting belong; as a result, they take on the character of free-floating entities. Think of a close-up of the Rubens woman: assuming its position in the portrait remains undefined, it inevitably challenges our imagination to complement its fragmentary existence by incorporating it into contexts of our choice. Here is where the moviegoer's expectations come in. They are largely responsible for his impression that the isolated head partakes of the indeterminacy of real-life phenomena and thus keep him further away from the head in the portrait, where it is part and parcel of an artistic composition which determines its functions and meanings. Precisely by decomposing any such whole, the film maker endows the imagery with a semblance of life as it evolves outside the aesthetic dimension.

Third, one might ask whether slide projections of the details of a painting are not on a par with film shots of the same details in this respect.[5] A few random observations tend to suggest that, all other conditions being equal, the film pictures exceed the slides in naturalness. The reason is presumably the addition of movement in film. There is no film on art in which the camera would not do a great deal of panning, traveling, and tilting. And these movements infallibly call forth kinesthetic responses—a "resonance effect" which causes the spectator to project the spatial sensations he experiences in its wake into his simultaneous perceptions. So he will attribute natural fullness to a group of flat figures or fancy himself meandering through a painted valley.

This partiality for the three-dimensional even persists when the camera occasionally discontinues its rambling to dwell on some significant detail; the resultant "stills" then affect us as transient lulls in an over-all movement rather than regular slide projections and, hence, retain the quality of pictures taken by the moving camera. Certain movements are particularly fit to breathe life into a painting. No sooner does the camera approach a stationary object or move away from it at right angles than we are confident that it is the object itself which changes its place. The use of these devices in art films benefits the illusion that painted people are on the point of moving about like real people, or just now stop moving to compose a *tableau vivant*.

The experimental trend

The experimental film maker approaches a painting not with the intention of rendering it in some way or other so as to reveal its inherent

values but out of a desire to use it as a point of departure for new creations. Exactly like the *avant-garde*, which was not content with exploring
nature, he refuses to be cast in the role of a "reader" who acknowledges
the given work of art as a sacrosanct text. To him the art work is nothing
but raw material[6] which he shapes according to his visions. This he can
accomplish only if he "atomizes" the work and reintegrates the atoms or
elements thus isolated into films which may or may not refer back to the
original. The film of this type, says Read, "exploits art purely for its own
filmic purpose. It may be that it seeks to achieve effects which have little
to do with the spirit of the work it uses."[7] As an objection to the experimental art film this statement is hardly conclusive, for it fails to take into
account the fact that within the traditional arts themselves transfers of
works of art from their own medium to another are fairly frequent and
are considered quite legitimate. Piranesi in his engravings utilized pieces
of antique architecture to compose his baroque prospects and operatic
vistas; Watteau in his *Fêtes champêtres* drew French and Italian fountain
sculptures into the festive bustle about them so that they seemed to
mingle with the humans. Why should not the cinema be entitled to effect
such transfers?

Judging from the available evidence, experimental art film makers
proceed in ways which are in a measure cinematic. As has already been
mentioned above, they keep the camera moving all the time, thereby
counterbalancing the intrinsic immobility of the material presented. Add
to this the systematic exploration of editing possibilities and various
cinematic devices. There are transitions from reality as suggested by the
art works to "reality of another dimension," shifts of emphasis from the
meanings, say, of a painted face to its material qualities, etc. It almost
looks as if the run of experimental art films surpassed the bulk of feature
films in knowingly involving the technical properties of the medium.

And what is cinematic language used for? Sometimes the art film
maker aims at reconstructing a historical period with the aid of contemporary paintings and drawings; whenever this happens, his formative aspirations are obviously geared to near-realistic intentions. A good case in point
is Luciano Emmer's GOYA, which depicts life in eighteenth-century Spain
as formed by the painter. This film is of interest technically because
Emmer tries hard to redeem the Goya figures from their stationary existence. He handles them as though they were real-life people engaged in
action. A scene with a pierrot thrown up into the air by girls, who hold
out a net to catch him again, is rendered by a quick succession of shots
from different angles which so animate the scene that you seem to follow
the pierrot's trajectory and expect him to land in the net any moment. An
accelerated montage of details of bullfight etchings comes close to creating

the dramatic suspense inseparable from the actual event. And as with real crowds, a mixture of long shots and close-ups is used to capture the painted ones. Or to cite another example, remember that sequence in MOULIN ROUGE in which, in Parker Tyler's words, "Lautrec's dance-hall figures are run swiftly before the eye and intercut to produce the *impression* of real action in the famous café"[8] Since altogether these technical procedures are instrumental in establishing physical reality itself on the screen, the spectator, accustomed to the use normally made of them, will all the more be disposed to take for granted what is insinuated in their application to paintings—that the objects he sees are "drawings brought to life" and therefore form part of unstaged reality. Art films in the manner of GOYA have much in common with those historical films which, like Dreyer's DAY OF WRATH, are patterned on period paintings. Consequently, all that has been said about the cinematic qualities of the Dreyer film* also holds true of them: they make the spectator (who naturally knows that the whole real-life magic is derived from lifeless material) experience nascent movement; and they have the ring of authenticity. One might conceive of these art films as historical documentaries, in a sense. In about the same vein are such "montage" films as Mercanton's *1848*, the biographical sequences of THE TITAN, or LINCOLN SPEAKS AT GETTYSBURG by Lewis Jacob and Paul Falkenberg: they resuscitate the spirit of a bygone era through an appropriate assemblage of its remains, artistic or otherwise, and thus profit by the camera's faculty of reproducing faithfully everything before the lens.

Other experimental art films give the impression of resulting from two divergent pursuits. Their authors, it appears, not only aspire to free artistic compositions but go in for indoctrination as well. On the one hand, they indulge their creative urges, often fragmentizing the art work with little regard for its peculiar structure (which may be in a cinematic interest); on the other, they play the part of the art critic or historian of art, trying to arrange the material accordingly (which may serve an educational purpose). Storck-Haesaerts' RUBENS, for instance, combines cinematically brilliant camera penetrations of the painter's world with an attempt to drive home his predilection for gyrational movements. Note that this film is neither pure cinema nor merely a teaching instrument. It is a glamorous hybrid. From an educational angle such hybrids are problematic, for they half-heartedly assume functions which the instructional film, with its straight exposition of all relevant data, is better equipped to fulfill.

The experimental art film comes fully into its own when its creator,

* See pp. 81–2.

unconcerned for any outside purpose, aims at building from the elements of the paintings used a self-contained whole as valid artistically as the originals. Like experimental films in general, these creations may emphasize rhythm or content. To begin with the former, think of those sequences of THE TITAN focusing on Michelangelo's sculptures: gliding at close range along them, the camera distils from their surfaces flat rhythmical patterns of lights and shadows.[9] Small wonder that Calder's mobiles, which are a natural for abstractions, have repeatedly given rise to similar exercises.[10] Compositions featuring content usually evoke a sort of spiritual reality; as Bolen puts it, they mold the art material according to "metaphysical, esoteric, and philosophical considerations."[11] In his CARPACCIO'S LEGEND OF ST. URSULA, Emmer juxtaposes scattered details of the paintings so as to make them bear out the legend narrated by an invisible speaker. (To simplify matters, the relations between sound and visuals in art films will not be covered here.) Of DEMON IN ART Bolen rightly says that its author, Enrico Castelli Gattinara, "does not hesitate to express his own conception of the world with the aid of materials borrowed from Bosch, Memling, or James Ensor."[12] This trend reaches, perhaps, its climax with Storck-Micha's LE MONDE DE PAUL DELVAUX in which, to the accompaniment of a poem by Paul Eluard, figures, objects, and fragments of the artist's works jell into a dream-like universe. Is it Delvaux's, experienced from within? In any case, it is not his paintings. Configurations of phenomena all but unidentifiable in them jut out on the screen and challenge the audience to guess their meanings; and camera movements establish contexts of which the painter himself may have been entirely unaware. The films of this last group employ cinematic language not to transfer the work of art from the orbit of the fine arts to that of the cinema but to metamorphose it into an autonomous screen work which again claims to be Art. Whether abstractions or compositions with a surrealistic flavor, they are an extension of contemporary art rather than genuine films. The center of the medium lies elsewhere.

The documentary trend

Nearer to the center are those art films which, according to Read's definition, are made "for the same reasons that one makes films about ships and shipbuilders or savage tribes." And for what reasons does one make them? They are made not simply to represent ships—or primitive masks, for that matter—but to incorporate these objects with the real-life developments from which they emerge. Similarly, films on art which follow the documentary tendency do not isolate the work of art and feature it as an autonomous entity; rather, in keeping with the medium's affinity for natural material they try to make the work appear as an element of actuality. Paintings resemble musical production numbers in that they do not essentially belong to the common everyday world which attracts the camera; hence the need for reintegrating them into that world in which they have a foothold also, after all. So it is not surprising that the methods used for the adjustment of musical performances to camera-life are applied in art documentaries as well.*

Two of them have become standard practice; they frequently concur in one and the same film. First, representations of paintings are embedded in a narrative devoted to their creator—his life circumstances, his ideas, etc. A typical film of this kind is GRANDMA MOSES, which mingles glimpses of the venerable lady's art with scenes of her life in the countryside. In order to intensify the real-life atmosphere in which the camera can breathe, the biographical statements are sometimes supplemented by shots of the people and landscapes from which the artist has taken his inspiration. LUST FOR LIFE, a feature film about Van Gogh, indulges in such confrontations of art and reality. Along with the Toulouse-Lautrec film, MOULIN ROUGE, this screen biography can be considered a counterpart of the many music films whose renditions of concert pieces and the like seem organically to grow out of the romanticized life of a virtuoso or singer. It need not be a biographical sketch; occasionally the artist is introduced as his own commentator, with the emphasis on his thoughts, his whole outlook. Numbers of art documentaries thus meet John Read's dictum, which he himself follows in his HENRY MOORE, WALTER SICKERT, etc.—that "the film on art should be about art and artists."[13] The art works exhibited in these films either function like stage interludes, increasing, by way of contrast, the spectator's sensitivity to the incidental events about them, or help implement the human-interest story with which they are interwoven. (Whether this gain in cinematic quality always serves the cause of art appreciation is quite another question.)

Second, as with Duvivier's THE GREAT WALTZ, which shows Johann Strauss composing his *Tales from the Vienna Woods*, other art documentaries concentrate on the genesis of a work of art rather than the work itself. The principle is the same here and there: since the finished work lends itself to being rendered on the screen only in as much as the cinema is also a reproduction technique, the film maker prefers to present the work not as it is but as it becomes; in other words, he has us witness the creative processes from which it arises. In picturing the prenatal stages of a painting, he lures it back into the very dimension which is the camera's hunting ground. This procedure is strikingly illustrated by Henri-Georges Clouzot's THE MYSTERY OF PICASSO, in which the camera, often placed be-

* Cf. pp. 149–51.

hind the translucent "canvas" on which the artist is painting, faithfully records his activities. [Illus. 37] So we are permitted to watch the act of creation. It is a most exciting spectacle. Once Picasso has outlined what he appears to have in mind, he immediately superposes upon his initial sketch a second one which more often than not relates only obliquely to it. In this way it goes on and on, each new system of lines or color patches all but ignoring its predecessor. It is as though, in creating, Picasso were overwhelmed by a cataract of intentions and/or impulses so that the ultimate product may well be a far cry from the first draft now buried under a mass of seemingly incoherent structures.

If an artist's creative labors cannot be observed directly, there still remains the possibility of conveying an impression of them through a "montage" of his successive attempts to substantiate his vision. "In a documentary on Matisse," says Tyler, "we are shown how the artist developed his conception of a head in a series of sketches from a quasi-naturalistic version to the final form. This was done by superimposing the finished sketches transparently so that an illusion of the organic evolution was obtained."[14]

DOCUMENTARY

Whatever their purpose, documentaries have a penchant for actuality. And do they not rely on non-actors? To all appearances they cannot help being true to the medium. Upon closer inspection, however, this bias in their favor turns out to be unwarranted. Aside from the fact, to be considered later on, that documentaries do not explore the visible world to the full, they differ strongly in their behavior toward physical reality. To be sure, part of them manifest sincere concern for nature in the raw, carrying messages which palpably emanate from their camera work, their imagery. But numbers of documentaries seem to be motivated by other concerns. Even though their authors also resort to natural material as a matter of course, they care little about utilizing it for the implementation of their objectives. In these films formative impulses dissociated from the realistic tendency assert themselves at the expense of the latter.

Concern about material reality

REPORTAGE

There are then, roughly speaking, two groups of documentaries, one conforming to the cinematic approach, the other indifferent to it. To begin with the films of the first group—those in which the visuals serve as the main source of communication—many among them are hardly more than straight pictorial records of this or that segment of the world around us. No doubt their "objectivity" is bought at the price of intensity. Yet impersonal as they may be—recalling the image which Proust's narrator formed of his grandmother when watching her with the eyes of a stranger—they do meet the minimum requirement of the medium.

A perfect example is the early British documentary HOUSING PROBLEMS, a plea for better housing done mostly by interviewing housewives of the London slums in front of the camera. Cinematically, this report is anything but exciting, for it confines itself to photographic statements which could not be plainer. [Illus. 38] Now note that their plainness is in harmony with the whole character of the film. HOUSING PROBLEMS visibly rests upon the conviction that you cannot get mature people interested in the issues at stake unless you show them what life in the slums is like. So Edgar Anstey and Arthur Elton, the directors of this documentary, quite sensibly confront the spectator with real slum dwellers and have him listen to their complaints about rats, broken ceilings, and plumbing.[15] (The large role assigned to the verbal contributions may be discounted here for the sake of argument; this is all the more possible since much information flows from the visuals also.) The thing that matters is veracity; and it is precisely the snapshot quality of the pictures which makes them appear as authentic documents. An aesthetically more impressive depiction of the slums might indeed have interfered with the intended effect by inducing the audience to conceive of the film as a subjective comment rather than an unbiased report. The commonplace photography in HOUSING PROBLEMS is a product of deliberate self-restraint on the part of its directors. Significantly, Graham Greene praises Anstey for having been "superbly untroubled by the aesthetic craving."[16] Perhaps the film is free from any such craving also because of its theme. Joris Ivens relates that during the shooting of BORINAGE, a documentary about the miners in this Belgian coal district, he and Henri Storck realized that their very subject demanded that they turn from aesthetic refinement to photographic "simplicity." [Illus. 39] "We felt it would be insulting to people in such extreme hardship to use any style of photography that would prevent the direct honest communication of their pain to every spectator."[17] Human suffering, it appears, is conducive to detached reporting; the artist's conscience shows in artless photographs.

IMAGINATIVE READINGS

However, self-restraint is not always a virtue. His preference for strict veracity notwithstanding, the documentary maker may approach the locales before his lens with an irrepressible sense of participation. There are in fact documentaries which mark a transition between straight records and more personal readings. For instance, IN THE STREET, a documentary about New York City, has an emotional quality absent, or at least largely subdued, in HOUSING PROBLEMS. On the one hand, this film is nothing but a reportage pure and simple; its shots of Harlem scenes are so loosely juxtaposed that they almost give the impression of a random sample. A child behind a window is seen licking the pane; a woman with a terrible face passes by; a young man languidly watches the spectacle in the street; Negro children, intoxicated by their Halloween masks, dance and romp about with complete self-abandon. On the other hand, this reporting job is done with unconcealed compassion for the people depicted: the camera dwells on them tenderly; they are not meant to stand for anything but themselves. (As a notebook-like assemblage of on-the-spot observations, the film is also expressive of an outspoken, very cinematic susceptibility to street incidents. These assets, however, are not without a drawback; the lack of structure which results is at variance with, and weakens, the film's emotional intensity.)

Documentaries like IN THE STREET still cling to the form of the matter-of-fact account. But this need not be so. The film maker's concern for unbiased reporting (which inevitably entails straight photography) may yield to an urge to picture reality in the light of his views and visions. His formative impulses will then prompt him to select the natural material according to his inner images, to shape it with the aid of the techniques available to him, and to impose upon it patterns which would not be fitting for a reportage. As long as his imagination is kindled by the given objects his film will more likely than not realize potentialities of the medium. Veracious reproductions are thus superseded by pictorial penetrations or interpretations of the visible world.

Documentaries of this kind—part of them can be traced to the *avant-garde* of the 'twenties—are not infrequent. Here belongs, for instance, Ivens's RAIN, whose theme represented a challenge to his "aesthetic craving" rather than an obligation for him to revert to photographic "simplicity"; Painlevé's THE SEA HORSE, which reveals the wonders of the submarine universe; and NIGHT MAIL, in which Basil Wright and Harry Watt evoke the nightly run of a postal train from London to Edinburgh as it might be experienced by those in love with the road. In all three films the directors' quest for poetic expression is subordinated to their involvement in the objects themselves. The poetry of NIGHT MAIL, which at the end even emancipates itself from the visuals to assume independence of a sort in Auden's spoken verse, is still the poetry of the real postal train and of the night enveloping it. What characterizes these films is indeed their devotion to the hieroglyphs of the train, the sea horse, and the rain—the very devotion which once caused Rossellini to reprimand a cameraman for removing an isolated white rock which seemed to him inconsistent with all the dark rocks that covered the field they were about to shoot.

This field, Rossellini told the cameraman, had been there a hundred, maybe a thousand years, and it had taken nature that long to fashion the field and to distribute and color the rocks, and what right had he, the cameraman, to think he could improve on nature?[18] (Confront Rossellini's attitude toward nature with Eisenstein's: when the latter was shooting the road scenes of BEZHIN MEADOW he insisted on the removal of two kilometers of telephone poles because he believed them to deface the scenery. It should be noted that the film features an episode of the contemporary Soviet campaign for farm collectivization and that telephone poles have a way of fusing with the landscape to which they belong. While Eisenstein unhesitatingly reshapes the given environment to make it conform to what his biographer Marie Seton calls his "creative vision,"[19] Rossellini starts from the premise that the cinema opens its lens on the physical world and only through it, perhaps, on the spirit. With Eisenstein nature is imperfect as compared to a freely created theatrical design, whereas for Rossellini the design of nature is the fountainhead of all visions.)

As penetrations of the "wide world"[20] which pay respect to the stray rock in the field, Flaherty's documentaries are a unique achievement. From NANOOK OF THE NORTH to LOUISIANA STORY they affectionately acknowledge that which exists—still exists, one is tempted to add in view of their absorption in primitive cultures. Their singular beauty is a reward for patient waiting till things begin to speak. There is much time invested in them, and, of course, the patience goes together with sensitivity to the slow interaction between man and nature, man and man.

In the films considered so far devotion to the natural world sets the tune. Now imagine that the documentary maker's desire to express his visions or ideas steadily gains momentum, even though what he wants to express may resist cinematic treatment: when a certain point is reached, this desire will almost match in strength his otherwise realistic inclinations. But since, according to premise, at that point the latter are still more powerful, if by a narrow margin, than his disengaged formative intentions, the balance established between the two antagonistic tendencies does not run counter to the preferences of the medium. It is a precarious balance, though; and the films in which it materializes are borderline cases.

Such a case is, perhaps, SONG OF CEYLON. This beautiful documentary about Singhalese life includes an apparently Russian-inspired "montage" sequence which tries to epitomize the impact of Western civilization on native custom. European voices from the London Stock Exchange, ship-ping agencies, and business offices form a crisscross pattern of sounds which is synchronized with shots illustrating the actual spread of indus-trialization and its consequences for a pre-industrial population. Com-pared with Louisiana Story, where the inroads made by industry in a primitive society are pictured in purely cinematic terms, this sequence has the character of a construction; intellectual argument prevails over visual observation. Yet the whole sequence is embedded in passages featuring camera-reality. Thus it acquires traits of an interlude. And as such it deepens the impression of cinematic life around it.

Another case in point is the UNESCO film World Without End made by Paul Rotha in Mexico and Basil Wright in Thailand. The film depicts ordinary people in these underdeveloped countries—their daily life as well as the beneficent help they are receiving from the advisers and medical teams sent out to them by UNESCO. As Rotha puts it, World Without End carries the basic theme "of there being one world in which we are all neighbours."[21] It is an ideological theme; and the commentator, aside from doing a great deal of explaining, drives home the message of goodwill in sententious statements. So there is a real danger lest his pleas might lure the spectator into realms where material phe-nomena no longer count much. However, this bent toward the spiritual, as transmitted through words, is counterbalanced in several ways. First, the two directors implement the one-world idea within the visual dimension itself by linking areas 10,000 miles apart through meaningful similari-ties and common topics. Mexicans and Siamese alike catch fish for a liv-ing and crowd the colorful markets; and, time and again, United Nations experts fight the drought in Mexico, the skin disease in Thailand, and ignorance everywhere. Note that this cutting on resemblances, elementary needs, and humanitarian efforts does not level all exotic charms and cul-tural differences: a squatting Buddha puts up with the trucks on the highway; a dilapidated Mexican village church glistens in the harsh light as if petrified with eternity.

Second, the spoken word is frequently superseded by actual sound; firecrackers explode noisily, and people are singing and dancing in their leisure time. Far from being merely a digression, these spectacles bear out the basic theme; and they call all the more for attention since they occur in the absence of purposeful speech. Third, Wright and Rotha seem to have fallen in love with the people they picture. Their camera lingers on cured Siamese children aglow with happiness and visibly hesitates to turn away from a group of old and young Indian faces. Shots like these radiate a warmth which by itself suggests the idea behind the film. True, World Without End spreads a message which may be put across effectively without elaborate references to the physical world, but the directors manage to discover in this very world much of what they are supposed to convey. Their formative intention to propagate the ideal of the "family of man" is largely reconciled with their realistic attitude, their insistence on camera-life.*

Within this border region a slight shift of emphasis suffices to upset the precarious "right" balance between the realistic and formative tendencies. In Willard Van Dyke's VALLEY TOWN they overtly vie with each other for ascendancy. As long as this documentary about an American industrial town in depression surveys the past—work in the factories, the years of prosperity, increasing unemployment caused by improved machinery—it is a first-rate visual report with sparse commentary. But no sooner does Van Dyke arrive at the era of depression, with its misery and suffering, than the artist in him seems to rebel against the limitations of a medium requiring him to cling to the epidermis of things. He himself relates the experiences that led him and his collaborators to change their approach while the film was taking shape: "There was one thing missing. We felt that somehow we must get inside the people's minds. . . . What does the workman think when he begins to lose his skill? We knew well enough what he would say, but that wasn't enough. We'd have to find a way to let his thoughts speak for him."[22] They found a way, alas. The second and main part of VALLEY TOWN culminates in episodes of the depression period which revolve around a worker and his wife—to be precise, around their inner life, for the shots of them are synchronized with echo-chamber voices designed to verbalize the thoughts and emotions of these two people. Something inside them, we are asked to believe, speaks up and screams or even indulges in singing. Yet in exposing the minds of the worker and his wife, Van Dyke strips their outward appearance of meaning, which is all the more confusing since he often fills the whole screen with their faces. Of course, these close-ups and big close-ups—which, were they left to themselves, would be quite able to do all the talking needed—are lost on a spectator whom the ghostly soliloquies transform, willy-nilly, into a mind reader.

Indifference to material reality

VALLEY TOWN marks a divide within this grouping of documentaries. From there the way leads straight to films indifferent to the visible world. Among the possible reasons for their indifference two are of interest here: the one-sided concern with formal relationships between the images uti-

---

* There are also recent imaginative readings which border on the experimental film. A fine example is Shirley Clarke's SKYSCRAPER which resumes, somehow, the traditions of the *avant-garde* documentary of the 'twenties. (See pp. 180–81.)

lized and, much more frequent, the preoccupation with mental rather than physical reality.

PREVALENCE OF FORMAL RELATIONSHIPS

Walter Ruttmann's classic, BERLIN, once and for all illustrates the implications of a formalistic approach. This "Symphony of a Great City" is particularly intriguing because it has the makings of a truly cinematic documentary: its candid shots of streets and their extensions are selected and arranged with an admirable sense of photographic values and transient impressions. And yet the film does not fulfill its promise. Ruttmann establishes his cross sections of Berlin everyday life by juxtaposing shots which resemble each other in shape and movement; or he uses crude social contrasts as linkages; or he turns, LA MARCHE DES MACHINES fashion, parts of moving machinery into near-abstract rhythmical patterns.

Now it is inevitable that such cutting on analogies, extreme differences and rhythms should divert audience attention from the substance of the images to their formal characteristics. This perhaps accounts for Rotha's verdict on the "surface approach" of BERLIN.[23] Due to Ruttmann's formalistic approach, which may have resulted from his notions of art as well as his fear of committing himself, the objects pictured function mainly as the constituents of such and such relationships so that their content threatens to evaporate. True, these relationships seem intended to render the "tempo" of Berlin, but tempo is also a formal conception if it is not defined with reference to the qualities of the objects through which it materializes.[24] Compare BERLIN with ENTR'ACTE: like Ruttmann, Clair interlinks dissimilar objects according to their surface similarities; yet unlike Ruttmann, he does so in a playful spirit. ENTR'ACTE toys with real-life phenomena, thereby acknowledging them in their integrity, whereas BERLIN, with a complete lack of playfulness, emphasizes resemblances and contrasts of phenomena, and thus superimposes upon them a network of ornamental relationships that tend to substitute for the things from which they are derived.

PREVALENCE OF MENTAL REALITY

Documentary makers are often so exclusively concerned with conveying propositions of an intellectual or ideological nature that they do not even try to elicit them from the visual material they exhibit. In this case mental reality takes precedence over physical reality. Even before the appearance of sound such messages were delivered from the screen with complete indifference to the content of the images; then the task of disseminating them naturally fell to the subtitles and the visuals themselves. In the 'twenties, possessed with the idea of an "intellectual cinema" that would culminate in the adaptation of Marx's *Capital*, Eisenstein relied mainly on pictures to touch off thought processes and attitudes in the spirit of dialectical materialism. He had learned too well the lesson of Griffith's INTOLERANCE: along with its admirable "montage" methods, he also assimilated its less exemplary lapses into pictorial symbolism. Remember the ludicrous recurrent image of the rocking cradle in INTOLERANCE, used to symbolize the mysterious births and rebirths of time, or history, or life: out of this very cradle come many shots in Eisenstein's own films TEN DAYS THAT SHOOK THE WORLD and OLD AND NEW. One shot shows Kerensky together with a peacock spreading its plumage, the stereotyped symbol of vanity; hands playing harps satirize the futility of Menshevist peace pledges; an enoromus typewriter dwarfs the typist behind it, evoking the notion of dehumanized bureaucracy. Yet the use of these objects as signs or symbols voids the shots of them of their inherent meanings. They stand for something outside them; any peacock would do, indeed. While the peacock is a familiar symbol, other elements of Eisenstein's picture language are all but unintelligible. There is, in TEN DAYS, a sequence picturing the deities of various peoples; it ranges from a baroque Christ whom we accept unquestioningly down to an exotic Eskimo idol. And what is the sequence intended to signify? This chain of images, says Eisenstein himself, "attempted to achieve a purely intellectual resolution, resulting from a conflict between a preconception and a *gradual discrediting of it in purposeful steps*."[25]

In other words, he is confident that the sight of the primitive idol at the end of the descending series will alienate the audience from the Christ at its beginning. Yet the odds are that, at least in democratic countries, the purpose of the sequence eludes the grasp of the spectator; it impresses him as an aimless assemblage of religious images rather than an attack on religion. Eisenstein overestimates the signifying power of images and accordingly goes the limit in overlaying their intrinsic meanings with those he sees fit to confer upon them. Pudovkin also indulged in symbolism. In the Russia of the period, revolutionary reality did not seem real unless it could be interpreted as an outgrowth of the Marxist doctrine. Hence the inclination of the Russian film directors to misuse the visuals as references to the ruling ideology. Small wonder, for the rest, that it is precisely the symbolic shots and scenes in the Eisenstein films which have least withstood the passing of time. They now affect us as the artifices they are—rebuses which, once solved, lose all their magic. (Under the impact of "social realism" Eisenstein was later to recant his dream of an "intellectual cinema";[26] this did not prevent him from assigning further symbolic functions to the pictures, though. His upward drive toward the significant, cinematic or not, was irrepressible.)

Upon the advent of sound, documentary makers preoccupied with mental reality were in a position to resort to the spoken word, decidedly the most suitable vehicle for conceptual reasoning and ideological communications. It was the easiest way out. So pictorial symbolism by and large yields to excessive commentary—a change in style which has given rise to the misconception that the uncinematic neglect of the visuals must be laid to the dominance of speech. This is not so. Rather, the example of the silent Russian films proves conclusively that the dominance of speech itself results from the primary concern with intellectual or ideological topics and that it is essentially the absorption in the latter which accounts for that neglect.

Documentaries exploring mental reality with the aid of speech have already been discussed in chapter 9; it has also been mentioned there that they usually follow the pattern set by the MARCH OF TIME.* What still remains to be considered is the sad fate of their imagery. Do the visuals at least illustrate the self-contained verbal narration which is the very backbone of these films? Take OUR RUSSIAN ALLY, one of the Canadian WORLD IN ACTION documentaries which Grierson produced or supervised during World War II in an effort to imbue topical information with propaganda appeals: it includes a passage in which a few shots of Russian soldiers and tanks moving through the snow languish on the screen while the commentator holds forth:

From the trenches of Leningrad to the gates of Rostov they stood to arms all through the bitter winter of 1941. All winter long they wrote across the blood-stained snow a chapter of heroism of which the greatest armies of history might be proud. And come what may, on this two thousand mile battlefront where the titanic forces of the swastika and the red badge of courage struggle for dominion over one-sixth of the earth's surface, Russia knows that her true war power lies not alone in arms and equipment but in the inner spirit of a people.[27]

This scene with the voice from the tomb is quite typical, as can be inferred from the verdict which Richard Griffith passes on many films of the WORLD IN ACTION series. Their visuals, says he "were slapped to the portentous, stentorian commentary in a fashion so meaningless as to leave the spectator neither knowing nor caring what he was looking at; he might as well have been at home listening to a broadcast."[28] Griffith's criticism is very much to the point. The few shots of Russian soldiers and tanks in the above example have no recognizable bearing whatever on the wordy eulogy of Russian heroism with which they are synchronized. Not only does the sheer impact of the commentator's oratory automatically smother

* See p. 119.

all communications they might be able to make on their own, but his statement involves subjects and ideas which elude pictorial representation. Accordingly, the scattered tank and soldier columns in the snow are not even illustrations; they do not, and indeed cannot, illustrate the two thousand mile battlefront or the titanic struggle.

Nor does the presence of sweeping symbolic language permit them to function as symbols. What, then, is their function? They are stopgaps. The recourse to such stopgaps is by no means a consequence of the frequent necessity for the documentary maker to utilize stock material; granted that this necessity represents a serious handicap, he is still in a position to draw on the meanings of the footage available. And it need not be a lack of craftsmanship either which makes him insert plain duds. Rotha's sense of the medium is unquestioned, but in his documentary on food, WORLD OF PLENTY, made in the middle of the last world war, even Rotha is obliged to combine the running verbal argumentation with images of crowds and cornfield which are as unspecific as they are meaningless. Visual stopgaps become inevitable whenever dominant speech ventures into unpicturable dimensions. The reason is obvious: as the speaker proceeds, something has to be put on the screen, yet nothing visible really corresponds to his words.

This reliance on speech and the concomitant indifference to the visuals finds support in Grierson's idea of documentary. Grierson, who initiated and promoted the British documentary movement, instilled new life into the genre while at the same time estranging it from its cinematic roots. He himself admits his relative unconcern for film as film. In Grierson's words, the "documentary idea," meaning his own, "was not basically a film idea at all, and the film treatment it inspired only an incidental aspect of it. The medium happened to be the most convenient and most exciting available to us. The idea itself, on the other hand, was a new idea for public education: its underlying concept that the world was in a phase of drastic change affecting every manner of thought and practice, and the public comprehension of that change vital."[29] To him and his collaborators, then, film, in particular documentary, is a medium of mass communication like the newspaper or the radio, a propitious means of spreading civic education in a period and world in which the strength of democracy more than ever depends upon the spread of information and universal goodwill.

From the angle of the Grierson approach Rotha's "argument film"[30] WORLD OF PLENTY with its "multi-voiced narration"[31] is of course perfect screen propaganda. In this brilliant intellectual reportage, plain people, farmers, politicians, and food experts from various corners of the Anglo-Saxon world are seen—or rather, heard—discussing problems of food

production and distribution—an orderly sequence of arguments which culminates in a humane and passionate plea for a "world food plan" once
the war is over. The film makes good use of the cinematic device of "creative geography,"* without, however, being a genuine film. Nor was it
intended as such; rather, it was a deliberate extension of the American
"Living Newspaper" series of the 'thirties, those stylized stage productions
which dramatized crucial issues of the New Deal era. Now it is quite
true that genuine films cannot deliver language-bound messages in the
manner of the WORLD IN ACTION films or WORLD OF PLENTY; but is it not
equally true that the restrictions imposed upon them are more than compensated for by the incomparable power of their visual appeals and suggestions? Grierson is aware of this, as follows from his observation, already
quoted in earlier contexts, that "in documentary you do not shoot with
your head only but also with your stomach muscles."**

Evidently, his dictum applies not so much to documentaries over-
saturated with verbal communications as to propaganda films steeped in
physical reality—POTEMKIN or WORLD WITHOUT END. Perhaps Grierson's
greatest merit is that his uncinematic documentary idea did not blind
him to the contributions of film directors whom he considers impression-
ists or "aesthetes"; NIGHT MAIL and SONG OF CEYLON were made under his
auspices. "I may say," he remarks in retrospect, "that we soon joined
forces with men like Flaherty and Cavalcanti. . . . They were concerned
with the film patterns which went deeper than the newsreel . . . and arrived perhaps at the idyll and the epic. The educators have never from
that day altogether strait-jacketed the aesthetes in documentary and it
would be a loss if they ever succeeded."[32]

Re-emergence of the story

In both the preceding chapter and the present one the two major
non-story film types—the experimental film and the film of fact—have
been analyzed with a view to testing the hypothesis, tentatively established
at the outset, that story telling runs counter to the cinematic approach.
The results obtained so far can be summed up as follows:

(1) The experimental film gravitates toward achievements which, it
is true, shun story telling but do so with little regard for the affinities of
the medium. They omit camera-reality. Whether abstract compositions
or projections of dream life, they are not so much films as an extension of

* See p. 48.
** See p. 160.

contemporary painting or of literary designs. They abolish the story principle only to enthrone instead the art principle. Perhaps Art gains by this *coup d'état*. The cinema does not, or, if it does, only by indirection.

(2) The film of fact in the form of the film on art is likewise a problematic hybrid as long as it is patterned on the experimental film. But art films may well acquire a cinematic quality if they assume the character of regular documentaries, with the works of art being embedded in real-life processes.

(3) There remains documentary itself, the main genre of the film of fact. Suffice it to repeat that all such documentaries as show concern for the visible world live up to the spirit of the medium. They channel their messages through the given natural material instead of using the visuals merely as a padding. Moreover, relieved from the burden of advancing an intrigue, they are free to explore the continuum of physical existence. The suppression of the story enables the camera to follow, without constraint, a course of its own and record otherwise inaccessible phenomena.

And this would be all that is to be said were it not for the fact that documentary suffers from a limitation in range. Confined, by definition, to the rendering of our environment, it misses those aspects of potentially visible reality which only personal involvement is apt to summon. Their appearance is inseparable from human drama, as conveyed by an intrigue. The suppression of the story, then, not only benefits documentary but puts it at a disadvantage also. "One of the most serious shortcomings of the documentary film," says Rotha, "has been its continued evasion of the human being."[33] How can this shortcoming be remedied? Paradoxically, the desire for story telling develops within a genre which repudiates the story as an uncinematic element.

On the one hand, the documentary maker eliminates the intrigue so as to be able to open his lens on the world; on the other, he feels urged to re-introduce dramatic action in the very same interest. It is again Rotha who requests documentary to "embrace individuals"[34] and to "broaden its human references."[35] Similarly, Bernard Miles submits that the aims of documentary "can best be served from the screen point of view by a marriage of documentary as we know it with a more . . . human story value."[36] Consider also René Clair's change of attitude: the Clair of 1950 reproves the Clair of 1923 for having scorned any *"sujet"* or intrigue out of the then fashionable intoxication with visual exercises in documentary style.[37]

This dialectic movement away from the story and again back to it can be traced to two conflicting principles, both well founded. The first move—suppression of the story—conforms to Proust's profound observation that revealing camera statements presuppose emotional detachment on the photographer's part. Photography, Proust has it, is a product of alienation,* which implies that good cinema is inconsistent with the enticements of an intrigue. The second move—acceptance of the story—finds support in Ortega y Gasset's judicious remark to the effect that our ability to perceive and absorb an event profits by our emotional participation in it: "It appears that those elements which seem to distort pure contemplation—interests, sentiments, compulsions, affective preferences—are precisely its indispensable instruments."[38]

The conflict between these two antinomic moves, which are natural outlets for the realistic and formative tendencies respectively, materializes in the very form of the musical. No sooner does the real-life intrigue of a musical achieve a certain degree of consistency than it is discontinued for the sake of a production number which often has already been delineated at a prenatal stage, thereby corroding the intrigue from within. Musicals reflect the dialectic relation between the story film and the non-story film without ever trying to resolve it. This gives them an air of cinema. Penelope fashion, they eternally dissolve the plot they are weaving. The songs and dances they sport form part of the intrigue and at the same time enhance with their glitter its decomposition.**

The demand for the story, then, re-emerges within the womb of the non-story film. In fact, the body of existing documentaries testifies to a persistent tendency toward dramatization. But how is it possible for the film maker to follow this tendency—tell a story, that is—and yet try to capture the flow of life? Or to put it this way, how can he do justice to the two conflicting principles according to which the story both obstructs and stimulates camera explorations? In rendering the world around us, he seems to be faced with the dilemma of having to sacrifice either its alienation or its fullness.

Note that the two opposite principles are not as irreconcilable as the form of the musical which mirrors them tends to suggest. And of course, the same holds true of the dilemma in their wake. It would be insoluble only if the tentative hypothesis that the story as such goes against the grain of the medium could be upheld. Then the recourse to a story—any story—would automatically preclude the display of cinematic life, and the dilemma confronting the film maker would indeed be a genuine one. Upon closer inspection, however, this hypothesis turns out to be too broad to cover all the relevant cases. It requires qualification. It must be replaced

* See pp. 14 ff.
** For this passage, see pp. 148–9.

by the more discriminating proposition that there are different types of stories, some of which, in keeping with that hypothesis, resist cinematic treatment, while others do prove responsive to it. Even Maurois and Sève who reject the story film admit that much; they inadvertently modify their anti-story dictum by exempting Balzac stories and Chaplin films from the general rule.*

* See pp. 176–7.

The Theatrical Story

INTRODUCTION

Form and content

THE TIME-HONORED differentiation between form and content of artistic achievements affords a convenient starting-point for an analysis of story types. It is true that in any given case these two components of the work of art interpenetrate each other insolubly: each content includes form elements; each form is also content. (Hence the legitimate ambiguity of such terms as "comedy," "melodrama," and "tragedy"; they may point to the peculiar contents or the formal aspects of the genres they designate or cover both of them indiscriminately.) But it is no less true that the concepts "form" and "content" have a basis in the properties of the artistic work itself. And the near-impossibility of neatly validating these concepts in the material is rather a point in their favor. With complex live entities the accuracy of definitions does not suffer from the fact that they retain a fringe of indistinct meanings. Quite the contrary, they must be elusive to achieve maximum precision—which implies that any attempt to remove their seeming vagueness for the sake of semantically irreproachable concepts is thoroughly devious.

This chapter and the two following will be devoted to a breakdown of story types according to differences in form. Since these types should be expected to be relevant cinematically, they must be definable in terms which bear on the inherent affinities of film. They constitute types only if they reveal themselves as such from the angle of cinema.

An uncinematic story form

To begin with uncinematic story forms, only one such type stands out distinctly—the "theatrical story," so called because its prototype is the theatrical play. Uncinematic stories, then, are patterned on a traditional literary genre; they tend to follow the ways of the theater. Significantly, the literature on film abounds with statements which place all the emphasis on the incompatibility of film and stage, while paying little attention, if any, to the obvious similarities between the two media. Thus Eisenstein, Pudovkin, and Alexandrov in their 1928 manifesto voice misgivings lest the advent of sound might engender a flood of " 'highly cultured dramas' and other photographed performances of a theatrical sort."* In Proust the narrator compares the impression his grandmother makes on him after a long absence with a photograph picturing her as the sick, old woman she is. But this is not the way, he continues, in which we usually perceive the world, especially things we cherish. Rather, "our eye, charged with thought, neglects, as would a classical tragedy, every image that does not assist the action of the play and retains only those that may help us to make its purpose intelligible." He concludes by calling his lapse into photographic perception a chance event which is bound to happen when our eyes, "arising first in the field and having it to themselves, set to work mechanically like films."** This passage is important because it specifies the sort of theater least amenable to cinematic treatment. Proust identifies it as the classical tragedy. To him the classical tragedy is a story form which, because of its tight and purposeful composition, goes the limit in defying the photographic media. By the way, the Eisenstein of 1928, who had not yet succumbed to the pressures of Stalinism, may have referred to this very compositional entity when he predicted an increase of "highly cultured dramas" in the wake of sound.

ORIGINS AND SOURCES

The trend in favor of the theatrical story was initiated as early as 1908 by *Film d'Art*, a new French film company whose first production, the much-praised and much decried† ASSASSINATION OF THE DUC DE GUISE, represented a deliberate attempt to transform the cinema into an art medium on a par with the traditional literary media. [Illus. 40] The idea was to demonstrate that films were quite able to tell, in terms of their own, mean-

* See pp. 102–3.
** See p. 14.
† See p. 179.

ingful stories after the manner of the theater or the novel. An academician wrote the scenario of this ambitious film; actors of the *Comédie-Française* impersonated its historical characters; and dramatic critics of high repute published enthusiastic reviews. From the lower depths the cinema thus rose to the regions of literature and theatrical art. Cultured people could no longer look down on a medium engaged in such noble pursuits.

Duc de Guise, then, aimed at rehabilitating the cinema in the name of Art. And since its authors were saturated with stage traditions, it was natural for them to believe that, to be art, the cinema would have to evolve along much the same lines as the theater. The action of Duc de Guise is strongly reminiscent of historical dramas, as they unfold on the stage. And so is the *mise-en-scène*. Méliès's insistence on advancing the narrative with the aid of specifically cinematic devices seems forgotten; instead an immobile camera captures the drama from the angle of the spectator in the pit. The camera *is* the spectator. And the characters themselves move in settings which for all their realism never let you ignore that they are painted canvas—a *Château de Blois* intended to impress the theatergoer, not the moviegoer, as the real thing.[1]

It should be noted, though, that, its theatricality notwithstanding, Duc de Guise testifies to a certain awareness of the differences between the two media. The story of the conspiracy against the Duke and his ultimate liquidation appears to have been fashioned with a view to acclimatizing theatrical art to the screen. In any case, the jerky succession of isolated *tableaux vivants*, customary then, is here superseded by a sort of pictorial continuity which does not depend upon lengthy captions to make itself understood. Also, the actors play their parts with a sense of detailed characterization and a minimum of gestures, thus breaking away from stage conventions.[2]

A tremendous success, Duc de Guise fathered hosts of period pictures and "highly cultured dramas" in France. America followed suit. D. W. Griffith let himself be inspired by this first *film d'art*; and Adolph Zukor began to feature "famous players in famous plays." Producers, distributors, and exhibitors were quick to realize that Art meant big business. Films capitalizing on the prestige of literary works or imitating them attracted the culture-minded bourgeoisie which had shunned the moviehouses before. The moviehouses themselves became more and more sumptuous in the process.[3] Their cheap, if expensive, glamour was a condoning factor in as much as it denounced the falsity of these cultural aspirations. (Yet in stigmatizing the commercialization of art, the discerning critic will have to acknowledge that it does not necessarily do away with art. Many a commercial film or television production is a genuine achievement besides being a commodity. Germs of new beginnings may develop within a thoroughly alienated environment.)

The *film d'art* movement persists, unbroken, to the present day. As might be expected, numerous films of this type, such as PYGMALION, DEATH OF A SALESMAN, etc., are actually theatrical adaptations. There is practically no Broadway hit that would not be exploited by Hollywood. Or think of the uninterrupted series of Shakespeare films, down to JULIUS CAESAR, MACBETH, and RICHARD III. However brilliantly executed, in spirit and structure all such screen dramas can still be traced to DUC DE GUISE. They need not be theatrical adaptations. Films like THE INFORMER, THE HEIRESS, GREAT EXPECTATIONS, and ROUGE ET NOIR take their inspiration from novels and yet recall the stage as vividly as does any screen version of a play. About the same applies to MOBY DICK; despite its cinematic elaborations it renders the Melville novel in terms of a dramatic action which would be a natural for the theater. Other theatrical films do not borrow from literary sources at all, as is illustrated by DUC DE GUISE itself. Similarly, Eisenstein's last films, ALEXANDER NEVSKY and IVAN THE TERRIBLE, are original screen works; nevertheless, they seem to be patterned after nonexistent plays or operas. [Illus. 41] It is not by accident that shortly before his death Eisenstein directed Wagner's *Die Walküre*. He once rebelled against the theater; he reverted to it at the end.

CHARACTERISTICS

Emphasis on human interaction

As viewed from both photography and film, one of the main features of the theatrical story form is its strong concern for human characters and human interrelations. This is in accordance with stage conditions. To repeat what has already been said, theatrical *mise-en-scène* cannot re-create full physical reality in all its incidents. Huge crowds transcend the given frame; tiny objects are lost in the total impression of it. Much must be omitted and much is an allusive substitute rather than the real thing. The stage universe is a shadowy replica of the world we live in, representing only such parts of it as sustain the dialogue and the acting and through them an intrigue which inevitably concentrates on events and experiences purely human.[4]* But all this has a restrictive effect on film. The theatrical story limits the appropriate use of a medium which does not differentiate between humans and inanimate objects.

* See pp. 45, 51, 96–7.

Complex units

The smallest elements of the stageplay—and consequently the theatrical story—are complex units as compared with the elements accessible to the camera. The reason is that, because of its dependence upon stage conditions and its concomitant emphasis on humanly significant action, the theatrical play does not admit indefinite breakdowns. Of course, it may suggest them in varying degrees. Shakespearean plays, for instance, are relatively transparent to unstaged nature, introducing characters and situations which might as well be dispensed with in a strictly compositional interest; and these seeming diversions and excursions evoke, somehow, life in the raw—its random events, its endless combinations.[5] Also, a *Kammerspiel* may come so close to its characters that it sensitizes the spectator to imperceptible psychological undercurrents and their physiological correspondences. Yet even the most subtle, most open-ended stage play is hardly in a position to implement its suggestions and carry analysis beyond a certain point.

The fact that the elements of which it consists—behavior patterns, passions, conflicts, beliefs—are highly complicated aggregates can easily be seen. Take the modern novel: Joyce, Proust, and Virginia Woolf coincide in decomposing the smallest units of older types of the novel—those which cover a series of developments as they occur in chronological time. These modern writers, says Erich Auerbach, "who prefer the exploitation of random everyday events, contained within a few hours and days, to the complete and chronological representation of a total exterior continuum . . . are guided by the consideration that it is a hopeless venture to try to be really complete within the total exterior continuum and yet to make what is essential stand out. Then too they hesitate to impose upon life, which is their subject, an order which it does not possess in itself."[6] But the theater goes far beyond any epic genre in forcing such an order on life in its fullness. A glance at the microscopic elements of, say, the Proust novel suffices to reveal the gross nature of the units which form the irreducible cells or nodal points of the stage play.

Film not only transcends human interaction but resembles the novel, modern or not, in that it tends to render transient impressions and relationships which are denied to the stage. From the angle of film the theatrical play is composed of units which represent a crude abbreviation of camera-life. To say the same in cinematic terms, the theatrical story proceeds by way of "long shots." How should it proceed otherwise? It is constructed for the theater, which indeed requires that analysis be curtailed for the sake of dramatic action and that the world onstage be visible from an inalterable, rather remote distance. This is what the young Eisenstein experienced when, as a theater director, he felt increasingly urged to stage the kind of reality germane to the cinema. He removed a wrestling match from the stage to the middle of the auditorium so as to transform it into a real-life event; he even tried—an impossible artifice—to isolate hands, pillars, legs, house façades in an effort to create the illusion of close-ups. But it just did not work. So he left the stage for the screen, while at the same time turning his back on the story as such which, he then believed, was bound to feature individual destinies. His goal, a cinematic one, was the depiction of collective action, with the masses as the true hero.[7]

Complex units interfere with cinematic narration. Hence the jerkiness of films advancing a theatrical intrigue. It is as if they jumped from unit to unit, leaving unexplored the gaps in-between—whereby it does not in the least matter whether the films are silent or follow the lead of dialogue. And each jump affects the spectator as an arbitrary change of direction, because the units which mark the joints of the intrigue are by far not the last elements at which cinematic analysis may arrive. In the play *Romeo and Juliet* the Friar's failure to pass on Juliet's letter in time is acceptable because it suggests the workings of Fate. But in ROMEO AND JULIET, the Castellani film, the same event does not stand for anything; rather, it appears as an outside intervention unmotivated by what goes before, a story twist which for no reason at all abruptly alters the course of action. The whole affair with the letter belongs at best to an ideological continuum, not the material one to which film aspires. It is a sham entity which would have to be broken down into its psychophysical components to become part of camera-reality. This does not imply, of course, that the cinema can afford completely to ignore units which, so to speak, are given only in long shots. These units, which resemble intricately structured molecules, transmit common thoughts, emotions, visions. If the film narrative did not occasionally avail itself of them as points of arrival or departure, the spectator would be at a loss how to assimilate the succession of camera revelations.

Detachable patterns of meanings

In progressing from complex unit to complex unit, the theatrical story evolves distinct patterns of meanings. From the angle of film these patterns give the impression of being prearranged because they assert themselves independently of the flow of visuals; instead of seeming to grow out of it, it is they which determine the direction of that flow, if flow it still is. Compare ROMEO AND JULIET with UMBERTO D.: the Shakespeare film relates a self-sufficient story which is significant in its own right, whereas the significance of the De Sica film lies in the penetration with which it pictures the everyday existence of an old man condemned to live on a pension which does not permit him to live; here the story consists in what the camera makes us see. Unlike this truly cinematic story, the theatrical intrigue is detachable from the medium; accordingly, the imagery conveying it illustrates rather than releases its meanings. When looking at a theatrical film, our imagination is in fact not primarily stimulated by pictures of physical reality so that, following their suggestions, it would work its way from them toward significant story contexts; conversely, it is first attracted by these contexts and only then takes cognizance of the pictorial material bearing them out.

A whole with a purpose

Much as theatrical intrigues may be given to meandering and thus acquire an almost epic quality, when compared with film they all appear to be modeled on the classical tragedy which, Proust has it, neglects "every image that does not assist the action of the play and retains only those that may help us to make its purpose intelligible."* The story form he has in mind is not only a whole—all works of art are, more or less—but a whole with a purpose; its every element, that is, has the sole function of serving that purpose. Now the term "purpose," as used by Proust, evidently refers to the significance of the story. So one might as well say that, viewed from film, the theatrical intrigue revolves around an ideological center toward which all its patterns of meanings converge. In other words, it must be tightly organized; it is essentially a closed story.

From the early 'thirties on, when the individual hero began to supersede the heroic masses on the Soviet screen, Eisenstein under the pressure of terrorist totalitarianism expressly championed this story type and its compositional implications. He requested each fragment of a film to be "an organic part of an organically conceived whole."[8] And he declared toward the end of his life: "For us montage became a means . . . of achieving an organic embodiment of a single idea conception, embracing all elements, parts, details of the film-work."[9] In his youth Eisenstein had been less idealistic-minded, less totalitarian. Legitimately so, for a film built from elements whose only *raison d'être* consists in implementing the (pre-established) "idea conception" at the core of the whole runs counter

* See p. 216.

to the spirit of a medium privileged to capture "the ripple of leaves in the wind."* There is a nice observation by Béla Balázs to the effect that children linger over details while adults tend to neglect the detail in some big design. But since children see the world in close-ups, he argues, they are more at home in the atmosphere of film than in the long-shot universe of the theater.[10] The conclusion, not drawn by Balázs himself, would be that the theatrical film appeals to adults who have suppressed the child in themselves.

ATTEMPTS AT ADJUSTMENT

The "most marvelous things"

FEYDER'S DICTUM

Jacques Feyder, the French film director, once postulated that "everything can be transferred to the screen, everything expressed through an image. It is possible to adapt an engaging and humane film from the tenth chapter of Montesquieu's *L'Esprit des lois* as well as . . . a paragraph of Nietzsche's *Zoroaster*." Yet to do this, he cautiously adds, "it is indispensable to have the sense of the cinema."[11]

Assuming for the sake of argument that Feyder is right, the theatrical story would certainly not resist cinematic treatment. But how can it be transformed into authentic cinema? In narrating such a story, any film maker who has the sense of the medium is obviously faced with two different, if not incompatible, tasks. He will have to put across the story as the purposeful whole it is—a task requiring him to reproduce its complex units and patterns of meanings in a straight manner. At the same time he will have to follow the realistic tendency—a task which prompts him to extend the story into the dimension of physical existence.

STRAIGHT REPRESENTATION OF THE INTRIGUE

Many theatrical films, among them some executed with consummate skill, live up to the first task without even trying to pursue the second. They adequately impart the intrigue, with all its inherent meanings but, as if completely absorbed in its straight representation, fail to explore the world around us. THE INFORMER, GLASS MENAGERIE, MOURNING BECOMES ELECTRA, DEATH OF A SALESMAN, ROUGE ET NOIR, etc., are hardly more than custom-made adaptations of tightly composed stories detachable from the medium; they fit the story like a well-tailored suit. Hence an atmosphere

* See p. 31.

which induces claustrophobia in the viewer. This must be laid to the way their imagery is handled.

In the old Griffith film, BROKEN BLOSSOMS, the superb shots of the fog enveloping the Thames and the London East End streets seem to have no other function than to picture the environment in which the action takes place. Whatever they may contribute to establish the action, they do not exhaust themselves in supporting it. They really record city nature. What a contrast between this natural fog and the fog which plays so conspicuous a role in Ford's THE INFORMER! It is a symbolic fog expressly selected or concocted to point beyond itself toward the "idea conception" of the intrigue.[12] Griffith's lens opens upon the world, while Ford shuts it out in the interest of theatrical composition. Yet at least THE INFORMER does not pretend to camera-reality. Other films in the same vein do. Thus Kazan leans over backward in an attempt to pass off his ON THE WATERFRONT as a semi-documentary. The film, a veritable *tour de force*, is shot on location and utilizes techniques appropriate to a film of fact. Actually it is nearly the opposite. Every shot of it is calculated to enhance the dramatic impact of a contrived intrigue. There is no air about these shots. True, they let in material reality, but they do so only to drain it of its essence. Reality itself is here employed to build a universe as hermetically closed as that of THE INFORMER.

In sum, films which aim at the straight implementation of a theatrical story have the following, easily recognizable features in common. They emphasize the actors and their interplay. In keeping with this main concern, they further coincide in assigning to inanimate objects and environmental factors a subsidiary role. Finally and most important, they include practically no image that would not serve the ends of story construction. This is to say, each image, instead of being established as a fragment of reality which may yield multiple meanings, must assume a meaning derived from contexts alien to the medium—contexts which gravitate toward an ideological center.

EXTENSION OF THE INTRIGUE

"I am rewriting Shakespeare," said Zecca, the contemporary of Lumière and Méliès, to a friend who found him blue-penciling a manuscript. "The wretched fellow has left out the most marvelous things."[13] Zecca had the feel of the medium; what he did was simply to devote himself to the task of extending the theatrical story in the direction of camera-life. There is little doubt indeed that his "most marvelous things" are identical with the specifically cinematic subjects treated in chapter 3: objects moving, the small, the big, the familiar, etc. The necessity of incorporating these subjects, should even the script not provide for them, has been recognized, if with less candor, by modern film makers and critics as well. "The content of theater material," said Hitchcock to an interviewer, "is much slighter than that of movies. One good movie may need as much material as four plays."[14] And Panofsky holds that "in a film it does not interrupt but rather intensifies the action if the shifting of the scene from one place to another—meaningless as it is psychologically—is thoroughly depicted as an actual transportation with car-driving through heavy street traffic, motor-boating through a nocturnal harbor, galloping on horse back, or whatever the case may be."[15]

Not every extension of a theatrical intrigue, however, is an extension which causes "reality itself to participate in the action."[16] If, for instance, a play includes a verbal reference, indispensable for its understanding, to World War II, and the film version of that play shows a few typical battle scenes, these supplementary shots are unlikely to exert a noticeable impact; they illustrate rather than extend the verbal reference.* The whole issue is intelligently paraphrased in the late Norbert Lusk's memoirs. Reminiscing about the silent 1923 adaptation of O'Neill's *Anna Christie*, Lusk observes that the film version comprises two episodes not given on the stage: Anna as a child in her Swedish native village and, somewhat later, Anna being raped by a degenerate. Are these additions in the nature of extensions?

The point he makes is that they are not. As he sees it, they just serve to tell in pictures what the play is able to convey through words—that Anna "was a foreigner but wholesome" and that "her subsequent life was no fault of her own." The playwright himself shared this view. "With quick perception of a medium new to him," relates Lusk, "Mr. O'Neill quietly pointed out that the interpolation was necessary to round out the story in terms of photographed action. He . . . accepted the film for the sincere transcription it was."[17] The two episodes, then, were added for the sole purpose of transcribing faithfully the intentions of the original in a medium which could not yet express them otherwise. For lack of sound, pictures were required not to extend the play but to reproduce it. The excess amount of visuals did not result from a concern with cinematic subjects.

Yet, more often than not, theatrical films do manifest such a concern. Their authors really extend the story to include the "most marvelous things." This may be achieved in a hundred of ways. A run-of-the-mill procedure, referred to by Panofsky, is the insertion of street scenes in films whose plots would be fully intelligible if the protagonists stayed indoors all the time. Whenever film makers want to "take an action out

* See p. 118.

of stylized presentation (however effective) and make it completely natural,"[18] they feel irresistibly attracted by the street and its extensions. Presumably the sharp contrast between unstaged street life and purposeful stage action is responsible for this common preference.

To mention also a few less typical efforts along similar lines, Laurence Olivier in his HAMLET has the camera incessantly pan and travel through the studio-built maze of Elsinore castle, with its irrational staircases, raw walls, and Romanesque ornaments, in an effort to expand the play into the twilight region of psychophysical correspondences. Or remember Eisenstein's script of AMERICAN TRAGEDY, which clearly centers on an "idea conception": his desire to externalize Clyde's inner struggle in the form of a *monologue intérieur* marks an attempt to dissolve one of the most decisive complex units of his script into an all but unlimited succession of cinematic elements uncalled-for by the story construction. It sometimes is as if these extensions were considered more essential than the story itself. Stroheim confessed to an interviewer that he was possessed with a "madness for detail."[19] And Béla Balázs praises a silent American film for leaving on two occasions its story behind and indulging instead in a "thin hail of small moments of . . . material life"[20] which were to bring the environment into play.

No doubt these cinematic elaborations have the function of adjusting the theatrical intrigue to the medium. But what about their relation to the intrigue proper? From the angle of the story they are much in the nature of gratuitous excursions. The story does not depend upon their inclusion to cast its spell over the audience.[21] On the one hand, then, such extensions prove desirable, if not indispensable, cinematically; on the other, they are inconsistent with a story form which for full impact requires straight representation. The concern for the extensions and the regard for the fabric of story motifs tend to conflict with each other.* This conflict shows in two ways both of which press home the difficulty of a solution.

Two alternatives

THE STORY COMPOSITION OVERSHADOWING THE CINEMATIC ELABORATIONS

"*Nevsky* I found too stylized and too prearranged," says Rotha. And comparing it with Eisenstein's earlier films, POTEMKIN and TEN DAYS, he adds: "The well-known Battle on the Ice never roused me to heights of response as did the Odessa Steps or the Storming of the Winter Palace."[22]

---

* See the Sève quote, p. 176.

His different reactions must be laid to a difference in story form between NEVSKY and the two other films—a difference which Eisenstein himself tried to blur later on. At the time he made NEVSKY, he still admitted, it is true, that POTEMKIN looks like a chronicle or a newsreel but then insisted that it was in reality a "tragic composition in its most canonic form—the five-act tragedy."[23]

No definition of this film could be more misleading. Even though POTEMKIN culminates in moments of tragic suspense and is, all in all, a masterpiece of intense and deliberate cutting, it is anything but a tragedy in the sense of Proust—a theatrical composition, that is, which radically obstructs the photographic or cinematic approach. Evidence of this may be found in Eisenstein's sudden decision to change his script upon seeing the historic Odessa steps. The sight of them moved him to discard much of the work already done and concentrate on the mutiny of the *Potemkin* sailors, which is a nontheatrical episode rather than a classical drama.[24]

The testimony of his eyes seems to have convinced him that the cinema has a special affinity for episodes quivering with life in the raw. POTEMKIN is a real-life episode told in pictures. One must have seen the sailors' revolt or the sequence of the Odessa steps to grasp the action. The fact that these pictures embody the intrigue instead of merely illustrating it can be inferred from the indeterminacy of many shots. Not forced to lend color to given story lines, the rising mists in the harbor, the heavily sleeping sailors, and the moonlit waves stand for themselves alone. They are part and parcel of the wide reality involved; and they are under no obligation whatever to serve an extraneous purpose that would impinge on their essence. They are largely purposeless; it is they and their intrinsic meanings which *are* the action.

The same applies to the famous close-up of the surgeon's pince-nez dangling down the ship rope. [Illus. 42] A decade or so after POTEMKIN Eisenstein would refer to this particular close-up to exemplify the artistic merits of the *pars pro toto* method. By showing only part of an object or a human figure, says he, the artist compels the spectator to retrogress to primitive modes of thinking—a state of mind where the part is at the same time the whole. "The pince-nez, taking the place of a whole surgeon, not only completely fills his role and place, but does so with a huge sensual-emotional increase in the intensity of the impression."[25] Here too Eisenstein overemphasizes the importance of the whole at the expense of the parts and fragments. To be sure, the pince-nez caught up in the rope signifies the death of its owner. But the haphazard tangle, rich in contrasts, of materials—part rough, part fine—is also significant in its own right; it carries various implications and only one of them points in the direction which Eisenstein has in mind.

Now consider the Battle on the Ice in NEVSKY. Unlike the Odessa steps, it marks the pictorial climax of an intrigue which conforms better than POTEMKIN to Eisenstein's misinterpretation of the latter—that POTEMKIN is not so much a "chronicle" as a "composition in its most canonic form." NEVSKY is not strictly a five-act tragedy, yet it is a historical drama conceived in terms of the stage. It is a whole with a purpose. Its characters comprise a closed orbit; all its interlinked motifs radiate from an ideological center. Nevsky is utterly remote from a real-life episode. Within this self-contained universe, then, there appears the Lake Peipus Battle, a cinematic elaboration in grand style. It is definitely an extension of the intrigue; for all its thoroughness, however, it does not add anything essential to the story developments. Regarding its structural function, it resembles the battles in Shakespeare plays which need not be seen to produce a dramatic effect; summary eye-witness reports fully do the job. The whole extension is clearly intended to drag an otherwise theatrical narrative through the region of camera-reality. As a matter of fact, it is rather lifeless.

Far from reflecting transitory life, the imagery affects you as a (re-) construction meant to be life; each shot seems predetermined; none breathes the allusive indeterminacy of the POTEMKIN pictures. (This is not to belittle the incomparable beauty of the long-distance shot of the plain on which the sequence opens.) Yet the decisive point is the following: the patterns of motifs and themes which make up the NEVSKY story are so pronounced that they subdue everything that comes their way. Hence, even assuming that the Battle on the Ice were cinematically on a par with the episode of the Odessa steps, these patterns which spread octopus-like would nevertheless corrode its substance, turning it from a suggestive rendering of physical events into a luxuriant adornment. Owing to the given compositional arrangements, the Battle sequence cannot possibly exert the impact of that POTEMKIN episode and thus on its part upset the theatricality of the action. It is nothing but an excrescence on the body of an intrigue imposed upon the medium. (Such "useless"[26] extensions are rather frequent. The battle in HENRY V, for instance, is just a decorative pageant. And the final hunt of the whale in MOBY DICK is under a cloud of symbolic references which nearly obscure it; its realism is wasted.)

CINEMATIC ELABORATIONS OVERSHADOWING THE STORY CONSTRUCTION

The Griffith chase A classic example of the other alternative— cinematic extensions overshadowing the story meanings– is the stereotyped chase sequence in D. W. Griffith films. Griffith indulges in theatrical intrigues; for long stretches he is content with rendering, one by one, dramatic actions and situations which are highly complex units from a cinematic point of view. Yet beginning with THE LONELY VILLA,[27] all his major films invariably conclude on a drawn-out chase which owes its particular thrill to the device of accelerated parallel cutting. While we are witnessing the agony of some innocent character doomed to death, we are at the same time permitted to watch the advance of his prospective rescuers, and these alternating scenes, or flashes of scenes, follow each other in ever shorter intervals until they ultimately merge, with the victim being redeemed. The Griffith chase dramatizes an intrinsically cinematic subject: objective physical movement.

More important, it is an ingenious attempt not only to extend theater into dimensions where material phenomena mean everything but to make the extension itself appear as an expression of the story's ideological climax. Griffith aspires to nothing less than to reconcile the requirements of the theater with those arising from the cinema's preference for physical reality and the flow of life. His attempt proves abortive, though. He does not, and cannot, succeed in bridging the gap between the theatrical and the cinematic narrative. True, his chases seem to transform ideological suspense into physical suspense without any friction; but upon closer inspection they represent an excess amount of the latter. Thus the "last-minute-rescue" in the "modern story" of INTOLERANCE is by no means a translation into cinematic terms of the conclusion at which the story itself arrives; rather, this finale captivates and thrills the spectator as a physical race between antagonistic forces. It provides sensations which do not really bear on, and bring out, the "idea conception" of the story—the triumph of justice over the evil of intolerance. The Griffith chase is not so much the fulfillment of the story as a cinematically effective diversion from it. It drowns ideological suspense in physical excitement.[28]

Pygmalion   The screen adaptation of *Pygmalion* is a case in point also. This film adds to Shaw's comedy a montage of recording machinery in close shots, a detailed depiction of Eliza's phonetic education, including her suffering under its ruthlessness, and the whole embassy ball episode replete with amusing trifles—sequences, all of which feature the physical life and the environment of the stage characters. What is the good of them? Since Shaw states everything he wants to impart in his play, they are certainly not needed to clarify his intentions. Yet there they are. And the embassy ball and the sequence of Higgins pouncing on Eliza are easily the most impressive episodes of the film. Erwin Panofsky has it that "these two scenes, entirely absent from the play, and indeed unachievable on the stage, were the highlights of the film; whereas the Shavian dialogue, however severely cut, turned out to fall a little flat in certain moments."[29]

On the screen, then, the brilliant satire of middle-class morals loses much of its impact, and what remains of it at all affects us as a leftover from the theater rather than genuine cinema. Or in more general terms, the metamorphosis of the play into a film entails a shift of emphasis from the dimension of intellectual messages to that of photographable objects. Sociological notions are overwhelmed by environmental facts; conceptual reasoning succumbs to the ambiguous manifestations of nature. The stage play evolves, so to speak, *above* the level of physical existence, while the film tends to pass right *through* it in an effort to record it exhaustively. Unlike the film, which brings the embassy staircase, Eliza's nightmares, and Higgins's gadgets into focus, the play takes all this for granted as a background to sophisticated dialogue. It is as if the screen version sprang from a desire to retrieve the raw materials out of which Shaw has carved his comedy and as if this desire automatically weakened the concern with the topics and arguments which keep the comedy going. Those "most marvelous things" which Zecca tried to graft upon Shakespeare are evidently the most ephemeral ones. And sure enough, their insertion calls for a sacrifice.

Running controversy   The extensions of this second type have time and again been categorically rejected or wholeheartedly acclaimed—a smoldering controversy which confirms the depth of the conflict between theatrical and cinematic designs. In the camp of the theatrical-minded, who value above all the straight representation of the intrigue, elaborations which, PYGMALION fashion, becloud the intentions of the original are not readily tolerated. These critics condemn the spread of incidentals which do not seem to be integrant elements of the whole. "Is this the experts' way of telling a story?" asks one of them indignantly. And he answers: "The living story is told in people and the things they say, with an occasional essential prop necessary for the progress of the story."[30]

The cinematic-minded on their part are interested not so much in story composition as the incidence of "small moments of material life." They prefer a straying from the preordained course of action toward camera-reality to the rigidity of films which confine themselves dutifully to following that course. Lang's FURY, says Otis Ferguson, "has the true creative genius of including little things not germane to the concept but, once you see them, the spit and image of life itself."[31]

This perennial dispute acquires a peculiar poignancy if it comes into the open on occasion of one and the same film. Take the reviews of

Vincente Minelli's 1945 film, THE CLOCK: whether or not its boy-meets-girl story is a theatrical story proper, the cinematic excursions from it made themselves strongly felt as such at the time and gave rise to diametrically opposed opinions. The theatrical-minded Stephen Longstreet, angry at the director's apparently aimless indulgence in New York street life, requested of him that he should in future shoot scripts that have "honesty, density and depth," shoot them with "old standing sets, some lights and shadows, and a dumb cameraman."[32] Not so Louis Kronenberger. More cinematic-minded, he delighted in Minelli's gift for "incident and detail" and his ability to get "something into *The Clock* that transcends its formula."[33]

CONCLUSIONS

Insoluble dilemma

The upshot is that Feyder is wrong in contending that everything can be transferred to the screen in a cinematic spirit. His dictum breathes complacency; it is that of a man of all too catholic tastes. The theatrical story stems from formative aspirations which conflict irrevocably with the realistic tendency. Consequently, all attempts to adjust it to the cinema by extending its range into regions where the camera is at home result at best in some compromise of a sort. The extensions required for the adjustment either disintegrate the intrigue—the case of PYGMALION—or are, themselves, rendered ineffective by its indelible suggestions—the case of the NEVSKY story themes overgrowing the Battle on the Ice.

In spite of these difficulties there are no end of films which follow the tradition of the *film d'art*. Their undeniable popularity, however, is by no means an indicator of their aesthetic validity. It only proves that a mass medium like the film is bound to yield to the enormous pressures of social and cultural conventions, collective preferences, and ingrained habits of perceiving, all of which combine to favor spectacles which may be high-level entertainment but have little to do with films. Within this context an argument by Pierre Bost, the well-known French scenarist, deserves mentioning.

Bost collaborated with Jean Aurenche on two scripts differing radically in cinematic quality—the script of GERVAISE, an excellent film drawn from Zola's *L'Assommoir*, and that of ROUGE ET NOIR, a Stendhal adaptation which is theater pure and simple. In a conversation with Bost, I was pleasantly surprised at learning that he was against using Stendhal in the first place and that he too does not consider ROUGE ET NOIR true cinema, as are, say, LA STRADA or UMBERTO D. Yet the point of interest is one of his arguments in defense of the Stendhal film. Bost holds that adaptations from literary classics cater to a lasting demand of the public; at any rate, they are an established French film genre. And this would account for their relative legitimacy, even if they fall back on the ways of the stage. The yardstick by which to appraise them is not primarily their adequacy to the medium but their closeness to the essence of the original (and of course the quality of their execution).

D. W. Griffith's admirable nonsolution

Griffith is generally recognized as the first to narrate a given story—mostly a theatrical one—in cinematic terms. But perhaps his greatest merit is that, unlike many of his successors, he remains keenly aware of the gulf which separates the theatrical story from the cinematic narrative. Except for his chase finales in which he tries in vain to blend these two incompatible modes of representation, he always keeps apart what does not belong together. His films are full of fissures traceable to his cinematic instinct rather than technical awkwardness. On the one hand, he certainly aims at establishing dramatic continuity as impressively as possible; on the other, he invariably inserts images which do not just serve to further the action or convey relevant moods but retain a degree of independence of the intrigue and thus succeed in summoning physical existence. This is precisely the significance of his first close-up.* And so do his extreme long shots,[34] his seething crowds, his street episodes and his many fragmentary scenes[35] invite us to absorb them intensely. In watching these pictures or pictorial configurations, we may indeed forget the drama they punctuate in their own diffuse meanings. Eisenstein did, for one. Years after having seen INTOLERANCE, he no longer remembered who is who in the street sequences of this film's "modern story"; but the figure of a passer-by visible only "for a flashing glimpse" still stood vividly before his inner eye.**

* See pp. 46–8.
** See p. 63.

Interlude: Film and Novel

SIMILARITIES

Like film, the novel tends to render life in its fullness

Great novels, such as *Madame Bovary, War and Peace,* and *Remembrance of Things Past,* cover wide expanses of reality. They aim, or seem to aim, at unfolding life on a scale which exceeds their intrigue proper. So does film. This glaring similarity between the two media is corroborated by the fact that in the novel too the story turns out to be a double-edged proposition.

No doubt it is indispensable for the novel, if only as a thread through the maze of life. Yet much as it is needed, it threatens to substitute an ordered sequence of events for life's unfathomable contingencies and thus to blur, in E. M. Forster's words, the "finer growths"[1] it is supposed to bring out. "Oh, dear, yes—the novel tells a story," says Forster, calling the latter a "low atavistic form."[2]

Accordingly, in creating a dramatic intrigue the novelist, as well as the film maker, is faced with the difficulty of reconciling two divergent, if not opposite, requirements. In defining them, I might as well continue to follow Forster, who, from his own practice in the field, is particularly sensitive to the conflicting tasks involved in novel writing. First, since the novelist cannot do without a story, he must in the interest of its significance "leave no loose ends" in narrating it. "Every action or word ought to count; it ought to be economical and spare."[3] Second, since a sustained pursuit of these compositional efforts would bring the novel dangerously close to the theatrical story the novelist is simultaneously obliged to move in the reverse direction also. He must break away from the story. He must not permit the story construction to overwhelm open-ended reality and replace it by a closed universe. Instead of investing too heavily in the texture of story developments (which he must not neglect either, of course), he will therefore profit by "ragged ends,"[4] say "things that have no bearing on the development,"[5] and feature "round"[6] characters apt to surprise the reader. Only in subduing the exacting story patterns will he be able to suggest the "incalculability of life."[7] It is logical that Forster should blame Thomas Hardy for reflecting Fate through a plot so tight that it encroaches on the characters of his novels; "their vitality has been impoverished, they have gone dry and thin."[8]

Like film, the novel aspires to endlessness

The novel's tendency toward endlessness is of a piece with its inherent nostalgia for the vast spaces of life. George Lukács in his *Die Theorie des Romans*, written before his conversion to Communism, says this is so because of the place the novel occupies in the historical process, as he conceives of it. His theological outlook on history leads him to assign the novel to a different era from that of the epic. The latter era he identifies as an age filled with significance—an age in which the notion of chronological time is still powerless because all humans and objects are oriented toward eternity and virtually partake of it. The novel on its part is the form of expression of a later age which no longer knows of ultimate meanings, so that the life it contains—the very life rendered by the novel—does not manifest itself in a rounded-out cycle of eternal presences but evolves in chronological time without beginning and end.[9]

This concern for endlessness has repercussions affecting the course of the story. The novelist naturally wants to bring his story to a conclusion which will put the seal on its wholeness. But in genuine novels it is precisely this conclusion that makes the reader feel uneasy; it strikes him as an arbitrary intervention, cutting short developments that might, or indeed should, be carried on and on. It is as if the story of the novel were meant to destroy the integrity it is about to achieve. "Why has a novel to be planned?" asks Forster. "Cannot it grow? Why need it close, as a play closes?"[10] And referring to that central passage of Gide's *The Counterfeiters* where Edouard expresses his desire to plunge into the (endless) stream of life rather than comply with the demands of the story, he exclaims, entirely in keeping with Edouard-Gide: "As for a plot—to pot with the plot. . . . All that is prearranged is false."[11]

If these resemblances between the two media were alone decisive, the novel would indeed be a cinematic story form. Yet novel and film also differ from each other: their formal properties are anything but identical. And the worlds to which they reach out do not coincide either. What exactly is the nature of these differences? And are they strong enough to neutralize the existing similarities?

DIFFERENCES

Formal properties

SOURIAU'S PROPOSITION

The difficulties confronting the adapter of novels are frequently traced not to the kind of universe which the novel renders but to the specific ways in which it shapes any world it encompasses. In order to find out whether this school of thought gets at the core of the matter, let me discuss the proposition of one of its exponents. In his paper, *Filmologie et esthétique comparée*, Etienne Souriau, the French aesthetician, submits that the novel has four formal (or structural) properties which resist stubbornly translation into cinematic language; and from all that he says, it is evident that he believes them to be the main source of trouble.[12] These properties show in the novel's dealings with the elements of (1) time, (2) tempo, (3) space, and (4) the angle of approach (*point de vue*). I shall comment only on the first and last elements, which the author himself considers particularly important.

TIME

Souriau contrasts the novel's flexibility in handling all imaginable modes of time with the rigidity of films. Thus the novelist may characterize some action as a customary one, be deliberately vague about the moment of its emergence, interrelate things present and past whenever he wants to, etc. All this film cannot do. What appears on the screen has inevitably the earmarks of an actual event. The only means by which film can evoke the past is the flashback—which Souriau calls a pretty clumsy device.

Yet even though the cinema lacks the possibility of exploring time with the sovereignty of the novel, it is nevertheless much more flexible than he is prepared to admit. The manner in which one of the gunmen in SCARFACE tosses a quarter suggests that he plays with the coin also when we are not looking at him; we immediately identify his present action as a compulsive habit. PATHER PANCHALI presents a chronologically ordered **sequence of episodes in such a way that the spectator feels continually** urged to relive what has gone before. His imagination moves to and fro, weaving the fabric of a time which has little in common with that of the sequence. And steeped in this inner time, he is no longer able, nor does he any longer care, to establish in chronological time the events that pass across the screen. They drift, unlocalizable, through a temporal realm in which the past and the present inextricably fuse with each other. (Compare this film with Bresson's UN CONDAMNE A MORT, which confines itself to a purely linear chronology as irreversible as it is empty.)

In his TEN DAYS Eisenstein takes whole passages—for instance, the drawbridge episode—out of the time of action and, as does the novel, dilates them to magnify an emotion or drive home a thought. In many an otherwise insignificant story film the continuity is suddenly disrupted, and for a short moment it is as if all clocks ceased to tick; summoned by a big close-up or a shot of heterogeneous fragments, strange shapes shine forth from the abyss of timelessness. There are flashbacks which do not just resuscitate the past but manage to integrate it into actuality. The pictorial reconstructions of the alleged crime in RASHOMON are so executed and interlinked that you cannot follow them without acutely realizing their relevance to the ongoing search for truth. These retrospects are part and parcel of the present.

Films may even achieve what seems exclusively reserved for the novel: they may show a character in company with the people he recollects. The old doctor in Ingmar Bergman's WILD STRAWBERRIES, suffering from the emptiness in and about him, is haunted by memories which increasingly close in on him. Yet these flashbacks are more than isolated inserts: he enters them in the flesh, watching from close by his onetime friends, the youngster he was, and the loving girl he did not know how to keep. [Illus. 43] Were he only a specter among apparitions unaware of his presence, the past would still be at a distance. This distance, however, is eliminated also. From an observer the dreamer turns into a participant who resumes contact with at least one of those pale figures. No longer a secluded province, the past thus takes on life in a literal sense and, as it develops, makes the old man himself undergo a change. Evidently, the different treatment of time in novel and film is only a difference in degree, not in essence.

ANGLE OF APPROACH

Souriau further points out that the novelist is at liberty to place himself inside any of his characters and, accordingly, set the outer world, or what then appears of it, in the perspective of the latter's inward being (*intériorité*). Film on its part, the author continues, is incapable of proceeding from this particular angle of approach. The camera cannot achieve complete identification with a screen character in the fashion of the novel; all that it can do is to suggest intermittently what he sees and how he feels about it. In support of his thesis Souriau refers to Sacha Guitry's THE STORY OF A CHEAT, which is passed off as an autobiography told by the film's protagonist. He is certainly right in arguing that, except for the framing verbal statements and several arrangements involving only the intrigue, nothing in the film bears out the claim that the cheat, its hero, is identical with the narrator. The cheat is perceived from without like the rest of the cast; nor does the imagery strike one as a projection of his inner states of mind. Here as elsewhere, the role of the camera is that of an independent, if secret, witness.[13]

Again Souriau underestimates the potentialities of film. Even granted that the film maker is much less free than the novelist to become one with a character of his choice, he may go far in giving the impression of such mimetic transformations. Of course, Robert Montgomery's THE LADY IN THE LAKE is anything but a case in point. In this film the camera simply substitutes for the eyes of the leading character, so that he himself remains almost invisible while his environment looks exactly the way it would appear from where he is standing or moving. The identity thus established is purely external; it does not permit us really to identify with that character. Yet the failure of the Montgomery picture to come to grips with the problem it poses should not lead one to infer that this problem is out of bounds for the medium.

Some films do tackle it with a measure of success. Take CALIGARI: true, the narrator of the CALIGARI story mingles in person with the other characters of the film, but even so we cannot help feeling that they are products of his imagination and that the bizarre world enveloping him as well as these phantoms emanates from the core of his self. The whole film seems to grow out of the narrator's interior life, reflecting in its light the universe it releases. UEBERFALL accomplishes about the same in a more cinematic, less painterly spirit. Here too it is as if the sordid real-life streets, rooms, and underpasses that crowd the film were hallucinated by its panicky protagonist. All these shots converge toward his mind; in a manner of speaking his mind is the seat of the camera generating them. And does not RASHOMON prevail upon the spectator to scrutinize the murder scene from the divergent viewpoints of the successive narrators? Whether he knows it or not, he is adopting their varying attitudes in the process.

Inwardness, then, is not entirely inaccessible to film either. This justifies the conclusion that, in general, the differences between the formal properties of film and novel are only differences in degrees. As such they carry less weight than the substantive similarities between the two media.

They are secondary differences; were it for them alone, the novel would offer little resistance to adaptations conforming to the cinematic approach.

But the two media also embrace different worlds. And this difference between them is crucial indeed.

Two worlds

THE MATERIAL AND THE MENTAL CONTINUUM

The fact that both film and novel feature the flow or stream of life does not imply that they focus on the same aspects of it. As mentioned earlier, film gravitates toward a kind of life which is "still intimately connected, as if by an umbilical cord, with the material phenomena from which its emotional and intellectual contents emerge."* Cinematic films, that is, capitalize on the suggestive power of these phenomena to convey all that which is not visible and material. In DIARY OF A COUNTRY PRIEST, for instance, it is the allusive expressions of the young priest's face rather than his explicit diary entries, which succeed in evoking and impressing upon us his spiritual struggles and sufferings; everything here hinges on the transparence to beliefs and values of a physical entity. Life, as captured by the camera, is predominantly a material continuum.

To be sure, the novel too is frequently engrossed in physical existence —faces, objects, landscapes and all. But this is only part of the world at its command. A composition in words, it is able, and therefore disposed, directly to name and penetrate inner-life events that range from emotions to ideas, from psychological conflicts to intellectual disputes. Practically all novels lean toward internal developments or states of being. The world of the novel is primarily a mental continuum. Now this continuum often includes components which elude the grasp of the cinema because they have no physical correspondences to speak of. Unlike the country priest's spirituality, they cannot be intimated by facial expressions or so; there is nothing in camera-reality that would refer to them. (The counterargument that they are within the reach of dialogue and, hence, easily accessible to the screen is flimsy, for it means endorsing uncinematic films—those with verbal statements in the lead.) Consequently, the differences between the universes of the two media threaten to outweigh their resemblances.

REMEMBRANCE OF GREGORIAN CHANTS

That life, as depicted in literary narratives, may always extend into cinematically irreproducible regions, is strikingly illustrated by the Proust

* See p. 71.

novel. Somewhere in the part entitled *The Captive* Marcel describes him-self as lying awake at dawn and listening to the cries of the street vendors that penetrate his bedchamber.[14] So far this episode seems predestined to be filmed. Yet Proust details the hawkers' stereotyped exclamations and intonations mainly for the sake of the memories they evoke in him. They remind him of Gregorian chants. Accordingly, the episode leads up to comparisons between the Paris street cries and these liturgical divisions. But in thus weaving the infinite fabric of observations and recollections in which his life fulfills itself, Proust evolves a continuity impervious to the camera.

The cinema cannot possibly suggest those comparisons and the meditations in their wake without resorting to devious expedients and artificial devices; and of course, no sooner does it draw on them than it ceases to be cinema. What it can represent adequately is not the mental continuum in its entirety but only the physical incidents occasioning it—the vendors in the early street, their sung phrases heard through shutters and curtains, and the narrator's spontaneous response to them. The shots of these incidents may then stir the spectator to embark on the route they throw open to him; in imagining their meanings and implications, however, he will hardly come across the mental images called forth in the novel. So the adapter is in a dilemma. If he features the vendors and their cries he stands little chance of incorporating organically the memories with which they are interwoven; and if he wants to highlight the latter he is heading for uncinematic eleborations which of necessity relegate the street and its noises to the background. Any attempt to convert the mental continuum of the novel into camera-life appears to be hopelessly doomed.

The whole episode is symptomatic of Proust's ambiguous relation to the cinema. On the one hand, he insists that insignificant physical and physiological events—a madeleine dipped in tea, the peculiar position of a limb, the sensation of slightly uneven flagstones—touch off momentous involuntary memories; and it goes without saying that, because of their material character and their very smallness, these events are a natural for the camera. On the other hand, he follows the train of memories, reveling in experiences and thoughts which no longer have an equivalent in the visible world. They are language-bound; even the most ingenious camera work would be only a poor substitute for the visions roused by the words. A contemporary of the rising new medium, Proust acknowledges film in more than one way; at the same time he completely ignores it in his capacity as a writer. His affinity for the cinema makes him sensitive to transient impressions, such as the three trees which look familiar to him; but when he identifies the trees as yet undeciphered phantoms of the past "appealing to me to take them with me, to bring them back to life"[15] he exchanges the world of the cinema for dimensions alien to it.

The novel, then, is not a cinematic literary form. This conclusion immediately brings into focus the issue of adaptations, an issue so complex that there is no purpose in discussing every facet of it.

ABOUT ADAPTATIONS FROM NOVELS

Difference in cinematic quality

Many an adaptation cares little about the spirit of the literary work from which it is drawn. Thus DEVIL IN THE FLESH introduces motifs and messages not found in the Radiguet novel—which, incidentally, may well account for the fact that it is so enjoyable as a film.[16] Let us eliminate such free variations at the outset and concentrate instead on the relatively faithful adaptations. To be sure, they are not literal translations either, but despite all their deviations from the original—deviations partly made necessary by its transfer to the screen—they nevertheless represent an effort, successful or not, to preserve intact its essential contents and emphases. In considering these adaptations in the strict sense of the word, let me examine only one aspect: the extent to which they meet the requirements of the film medium. A glance at the existing film versions of distinguished novels shows that they differ radically in cinematic quality. THE GRAPES OF WRATH and GERVAISE are remarkable films, whereas Jean Renoir's MADAME BOVARY, Claude Autant-Lara's ROUGE ET NOIR, or John Huston's MOBY DICK can hardly be called genuine cinema. Note that these three directors are outstanding professionals with superior films to their credit and that the scripts of ROUGE ET NOIR as well as GERVAISE have been prepared by the same scenarists.* It is therefore highly improbable that uncinematic adaptations should result from a lack of film sense or competence on the part of their authors. So the only remaining way of explaining the difference in cinematic quality between, say, THE GRAPES OF WRATH and MADAME BOVARY is to trace it to a difference inherent in the adapted novels themselves.

The content of novels

Remember that the mental continuum through which novels are ranging may comprise elements which cannot be assimilated by the

* See p. 230.

cinema. Now these elements do not always have to be dominant in a novel. True, many existing novels do involve or indeed feature such untranslatable aspects of life, but there are enough literary works which prefer to bring other aspects into focus. They avoid touching on situations, events, and relationships which are not in a measure transparent to physical reality; they depict a mental continuum which lends itself to being represented and intimated by a continuity of material phenomena. Novels of the first type, then, are rather remote from film, while those of the second come close to it. It is evident that these two types differ with respect to their adaptability. And what do their different contents imply for the adaptations themselves? In trying to answer this question, let me assume throughout that both adapter and director are consummate and sensitive craftsmen.

Cinematic adaptations

To begin with, novels which keep within the confines encompassed by film can naturally be expected to favor cinematic adaptations. In case of such novels the similarities between the literary and the cinematic medium tend to prevail over the differences between the respective universes.

This is confirmed, for instance, by John Ford's THE GRAPES OF WRATH —a classic of the screen as well as a faithful adaptation from the Steinbeck novel of the same title. Among the reasons why Ford was in a position to follow the novel without betraying the cinema, George Bluestone lists the affinity of Steinbeck's main themes for cinematic expression; his insistence on conveying character through physical action; his concomitant reluctance to get inside the minds of his people; and his indulgence in a scenario-like style free from meditations.[17] "There is nothing here," says Bluestone, "which could not be turned into images of physical reality."[18]

He might have been even more specific on two counts. First, Steinbeck's novel deals in human groups rather than individuals. But, as compared with the possible experiences of an isolated person, those of the group are relatively primitive; and they exceed the former in visibility because they must manifest themselves in terms of group behavior. Are not crowds a cinematic subject par excellence? Through his very emphasis on collective misery, collective fears and hopes, Steinbeck meets the cinema more than halfway. Second, his novel exposes the predicament of the migratory farm workers, thus revealing and stigmatizing abuses in our society. This too falls into line with the peculiar potentialities of film. In recording and exploring physical reality, the cinema virtually challenges us to confront that reality with the notions we commonly entertain about it —notions which keep us from perceiving it. Perhaps part of the medium's significance lies in its revealing power.

René Clément, who directed GERVAISE, calls this film version of Zola's *L'Assommoir* a "naturalistic documentary."[19] [Illus. 44] The same might be said, with even greater accuracy, about the novel itself. It is a fictionalized study of alcoholism which traces its origins to environmental conditions and shows its disastrous consequences for health and family life. As always with Zola, the characters he uses for demonstration purposes are composite types rather than complex individuals; and, as always, he highlights the crudest physical influences and effects. The novel is a boon to adapters. In fact, it is so saturated with photographable things, events, and relationships that Aurenche-Bost and Clément can afford to venture further into the psychological dimension than Zola did without deserting the material continuum he establishes. Aside from other, less important changes, they tone down his emphasis on sociological revelations—stuff eminently suitable for the screen—and feature instead Gervaise's valiant effort not to let herself be contaminated by the decay about her.[20] Thus they create a heroine with a touch of human depth. (Whether Zola would have approved such a digression from his main concerns is another question.)

Yet this shift of emphasis notwithstanding, GERVAISE is pure Zola and good cinema to boot. That its truth to the medium goes together with loyalty to the novel must be laid to the latter's indestructible cinematic substance. The major strands of the story, as well as the descriptions of contemporary milieus, are easily woven into the broad pictorial continuity; and the scenes of violence and animal horror in particular turn out to be genuine film material. In the case of these scenes which seem to come into their own when they are transferred from word to image the translation surpasses the original in impact and indeed aesthetic adequacy. Only the camera is able to record dispassionately the repulsive spectacle of the delirious Coupeau wrecking the laundry shop and tumbling down with the cupping glasses on his back. Of course, all this is not to underestimate the director's sensibility, which shows, for instance, in his exquisite handling of the child Nana. Nor should it be forgotten that GERVAISE benefits by being located in that period of the past which still reverberates in our early memories and therefore favors cinematic treatment.*

These two examples would be thoroughly misleading if they gave the impression that only realistic and naturalistic novels can be made into satisfactory films. This is not so. Actually, the adaptability of a novel

* Cf. pp. 56–7.

depends not so much on its exclusive devotion to the material world as on its orientation toward contents which still fall into the dimension of psychophysical correspondences. An apparently realistic novel may indulge in externals for the sake of themes and motifs which defy congenial representation on the screen. Conversely, the fact that a novel involves inner-life processes does not by itself alone mark it as an unadaptable narrative.

Robert Bresson's DIARY OF A COUNTRY PRIEST, drawn from the Bernanos novel of this title, illustrates the posibility of translating certain religious experiences and modes of spirituality into the language of film. It illustrates something else also—that such states of mind are not fully transferable. The country priest's ubiquitous face, by far the most important, most cinematic element of the film, reflects, it is true, the exalted character of his mental preoccupations but fails, necessarily so, to specify their peculiar content. His thoughts, temptations, and aspirations —the *raison d'être* of the novel itself—have no equivalent in his appearance. [Illus. 45] In order to keep us posted on them nevertheless, Bresson has to resort to an expedient. Every now and then he reproduces the notes which the priest is entrusting to his journal—inserts which call to mind many a silent film crammed with captions. Their obtrusive presence points to the elusiveness of part of the novel, thus raising the issue of uncinematic adaptations.

Uncinematic adaptations

Such uncinematic adaptations as aim at a faithful rendering of the original and are carried out by skillful and film-minded adapters are inevitably derived from novels which construct a cinematically unmanageable universe in the manner of Proust's. There is no question about this. The question is, rather, how do the adapters cope with the tremendous difficulties confronting them? It almost looks as if the predicament they are in forced them to adopt a uniform line of conduct. The "solutions" at which they arrive are mostly adaptations in a theatrical vein.

Jean Renoir's adaptation of *Madame Bovary* exemplifies this tendency all the more convincingly since the Flaubert novel not only devotes much space to the drabness of provincial life but also pays great attention to physical detail. Add to this that all environmental phenomena are made to appear as Emma might experience them; they help project her inward being. So it would at first glance seem relatively easy for a film maker to establish a material continuum by following Flaubert's realistic descriptions and to suggest through it the main contents of the original. (Even though the various external happenings in the novel are not so much actual facts succeeding each other in chronological time as projections characterized and interlinked in terms of Emma's response, there is no serious obstacle to their transformation into film imagery.) Yet this impression is deceptive. For unlike the Steinbeck and Zola novels, Flaubert's culminates in psychological events which no combination of physical data would be able to connote.

Those descriptions of the environment are embedded in a narrative whose declared objective is to drive home the "formless tragedy"[21] of Emma's existence—her boredom, her futile attempts to achieve happiness, her disappointments, and her inexorable doom. What the novel is about is the history of a soul. As Erich Auerbach puts it, "If Flaubert . . . lingers as a matter of principle over insignificant events and everyday circumstances which hardly advance the action, there is nevertheless to be sensed throughout *Madame Bovary* . . . a constant slow-moving chronological approach first to partial crises and finally to the concluding catastrophe, and it is this approach which dominates the plan of the work as a whole."[22] And how do the dominating developments materialize? They are transmitted through the whole of the plot, which, along with the many elaborations on Emma's milieu, comprises a plethora of verbal images and language-bound observations as remote from camera-reality as are Proust's references to the Gregorian chants.

This accounts for the uncinematic character of Renoir's MADAME BOVARY. It may be taken for granted that the film represents an effort to reproduce as faithfully as possible the novel's "slow-moving chronological approach" to the processes that lead to Emma's self-destruction. But these processes make up a universe which resists translation into a cinematic continuity. Renoir cannot transfer it wholesale to the screen. In dealing with the total plot all he can lay his hands on is its skeleton—the bare story line, that is. The novel is such that his very desire to get at its core compels him to concentrate—"oh, dear, yes"—on the intrigue threading it. To this end he must isolate the intrigue from the "finer growths" of life with which it is insolubly interwoven in the novel and organize it according to the purposeful evolution of the bulk of the narrative. The inevitable result is an adaptation which has all the traits of a theatrical film.

His film consists of a succession of actions and episodes which completely lack cohesion. There are gaps between these units, and, in addition, from the angle of film, most of them are very complex indeed. The reason is that they are culled from the novel with a view to implementing the essentially unadaptable tragedy of Emma's life. Hence, if they form a continuity, it is certainly not a material one. The patterns of meanings they convey are detachable from the medium. Of course, Renoir would not be the film maker he is did he not try to restore the environment to the role it plays in the novel. He incorporates the agricultural fair and continually reverts to the country road; nor does he forget the street singer or the meetings in theater and cathedral. Due to their transfer from book to screen, however, these settings and incidents undergo a change of function. In the novel they are fully integrated into the epic flow of the whole, while in the adaptation they serve either to fill a gap between the units of the intrigue or to sustain its patterns of meanings. The first alternative is illustrated by the fair scenes, which affect one as sheer background commotion; the second by the repeatedly shown country road which in its capacity as a meaningful story motif loses its reality character. The intrigue abstracted from the novel prevails throughout and drains it of life.

About the same might also be said of GREAT EXPECTATIONS, THE HEIRESS, ROUGE ET NOIR, etc. [Illus. 46] In his comment on the latter—an outright theatrical dialogue film which even goes so far as to verbalize the hero's thoughts—Gabriel Marcel poignantly epitomizes the detrimental consequences for adaptations of any original whose universe extends beyond the reach of the camera. Stendhal's *Le Rouge et le Noir*, Marcel remarks, "was the very type . . . of novel which should not have been brought to the screen." Why? Because all that counts with Julien Sorel, its protagonist, is "a certain interior life very little of which can, by definition, be exteriorized; I should almost say, it is the deviation of his appearance from his reality [which counts]. The novelist is quite in a position to reveal to us this reality . . . whereas the film maker must stick to the appearances; and only by his recourse, fraudulent in a way, to the text, will he be able to render intelligible—incidentally, in an inevitably schematic manner—the interior world which is Julien Sorel's. . . . In consequence, the substance of Stendhal's masterwork becomes terribly thin, and what constitutes the interest of the book is not really retained."[23]

The Found Story and the Episode

LIKE THE NOVEL, the short story may dwell on unadaptable aspects of inner life. There are no genuinely cinematic literary forms.

Yet, of course, this does not exclude the possibility of cinematic story forms which assert themselves independently of the established literary genres. Now note that such story types are only rarely referred to in the literature on film; in fact, they do not even carry names by which to recognize them. Is one to infer from this that they are actually non-existent? By no means. Rather, there is evidence that the prevailing unconcern for them stems from a widespread and deep-rooted bias. Most critics have thought of film as an art in the traditional sense, and, as a result, they have not seriously tried to trace and identify cinematic story forms. So why not proceed from the perfectly sound assumption that they do exist after all? In the following, an attempt will be made to drag these story forms out from their undeserved anonymity. Obviously they must be definable in terms which bear on the preferences of film. And they must by their very nature permit or indeed stimulate the representation of camera-reality on the screen.

THE FOUND STORY

Definitions

The term "found story" covers all stories found in the material of actual physical reality. When you have watched for long enough the surface of a river or a lake you will detect certain patterns in the water which may have been produced by a breeze or some eddy. Found stories are in the nature of such patterns. Being discovered rather than contrived, they are inseparable from films animated by documentary intentions. Accordingly, they come closest to satisfying that demand for the story which "re-emerges within the womb of the non-story film."*

Since the found story is part and parcel of the raw material in which it lies dormant, it cannot possibly develop into a self-contained whole—which means that it is almost the opposite of the theatrical story. Finally, due to its symbiosis with documentary, it tends to render incidents typical of the world around us. Perhaps the earliest example of a story film of this kind is Lumière's TEASING THE GARDENER, whose action, a chance constellation of comic happenings, seems to be drawn straight from unstaged everyday life.

Found stories differ from each other by their degree of compactness or distinctness. They may be arranged along a continuum which extends from embryonic story patterns at one pole to fairly well-contoured stories, often packed with dramatic action, at the other. Somewhere in-between lies Flaherty's "slight narrative."

Types

EMBRYONIC PATTERNS

Many a documentary includes found stories in a pupa state—"stories" which hardly detach themselves from the flow of environmental impressions. Thus Arne Sucksdorff's PEOPLE IN THE CITY, a "city symphony" picturing Stockholm street life in documentary fashion, evolves three such storylike textures: (1) A young man who has sought shelter from the rain in a doorway follows a young girl standing beside him after the rain has ceased. (2) Schoolchildren in a church, awed by the organ music and the sanctity of the place, search stealthily for a marble which one of them believes he has dropped. (3) A fisherman spreads his small haul on the river bank and then busies himself with other things; suddenly he discovers that sea gulls have taken advantage of his negligence and now are flying away with the fish. [Illus. 47] These "most fascinating news stories of the week," as *The New Yorker* would call them—but what is wrong in literature is often the right thing for film—are just articulate enough to convey a shade of human interest apt to lend color to the juxtaposed documentary shots; and they are sufficiently sketchy and inconsequential to dissolve again into the general city life within which they accidentally

* See p. 213.

crystallized. Whether their elusiveness proves entirely satisfactory to the spectator is another question; he may feel he is being let down by suggestions and promises which invariably fail to come true.

FLAHERTY'S "SLIGHT NARRATIVE"

The term "slight narrative" originates with Rotha, who says of Flaherty that "he prefers the inclusion of a slight narrative, not fictional incident or interpolated 'cameos,' but the daily routine of his native people."[1] Rotha's observation amplifies part of a summary key statement by Flaherty himself: "A story must come out of the life of a people, not from the actions of individuals."[2] Out of the life of a primitive people, Flaherty should have added, in order to present to the full the formula underlying his major films. This formula was of a piece with his passions and visions. Besides enabling him to satisfy his explorer instincts, it was rooted in his Rousseauan conviction that primitive cultures are the last vestiges of unspoiled human nature and in his sustained desire to show "the former majesty and the character of these people, while it is still possible."[3] [Illus. 48]

Flaherty has been called a romantic and indicted for escapist leanings, because of his withdrawal from our modern world, with its pressing needs.[4] To be sure, he *was* the rhapsodist of backward areas in a sense, but this does not impinge on the integrity of his films. Their inherent romanticism notwithstanding, they are cinematic documents of the highest order. Hence the general significance of Flaherty's formula. Now what matters here is exclusively his conception of a cinematic story, as defined in his programmatic statement quoted just above. This statement carries four important implications.

First, in immediately raising the issue of the story, Flaherty seems to take it for granted that a story is desirable for documentary. His own work bears witness to this belief; there is practically no Flaherty film that would lack structured sequences in the nature of an empathic narrative. Moreover, his films show an increasing tendency toward distinct story patterns. While NANOOK still confines itself to a thoroughly coherent and understanding representation of the Eskimo way of life, LOUISIANA STORY narrates the encounter between a Cajun boy and an oil derrick in terms which almost transcend Flaherty's program; one further step in this direction and the documentary would turn into an outright story film.

Second, a story must come out of the life of a people, says Flaherty, whereby it is understood that he means primitive people. Now primitive life unfolds in a natural setting and plays up bodily movements as well as events close to nature; in other words, one of its relevant features is its affinity for photography. Accordingly, if this part of Flaherty's statement is extended, it can be applied to stories which cover human reality as it manifests itself significantly in the physical world. So the narrative may not only grow out of primitive people but take its cue from crowds, street scenes, and what not.

Third, the story must not come from the actions of individuals. That this was tremendously important to Flaherty is corroborated by a biographical fact. Even though he was known to be "one of the greatest yarn-spinners of our times,"[5] he never displayed his brilliant gifts as a story-teller on the screen. His refusal to yield to this temptation, if temptation it was, is completely incomprehensible unless one assumes that he believed individual actions to be inconsistent with the spirit of his medium. Generally speaking, he shunned the full-fledged intrigue which traditionally features the individual. As a film maker he certainly felt the need for a story, but he seems to have been afraid lest fully developed, rounded-out stories, which often have very pronounced patterns of meanings, prevent the camera from having its say. This helps explain why he preferred the "slight narrative," which sticks to the typical.

Fourth, the deliberate use of the verb "come out" in Flaherty's statement testifies to his insistence on eliciting the story from the raw material of life rather than subjecting the raw material to its pre-established demands. "There is a kernel of greatness in all peoples," says he, "and it is up to the film maker to . . . find the one incident or even the one movement that makes it clear."[6] His idea of "discovering the *essential human story from within*"[7] led him to evolve it during an incubation period in which he assimilated the life of the people he wanted to picture.[8] And he was so averse to letting story requirements interfere with the experiences thus gathered and with his concurrent camera explorations that, in shooting the story, he used a working outline which could always be changed as he proceeded. It is as if the medium itself invited this kind of approach: in any case, Flaherty is not the only one to rely on improvisation in immediate contact with the material. When shooting THE BIRTH OF A NATION, D. W. Griffith "improvised freely as he went along"; by the way, Lewis Jacobs who mentions this adds that Griffith's confidence in his intuition also accounts for many an absurdity in his films.[9] Similarly, the Rossellini of OPEN CITY, PAISAN, and GERMANY YEAR ZERO develops his scenes on locale, with only a rudimentary story serving him as a guide.[10] Nor does Fellini want to be incommoded by a well-written story: "If I know everything from the start, I would no longer be interested in doing it. So that when I begin a picture, I am not yet sure of the location or the actors. Because for me, to do a picture is like leaving for a trip. And the most interesting part of a trip is what you discover on the way."[11]* And did not Eisenstein undergo a change of mind when he saw the Odessa steps?

If put into words, Flaherty's "slight narrative" would be something like an interpretative account bordering on poetry. The unavoidable consequence of his solution is that it does not involve the audience as intensely as might a more outspoken story film. To the extent that his films evade the individual, the individual may not feel urged to surrender to them.

DRAMATIZED ACTUALITY

The limitations of films about the world around us have long since stirred documentary makers to cross the boundaries which Flaherty respected. Rotha, who already in the 'thirties advocated documentaries which "embrace individuals,"** declares over twenty years later that in his opinion "socially and aesthetically the so-called story film and the true documentary are growing closer and closer together."[12] Whether or not this will happen, there are numbers of documentary-like films with stories which go beyond the "slight narrative." To be sure, they still are found in reality and do highlight events typical of it, but at the same time they are almost as compact and distinct as many a contrived intrigue. POTEMKIN, MOTHER, and other Russian films of the Revolution may well belong here; or think of Cavalcanti-Watt's NORTH SEA, one of the first British documentaries to dramatize actuality. In these films compositional aspirations merge, or rival, with the underlying documentary intentions, and fictional elaborations tend to complement and intensify the given incidents. Clearly, films like NORTH SEA or FARREBIQUE or TOGETHER lie in the border region that separates documentary from feature film, especially the episode film.

Hence the difficulty of classifying them. "Where does fiction begin in the dialogue and action of *North Sea* . . . ?" asks Roger Manvell, who then immediately raises the corresponding question: "Where does documentary begin . . . in *The Grapes of Wrath* . . . ?"[13] If dramatic documentaries picture a found story which seems constantly to dissolve into the environment from which it is being distilled, they must certainly be considered true to type. This is how Rotha conceives of NORTH SEA; he defines it as a documentary "on the verge of being a story-film."[14] Georges Rouquier's FARREBIQUE, which renders the life of a French farm family

---

* James Agee in *Agee on Film*, p. 401, quotes the film director John Huston as saying: "In a given scene I have an idea what *should* happen, but I don't tell the actors. Instead I tell them to go ahead and do it. Sometimes they do it better. Sometimes they do something accidentally which is effective and true. I jump on the accident."

** See p. 212.

throughout a year and, along with it, the farm itself and the seasonal changes of nature, might be entered under the same title. It delicately molds the rural life cycle it self-forgettingly records; and its invented incidents enhance rather than belie its "reverence for unaltered reality."[15]

If, on the other hand, the found story of films in that border region attains to such a solidity that it threatens to obscure their non-story character and their primary concern for actuality, these films give the impression of episode films on the verge of being documentaries. A case in point in Lionel Rogosin's ON THE BOWERY, an admirable report on the flophouses and bums in downtown New York. [Illus. 49] It is as if its story—a spun-out anecdote centering on the protagonist—involved the environment instead of being part of it; like a magnet, the film's fictional core attracts its reportorial elements which group themselves accordingly. The Russian films of the Revolution dramatize re-enacted actuality in a similar way, with the difference that in them Marxist argumentation substitutes for the story proper.

FINIS TERRAE

All these attempts at a fusion of the story film and documentary are faced with a problem which Flaherty avoided. Since he found, or believed to find, his story by exploring, with the assistance of his camera, the life of the people in whose midst he lived, his documentary account and his "slight narrative" interpenetrate each other from the outset. What the task of effecting this kind of interpenetration amounts to once the "slight narrative" yields to a story which encompasses individuals—or an ideology, for that matter—is drastically demonstrated by an extreme case: Jean Epstein's FINIS TERRAE. In this film Epstein tries to blend a full-grown documentary on Breton fishermen with an equally full-grown story found in the reality covered—at least found in the sense that it was drawn from the columns of a local newspaper.

The story features a rescue action: a wounded young fisherman staying with his three companions on a lonely island would be lost were it not for the old village doctor who braves the storm to come to his aid; the documentary on its part records the stony island, the Breton village community, the lighthouse, the ocean. Now the point is that, in spite of the fact that a documentary and a story require different styles of representation—the latter consuming the very raw material which the former is supposed to bare—Epstein aims at a reconciliation between these styles without apparently being willing to sacrifice any of the specific virtues of either. He goes the limit in embroidering his tale and he never refrains from elaborating on depictions in documentary fashion. So of course he does not succeed in closing the gap between the two forms of narration involved. Far from achieving their fusion, Finis Terrae is, all in all, a mechanical and rather clumsy mixture of actuality and fiction. But as such it offers great interest for laying open the difficulty against which film makers run who want to weave some highly distinct found story into a non-story texture of factual shots. Immense tact is required on their part to fuse these divergent modes of continuity of which a dramatic documentary necessarily consists.

That approximate solutions are possible is evidenced, for instance, by Lorenza Mazzetti's Together, a movie about two deaf-mute London dock workers in which long passages devoted to their dreary everyday existence alternate with sequences in a feature-film vein. [Illus. 50] One of the deaf-mutes indulges in a dream of love-making; at the end playing children push him into the Thames, as if he were a plaything, and he drowns in silence, unseen by the crew of a near-by barge. Thanks to the wise selection of story motifs, all of which are potential implications of deaf-mute-ness, the balance between drama and reportage is nearly perfect. And the two kinds of continuities would indeed jell into a unified flow of pictures were it not for the difference between the concepts of time in the film's story and documentary parts. The emphasis, within the latter, on the limbo enveloping the deaf-mutes results in repetitious scenes which denote an indefinite span of time markedly at variance with the short and well-defined time periods in which the story episodes take their course.

THE EPISODE

Definitions

Webster defines "episode" as a "set of events having distinctness and moment in a larger series, as in one's life, in history or in creation." Accordingly, this term will be applied to stories whose common property it is to emerge from, and again disappear in, the flow of life, as suggested by the camera. It is their bearing on camera-life which accounts for their adequacy to the medium. This implies that otherwise episodic films become problematic aesthetically if they feature some unadaptable inner conflict or thought instead of that life; their uncinematic content threatens to overshadow their cinematic form. Such an episode film is, for instance, The Defiant Ones, which pictures the escape from a Southern prison camp of a white man and a Negro who are chained to each other, their desperate, if futile, attempts to reach safety, and their inevitable capture at the end.

This episode in the convicts' lives is plainly told with a view to driving home the change of mind they are undergoing during their flight: the white man learns to accept the Negro as a human being worthy of his friendship, while the Negro sheds off distrust and repays loyalty with confidence. Now it would be easy to show that the ideology behind the film does not grow out of the reality depicted but, conversely, assumes the role of a prime mover; the inner change of the two runaways is a foregone conclusion which predetermines the order and meaning of the successive scenes. Hence the impression that the film is a tale of human dignity, a sermon against the evil of race bias. By the same token its episodic story ceases to point up the flow of life and turns instead into a theatrical morality play whose realism strikes one as simulated.

In the border region between episode films and documentaries dramatizing actuality, transitions are so fluid that there is no purpose in trying to arrive at clear-cut distinctions. Any documentary with a found story of high compactness, such as NORTH SEA or TOGETHER, may also be considered an episode film; and numbers of movies in a palpably episodic vein—e.g. MENSCHEN AM SONNTAG, THE QUIET ONE, LITTLE FUGITIVE, OPEN CITY, etc.—have a marked documentary quality. [Illus. 51] Yet their overlaps notwithstanding, the two genres differ in two respects. First, unlike the found story, the episode may be a contrived intrigue, as illustrated by BRIEF ENCOUNTER, CAVALCADE, the Roman story of PAISAN, etc. Similarly, the old *avant-garde* films FIEVRE, EN RADE, and MENILMONTANT narrate fictitious incidents embedded in poetized actuality; or remember the ingenious episodes of silent comedy, tangles in a topsy-turvy world in flux not identical with documentary reality either. Second, unlike the found story, the episode is by no means bound to render events and situations typical of the environmental life to which it refers. The fantastic stories of DEAD OF NIGHT run true to type; and the episode with the lady high-diver in ENCORE is as genuine as that of the old dancer in the mask of a youth in LE PLAISIR.

Types

Episode films may consist of a single episodic unit—an episode, that is, which resembles a monad or cell in that it resists further division—or be composed of a number of such units. To begin with the first alternative, it does not occur frequently because it makes for shorts rather than feature-length films. THE RED BALLOON, a weak 34-minute fairy-tale about a miraculous balloon befriending a Paris urchin, figures among the exceptions. In order nevertheless to profit by this effective—and cinematic—

story form, the film industry has fallen on the device of assembling, anthology fashion, several short units under a common heading. The just-mentioned films Le Plaisir and Encore are nothing but mechanical pack-ages of self-sufficient episodes. True, all the episodes are adapted from Maupassant and Maugham respectively, but this does not confer on either package a semblance of unity. What appears here and there is not so much a film as an expedient collection of independent little movies. (Incidentally, the fact that many episodic units are drawn from short stories should not blind one to the cinematically neutral character of this literary form.)

The second alternative comprises episode films built from a series of episodic units. These units may be relatively autonomous entities which are strung together like beads so that they attain to a degree of cohesion. Or they may relinquish their independence and, often hardly distinguish-able from each other, become parts of a story into which they are inte-grated like the cells of a living organism.

THE UNITS ARE STRUNG TOGETHER

Sometimes a minimum of unity is achieved in terms of space, differ-ent stories being laid in one and the same locality. In Gold of Naples and It Happened in the Park it is the *genius loci* of Naples and the Borghese Gardens respectively which provides a fragile bond between otherwise separate units. Instead of a place, the common denominator may also be an identical period of time. Thus all the six episodes of Paisan are set against the common background of war—a diffuse and very cinematic frame of reference.

Or the unifying link is a story of a sort. Such stories as silent film comedy advances have merely the function of interrelating somehow their gags or monad-like units of gags. What matters is that the units follow each other uninterruptedly, not that their succession implements a plot. To be sure, they frequently happen to develop into a halfway plausible intrigue, yet the intrigue is never of so exacting a nature that its sig-nificance would encroach on that of the pieces composing it. Even though The Gold Rush and City Lights transcend the genre, they climax in epi-sodes like the dance with the fork or the misdemeanor of the swallowed whistle, gag clusters which, for meaning and effect, depend so little on the narrative in which they appear that they can easily be isolated without becoming less intelligible or losing any of their flavor. For the rest, film comedy indulges in absurdity, as if to make it unmistakably clear that no action is intended to be of consequence. The nonsensical frolics of Mack

Sennett's bathing girls smother the tender beginnings of comprehensible plots.

Once a story is used to string episodic units together, the idea of giving it more scope suggests itself immediately. There are films which mark a transition between an aggregate and a coherent whole. If Mr. Hulot's Holiday, this amazing late offspring of silent comedy, lacks a real intrigue, yet it carries a message which unifies the colorful diversity of its incidents and seeming impromptus: all of them denounce the melancholy void pervading middle-class life in a state of relaxation. The framing story of Dead of Night almost matches in impact the several episodes it threads. Does Cavalcade belong here? Its over-all story assumes such proportions that it not only connects the war, drawing-room, and street episodes of which it consists but determines their emotional content, their course.

THE UNITS ARE INTEGRATED INTO A STORY

In fact, Cavalcade might as well be called an integrated episode film. Complex products of this type are fairly frequent. Some of them—for instance, Cabiria and Pather Panchali—resemble Cavalcade in that their episodic units preserve a certain distinctness, while at the same time constituting a perfectly consistent sequence of events. In others, such as The Bicycle Thief, Brief Encounter, La Regle du jeu, the units tend to fuse so that it is as if each film they make up were a single episode. Not that this structural difference would matter much. All that counts is, rather, that the units form part and parcel of an open-ended narrative — open-ended in the sense that it relates in its entirety to the flow of life. Sensitivity to this flow seems to be an inherent feature of Italian neorealism. To Rossellini, De Sica, and Fellini life that concerns us is essentially the kind of life which only the camera is capable of revealing. Their films time and again probe into significant aspects of it.

Structure

PERMEABILITY

An episode is all the more in character if it is permeable to the flow of life out of which it rises. This means that its cinematic quality varies in direct ratio to the degree of its permeability, any increase of the latter being tantamount to an increasing influx of camera-reality. Take Brief Encounter: one of the reasons why it is good cinema lies in the fact that it is punctuated by references to the physical world from which its story stems—references which help characterize the story as an episode. Furthermore, because of its permanent movement, the inflowing environment it-self figures among the cinematic subjects. BRIEF ENCOUNTER, says the French critic Albert Laffay, "practically confines itself to two or three sets, not more . . . Yet these settings are 'open'; people circulate in them; one is constantly aware that they are replaceable any moment. They send you away because they are being penetrated by movements or the vibration of trains."[16]

Railway stations belong in the orbit of the "street,"* that province of reality where transient life manifests itself most conspicuously. Hence the affinity of episode films for places with accidental, ever-changing patterns. FIEVRE incessantly reverts to the customers in the bar; in L'ATALANTE the street-like river is virtually omnipresent; UEBERFALL would cease to breathe without its reiterated shots of desolate streets and dilapidated houses. And what about the great Italian films? From OPEN CITY to CABIRIA, THE BICYCLE THIEF to LA STRADA, they are literally soaked in the street world; they not only begin and end in it but are transparent to it throughout. Fellini once expressed to an interviewer his preference for nocturnal scenery and the solitude of empty streets.[17] One of his main themes is in-deed human loneliness, as experienced in streets, empty or not.[18]

Permeability calls for loose composition. Renoir's insistence on it, as manifest in his LA REGLE DU JEU or LA GRANDE ILLUSION, is all the more noteworthy since his stories, their episodic tenor notwithstanding, come close to rounded-out fiction. It almost is as if he wanted to get away from his story while narrating it; as if, in a state of absent-mindedness, he con-stantly permitted unrelated incidents to slip in and blur the story patterns proper. His aversion to straight story construction has given rise to critical comment. Yet, as Henri Agel judiciously remarks, the "conserva-tive critics who wonder at the extreme liberty and indeed negligence which Renoir displays with respect to the course of his stories . . . do not understand that for Renoir all is moving . . . and that it is this process of molting [mue] . . . which must be communicated by an absolutely dis-engaged and dilated style."[19] The true film artist may be imagined as a man who sets out to tell a story but, in shooting it, is so overwhelmed by his innate desire to cover all of physical reality—and also by a feeling that he must cover it in order to tell the story, any story, in cinematic terms—that he ventures ever deeper into the jungle of material phenomena in which he risks becoming irretrievably lost if he does not, by virtue of great efforts, get back to the highways he has left. Renoir has traits of this type of artist.

The episode film, then, is full of gaps into which environmental life

* See pp. 62–3, 71–3.

may stream. This raises the question as to how the elements of an episodic unit and, in a complex episode, the units themselves are interrelated. Sure enough, they do not implement pre-established story patterns or else there would be no air between them. The story they narrate is inherent in their succession. So we inevitably get the impression that they follow a course strangely devoid of purpose and direction; it is as if they drifted along, moved by unaccountable currents. Only a few critics—foremost among them Henri Agel—have recognized, let alone endorsed, this process of drifting, which runs counter to the cherished conceptions of traditional aesthetics. Referring to Fellini's I VITELLONI, Agel says: "The whole film is composed of instants whose only *raison d'être* is their instantaneousness: the thunderstorm which bursts during the election of the beauty queen, the billiard game, the gloomy walk in the nocturnal streets. These are the facts which glide into each other and join one another with no other linkage than the circumstances. . . . all appears to be interlinked at random, without any logic, any necessity."[20] (Perhaps the Fellini films, with their relatively distinct episodic parts, demonstrate best the kind of loose construction inseparable from permeability; but it is understood that all other episode films, say, PAISAN or UMBERTO D. or Jean Vigo's beautiful L'ATALANTE, proceed in similar ways.) Agel supplements his description of the drifting and gliding processes by contrasting the episode, which he calls "chronicle," with films conveying a tragedy or a philosophy; unlike the latter, he declares, the chronicle has "the style of a proposition; it permits us to entertain imperfect notions [of the things we see]."[21]

But what about the flow of life which is supposed to permeate the episodic story? It is both suggested and represented within its framework. Suggested: the random way in which the elements of the story succeed each other stirs us to imagine, however confusedly, the circumstances responsible for their succession—circumstances which must be traced to that flow. Represented: diffuse physical reality as a rule enters the scene in the form of incidents which are drawn from the wider environment. These incidents may extend the episode into the material world at large, or belong among the chance currents changing its direction, or be not directly related to it at all. In the Italian neorealistic films—not in them alone, of course—they are sometimes so selected and inserted that they take on the function of ideograms. Here is where Rossellini's remark on Fellini acquires a specific meaning. Fellini, he said, "is at once imprecise and precise"[22]— an observation which presumably holds true also of De Sica and Rossellini himself. In any case, all of them are, or appear to be, imprecise in that they fail to connect the elements or units of their narratives in a rational manner. A straight line seems unimaginable to them; nothing really dovetails in their films. At the same time, however, it is as if they possessed a divining rod enabling them to spot, on their journey through the maze of physical existence, phenomena and occurrences which strike us as being tremendously significant.

The lone horse passing by the abandoned Gelsomina at dawn and the sick child with the eyes of a scared small animal which has never left its cave (La Strada); the street invading the rooming house and the rows of Roman façades, as seen from a moving streetcar (Umberto D.); the group of German-speaking priests in the rain (The Bicycle Thief); the Naples marionette theater where the drunken American Negro soldier mistakes the puppets for real warriors and joins in the battle (Paisan)—these scenes and images, found in the world around the story proper, are singled out with unrivaled precision. Selected from among the many incidents with which the environment teems, they are very special samples indeed. They are beckoning us with great urgency, like the three trees in the Proust novel.

Looking at the lone horse, the group of priests, the puppet show, we feel that they desperately want to impart to us an important message. (The same may be said, for instance, of the appearance of the candy man in Pather Panchali, or the shots of the populous Paris market quarter in the silent film The Love of Jeanne Ney, whose tendency toward the episodic grew out of G. W. Pabst's then marked preference for camera-realism.) Is the message decipherable? Any attempt at an allegorical interpretation would drain these ideograms of their substance. They are propositions rather than rebuses. Snatched from transient life, they not only challenge the spectator to penetrate their secret but, perhaps even more insistently, request him to preserve them as the irreplaceable images they are.

THE DANGER OF SELF-CONTAINMENT

Since the cinematic quality of an episode depends upon its permeability, it is bound to deteriorate if it shuts out the flow of life from which it emerges. If its pores are closed, the episode becomes self-contained; there is nothing that would prevent it from turning into a theatrical intrigue pure and simple.

No doubt the Roman story of Paisan is a war story like all the other episodes of this film, but you cannot help noticing that it has a peculiar cachet: it is a highly contrived story, not the kind of sketchy and nervous reportage in which most of Paisan excels. A tipsy American soldier, picked up by a prostitute, tells her about Francesca, the girl he met when he arrived in Rome with the army half a year before, riding in a tank which happened to stop just before Francesca's house. [Illus. 52] Flashback: we see the soldier enter the house and then watch the charming and innocent beginnings of a love story which never develops into one, for the soldier is called back to his tank and all his later attempts to find the house with Francesca in it prove abortive. This he tells the prostitute in a mood of disillusionment over the virtue of the Roman girls; they are no good anymore. The prostitute says she knows Francesca and the house he is talking about; she also says that many girls have remained decent in their struggle for survival; and she asks the soldier to come to Francesca's house where Francesca will be waiting for him tomorrow. He succumbs to his stupor and falls asleep. Francesca withdraws, leaving instructions behind that he be given her address upon awakening. Next day she waits in vain for the soldier—the hours are passing and he does not come. Along with other soldiers, he lingers about near the Colosseum, on the point of leaving the city. Their army outfit is moving on into the war.

Now this negative love story with the Maupassant touch is anything but the war episode it pretends to be. And what does prevent it from being one? Its indulgence in fictitious events? Certainly not. Think of BRIEF ENCOUNTER, which clearly shows that films with a contrived intrigue may well be episodic in spirit. The non-episodic character of the Roman story must be traced to its lack of porosity, which is all the more striking since the story simulates a genuine episode. In fact, it claims special interest for conveying an anti-episodic attitude with the aid of thoroughly episodic material. The American soldier meets Francesca in the turmoil of the Liberation; loses sight of her; finds her unexpectedly; leaves her for the front—these incidents all of which are characteristic of the flow of life in times of war, times of chronic instability, thread the story, so that at first glance it is as if the story were permeated by that flow.

But what really happens is just the reverse. Instead of illustrating free-flowing life, the incidents contingent on it are made to figure as elements of a forcedly significant composition. The Roman story is not so much a suggestive flow as a closed system: its accidents are premeditated, its random coincidences a matter of sophisticated choice. All these chance occurrences defy chance; they seem expressly assembled to implement the idea that under the duress of war nothing that is tender, human, and beautiful is permitted to grow and subsist.

The story is a self-contained whole rather than an open-ended episode. This follows conclusively from the way in which we are made to conceive of the final scene. The American soldier appears in a group of G.I.'s near the Colosseum. They are standing in the rain. He negligently drops the slip of paper with Francesca's address and then boards the bus or jeep come to fetch him and his comrades. The paper floats in a puddle. If the story were an authentic episode, these magnificent last shots would **make it look like a bubble dissolving into the elegiac life from which it** rose a moment before. For an episode thus to disintegrate is a fully adequate ending. Actually, however, this ending impresses us not as the natural submersion of an episodic story in environmental currents but as the contrived conclusion and very climax of the narrative itself. The Roman story is palpably calculated to demonstrate the decay of humanity in a period of war. So it is inevitable that the image of Francesca's address floating in the puddle should turn from a real-life shot for its own sake into the ultimate symbol of the all-pervading idea of that decay.

A number of semi-documentaries belongs here also. One of the reasons for the rise of this genre after World War II was presumably the desire of the film industry to cash in on the success of the war documentaries and neorealistic films. Why not exploit the trend in their favor and produce movies along similar lines? Semi-documentaries are films of fiction which try to let in life in the raw and preferably center on topical issues; because of their inherent concern with actuality, they have, or ought to have, an affinity for the episode. Note that, due to its hybrid character, the genre requires a fusion of story and non-story elements difficult to reconcile with each other. Among the best solutions so far is Louis de Rochemont's BOOMERANG, directed by Elia Kazan; an almost improbable blend of episodic action and factual account, it gives the impression of rendering, newsreel fashion, real-life events which jell into a dramatic sequence of their own accord. BOOMERANG is good cinema.

Yet compared with this product of ingenuity and opportunity, most so-called semi-documentaries are outright sham. What is wrong with them? They miss something essential to the genre—the episodic story form. Instead they fall back on the self-contained intrigue which, as a more or less closed entity proves impermeable to camera-reality, fitting the theater rather than the screen. Semi-documentaries mingle fiction and fact mechanically; to be precise, their plot, with its exacting patterns of meanings, unavoidably dominates their documentary contributions. Thus THE SEARCH, a typical semi-documentary, is nothing but a regular feature film, with some documentary material thrown into the bargain.

Much as such films play up prima-facie takes in the documentary sections, these takes never assume any vital function. Far from penetrating the story so that the flow of life begins to assert itself, they remain inserts which represent at most an attempt to adjust the story to the medium. To be sure, they may seem to add a whiff of fresh air, thereby acting as a stimulant, but then again they may, by way of contrast, increase our awareness that the intrigue they are seasoning is a construction indifferent to documentary truth. This is what Flaherty means when he declares that "you can not superimpose studio-fabricated plots on an actual setting without finding that the reality of the background will show up the artificiality of your story."[23]

A framing device

Further evidence that the episode film is more in keeping with the cinematic approach than the theatrical story film may be found in a device which has been occasionally used to mitigate the uncinematic character of the theatrical story. The device consists in framing the theatrical film by scenes which are apt to divert our attention from its staginess and indeed pass it off as an episode. These surrounding scenes usually establish a real-life situation in such a way that the action in between them seems to grow out of it. An Ideal Husband, for instance, opens with a prelude in documentary style which affords a glimpse of Victorian splendor in Hyde Park. Dowagers in their carriages exchange greetings with men on horseback, and groups of well-to-do people are leisurely bandying small talk. Then some of these people, already recognizable as members of the cast, come increasingly into focus. The environment recedes and the Wilde comedy, a sheer drawing-room affair, takes its preordained course. It concludes as it began: Hyde Park with its cavalcades, carriages, and chance gatherings re-emerges. The idea is naturally to create the illusion that the comedy itself is not so much a theatrical job as an episode involving the Victorian smart set on display—an episode expressly marked as such by the fact that it issues from, and eventually rejoins, the glittering flow of life in the street-like Park. Does the magic work? The spell which the framing documentary shots cast over the spectator is likely to be destroyed by the penetrant theatricality of the bulk of the film.

Similarly, the opening scenes of Olivier's Henry V show the London Globe Theatre in the times of Shakespeare, with the audience waiting for the curtain to rise; and when the performance is over, an appended finale reverts to the theme of the beginning. This frame is clearly intended to make the play appear as an episode in the everyday life of contemporary London. The whole arrangement does credit to Olivier's film sense. It is an attempt to put the theatrical spectacle in brackets and offset the effect of its stylizations by a touch of camera-reality.[24]

A striking counter-example is the Italian film Side Street Story (Napoli Milionaria), which features a number of people in a small and crowded Naples street and casually relates their destinies before, during, and after World War II. Nobody would believe this film, with its loosely connected episodic units, was adapted from a stage play were it not for its theatrical framing scenes. At the beginning and end the two protagonists converse about the questionable state of the world, which in their opinion remains invariably the same, wars and revolutions notwithstanding. [Illus. 53] In other words, they tell us what should be considered the moral of the film, thus imposing a meaning on it which threatens to obscure the inherent multiple meanings of the pictures themselves. Hence the nuisance character of the framing scenes: they reduce the film to an illustration; they force it to illustrate the very message you would expect it to convey on its own account. These scenes transform the film from a cinematic communication into a whole with an ideological center.

Matters of Content

THREE ASPECTS OF CONTENT

So much for story types according to form. Now I come to the issue of story content. Small wonder that this major issue has already been touched on* and that it has become evident that different kinds of content differ in their adequacy to the medium. So it may be taken for granted that the screen attracts certain types of content, while being unresponsive to others.

To begin with, let us distinguish between three aspects of content. There is, first, the content *area*. Does the story involve actual reality? Or does it belong to the realm of fantasy? After all that has been said before, the significance for photographic film of the area to which its material belongs is rather obvious. A second aspect of content bears on the *subject matter* of the story. People refer to this aspect when they say of a movie that it pictures a psychological conflict, a war adventure, a murder case, and the like, or simply define it in terms of some established genre, such as science-fiction, a Western, a musical, etc. Because of their dependence on changing social and historical circumstances, these subjects or topics elude systematic classification. Finally, content asserts itself in the form of *motifs*—salient story features which, it is true, materialize in the subject matter of the story but are by no means identical with it. Thus the guiding motif of a war film may be the concern for what happens to individuals in times of war; the preoccupation with the havoc wrought by war on whole populations; the glorification of heroism; a plea for mutual understanding between peoples; and so on.

The first of these aspects—content areas—has been discussed in chapter 5, where it was shown that, due to the medium's affinity for actual

* See pp. 209 ff., 237, 239 ff., and *passim*.

physical reality, content in the realms of history and fantasy is amenable to cinematic treatment only under certain conditions. Accordingly, it will suffice here to concentrate on the remaining two aspects of content. In the following the term "content" applies exclusively to subjects and/or motifs. To simplify matters, they may, where not otherwise stated, be thought of as occurring in feature films which fall into the area of actuality.

UNCINEMATIC CONTENT

As with story forms, it may perhaps be best to start by looking for uncinematic content. The task of tracing it will be facilitated by a summary recapitulation of several basic ideas which point in this direction. Much emphasis has been placed throughout on the fact that film shots of material phenomena are surrounded by a fringe of indeterminate meanings and that, thanks to their psychological correspondences and mental connotations, they may well lure us into remote provinces of the mind. The representation of the inner world, that is, conforms to the cinematic approach as long as the phenomena of this world can be derived, somehow, from pictures of the outer world. Things change, as I have likewise stressed, if the relation between the two worlds which comprise actuality is reversed. No sooner do the events which make up mental reality pretend to autonomy than they on their part determine the character and succession of the shots of physical reality; instead of being suggested by a flow of images, they force the imagery to externalize their flow. And yet another point has been impressed upon the reader, namely, that mental reality includes components which indeed must claim ascendancy in order to be represented at all. The reason is that they lack correspondences in the physical world.*

Uncinematic content is identical with these particular components of the mental continuum. It is content which does not stand a chance of making itself known unless it is communicated in its own terms. Wherever such content is required, it automatically occupies the leading position. The visuals may signify it in one way or another but are incapable of evoking it by indirection. Two varieties of uncinematic content stand out clearly—conceptual reasoning and the tragic.

Conceptual reasoning

Conceptual reasoning, a mode of conveying thought processes rather than a mental entity like the tragic, is by itself neither subject matter nor

* See especially p. 237.

motif. But, of course, it may help define either. Now such reasoning is of interest here only to the extent that it really proves indispensable. And it is indispensable only if it relates to motifs which must be argued out to become intelligible. This is illustrated by a comparison between the film PYGMALION and the play from which it is adapted. The message of the play arises not so much from its characters and situations as from the arguments and counterarguments bandied about in the conversation; the screen version on its part skips a great deal of the dialogue (for reasons which do credit to the adapter's film sense): hence its complete failure to put across that message. Yet, for instance, MAJOR BARBARA, more faithful to Shaw and less true to the cinema than PYGMALION, indulges in conceptualizations. In MONSIEUR VERDOUX and LIMELIGHT Chaplin too resorts to them for the sake of otherwise incommunicable thoughts which elucidate the moral of these films.* And remember the many ideological documentaries, including Rotha's "argument-film" WORLD OF PLENTY, which would never succeed in driving home the thesis they champion were it not for their reliance on explicit argumentation.

To be sure, conceptual reasoning must be verbalized, but this alone does not sufficiently account for its uncinematic effect. As has been shown in chapter 7, the difficulties raised by dialogue can in some measure be surmounted. All that is needed is to divest the spoken word of its leading role. Dialogue ceases to be a total liability if its content is de-emphasized in favor of that of the visuals or of the material qualities of speech. Here is where the real problem lies. For what matters in dialogue featuring conceptual reasoning is precisely its content—the argument which, according to premise, clarifies a significant motif. In this case everything hinges on the words and their meaning. If they are blurred in a cinematic interest, the all-important thought they transmit remains unexpressed. So they are bound to take the lead.

Conceptual reasoning is an alien element on the screen. "Let us imagine," says Gabriel Marcel, whose awareness of its incompatibility with the medium is surpassed by no one, ". . . that I would make a professor of history of philosophy at the Sorbonne appear in a film. Of course, nothing will prevent me from having him discuss the doctrine of Kant. From the viewpoint of the aesthetics of film, however, this would be a ridiculous misuse. Why? Because the spectator does not go to the movies to listen to explications." Marcel supplements this comment by a no less trenchant proposition concerning the possibility of nevertheless acculturizing the professor to the ways of the cinema. "Most assuredly a historian of philosophy can be a film character, but [only] under [certain]

* Cf. p. 108.

conditions or under a very strictly controlled aspect. What must be accentuated and thrown into full relief is his comportment in a behaviorist sense, his manner of walking, of sitting down, and with regard to speech, his intonations and perhaps his facial contractions—by no means and to no degree the content of what he is saying."[1]

The tragic

INTRODUCTION

The term "tragic" is used here in a strict sense, best illustrated by reference to such genuinely tragic figures as Shakespeare's Macbeth or Schiller's Wallenstein. True, sufferings in the wake of adverse circumstances and unfortunate destinies are often called tragic also. But are they? When in LIMELIGHT the aging Calvero renounces Terry against her desire, sacrificing his happiness to what life may have in store for her, his resignation, loneliness, and end are melancholy rather than tragic. Nor does the gangster who prefers death at the hand of the police to capture and punishment bear any resemblance to a tragic hero.

Narratives devoted to a tragic conflict may be built from very different materials in terms of milieus and people. But whatever their subject matter, they invariably utilize it to enhance that conflict as a unique experience, a mental entity of momentous significance. If the tragic comes true at all, it does so in the form of a guiding motif.

As such it has a natural affinity for the theatrical story which, in keeping with Proust's definition of the classical tragedy—its extreme fulfillment —retains only those images "that may help us to make its purpose intelligible." Being an inner event, the motif of the tragic is indeed predestined to be implemented by a story form which is a "whole with a purpose"*— more often than not an ideological purpose. That this motif is as much opposed to photography or film as is conceptual reasoning follows conclusively from its inherent characteristics.

CHARACTERISTICS

Exclusive concern with human interaction   The tragic is exclusively a human affair. In consequence, its adequate representation involves inanimate objects not as equal partners in the play but as stage requisites whose function it is to bear out, and attune us to, the inner drama in progress. What has been said about theatrical story films in this respect,**

* See pp. 221–2.
** See p. 218.

applies all the more to films with a tragic theme: they automatically fall
back on the ways of the theater. Revolving around an all-absorbing mental
event, they cannot help arranging the outer things to reflect what is
going on inside the minds. Their interiors reflect those of the protagonists;
their lighting sustains fitting moods; and, for instance, when in WUTHERING
HEIGHTS human passions reach a climax the elements of nature burst forth
also. There is rarely a screen tragedy without a symbolic storm.* The
degree to which films in this vein exploit camera-reality, or what remains of
it, in the interest of their guiding motif becomes immediately apparent if
you compare them with films which encompass both human action and
physical reality at large. The railway noises in BRIEF ENCOUNTER are not
intended to denote mental agitation; the streets in UMBERTO D. lead a
life of their own; and the furniture, staircases, and cars in slapstick comedy
behave exactly like actors in the flesh.

Cosmos vs. flow of life The tragic conflict materializes only in a
closed universe governed by mythical beliefs, moral principles, a political
doctrine, or the like. These binding, if frequently incoherent, rules of
conduct are not only responsible for the conflict but endow it with the
quality of the tragic; due to their existence, it appears to be meaningful as
well as inescapable. Tragedy presupposes a finite, ordered cosmos. And
film? Roland Caillois, one of the few critics raising this issue at all, insists
that "there is no Cosmos on the screen, but an earth, trees, the sky, streets
and railways: in short, matter.²** Hence the clash between the preferences of the medium and the tragic hero's death. His end marks an absolute end; time comes to a stop when he dies. It is evident that this ultimate
solution runs counter to the camera's ingrained desire for indefinite
rambling. In LIMELIGHT Chaplin knowingly avoids such a finale. He concludes with a shot which reintroduces the flow of life: the camera moves
away from the death scene in the wing toward Terry who is performing
onstage.

Elimination of the fortuitous The tragic precludes the fortuitous,
because, were random influences to alter the hero's fate, his destiny would

---

*Cf. p. 126.
** Contrary to Caillois' point of view—and my own, for that matter—Parker
Tyler holds that film, at least "creative" film, belongs essentially among the traditional arts and that, accordingly, it must obey the same laws as, say, painting. And
what do these laws prescribe? "Art," says Mr. Tyler, "The Film Sense and the
Painting Sense," *Art Digest*, Feb. 15, 1954, pp. 27–8, ". . . is produced by the con-
trolling principles of a *cosmos*, which underlies all casual aspects of confusion and
variety and represents destiny as opposed to chance, form as opposed to formlessness."
Quite so. The point is only that "there is no Cosmos on the screen."

become merely an incident. If tragedy acknowledges chance events, it does so by making them serve its own ends; chance is then an involuntary helper, not an independent agent. Yet this appropriation or indeed elimination of the accidental is most certainly against the grain of the cinema. It is again Caillois who exposes the discrepancy between film and the inherent determinism of tragedy: "The cinema emphasizes . . . the contingency of human relationships. The tragic heroes slay each other only among themselves; one locks them up like wild animals in the arena so that they may tear themselves to pieces. On the screen, as in the street, the passer-by is killed by the gangster because he happens to be there, for this world has no order, it is a place of movement and collision."[3]

What the difference between hero and gangster, arena and street, implies for cinematic treatment can be nicely demonstrated by a look at Thornton Wilder's novel, *The Bridge of San Luis Rey*, in which the street is passed off as a sort of arena. The bridge collapses, with five travelers being killed, and the account of their lives up to then is to convince us that the catastrophe was actually the work of divine providence. The disaster is thus reincorporated into a cosmos. (The fact that this particular cosmos relates to providence, not fate, is irrelevant here.) Now consider the pivotal event of the narrative—the collapsing bridge. Is it not a cinematic spectacle par excellence? No doubt it is, but only if it is conceived of and introduced as an accident in the dimension of physical reality; then indeed the shots of it will be an indispensable source of information and the nucleus of various meanings. Conversely, in a faithful screen adaptation of the Wilder novel in which the catastrophe is featured as an instrument of divine providence, the potential revealing power of these very same shots would be wasted on a spectator captivated by the catastrophe's predetermined significance. The collapsing bridge, that is, would withdraw from the realm of cinematic subjects into that metaphysical region which, among other ghosts, harbors Moby Dick.

Remoteness from the imagery Like conceptual reasoning, the tragic offers content which, because it lacks correspondences in the physical world, cannot be suggested by representations, however allusive, of this world. It eludes camera-life. An exclusively mental event, it must be communicated in a direct manner in order to come into view at all. But what about films, such as UMBERTO D., which convey their story primarily through a flow of images and yet manage to include a tragic theme? In the case of UMBERTO D. this theme is of course not the old pensioner's suffering under humiliating poverty; rather, it should be identified as the alienation which infects the whole world he lives in and manifests itself, for instance, in his relation to Maria, the wretched young servant. Supported only by casual dialogue, the visuals intimate that, their mutual sympathies notwithstanding, Maria and Umberto remain enclosed in their own lives without being able to overcome the solitude engulfing them. Umberto's love for his dog unmistakably originates in his loneliness.

Actually, however, the theme of alienation never claims priority; the many passages bearing on it are at most raw material for a tragedy, but not the tragedy proper. If De Sica had seen fit to build from the pertinent moods and incidents to which he confines himself a full-fledged tragedy, his UMBERTO D. would undoubtedly have lost its episodic character and developed into a theatrical film pure and simple. Far more than any other variety of this genre film tragedy requires an intrigue which substantiates content incommunicable in cinematic terms. It is therefore inevitable that the intrigue should be detachable from the medium; that the images that help advance it should, in Proust's words, serve merely to "make its purpose intelligible"; and that, where they prove powerless, the spoken word should take over. Tragedy on the screen involves a shift of emphasis from the images to language-bound meanings. Referring to Corneille's *Cid*, Caillois observes that in the theater "it does not matter to Chimène —or to us—whether she sees the corpse of Don Gormas; in the cinema the essential thing is that one is upset by the *image*."[4]

The question is whether, within the framework of a tragedy, the image can be made to produce an upsetting effect. The French film SYMPHONY PASTORALE, an adaptation from Gide with a cultured pseudo-tragic story, dwells upon beautiful mountain scenery, obviously for the purpose of redirecting audience attention toward the visuals. Yet this does not transform the drama into a cinematic affair. On the contrary, the obtrusive, if photogenic, beauty of the landscape shots only drives home their insignificance as elements of the composition. They have a purely decorative function. The center of SYMPHONY PASTORALE lies outside its imagery.

EXCURSION: NONTRAGIC ENDINGS

Contrary to tragic death, the happy ending makes you breathe the air of paradise and suggests at the same time that life will continue, thus catering to the camera's demand for limitless reality. In the famous German silent film, THE LAST LAUGH, an interesting attempt was made to combine these two opposite types of finale. The film ends logically with the extinction of the old hotel porter's hopes and his complete humiliation; or rather, it does not yet end: in an appended sequence the pathetic sufferer comes to riches and enjoys himself immensely. Does he dream all this? At any rate, the sequence is a farce which seems to have been intended as a sort of ironical comment on Hollywood's then declared preference for happy endings. But no matter what was meant with it, this "last laugh" still stands out as an ingenious, if crude, cinematic conclusion: it points beyond the near-tragic ending without obscuring its reality character. (The figure of the hotel porter is of course tragic only in a world saturated with authoritarian and militaristic notions—the very world which was one of the obsessions of the pre-Hitler German screen.)[5]

It need not be a dream of happiness. The main thing is that the ending does not mark the end. A classical example of such a finale is the ever-recurring concluding shot of Chaplin's old comedies; we see the Tramp waddle away and we know that he is indestructible. Similarly, all neorealistic Italian films which do not picture war feature characters who are given a new lease of life at the end; the ending of these films defies tragedy and is incompatible with the theatrical story in general.

An admirable achievement in terms of artistic intelligence and human delicacy is the last episode of UMBERTO D., in which De Sica manages, against heavy odds, to substitute a chance of survival for impending doom. [Illus. 54] At the end of his tether, Umberto, the old pensioner, sees no other way out than to do away with himself; and since his dog—a creature as unwanted as he—insists on keeping him company, he takes it with him to the railway outside the public park. The anguished animal whines and yelps as a train is approaching. "No," you hear the old man say. And he doubles back on his steps for the sake of the only being which connects him with the world of the living. Yet no sooner has he returned to the park than the dog, hurt by his master's unintelligible, nay, hostile conduct, refuses to play with him and proves unresponsive to all his advances. Like a rejected lover, Umberto continues his wooing with an urgency which cannot but kindle his will to live, as it were. Indeed, when he eventually succeeds in being re-admitted as a playmate, he seems almost happy, if one could apply such a term to him. Playing with each other, the man and the dog move toward the background, becoming ever smaller. Is doom only postponed? However pregnant with it, the future which opens before Umberto and us is unforeseeable.

The finale of Fellini's CABIRIA is no less indeterminate. As the heartbroken Cabiria walks through the nocturnal wood where young people are making music and dancing and drifting about in a Dionysian mood, we do not know what will happen to her; we only learn from a change of her facial expression that she will walk on and that there is no end to her story. Fellini himself says that his films never end; moreover, he explains why he deliberately avoids the kind of conclusion inseparable from the theatrical story: "I think it is immoral . . . to tell a story that has a conclusion. Because you cut out your audience the moment you present a solution on the screen . . . Conversely, by not serving them the happy ending on a platter, you can make them think, you can remove some of that smug security. Then they'll *have* to find their own answers."[6]

This existentialist argument is by itself insufficient. It is not just the lack of a ready-made ending which challenges the spectator; rather, he becomes "engaged" because of the nature of the qualities and processes which do not end: Cabiria's endurance and Umberto's fortitude—or, in LA STRADA, the capacity for maturing and inner awakening. [Illus. 55] Behind many nonsolutions, including those of the old Chaplin comedies, there lurks, perhaps, a desire to exalt the power of resistance of the seeming weak who time and again cheat destiny. Hence the emphasis of episode films in this vein on tenacity, resiliency, and indeed adaptability as weapons in an unending fight. No doubt such concerns are in accordance with the cinema's affinity for the flow of life, not to mention their bearing on a cinematic motif which will be discussed shortly.

This raises in turn the issue of cinematic content. As a matter of fact, most of mental reality admits of cinematic representation; even conceptual reasoning and the tragic may be put to good use as interludes.* Yet cinematic content differs from the run of subjects and themes in that it is particularly fit to be shown on the screen. Unlike uncinematic content, it asserts itself not only in the dimension of motifs but in the form of subject matter as well.

CINEMATIC CONTENT

Subject matter

CINEMATIC SUBJECTS

Content in the nature of subject matter is obviously cinematic if it pictures such elements of physical reality as the camera alone can capture. Now here we are on familiar ground, for these elements are to all intents and purposes identical with the "cinematic subjects" which have been discussed at length in chapter 3. Only one point concerning them still remains to be settled—the different positions they may occupy in the screen narrative.

To be sure, all cinematic subjects contribute to the subject matter of the films in which they figure, but not all of them have an equal share in it. In particular it is most unlikely that subjects which are bound up with technical procedures and camera devices will determine the character

---

* For interludes, see especially pp. 73–4, 86.

of a film's content. Much as cinematic films rely on the suggestive power of small material phenomena, they will hardly exhaust themselves in depicting these phenomena. Nor should inanimate objects, fleeting impressions, or special modes of reality be expected to fill the bill. And the same applies to the dissolution of conventional figure-ground schemata and the alienation of sights too familiar to be normally noticed. Of course, there are exceptions. UEBERFALL features throughout a special mode of reality—reality as it appears to the panic-stricken. Dreyer's silent JOAN OF ARC is essentially a story told in facial expressions. The world of the small, human or not, also attracts many an experimental film maker; Stan Brakhage's recent LOVING, for instance, consists almost exclusively of big close-ups. Yet scattered cases like these only confirm the rule.

Other cinematic subjects, such as the past still remembered or certain phenomena overwhelming consciousness,* behave differently: unlike the close-up, the transient, etc., they readily develop into major topics. Films resuscitating the Victorian era or the days before World War I are quite popular; and there is no end of films which culminate in the description of mass frenzy and elemental catastrophes. Some subjects belonging to this group recur so frequently that they constitute standing genres named after them. Thus people speak of dance films, chase films, horror films, films of violence, and so on.

The fact, however, that a film draws on cinematic subject matter does not by itself endow it with a cinematic quality. Equally evident is the fact that, in order to be true to the medium, films must permit their pictorial material to have, so to speak, its own way. Whether or not a film meets this requirement depends not only on the appropriateness of its material but on the form of its story and its underlying motif.

RELATION TO STORY FORMS AND MOTIFS

True, all story forms may carry cinematic subjects, yet it is no news either that the different types of narrative we have come to distinguish differ in the use they make of their visuals. While the found story and the episode let cinematic materials exert all the influence of which they are capable, the theatrical story, for its part, exploits rather than exposes these materials. The street scenes, big crowds, and night club episodes in theatrical films serve mainly to illustrate or sustain, somehow, the patterns of meanings which the intrigue is establishing independently of the imagery. Hence the futility of attempts to restore cinematic subjects to full significance within the framework of the theatrical story. As could be shown in chapter 12, such attempts tend to result in pictorial elabora-

* See pp. 56–8.

tions which either succeed in disintegrating the given story patterns or are largely overshadowed by them.*

However, not all traditional subgenres of the theatrical story form impair the integrity of their cinematic material with equal vigor. Comedy usually proves more permissive than tragedy in this respect. It accepts chance up to a point; and it may well admit inanimate objects among its actors. (That in spite of these concessions the genre remains a theatrical affair, can be seen if one compares any adaptation of a stage comedy with a genuine film comedy.) And there is melodrama. The sensational incidents which melodrama emphasizes reach deep into the physical world and go together with a plot too loose or crude to affect the relative autonomy of its parts. Add to this the genre's indulgence in strong emotions inseparable from those incidents and its partiality for a happy ending. Of all theatrical genres melodrama probably best lends itself to facilitating the display of cinematic subject matter.**

So far only uncinematic motifs have been treated—the tragic and any set of ideas or thoughts requiring explicit conceptualization. But these motifs alone are of interest here. It follows from what has been said about them that their ascendancy in films featuring cinematic subjects prevents the latter from becoming eloquent. In a film fashioned after Wilder's novel, *The Bridge of San Luis Rey*, the images of the collapsing bridge would have to implement the presupposed workings of divine providence and therefore not be able to put across messages of their own. Uncinematic motifs force co-existent cinematic subject matter into submission.

Motifs

INTRODUCTION

Definition   Motifs are cinematic if they are identical with, or grow out of, one or another property of film. To anticipate, the David-Goliath theme owes its cinematic flavor to the fact that it reveals the small as the hub of tremendous forces, which is to say that it can be interpreted as a derivative of the close-up. Intimately affiliated with the medium, cinematic motifs carry its preferences over into the dimension of meanings.

Relation to story forms and subject matter   There is an interesting difference between cinematic motifs and cinematic subjects, as regards

---

* See pp. 225–30.
** For theatrical genres, see also pp. 219, 221.

their relation to the theatrical story form. In any theatrical film the latter are inevitably neutralized, whereas the former not only retain their cinematic quality but tend to communicate it to the whole of the film, its theatricality notwithstanding. Evidence that motifs prove more pervasive and penetrant than subjects in this respect will be adduced subsequently.

On the other hand, no such rule governs the relations between cinematic motifs and uncinematic subject matter. Imagine a film in which a cinematic theme—e.g. sleuthing—is implemented by way of material which involves the dominance of dialogue. It is quite possible that, due to its contagious power, the motif of sleuthing mitigates the uncinematic effect of the obtrusive verbal statements. But it is equally possible that the prevalence of the spoken word deprives the sleuthing processes of their intrinsic appeal. Which alternative tips the balance depends upon its relative weight in each individual case.

THE FLOW OF LIFE

Among the cinematic motifs one occupies a unique position—the flow of life. It is the most general of all possible motifs and it differs from the rest of them in that it is not only a motif. This content corresponds to a basic affinity of film. In a manner of speaking it is an emanation of the medium itself.

As a motif pure and simple the flow of life materializes in films animated by no intention other than to picture some manifestation of it. For obvious reasons these films are usually documentaries, often in an impressionistic vein. To name a few examples, think of RAIN, BERLIN, and IN THE STREET. Arne Sucksdorff seems to be addicted to that flow, as is illustrated by his PEOPLE IN THE CITY, or a short he made in Kashmir, THE WIND AND THE RIVER. Cesare Zavattini, the theorist, might also be mentioned here for his championing a direct approach to dramatic sequences of environmental life. (His LOVE IN THE CITY, though, is a rather unconvincing piece of work.)

It almost looks as if these examples could easily be multiplied. Numbers of episode films and films with found stories give the impression of being nothing but variations on the theme: "Such is life." Flaherty's "slight narratives" portray or resuscitate modes of existence that obtain among primitive peoples; Rouquier's FARREBIQUE relates the round of experiences which a typical French farm family is undergoing year after year; De Sica's UMBERTO D. uncovers the conspiracy of minute incidents and circumstances which increasingly close in on the aged pensioner, etc. All these films feature life, especially everyday life, as a series of contingent events and/or a process of growth (e.g. Fellini's LA STRADA); and all of them feature it in such a way that it appears to be an end in itself.

Upon closer inspection, however, the such-is-life theme turns out to be not their only concern. The run of films devoted to this theme implement other motifs as well. Most Flaherty films are expressive of his romantic desire to summon, and preserve for posterity, the purity and "majesty"* of a way of life not yet spoiled by the advance of civilization. In keeping with the tradition of neorealism, UMBERTO D. raises a social issue; it exposes the plight of retired officials whom an indolent government condemns to starvation. As for Fellini, leftist Italian critics have accused him of breaking away from this traditional motif; they resent what they consider a heresy—that he avails himself of the neorealistic approach in the interest of individual values rather than social causes.[7] [Illus. 56]

As a rule, then, films which feature life as such also carry more specific messages. Note that these messages or motifs—De Sica's preoccupation with social justice, Fellini's involvement in human loneliness, etc.—may well be cinematically indifferent; indeed, many a theatrical film centers on the very problem of alienation which is at the core of LA STRADA or CABIRIA. What matters is that those messages are conducive to a symbiosis between them and the cinematic motif of the flow of life. No doubt the latter continues to partake of the nature of a motif in such combinations; were it otherwise, transparence to it would not be indispensable for episode films. But it is also something else. Whenever this symbiosis takes place, the flow of life becomes at the same time the matrix of the motifs associated with it—the stuff out of which they are woven. It is both a motif and intrinsically cinematic material or content. Films with themes suggested by this content are authentic cinema due to its dominant presence.

All other cinematic motifs have lesser generality; they can be supposed to have about the same limited range as the uncinematic motif of the tragic or the special propositions bound up with the flow-of-life theme. Their number is uncertain; their selection and formulation are contingent on a variety of uncontrollable factors, such as the prevailing social and historical conditions. Completeness being unattainable, the best thing to do is to illustrate the characteristics of these cinematic motifs by discussing two of them in greater detail—sleuthing and the David-Goliath motif.

SLEUTHING

Affiliation with film The motif of sleuthing, featured as early as 1908 by Victorin Jasset in his Nick Carter series,[8] is affiliated with film in several ways.

* Flaherty's term; already quoted, p. 247.

First, in order to trace a criminal or whoever is sought, the detective must look for material clues normally unperceived. "By a man's fingernails," asserts Sherlock Holmes, that uncontested authority on matters of detection, "by his coat-sleeve, by his boots, by his trouser-knees . . . by each of these things a man's calling is plainly revealed. That all united should fail to enlighten the competent inquirer in any case is almost inconceivable."[9] The implication is of course that films consecrated to sleuthing are obliged to exhibit physical phenomena for their own sake in the very interest of the action. Often close-ups are required to bring this cinematic material into focus.

Second, sleuthing constantly involves the accidental. Poe's master sleuth Dupin operates on the assumption that "the larger portion of truth arises from the seemingly irrelevant." And he elaborates as follows: "The history of human knowledge has . . . uninterruptedly shown that to collateral, or incidental, or accidental events we are indebted for the most numerous and most valuable discoveries. . . . *Accident* is admitted as a portion of the substructure."[10] The sleuthing motif, then, appears to best advantage in films which conform to the medium's preference for the fortuitous.

Third, Dupin refers to scientific inquiries as a model; so does Sherlock Holmes when he calls sleuthing the "Science of Deduction and Analysis."[11] Accordingly, detection has much in common with applied scientific research—a fact deliberately stressed in Lang's M and de Rochemont's The House on 92nd Street. The scientific character of sleuthing justifies the attention which films inspired by this motif are paying to physical detail; it is a dermatologist, not a detective, who, thinking in terms of big close-ups, compares the human skin to "a monumental façade that tells the age, the peaceful or calamitous past and the constitution of its owner."[12] More important here, these films are likely to reflect the virtual endlessness of scientific pursuits. In following the chain of causes and effects, they make us envision the unlimited continuum of physical reality.*

They thus live up to one of the affinities of photography and film alike. Significantly, perhaps the strongest effect produced by them is the suspense arising from the sleuthing process as such; the eventual discovery of the criminal is more or less in the nature of a letdown. Yet even so the discovery at the end is vitally important for the fulfillment of the process. Hence the strange futility of Lang's silent film, Spione, in which the process is all that counts. One party spies on the other, and soon you forget who is who and why. As an end in itself the endless process is mean-

* Cf. pp. 65–6.

ingless.[13] (Marie Seton, Eisenstein's biographer, relates that he loved detective stories. His "insatiable passion" for them, she says, "was not a response to their apparent plot, but a fascination with the processes they seemed to reveal to him." And she indicates that they did reveal to him not so much a concern for deduction and analysis as the workings of that "supernormal consciousness" by means of which the mystic gathers evidence from scattered clues in support of his experiences.[14] There may be some truth in this. Was not Poe a mystic? Sleuthing is the secular counterpart of theological speculations.)

Fourth, it is inevitable that detection should take on the form of a chase, with the sleuth pursuing the criminal or, conversely, a rogue, amiable or not, outwitting the representatives of the law.* Most crime or detective thrillers—think of THE THIRD MAN—include physical chases. So they add to their cinematic motif another appeal: they embody the motif in specifically cinematic subject matter.

Hitchcock thrillers   Alfred Hitchcock, who called the chase "the final expression of the motion picture medium,"** has set a grand pattern for thrillers indulging in sleuthing. What distinguishes him from the rest of film directors is not primarily his superior know-how but, more, his unrivaled flair for psychophysical correspondences. Nobody is so completely at home in the dim border region where inner and outer events intermingle and fuse with each other. This implies, for one thing, a perfect command of the ways in which physical data may be induced to yield their possible meanings. Hitchcock literally thinks in terms of suggestive environmental material; in 1937 he declared that he would like to make travelogues with a personal element in them, or a documentary about the Derby, or a film composed around a fire at sea.[15] By the same token, his preference for that borderland which marks the junction of corporeal and mental influences enables him to venture deep into the psychological dimension and there single out particulars apt to be thrust upon us by a gesture, a garment, an interior, a noise, or a silence. His chases are frequently psychological chases which are developed from a minimum of physical clues.

Undeniably, the typical Hitchcock plot is anything but significant. His films utilize emotions as stimulants, insert conflicts and problems for the sake of suspense, and on the whole either avoid touching on serious human concerns or fail to do justice to them. Much as the late James Agee

* The prototype of all screen rogues to come was Fantomas, the hero of a series by Louis Feuillade, which started its successful career in 1913. See Bardèche and Brasillach, *The History of Motion Pictures*, p. 69.

** See p. 42.

admired Hitchcock, he found his LIFEBOAT inadequate and his SPELLBOUND "disappointing"; of THE PARADINE CASE Agee said that in it "Hitchcock uses a lot of skill over a lot of nothing."[16]

This raises an intriguing question. Is it at all possible for Hitchcock to turn to meaningful narratives and yet continue to make the peculiar contributions which are the trade-mark of his thrillers? Does he perhaps prefer sleuthing, chases, and sensational effects out of a feeling that he would lose his essence if he met the requirements of really essential plots? (It is not necessary to repeat that such plots most certainly are susceptible to cinematic solutions.) In the case of the Hitchcock films I am tempted to assume that the very insignificance of their stories is inseparable from their impressive assets. Hitchcock himself once traced his habitual recourse to thrillers to his search for stories which will best "suit the film medium."[17]

Thrillers have satisfied his demand in two ways. Their suspense-laden sleuthing processes cause a stir in the region of psychophysical correspondences and thus challenge him to indulge his uncanny sense of the interplay between moods and surroundings, inner excitation and the look of objects.

But, even more important, precisely because of their insignificance thrillers permit him to highlight these moments of photographable reality without any regard for the obligations which intrigues with substantive issues might impose upon him. He need not assign to the close-up of a wrist-watch a symbolic function nor insert, say, a casual encounter in a train for the purpose of complementing or bolstering some predetermined action which can be detached from the medium. Consider also Hitchcock's susceptibility to quaint people, such as you meet in public places or at a party. Thus, his films culminate in material things and occurrences which, besides being traces of a crime and offering clues to the identity of the criminal, are pregnant with both external and internal life. The creepy merry-go-round; "the red tip of a murderer's cigar glowing ominously in a darkened apartment";[18] the bit-players reminiscent of D. W. Griffith's street characters whom Eisenstein recalled twenty years after last having seen them*—these poignant configurations of camera-life have an individuality and a glamour all their own; they spur our imagination, attuning it to the tales still half-enshrined in them. True, the Hitchcock thrillers lack deeper meaning, but they comprise a host of virtually significant, if embryonic, stories.

Search for truth At first glance, Akira Kurosawa's RASHOMON presents itself as a sophisticated crime story laid in medieval Japan. In the

_____
* See p. 63.

middle of a forest a bandit waylays a traveling samurai and his wife; inflamed by the woman's beauty, he rapes her after having struck down and tied the man. Later the samurai is found dead on the scene of the assault. But all this belongs to the past. RASHOMON (whose framing story may be neglected here) reviews in retrospect—to be precise, shortly after the inquest—the events that led to the murder, if murder it was. The story of what happened in the forest is told by the three participants and a woodcutter who pretends to have been an eye-witness; and each version is pictured in a straightforward manner from the respective narrator's angle. The bandit boasts of having killed the man in a fair sword duel. The woman declares that she herself stabbed her husband in a troubled state of mind, while the dead samurai, through a medium conveying his testimony, insists that he committed hari-kiri. On his part the woodcutter confirms the bandit's story, but with a difference: the bandit, he says, savagely murdered the warrior at the behest of his shameless wife. Altogether it looks as if these conflicting accounts were assembled for the express purpose of reconstructing the crime in the forest. The identity of the criminal never leaks out, however; no final attempt is made to reconcile the four versions. [Illus. 57]

But does RASHOMON really culminate in fact-finding processes? According to Parker Tyler's brilliant interpretation, the question of the killer's identity is entirely beside the point. RASHOMON, Tyler argues, is a work of art, not a crime thriller à la Hitchcock. It is meant to show that people under the shock of the evil they have done or suffered above all try to restore their moral dignity; that they, consciously or not, manipulate the evidence in the interest of their inmost needs; and that these needs prompt each of them to assume the role of a hero in the tragedy he helped enact. As Mr. Tyler puts it, "in the depths of each person's memory, in *Rashomon*, is recreated the image of what took place far away in the forest as consistent with his ideal image of himself."[19]

That RASHOMON has traits of the traditional work of art, however, does not automatically make it good cinema. On the contrary, more often than not such films amount to hybrids with palpably divided loyalties— think of Olivier's Shakespeare adaptations. Why, then, is RASHOMON something like a genuine film and not just an art-minded amalgam? Here is where the seemingly misleading impression that it is a crime film reasserts itself; indeed, first impressions are rarely unfounded. The RASHOMON story actually uses detection to arouse suspense, just as a Hitchcock thriller does. Granted that the Japanese film points to a mystery far beyond factual truth, it does so in the form of a crime mystery dedicated to the exposure of hidden material facts. Hence the tremendous importance of its visuals.

Strangely enough, we do not feel bored by the near-repetition of the same events; rather, our eyes are riveted to the screen in a constant effort to register all the differences and similarities between the successive versions of the drama. A facial expression may be revealing; a weighty, if minute, detail may have been overlooked. As the woodcutter, followed by the traveling camera, slowly walks through the forest, we watch the drawn-out and completely uneventful scene with an intensity we would hardly summon were the scene merely designed to endow an otherwise theatrical film with a semblance of camera-reality. Functioning as physical clues, all these shots preserve their indeterminacy; they invite us to absorb them; they seem to be elements of a sustained inquiry rather than components of a narrative with preconceived patterns of meanings and an ideological center. The inquiry itself resembles the scientific process in that it does not come to a close. And the notion of endlessness thus evoked bolsters the cinematic effect of sleuthing. (Rudolf Arnheim judiciously remarks that RASHOMON is cinematic also for reflecting, on the level of story-telling, the camera's ability to view any subject from different positions.[20])

One might ask here whether the preoccupation with sleuthing in RASHOMON does not obscure the film's lofty message. But whatever this message, RASHOMON strongly intimates that the search for it is of the essence; that the whole business is left unfinished if sleuthing is not carried over to dimensions transcending the literal reconstruction of the crime. As one version after another passes by, the spectator, becoming increasingly aware of the glaring contradictions between them, cannot help realizing that the diverse attempts to dig up reliable evidence are abortive because of the intrinsic nature of the characters and events involved. So his mind will be oriented toward truths to which factual truth is irrelevant. Now imagine for a moment that these truths, instead of being suggested by a veritable crime story, occupied a pivotal position from the outset and therefore determined the selection and course of the visuals in the same way as, for instance, the truths which Cocteau tries to illustrate in his THE BLOOD OF A POET. Then they would be imposed, not implied. Then RASHOMON might still be a significant artistic achievement in a sense, yet it would certainly not strike you as a product indigenous to the film medium.

RASHOMON perfectly illustrates the infectious power of the sleuthing motif. Generally speaking, this motif benefits films which, might easily fall into the ways of Art if they did not adopt it. CITIZEN KANE, for instance, is cinematically attractive because it conveys the esoteric truth at its core by means of detection. This truth which bears on the inner wretchedness of a man who belongs among the kings and rulers of the world is neither initially given nor virtually omnipresent; rather, it is sought; it is inferred from scattered pieces of evidence which yet fail to reveal it. Only at the film's very end does a final material clue casually answer the question that has motivated the search.

In WILD STRAWBERRIES Victor Sjoestroem as the old doctor—what an actor he is!—inquires into his past in order to find out why he is now being punished with loneliness, the complete absence of human warmth. He dreams his past, that is. And as he relives what he was and did or did not, he discovers that his crime was to have killed love in himself and in those who offered him theirs. Both detective and criminal, he traces the vacuum about him to sloth and selfishness. The cinematic appeal of this agonizing, and redeeming, self-investigation is all the stronger since it is made to appear as an outgrowth of the flow of life. Touched off by an event of great importance to the old man, the dreams in which the sleuthing takes place are incidental to his everyday existence; they pervade and influence it. The dream of the trial, it is true, falls flat because it is too stylized, too purposeful, but even so the whole admirably reflects that drift of loosely interrelated memories and actual happenings which constitutes the real-life process. An episode of its protagonist's life, WILD STRAWBERRIES has no beginning, and its ending is anything but an end. The flow continues, though death may be near.

DAVID—GOLIATH

Affiliation with film The venerable David-Goliath motif is a natural for film because of the analogy that obtains between the "triumph of the seemingly weak over the seemingly strong"[21] and the cinematic standard procedure of the close-up. In magnifying the small, the camera exposes to view fantastic shapes too tiny to be normally noticed. As they fill the screen, they cast their spell over the spectator, impressing upon him the magic of a leaf or the energies which lie dormant in a piece of cloth. Any close-up suggests that the small, far from being negligible, may match or indeed surpass in impact the big things and events that catch the eye.* In essence this is the moral of the story of little David who slayed Goliath with his sling. The story demonstrates that there is no direct ratio between size and strength; that, on the contrary, the apparently small and weak is

---

* Cf. pp. 46–50. The same idea has found a classical expression in Adalbert Stifter's famous "Vorrede" to his *Bunte Steine*. (See Stifter, *Bunte Steine/Nachlese*, Insel Verlag, Leipzig, especially p. 8.)

often superior to ostentatious bigness. Hence the cinematic quality of this motif. It parallels the close-up; or rather, it is a sort of extension of the close-up into the dimension of meaningful issues and values.

The Tramp et al.   In THE PILGRIM Chaplin's Tramp, posing as a clergyman, delivers willy-nilly a Sunday sermon on David's victory over Goliath in the form of a pantomime in which he enacts both the little man he is and his giant adversary. [Illus. 58] This marvelous solo performance highlights a major theme of the Tramp films by presenting the archetypal Biblical story on which it is patterned. Is not the Tramp wholly a David figure? And is not this figure seen in a way under the microscope? It is as if the screen image of the little fellow were a drawn-out close-up of his fears and daydreams, embarrassments and stratagems, handicaps and successes. Chaplin endows the close-up with human significance. Perhaps the most impressive trait of his Tramp is a truly unquenchable capacity for survival in the face of the Goliaths of this world; the life force which he embodies brings to mind films on plant growth, with their accelerated-motion shots of tender shoots sprouting forth through the soil. Here is where a link can be established between the old Chaplin comedies and certain neorealistic films: CABIRIA and UMBERTO D. resemble the Tramp in that they are as vulnerable as they are indestructible.* All these characters seem to yield to the powers that be and yet manage to outlast them.

True, the Tramp and Mickey Mouse, his two-dimensional next of kin, have long since passed away, but the motif they embodied continues to assert itself time and again. (This, incidentally, implies that their disappearance cannot be sufficiently explained from sociological reasons, such as the change of the social climate in the 'thirties and the concomitant change of audience tastes. Therefore it makes good sense to look for other, more immediate explanations; both screen personalities may have been abandoned because of the changing aspirations of their creators and certain related developments in the motion picture industry.) A fascinating incarnation of little David is, for example, the typical hero of the Westerns, who is invariably introduced to us as an easy victim. Alan Ladd's Shane in the film of this title cuts a pitiable figure among the toughs in the bar, and James Stewart in DESTRY RIDES AGAIN does not even carry a pistol. Similarly, the odds are that the lone sheriff in HIGH NOON will himself be killed in the suicidal fight he provokes. Yet no sooner do the Westerns reach their climax than the potential victims reveal themselves as the shining righters of wrongs. And the punishment they eventually inflict on the overwhelming forces of evil adds significance

* See p. 270.

to the eternal appeal of the chases, the galloping horses, and the long-distance shots of mountain ranges and plains.

The Winslow Boy   Like the motif of sleuthing, the David-Goliath theme may infuse film life into theatrical pictures. Take THE WINSLOW BOY: no visible attempt is made in it to transform the stage play from which it has been adapted into a real film. To mention only one instance of outright theatricality, the film does not show the final and decisive scene in court but has the old housekeeper report its glorious outcome—the time-honored stage device of the eye-witness informing those concerned of victory or defeat in unstageable battles. The moviegoer is thus cheated out of delights which he is entitled to enjoy. And despite the splendid acting he would feel completely frustrated were it not for the kind of spectacle he attends: once again little David—the Winslow boy—wins out over Goliath—the British Admiralty and public opinion at large. The glamour of this cinematic motif proves all the more irresistible since the film also involves sleuthing activities which point in the same direction. So the spectator will be inclined to forget the theatrical construction in features which afford him the experience of genuine cinema. With its beautiful story THE WINSLOW BOY is almost at home on the screen.

EPILOGUE

Film in Our Time

THE TIME HAS COME to take up a thread which was left hanging in mid-air at the end of chapter 9. That chapter closed with the remark that the spectator is not dreaming all the time and that the fact of his awakening naturally raises the question as to what film may mean to his conscious mind.* Relevant as the question then was, there would have been little purpose in pursuing it further at a time when the question was in a sense premature. Only now that the inner workings of film have been dealt with is it possible and indeed necessary to come to grips with this issue, which is the most central of all: what is the good of film experience?

PRIMACY OF INNER LIFE?

No doubt a major portion of the material which dazes and thrills the moviegoer consists of sights of the outer world, crude physical spectacles and details. And this emphasis on externals goes hand in hand with a neglect of the things we usually consider essential. In PYGMALION the scenes added to the original, scenes which ignored its moral to concentrate on incidental life, prove much more effective than the salient points of the Shavian dialogue, which is drowned in bagatelles; and what the adaptation thus loses in significance is plainly a boon to it from the cinematic viewpoint.** The cinema seems to come into its own when it clings to the surface of things.

So one might conclude that films divert the spectator from the core of life. This is why Paul Valéry objects to them. He conceives of the cinema as an "external memory endowed with mechanical perfection."

* See pp. 171–2.
** Cf. pp. 228–9.

And he blames it for tempting us to assimilate the manners of the phantoms that people the screen: how they are smiling, or killing, or visibly meditating. "What is still left of the meaning of these actions and emotions whose intercourse and monotonous diversity I am seeing? I no longer have the zest for living, for living is no longer anything more than resembling. I know the future by heart."[1] According to Valéry, then, by featuring the outer aspects of inner life, the cinema all but compels us to copy the former and desert the latter. Life exhausts itself in appearances and imitations, thus losing the uniqueness which alone would make it worth while. The inevitable result is boredom.* In other words, Valéry insists that, because of its exclusive concern for the exterior world, film prevents us from attending to the things of the mind; that its affinity for material data interferes with our spiritual preoccupations; that inner life, the life of the soul, is smothered by our immersion in the images of outer life on the screen. He, by the way, is not the only writer to argue along these lines. Georges Duhamel complains that the moving pictures no longer permit him to think what he wants to but "substitute themselves for his very thoughts."[2] And more recently Nicola Chiaromonte reproaches photography and film with making us "stare at the world entirely from the outside." Or as he also puts it, "the eye of the camera gives us that extraordinary thing: the world disinfected of consciousness."[3]

This argument would be tenable, however, only if the beliefs, ideas, and values that make up inner life occupied today the same position of authority they occupied in the past and if, as a consequence, they were presently just as self-evident, powerful, and real as are the events of the material world which film impresses upon us. Then indeed we might with justice condemn the cinema for alienating us from the higher objectives within our reach. But are they? But can it really be said that the relations between the inner universe and physical reality remain at all times essentially the same? Actually, they have undergone profound changes in the course of the last three or four centuries. Two such changes are of special interest here: the declining hold of common beliefs on the mind and the steadily increasing prestige of science.

Note that these two interrelated developments—they have already been referred to on an earlier occasion to account for the notion of "life as

* This verdict notwithstanding, Valéry has a pronounced sense of the flow of material life, as is illustrated, for instar   by his delightful description of Amsterdam streets and canals. Also, he is aware tha   visible shapes cannot be grasped to the full unless they are stripped of the meanings which commonly serve to identify them; and the idea of seizing upon them for their own sake rather appealed to him. See Valéry, "Le retour de Hollande," in *Variété II*, pp. 25–7.

such"*—radically invalidate Valéry's argument. If ideology is disintegrating, the essences of inner life can no longer be had for the asking; accordingly, Valéry's insistence on their primacy sounds hollow. Conversely, if under the impact of science the material components of our world gain momentum, the preference which film shows for them may be more legitimate than he is willing to admit. Perhaps, contrary to what Valéry assumes, there is no short-cut to the evasive contents of inner life whose perennial presence he takes for granted? Perhaps the way to them, if way there is, leads through the experience of surface reality? Perhaps film is a gate rather than a dead end or a mere diversion?

Yet these matters will have to wait. Let me begin at the beginning— modern man's intellectual landscape.

THE INTELLECTUAL LANDSCAPE

"Ruins of ancient beliefs"

From the ninetenth century on practically all thinkers of consequence, no matter how much they differed in approach and outlook, have agreed that beliefs once widely held—beliefs that were embraced by the whole of the person and that covered life in its wholeness—have been inexorably waning. They not only acknowledge this fact but speak of it with an assurance which is palpably founded on inner experience. It is as if they felt in their very bones the breakdown of binding norms.

Suffice it to select some pertinent views at random. Nietzsche, the Nietzsche of *Human, All Too Human*, claims that religion has had its day and that there "will never again be a horizon of life and culture that is bounded by religion."[4] (The later Nietzsche, though, would try to restore the patient to health by substituting the gospel of the Anti-Christ for abandoned Christianity. But had not Comte too declared religion to be a thing of the past and then made a new one of reason? *Le roi est mort! Vive le roi!*) What Nietzsche sweepingly postulates, Whitehead puts on the record in the manner of a physician consulting the fever chart. "The average curve marks a steady fall in religious tone," he observes within contexts devoted to the decay of religious influence in European civilization.[5] Freud on his part diagnoses the decay as a promising symptom. He calls religion the universal illusion of mankind and, with complete candor, compares it to a childhood neurosis. "According to this conception one might prophesy that the abandoning of religion must take place with

* See pp. 169–70.

the fateful inexorability of a process of growth and that we are just now in the middle of this phase of development."[6] And of course, to Marx religion is nothing but part of the ideological superstructure, destined to cave in when class rule is swept away.

If the impact of religion lessens, that of common beliefs in contiguous secular areas, such as ethics or custom, tends to become weaker also. Many are the thinkers who hold that our cultural traditions in general are on the decline; that there are indeed no longer any spiritual values and normative principles that would be unquestioningly sanctioned. Here is Spengler with his comparative survey of world cultures; his panoramic analogies culminate in the sad truth that, like previous cultures, ours is bound to die and that, as matter of fact, we have already reached the end of the way. Toynbee indulges in comparisons similar to Spengler's; and he would arrive at exactly the same conclusions were it not for his desire to uplift our morale, a desire which every now and then gets the better of his propensity for ominous historical parallels: he concedes the uniqueness of Western civilization, which in turn permits him to hold out to us a chance of survival (provided we seize it). Others, not given to such ambitious bird's-eye views of history, are nevertheless as strongly convinced as Toynbee or Spengler that ideological unity is in an advanced state of disintegration. Dewey, for instance, has it that the "disruption of consensus of beliefs" is at the bottom of what he considers the diffuseness and incoherence of contemporary art. "Greater integration in the matter and form of the arts depends consequently upon a general change in the direction of attitudes that are taken for granted in the basis of civilization. . . ."[7] (Ah, the enviable ease with which he makes out this prescription!) It is Durkheim who coins the metaphor of the "ruins of ancient beliefs."[8]

Vistas

Man in our society is ideologically shelterless. Need it be said that this is not the only aspect under which his situation presents itself? Yet before turning to the other major characteristic of his intellectual make-up, I should like to take a look at the divergent visions and speculations which the breakdown of overarching beliefs calls forth in him.

These speculations can roughly be divided into two groups. There is, first, the liberal outlook, traceable, as it were, to the days of the Enlightenment and strengthened by the surge, in the nineteenth century, of scientific conceptions more or less in keeping with it. Its exponents aspire to the complete secularization of public life and, accordingly, welcome the receding power of religious notions as a step forward in the evolution of mankind. They claim that religion should be superseded by reason; and they tend to identify reason with science, or at least were inclined to do so in the pre-atomic age. When speaking of the "ruins of ancient beliefs," Durkheim exhorts those who view them "anxiously and sadly" not to "ascribe to science an evil it has not caused but rather it tries to cure." And: "Once established beliefs have been carried away by the current of affairs [!], they cannot be artificially established; only reflection can guide us in life, after this."[9]

Guide us in what direction? Liberal-minded thinkers are confident that the human race is amenable to education; that education inspired by reason will launch it onto the way of progress; and that it will progress infinitely in a society which affords its members freedom from oppression, intellectual freedom and, not least, freedom from want, so that they may fulfill all their inherent potentialities. The "classless society" is basically a radical liberal's blueprint of the ideal social arrangement. Whatever the varieties of the liberal creed, they always revolve around the principles of reason, progress, democracy. This is not the place to elaborate on them. The salient point is, rather, that here you have a vision which interprets the loss of "ancient beliefs" as a gain in human prospects, with the ruins being deserted for lively communities where religion retires to the domain of private affairs.

Yet doubts mingle with optimism in the liberal camp itself. Ernest Renan, who had extolled the beneficent implications of science at the time of the 1848 revolution, recanted his youthful enthusiasm over four decades later. Human reason by itself alone, he would then declare, is hardly in a position to provide norms and sanctions able to regulate our moral life as effectively as did religion with its supernatural commandments; indeed, he goes so far as to submit that morality may deteriorate in inverse ratio to the advance of science.[10] Or think of Freud's late writings. True, he does not share Renan's nostalgia for the ruins left behind, but eventually he too takes a pretty dim view of the chances of reason and progress. Only two years after having expressed the genuinely liberal opinion that "in the long run nothing can withstand reason,"[11] he professes a cultural pessimism, in Civilization and Its Discontents, which testifies to a profound change of heart.

Disavowing his hopes of yesterday, Freud now avers that the realm of reason is forever threatened by man's innate tendency toward aggression. He derives this tendency from the "death instinct" and calls it "an overwhelming obstacle to civilization."[12] The disturbing function he assigns to it gives rise to the suspicion that in reality his instinct of aggression is nothing but an old acquaintance of ours—original sin. The religious definition of evil thrown out by the front door would thus slip in again in the guise of a psychological concept. (Be this as it may, Freud probes deeper than Marx into the forces conspiring against the rule of reason. But Marx, intent on widening that rule, could not well make use of discouraging profundities. When you want to travel far your luggage had better be light.) The misgivings entertained by a few luminaries have meanwhile trickled down to the rank and file. At a time when nuclear physicists worry about their moral responsibilities, people at large cannot help realizing that the science, which once seemed synonymous with reason, is actually indifferent to the form of our society and to progress other than technological. So reason itself eludes them all the more, turning from a substantive entity into an anemic notion. But this does not exactly strengthen people's confidence in its directive power, discredited also by social and political developments which rather vindicate Freud's ultimate forebodings.*

And there are, secondly, all those who plead for the rehabilitation of communal faith in revealed truth or in a great cause or in an inspired leader, as the case may be. In their eyes, the decline of "ancient beliefs" does not usher in a better, man-made future but, on the contrary, atomizes the body social, thereby corroding our spiritual energies. They reject natural reason as a guiding principle because it is unable to meet man's innermost needs; and they are afraid lest liberal reliance on progress, democratic equality, etc., might put a premium on uninformed mediocrity and contentment devoid of content. Whether or not they aim at the rebirth of religion proper, their messages are meant to kindle religious ardor in shiftless souls. Significantly, Sorel compares his social myth with the apocalyptic imagery that loomed large in the minds of the early Christians. (Instead of new Christians, though, his doctrine bred only Fascists, the syndicalists taking little notice of it.)

That anti-intellectualistic propositions fall on a fertile soil today must be laid to the very developments responsible for the crisis of liberalism. Their psychological effect is, as a liberal writer puts it, "a sense of drift and of drift without limits or direction."[13] It is, indeed, as if the atmosphere were impregnated with a feeling of uneasiness about the absence of unifying incentives that would set meaningful goals and thus contour the horizon. (More recently, by the way, this malaise, which no contemporary critic fails to dwell on, is being sustained by the spectacle

* Cf. p. 171.

of Soviet Russia, where people, much as they may suffer, do at least not seem to suffer from our "sense of drift." Yet were they even spontaneously devoted to the cause of Communism, their faith would be anything but a permanent emotional asset. For assuming Soviet Russia succeeds in achieving a state of well-being comparable to America's, then all the ideological incentives and pressures which now create suspense on the domestic scene are likely to falter for lack of purpose, and the resulting society, classless or not, will presumably be threatened with the same ideological exhaustion as the liberal democracies.)

Hence a will to believe, a preparedness for appeals summoning faith; exposed to the cold winds of emptiness, many a disenchanted intellectual has successively sought shelter in Communist party discipline, psychoanalysis, and what not. Nor is there a lack of faith-raising campaigns. Toynbee never tires of advising us that we will go to the dogs if we do not place again religion above all secular concerns. What religion? His historical analogies should prompt Toynbee to predict the emergence of a new "higher religion" superseding Christianity. But loath to desert the latter, he prefers to forget his own premises and, in a dizzying turnabout, proclaims flatly that in our particular case a new "higher religion" can be dispensed with because Christianity is not yet at the end of its rope.[14] It need not be Christianity. Others, alarmed by the fatal consequences of specialization, champion a renaissance of humanism; and still others refer us to mythology or get immersed in the religions of the Far East. Most of these movements are regressive in the sense that they revert to fashions of thought and argument preceding the scientific revolution. For the rest, it appears that the will to believe is matched by the incapacity for believing. Apathy spreads like an epidemic; the "lonely crowd"[15] fills the vacuum with surrogates.

Highways through the void

The other, less noticed characteristic of our situation can briefly be defined as abstractness—a term denoting the abstract manner in which people of all walks of life perceive the world and themselves. We not only live among the "ruins of ancient beliefs" but live among them with at best a shadowy awareness of things in their fullness. This can be blamed on the enormous impact of science. As the curve of "religious tone" has been falling, that of science has risen steadily. How could it be otherwise? Science is the fountainhead of technological progress, the source of an endless stream of discoveries and inventions that affect everyday life in its remotest recesses and alter it with ever-increasing speed. It is not too much to say that we feel the sway of science at each move we make or, thanks to science, are saved from making. Small wonder that an approach so productive in applications of the first magnitude should leave its imprint on the minds even in provinces not directly subject to its rule. Whether we know it or not, our way of thinking and our whole attitude toward reality are conditioned by the principles from which science proceeds.

Conspicuous among these principles is that of abstraction. Most sciences do not deal with the objects of ordinary experience but abstract from them certain elements which they then process in various ways. Thus the objects are stripped of the qualities which give them "all their poignancy and preciousness" (Dewey).[16] The natural sciences go farthest in this direction. They concentrate on measurable elements or units, preferably material ones; and they isolate them in an effort to discover their regular behavior patterns and relationships, the goal being to establish any such regularity with mathematical precision. If it holds true that units admitting of quantitative treatment are more abstract than units which still preserve traits of the objects from which they are drawn, one might speak of a tendency toward increasing abstractness within the sciences themselves. The social sciences, for instance, whose subject matter would seem to justify, or indeed require, a qualitative appreciation of the given material, tend to neglect qualitative evaluations for quantitative procedures apt to yield testable regularities (which, however, are often entirely irrelevant); in other words, they aim at achieving the status of the exact sciences. And the latter on their part aspire to further mathematization of the traces of reality they involve.

While scientific operations become more and more esoteric, the abstractness inherent in them cannot but influence our habits of thought. One of the main channels of this influence is of course technology. The pervasive growth of technology has given birth to an army of technicians trained to supply and service the innumerable contrivances without which modern civilization cannot be imagined. All these products are in the nature of tools which may be used for various purposes, meaningful or not; all of them are mechanisms and, as such, understandable only in terms of particular abstractions; and the essence of all of them is tantamount to their function.

The technician cares about means and functions rather than ends and modes of being. This cast of mind is likely to blunt his sensitivity to the issues, values, and objects he encounters in the process of living; he will be inclined, that is, to conceive of them in an abstract way, a way more appropriate to the techniques and instruments of his concern. It has frequently been remarked that ours is a technological age. There is some truth in this, as can be inferred from the constant influx of new technical terms, such as "fall-out," "plastics," "automation," etc.; the odds are, in fact, that terms in this vein make up a large percentage of the words which ordinary language is continually assimilating. Words canalize thought: the prominent place which technical nomenclature occupies in common speech suggests that the technician's mentality spreads far afield.

People are technological-minded—which, for instance, implies that the gratifications they derive from certain media of communications often bear no relation to the quality of the communications themselves. The transmitting apparatus overwhelms the contents transmitted. A case in point is the use which so many people make of canned music; as if tempted by its unlimited availability, they assign to it just the role of a background noise. Presumably the music not listened to satisfies their desire for companionship; when noise drowns the silence enveloping them, they need no longer suffer from loneliness. And why do they feel lonely? Much as they may miss human contacts, their loneliness is also a symptom of the abstractness which obstructs our intercourse with images and meanings.

Indeed, no sooner do we try to get in touch with mental entities than they tend to evaporate. In reaching out for them, we reduce them to abstractions as colorless as the noise to which radio music is commonly being reduced. This is illustrated by two popular approaches to things cultural or spiritual; both effect such reductions and both take their cue from science in a sense. One of them, which feeds strongly on Freud and depth psychology in general, voids all kinds of mental phenomena of their substance by passing them off as derivatives of psychological dispositions. To mention a few familiar examples, religious beliefs are identified as expressions or symbols of man's inborn fears and hopes (but what about the forms these beliefs assume, the degrees of truth to which they may attain?); wars are explained from irrepressible aggressivity (which does not explain historical wars at all); appraisals of the merits and shortcomings of our social order give place to considerations which largely revolve around the problem of whether we are adjusted or maladjusted to that order, no matter what it is like. It is all attitudes, behavior patterns, inner drives. Thus the specific content of the values surrounding us is psychologized away and the realm to which they belong sinks into limbo.

The other approach to this realm consists in what may be called the relativistic reduction. Along with progressive social mobility, the large-scale flow of information, so greatly facilitated by the media of mass communications, makes people realize that everything can be viewed from more than one angle and that theirs is not the only way of life which has a title to recognition. Accordingly, their confidence in absolutes is wavering; at the same time the broadening of their horizon challenges them to try to compare the different views and perspectives pressed home to them.* (Incidentally, scientific developments seem to parallel the relativistic preferences at large; it looks as if scholarly preoccupation with comparative studies were on the increase in such areas as religion, anthropology and sociology—all areas which involve various social groups, societies, cultures.)

This characteristic of modern mentality is difficult to pin down. Perhaps it partly accounts for the creeping apathy referred to above and also shows in the vogue which cultural comparisons and confrontations are enjoying; the theme of East and West has become a much-favored topic since World War II. Now the point is that these comparisons—which, for the rest, may spring from a desire for reorientation or such—are bought at a price. As we engage in them, we inevitably run the risk of missing the very essences of the diverse value systems to which we are exposed. Our interest in their comparable elements interferes with our readiness to absorb any such system for its own sake; but only by getting absorbed in it can we hope to assimilate it to the core. The wider the range of values and entities we are able to pass in review, the greater the chances that their unique features will withdraw from the scene. What we retain of them is hardly more substantial than the grin of the Cheshire Cat.

Artists have a way of sensing and baring states of mind of which the rest of us are only dimly aware. Abstract painting is not so much an anti-realistic movement as a realistic revelation of the prevailing abstractness. The configurations of lines in which it indulges faithfully reflect the nature of contemporary mental processes. It is as if modern painting aimed at charting the routes our thoughts and emotions are following. These routes have their counterpart in reality itself: they resemble those thruways and highways which seem to lead through the void—past untrod woods and villages concealed from view.

Challenge

This then is modern man's situation: He lacks the guidance of binding norms. He touches reality only with the fingertips. Now these two determinants of contemporary life do not simply exist side by side. Rather, our abstractness deeply affects our relations to the body of ideology. To be precise, it impedes practically all direct efforts to revamp religion and establish a consensus of beliefs.

* Cf. pp. 8–9.

The chimerical character of these efforts is fairly obvious. Those in a revivalist vein, as we have seen, are frequently regressive; they revert to pre-scientific modes of thought and seem prepared to sacrifice the principles upon which modern civilization rests. As if we could set back the clock of history even if we wanted to! Defending science against its accusers, Durkheim remarks that the "authority of vanished traditions will never be restored by silencing it; we shall be only more powerless to replace them."[17] Unfortunately, he does not supplement his judicious rejection of romantic illusions by an indication as to how we might manage to replace the traditional beliefs and yet continue to endorse science. But this is precisely the snag.

And of course, many candid attempts to renew faith in absolutes are predestined to fall flat because they palpably partake of the abstract spirit which they try to overcome. Consider Toynbee's, which is representative of this fallacy: The facile way in which he arranges and rearranges his "higher religions" into convenient patterns, now dwelling on the analogies between them, now stressing the uniqueness of Christianity, gives the impression that to him Christianity, Judaism, etc., are indeed nothing but "higher religions"; he reduces them to abstractions, that is; and as such they naturally lend themselves to being tossed about like coins or pebbles. Yet this detachment from their contents takes the life out of his exhortations. "What shall we do to be saved?" asks Toynbee. He answers that in the spiritual dimension we will have to "put the secular super-structure back onto religious foundations."[18] This counsel defeats its purpose; it refers to religion in terms negating it and thus dissolves the coveted goal before our eyes. To repeat, Toynbee stands for a whole trend; the air is filled with the thin preachings of ideologists, anti-liberal or not.

Does all this imply, one feels tempted to ask, that ideological unity has irretrievably been lost? But this question is irrelevant and unrealistic; it invites speculations which do not take into account the situation provoking them. Nevertheless, now that the question has been posed, one such speculation may be offered for what it is worth. It is quite imaginable that the radiating power of any value system obeys the second law of thermodynamics; which means that the energies which the system is losing in the course of time can no longer flow back to it. On this view, the "ancient beliefs" will become increasingly cooler. Considering the immense energies accumulated in them, their temperature is likely to decrease imperceptibly. Ideological fervor may continue to soar at intervals; and religious institutions may stay with us for an indefinite period. It is only that the cooling process is irreversible. (Note that the familiar opposite view has a convincing ring also; one might indeed argue that common beliefs are bound to re-emerge because man cannot breathe and live in an ideological vacuum. Speculations *sub specie aeternitatis* along these lines are rather gratuitious.)

Once again, the question as to whether or not ideology has had its heyday is a sham question which only obscures the issue at stake. This issue concerns not so much our relations to unifying beliefs as the conditions alone under which such beliefs are accessible to us today. We would on principle have free access to them were it not for the abstractness of our approach to things in and about us. It is this characteristic of modern man's mentality which frustrates his attempts to escape from spiritual nakedness. So our situation confronts us with a very immediate, very urgent challenge: if we want to assimilate values that delimit our horizon we must first rid ourselves of that abstractness as best we can. In trying to meet this challenge, we may still not be able to cast anchor in ideological certainties, yet at least we stand a chance of finding something we did not look for, something tremendously important in its own right— the world that is ours.

EXPERIENCE AND ITS MATERIAL

"Radiance of the sunset"

Evidently we can limit our all but compulsive indulgence in abstractions only if we restore to the objects the qualities which, as Dewey says, give them "their poignancy and preciousness." The remedy for the kind of abstractness which befalls minds under the impact of science is experience—the experience of things in their concreteness. Whitehead was the first to see our situation in this light and to comment on it accordingly. He blames contemporary society for favoring the tendency toward abstract thinking and insists that we want concretion—want it in the double sense of the word: "When you understand all about the sun and all about the atmosphere and all about the rotation of the earth, you may still miss the radiance of the sunset. There is no substitute for the direct perception of the concrete achievement of a thing in its actuality. We want concrete fact with a high light thrown on what is relevant to its preciousness."

And how can this demand be met? "What I mean," Whitehead continues, "is art and aesthetic education. It is, however, art in such a general sense that I hardly like to call it by that name. Art is a special example. What we want is to draw out habits of aesthetic apprehension."[19] No doubt Whitehead is right in thus emphasizing the aesthetic character of experience. The perception of "concrete fact" presupposes both detached and intense participation in it; in order to manifest its concreteness, the fact must be perceived in ways similar to those which play a role in the enjoyment and production of art.

Whitehead himself exemplifies this necessity by pointing to the multiple aspects of a factory with "its machinery, its community of operatives, its social service to the general population . . ." etc. Instead of dealing with it merely in terms of economic abstractions, as is the custom, we should learn to appreciate all its values and potentialities. "What we want to train is the habit of apprehending such an organism in its completeness."[20] Perhaps the term "completeness" is not quite adequate. In experiencing an object, we not only broaden our knowledge of its diverse qualities but in a manner of speaking incorporate it into us so that we grasp its being and its dynamics from within—a sort of blood transfusion, as it were. It is two different things to know about the habits and typical reactions of a foreign people and really to experience what makes them tick. (Here, incidentally, lies the problem of the currently fashionable cultural exchanges, with their claim to promote "mutual understanding.") Or take our relations to a city: the geometric pattern of New York streets is a well-known fact, but this fact becomes concrete only if we realize, for instance, that all the cross streets end in the nothingness of the blank sky.

What we want, then, is to touch reality not only with the fingertips but to seize it and shake hands with it. Out of this urge for concretion technicians often fall into playful animism, lending some motor with which they commune the traits of a whimsical person. Yet there are different realities or dimensions of reality, and our situation is such that not all of these worlds are equally available to us. Which of them will yield to our advances? The answer is, plainly, that we can experience only the reality still at our disposal.

Reality within reach

Because of the waning of ideology the world we live in is cluttered with debris, all attempts at new syntheses notwithstanding. There are no wholes in this world; rather, it consists of bits of chance events whose flow substitutes for meaningful continuity. Correspondingly, individual consciousness must be thought of as an aggregate of splinters of beliefs and sundry activities; and since the life of the mind lacks structure, impulses from psychosomatic regions are apt to surge up and fill the interstices. Fragmentized individuals act out their parts in fragmentized reality.

It is the world of Proust, Joyce, Virginia Woolf. Proust's work rests throughout upon the conviction that no man is a whole and that it is impossible to know a man because he himself changes while we try to clarify our original impressions of him.[21] In addition, the modern realistic novel insists on the "disintegration of the continuity of exterior events."[22] Erich Auerbach uses a section of *To the Lighthouse* to illustrate this point: "What takes place here in Virginia Woolf's novel is precisely what was attempted everywhere in works of this kind . . . —that is, to put the emphasis on the random occurrence, to exploit it not in the service of a planned continuity of action but in itself."[23]* The inevitable result is that the chance happenings narrated for their own sake do not add up to a whole with a purpose."** Or as Auerbach observes, "common to almost all of these novels is haziness, vague indefinability of meaning . . . uninterpretable symbolism."[24] (About the same might be said of any Fellini film — prior to his DOLCE VITA, that is.)

Now the world portrayed by the modern novel extends from sporadic spiritual notions all the way down to scattered material events. It is a mental continuum which comprises the physical dimension of reality, without, however, exhibiting it separately. But if we want to do away with the prevailing abstractness, we must focus primarily on this material dimension which science has succeeded in disengaging from the rest of the world. For scientific and technological abstractions condition the minds most effectively; and they all refer us to physical phenomena, while at the same time luring us away from their qualities. Hence the urgency of grasping precisely these given and yet ungiven phenomena in their concreteness. The essential material of "aesthetic apprehension" is the physical world, including all that it may suggest to us. We cannot hope to embrace reality unless we penetrate its lowest layers.

Physical reality as the domain of film

But how can we gain access to these lower depths? One thing is sure, the task of contacting them is greatly facilitated by photography and film, both of which not only isolate physical data but reach their climax in representing it. Lewis Mumford justly emphasizes photography's unique capacity for adequately depicting the "complicated, inter-related aspects

* Cf. p. 219.
** See pp. 221–2.

of our modern environment."[25] And where photography ends, film, much more inclusive, takes over. Products of science and technology, the two media are our contemporaries in every sense of the word; small wonder that they should have a bearing on preferences and needs arising from our situation. It is again Mumford who establishes a relation between the cinema and one of these needs; he argues that film may fulfill a timely mission in helping us apprehend and appreciate material objects (or "organisms," as he sees fit to call them): "Without any conscious notion of its destination, the motion picture presents us with a world of interpenetrating, counterinfluencing organisms: and it enables us to think about that world with a greater degree of concreteness."[26]

This is not all, however. In recording and exploring physical reality, film exposes to view a world never seen before, a world as elusive as Poe's purloined letter, which cannot be found because it is within everybody's reach. What is meant here is of course not any of those extensions of the everyday world which are being annexed by science but our ordinary physical environment itself. Strange as it may seem, although streets, faces, railway stations, etc., lie before our eyes, they have remained largely invisible so far. Why is this so?

For one thing, it should be remembered that physical nature has been persistently veiled by ideologies relating its manifestations to some total aspect of the universe. (Much as realistic medieval painters indulge in ugliness and horror, the reality they reveal lacks immediateness; it emerges only to be consumed again by arrangements, compositional or otherwise, which are imposed on it from without and reflect such holistic notions as sin, the last judgment, salvation, and the like.) Yet considering the breakdown of traditional values and norms, this explanation of our failure to notice the world around us is no longer convincing. In fact, it makes good sense to conclude that, now that ideology has disintegrated, material objects are divested of their wraps and veils so that we may appreciate them in their own right. Dewey jumps at this conclusion. He submits that our freedom "from syntheses of the imagination that went contrary to the grain of things"[27] is compensated for by our new awareness of the latter; and he attributes this development not only to the disappearance of false syntheses but to the liberating influence of science as well. Science, says he, "has greatly quickened in a few at least alertness of observation with respect to things of whose existence we were not before even aware."[28]

But Dewey fails to realize that science is a double-edged sword. On the one hand, it alerts us to the world of its concern, as he assumes; on the other, it tends to remove that world from the field of vision—a counterinfluence which he does not mention. The truly decisive reason for the elusiveness of physical reality is the habit of abstract thinking we have acquired under the reign of science and technology. No sooner do we emancipate ourselves from the "ancient beliefs" than we are led to eliminate the qualities of things. So the things continue to recede. And, assuredly, they are all the more elusive since we usually cannot help setting them in the perspective of conventional views and purposes which point beyond their self-contained being. Hence, were it not for the intervention of the film camera, it would cost us an enormous effort to surmount the barriers which separate us from our everyday surroundings.

Film renders visible what we did not, or perhaps even could not, see before its advent. It effectively assists us in discovering the material world with its psychophysical correspondences. We literally redeem this world from its dormant state, its state of virtual nonexistence, by endeavoring to experience it through the camera. And we are free to experience it because we are fragmentized. The cinema can be defined as a medium particularly equipped to promote the redemption of physical reality. Its imagery permits us, for the first time, to take away with us the objects and occurrences that comprise the flow of material life.

THE REDEMPTION OF PHYSICAL REALITY

Art with a difference

But in order to make us experience physical reality, films must show what they picture. This requirement is so little self-evident that it raises the issue of the medium's relation to the traditional arts.

To the extent that painting, literature, the theater, etc., involve nature at all, they do not really represent it. Rather, they use it as raw material from which to build works which lay claim to autonomy. In the work of art nothing remains of the raw material itself, or, to be precise, all that remains of it is so molded that it implements the intentions conveyed through it. In a sense, the real-life material disappears in the artist's intentions. To be sure, his creative imagination may be kindled by real objects and events, but instead of preserving them in their amorphous state, he spontaneously shapes them according to the forms and notions they call forth in him.

This distinguishes the painter or poet from the film maker; unlike him, the artist would cease to be one if he incorporated life in the raw, as rendered by the camera. However realistically minded, he overwhelms rather than records reality. And since he is free to indulge his formative aspirations, his work tends to be a significant whole. In consequence, the significance of a work of art determines that of its elements; or conversely, its elements are significant in so far as they contribute to the truth or beauty inherent in the work as a whole. Their function is not to reflect reality but to bear out a vision of it. Art proceeds from top to bottom. From the distant viewpoint of the photographic media this also applies to works which imitate nature, induce randomness, or, Dada fashion, obstruct art. The scrap of newspaper in a perfect collage is transformed from a sample of extraneous actuality into the emanation of an "idea conception," to use Eisenstein's term.*

The intrusion of Art into film thwarts the cinema's intrinsic possibilities. If for reasons of aesthetic purity films influenced by the traditional arts prefer to disregard actual physical reality, they miss an opportunity reserved for the cinematic medium. And if they do picture the given visible world, they nevertheless fail to show it, for the shots of it then merely serve to compose what can be passed off as a work of art; accordingly, the real-life material in such films forfeits its character as raw material. Here belong not only artistically ambitious experimental films— e.g. Buñuel-Dali's Un Chien Andalou—but all the innumerable commercial films which, though completely devoid of art, nevertheless half-unintentionally pay tribute to it by following the ways of the theater.

Nobody would think of minimizing the difference between Un Chien Andalou, a hybrid of great artistic interest, and ordinary screen entertainment along theatrical lines. And yet the routine product and the artist's work coincide in estranging the medium from pursuits which are peculiar to it. As compared with, say, Umberto D. or Cabiria, average theatrical films and certain high-level *avant-garde* films must be lumped together in spite of all that separates them. Films of this kind exploit, not explore, the material phenomena they insert; they insert them not in their own interest but for the purpose of establishing a significant whole; and in pointing up some such whole, they refer us from the material dimension back to that of ideology. Art in film is reactionary because it symbolizes wholeness and thus pretends to the continued existence of beliefs which "cover" physical reality in both senses of the word. The result is films which sustain the prevailing abstractness.

Their undeniable frequency should not lead one to underestimate the occurrence of films rejecting the "lie of 'art.' "[29] These range from plain films of fact—newsreels or purely factual documentaries—to full-grown feature films imbued with their authors' formative aspirations. The films of the first group, which are not even meant to be art, simply follow the

* See p. 221.

realistic tendency, thereby at least meeting the minimum requirement of what has been called the "cinematic approach."* As for the feature films, they are the arena of both the realistic tendency and the formative tendency; yet in these films the latter never tries to emancipate itself from, and overpower, the former, as it does in any theatrical movie. Think of POTEMKIN, silent film comedy, GREED, several Westerns and gangster films, LA GRANDE ILLUSION, the major productions of Italian neorealism, LOS OLIVDADOS, MR. HULOT'S HOLIDAY, PATHER PANCHALI, etc.: all of them rely largely on the suggestive power of raw material brought in by the cameras; and all of them more or less conform to Fellini's dictum that a "good picture" should not aim at the autonomy of a work of art but "have mistakes in it, like life, like people."[30]

Does the cinema gravitate toward films in this vein? In any case, their prominent features tend to assert themselves throughout the body of films and often in places where one would least expect them. It time and again happens that an otherwise theatrical film includes a scene whose images inadvertently tell a story of their own, which for a transient moment makes one completely forget the manifest story. One might say of such a film that it is badly composed; but its alleged shortcoming is actually its only merit. The trend toward semi-documentaries is, partly, a concession to the virtues of dramatic documentaries.** The typical composition of the musical reflects the precarious, if not antinomic, relations that obtain in the depth of the medium between the realistic and formative tendencies.† More recently, attempts are being made, or rather, resumed††, to get away from literature and rigid story construction by having the actors extemporize their lines. (Whether these attempts are likely to introduce genuine incident is quite another question.)

All this does not imply that camera-realism and art exclude each other. But if films which really show what they picture are art, they are art with a difference. Indeed, along with photography, film is the only art which exhibits its raw material. Such art as goes into cinematic films must be traced to their creators' capacity for reading the book of nature. The film artist has traits of an imaginative reader or an explorer prodded by insatiable curiosity.§ To repeat a definition given in earlier contexts, he is "a man who sets out to tell a story but, in shooting it, is so overwhelmed by his innate desire to cover all of physical reality—and also by a feeling

---

* See p. 38, and *passim*.

** Cf. pp. 259–60.

† See pp. 148–9, 213.

†† Cf. pp. 98 (reference to Pabst's *mise-en-scène* of his THE LOVE OF JEANNE NEY), 249 n.

§ See p. 16.

that he must cover it in order to tell the story, any story, in cinematic terms—that he ventures ever deeper into the jungle of material phenomena in which he risks becoming irretrievably lost if he does not, by virtue of great efforts, get back to the highways he left."*

Moments of everyday life

The moviegoer watches the images on the screen in a dream-like state.** So he can be supposed to apprehend physical reality in its concreteness; to be precise, he experiences a flow of chance events, scattered objects, and nameless shapes. In the moviehouses, exclaims Michel Dard, "we are brothers of the poisonous plants, the pebbles . . ."[31] Because of the preoccupation of film with physical minutiae† as well as the decline of ideology it is in fact inevitable that our minds, fragmentized as they are, should absorb not so much wholes as "small moments of material life" (Balázs).†† Now material life may be part and parcel of various dimensions of life in general. Query: do the "small moments" to which we surrender ourselves show an affinity for a particular orbit of life?

In feature films these small units are elements of plots free to range over all orbits imaginable. They may try to reconstruct the past, indulge in fantasies, champion a belief, or picture an individual conflict, a strange adventure, and what not. Consider any element of such a story film. No doubt it is intended to advance the story to which it belongs, but it also affects us strongly, or even primarily, as just a fragmentary moment of visible reality, surrounded, as it were, by a fringe of indeterminate visible meanings. And in this capacity the moment disengages itself from the conflict, the belief, the adventure, toward which the whole of the story converges. A face on the screen may attract us as a singular manifestation of fear or happiness regardless of the events which motivate its expression. A street serving as a background to some quarrel or love affair may rush to the fore and produce an intoxicating effect.

Street and face, then, open up a dimension much wider than that of the plots which they sustain. This dimension extends, so to speak, beneath the superstructure of specific story contents; it is made up of moments within everybody's reach, moments as common as birth and death, or a smile, or "the ripple of the leaves stirred by the wind."§ To be sure,

---

* See p. 255.
** See chapter 9, *passim*; especially pp. 165–6.
† Cf. pp. ɔ0, 297–8.
†† See pp. 89, 225.
§ Cf. p. 31.

what happens in each of these moments, says Erich Auerbach, "concerns in a very personal way the individuals who live in it, but it also (and for that very reason) concerns the elementary things which men in general have in common. It is precisely the random moment which is comparatively independent of the controversial and unstable orders over which men fight and despair; it passes unaffected by them, as daily life."[32] Even though his poignant observation bears on the modern novel, it holds no less true of film—except for the fact, negligible within this context, that the elements of the novel involve the life of the mind in ways denied to the cinema.

Note that Auerbach's casual reference to "daily life" offers an important clue. The small random moments which concern things common to you and me and the rest of mankind can indeed be said to constitute the dimension of everyday life, this matrix of all other modes of reality. It is a very substantial dimension. If you disregard for a moment articulate beliefs, ideological objectives, special undertakings, and the like, there still remain the sorrows and satisfactions, discords and feasts, wants and pursuits, which mark the ordinary business of living. Products of habit and microscopic interaction, they form a resilient texture which changes slowly and survives wars, epidemics, earthquakes, and revolutions. Films tend to explore this texture of everyday life,* whose composition varies according to place, people, and time. So they help us not only to appreciate our given material environment but to extend it in all directions. They virtually make the world our home.

This was already recognized in the early days of the medium. The German critic Herman G. Scheffauer predicted as far back as 1920 that through film man "shall come to know the earth as his own house, though he may never have escaped the narrow confines of his hamlet."[33] Over thirty years later Gabriel Marcel expresses himself in similar terms. He attributes to film, especially documentary film, the power of deepening and rendering more intimate "our relation to this Earth which is our habitat." "And I should say," he adds, "that to me who has always had a propensity to get tired of what I have the habit of seeing—what in reality, that is, I do not see anymore—this power peculiar to the cinema seems to be literally redeeming [*salvatrice*]."[34]

Material evidence

In acquainting us with the world we live in, the cinema exhibits phenomena whose appearance in the witness stand is of particular conse-

* See pp. 71–2.

quence. It brings us face to face with the things we dread. And it often challenges us to confront the real-life events it shows with the ideas we commonly entertain about them.

THE HEAD OF MEDUSA

We have learned in school the story of the Gorgon Medusa whose face, with its huge teeth and protruding tongue, was so horrible that the sheer sight of it turned men and beasts into stone. When Athena instigated Perseus to slay the monster, she therefore warned him never to look at the face itself but only at its mirror reflection in the polished shield she had given him. Following her advice, Perseus cut off Medusa's head with the sickle which Hermes had contributed to his equipment.[35]

The moral of the myth is, of course, that we do not, and cannot, see actual horrors because they paralyze us with blinding fear; and that we shall know what they look like only by watching images of them which reproduce their true appearance. These images have nothing in common with the artist's imaginative rendering of an unseen dread but are in the nature of mirror reflections. Now of all the existing media the cinema alone holds up a mirror to nature. Hence our dependence on it for the reflection of happenings which would petrify us were we to encounter them in real life. The film screen is Athena's polished shield.

This is not all, however. In addition, the myth suggests that the images on the shield or screen are a means to an end; they are to enable—or, by extension, induce—the spectator to behead the horror they mirror. Many a war film indulges in cruelties for this very reason. Do such films serve the purpose? In the myth itself Medusa's decapitation is not yet the end of her reign. Athena, we are told, fastened the terrible head to her aegis so as to throw a scare in her enemies. Perseus, the image watcher, did not succeed in laying the ghost for good.

So the question arises whether it makes sense at all to seek the meaning of horror images in their underlying intentions or uncertain effects. Think of Georges Franju's LE SANG DES BETES, a documentary about a Paris slaughterhouse: puddles of blood spread on the floor while horse and cow are killed methodically; a saw dismembers animal bodies still warm with life; and there is the unfathomable shot of the calves' heads being arranged into a rustic pattern which breathes the peace of a geometrical ornament. [Illus. 59] It would be preposterous to assume that these unbearably lurid pictures were intended to preach the gospel of vegetarianism; nor can they possibly be branded as an attempt to satisfy the dark desire for scenes of destruction.*

* Cf. pp. 57–8.

The mirror reflections of horror are an end in themselves. As such they beckon the spectator to take them in and thus incorporate into his memory the real face of things too dreadful to be beheld in reality. In experiencing the rows of calves' heads or the litter of tortured human bodies in the films made of the Nazi concentration camps, we redeem horror from its invisibility behind the veils of panic and imagination. And this experience is liberating in as much as it removes a most powerful taboo. Perhaps Perseus' greatest achievement was not to cut off Medusa's head but to overcome his fears and look at its reflection in the shield. And was it not precisely this feat which permitted him to behead the monster?

CONFRONTATIONS

Corroborative images Films or film passages which confront visible material reality with our notions of it may either confirm these notions or give the lie to them. The first alternative is of lesser interest because it rarely involves genuine corroborations. Confirmative images, that is, are as a rule called upon not to authenticate the truth to reality of an idea but to persuade us into accepting it unquestioningly. Remember the ostentatious happiness of the collective farmers in Eisenstein's OLD AND NEW, the enraptured crowds hailing Hitler in the Nazi films, the miraculous religious miracles in Cecil B. De Mille's THE TEN COMMANDMENTS, etc. (But what an incomparable showman was De Mille, alas!)

All of it is rigged evidence. These sham corroborations are intended to make you believe, not see. Sometimes they include a stereotyped shot which epitomizes their spirit: a face is so photographed against the light that hair and cheek are contoured by a luminous line intimating a halo. The shot has an embellishing rather than revealing function. Whenever the visuals take on this function we may be reasonably sure that they serve to advertise a belief or uphold conformity. For the rest, it is understood that not all corroborative images lack genuineness. In DIARY OF A COUNTRY PRIEST the face of the young priest substantiates, with a power all its own, the awesome reality of his religious faith, his spiritual tribulations.

Debunking Of course, the main interest lies not with corroborative imagery but with images which question our notions of the physical world. No sooner do films confront reality, as captured by the camera, with what we wrongly believe it resembles than the whole burden of proof falls to the images alone. And since it is their documentary quality which then counts, such confrontations are certainly in keeping with the cinematic approach; in fact, they can be said to be as direct a manifestation of the medium as is the flow of material life.

Small wonder that the body of existing films abounds in confrontations of this type. Significantly, silent film comedy, where they are used for comic effect, develops them from the technical properties of the cinema. In a ship scene of Chaplin's THE IMMIGRANT a traveler who, seen from behind, seems to go through all the motions of seasickness reveals himself to be engaged in fishing when shown from the opposite angle. A change of camera position and the truth comes out. It is a standardized gag—a shot dissolving some misconception deliberately fostered by the preceding shots.

Whether fun or censure, the principle remains the same. The first one to utilize the camera as a means of debunking was, as might be expected, D. W. Griffith. He considered it his task to "make you see";* and he was aware that this task required of him not only the rendering of our environment but the exposure of bias. Among the many prototypes he created at the time of the first World War is that scene of BROKEN BLOSSOMS in which he juxtaposes the noble and unassuming face of the film's Chinese protagonist with the close-ups of two missionaries whose faces exude unctuous hypocrisy. Griffith thus confronts the belief in the white man's superiority with the reality it allegedly covers and through this confrontation denounces it as an unwarranted prejudice.

The pattern set by him has frequently been followed for the purpose of exposing social injustice and the ideology from which it stems. Béla Balázs, who knowingly points to the cinema's "innermost tendency . . . toward revealing and unmasking," extols the Eisenstein and Pudovkin films of the 'twenties as the apex of cinematic art because of their concern with confrontations along these lines.[36]

Need it be said that many of their seeming revelations are actually vehement propaganda messages? Yet as with public opinion, documentary film material cannot be manipulated infinitely; some truth is bound to come to light here and there. In THE END OF ST. PETERSBURG, for instance, the scene with the young peasant walking past the columned palaces of the Czarist capital illumines in a flash the alliance that obtains between oppressive autocratic rule and architectural splendor.

It is not the Soviet cinema alone which favors camera exercises in social criticism. John Ford bares the plight of migratory farm workers in his THE GRAPES OF WRATH, and Jean Vigo in A PROPOS DE NICE stigmatizes the futile life of the idle rich by depicting random moments of it. One of the most consummate achievements in this vein is Georges Franju's L'HOTEL DES INVALIDES, a documentary commissioned by the French government. On the surface, the film is nothing but a straight record of a

---

* See motto, p. 41.

sightseeing tour through the historical building; surrounded by tourists, the guides, old war invalids, proceed from exhibit to exhibit, holding forth on Napoleon, armored knights, and victorious battles. Their worn-out comments, however, are synchronized with pictures which void them subtly of their meaning, so that the whole turns into an indictment of militarism and an insipid hero cult. [Illus. 60]

Or physical reality is revealed out of a desire to pierce the fabric of conventions. Erich von Stroheim in GREED and elsewhere has his camera dwell on life at its crudest—all that rankles beneath the thin veneer of civilization. In Chaplin's MONSIEUR VERDOUX, a film which revels in debunking, the long shot of the lake with the little boat in it conveys a Sunday photographer's dream of peace and happiness; but the dream is exploded by the subsequent close shot of the boat itself in which Chaplin as Monsieur Verdoux is just about to murder another victim. If you watch closely enough you will find horror lurking behind the idyll. The same moral can be distilled from Franju's slaughterhouse film, which casts deep shadows on the ordinary process of living.

Such exposures have a trait in common with cinematic motifs proper: their contagious power is so strong that even an otherwise theatrical film may be transformed into something like a film by virtue of their presence in it. True, Ingmar Bergman's THE SEVENTH SEAL is essentially a miracle play, yet the medieval beliefs and superstitions it features are questioned throughout by the inquisitive mind of the knight and the outright skepticism of his squire. Both characters manifest a down-to-earth attitude. And their secular doubts result in confrontations which in a measure acclimatize the film to the medium.

From bottom to top

All that has been said so far relates to elements or moments of physical reality, as displayed on the screen. Now much as the images of material moments are meaningful in their own right, we actually do not confine ourselves to absorbing them but feel stimulated to weave what they are telling us into contexts that bear on the whole of our existence. As Michel Dard puts it: "In lifting all things out of their chaos before replunging them into the chaos of the soul, the cinema stirs large waves in the latter, like those which a sinking stone produces on the surface of the water."[37]

The large waves roused in the soul bring ashore propositions regarding the significance of the things we fully experience. Films which satisfy our desire for such propositions may well reach into the dimension of ideology. But if they are true to the medium, they will certainly not move from a preconceived idea down to the material world in order to implement that idea; conversely, they set out to explore physical data and, taking their cue from them, work their way up to some problem or belief. The cinema is materialistically minded; it proceeds from "below" to "above." The importance of its natural bent for moving in this direction can hardly be overestimated. Indeed, Erwin Panofsky, the great art historian, traces to it the difference between film and the traditional arts: "The processes of all the earlier representational arts conform, in a higher or lesser degree, to an idealistic conception of the world. These arts operate from top to bottom, so to speak, and not from bottom to top; they start with an idea to be projected into shapeless matter and not with the objects that constitute the physical world. . . . It is the movies, and only the movies, that do justice to that materialistic interpretation of the universe which, whether we like it or not, pervades contemporary civilization."[38]

Guided by film, then, we approach, if at all, ideas no longer on highways leading through the void but on paths that wind through the thicket of things. While the theatergoer watches a spectacle which affects primarily his mind and only through it his sensibility, the moviegoer finds himself in a situation in which he cannot ask questions and grope for answers unless he is saturated physiologically. "The cinema," says Lucien Sève, ". . . requires of the spectator a new form of activity: his penetrating eye moving from the corporeal to the spiritual."[39] Charles Dekeukeleire points to the same upward movement with an awareness of its implications: "If the senses exert an influence on our spiritual life, the cinema becomes a powerful ferment of spirituality by augmenting the number and quality of our sense perceptions."[40]

"The Family of Man"

And what about the spiritual life itself? Even though the propositions which films evolve in proceeding from bottom to top lie outside the domain of this book, two remarks on them would seem to be indicated, if only to round out the picture. To begin with, all attempts to establish a hierarchy among these propositions or messages have proved futile so far. Béla Balázs's thesis that the cinema comes into its own only if it serves revolutionary ends[41] is as untenable as are the kindred views of those schools of thought, neorealistic and otherwise, which postulate an intimate relationship between the medium and socialism or collectivism.[42]* Nor

* Cf. p. 274.

does Grierson's definition of film, or rather, documentary film, as an educational instrument, a means of promoting responsible citizenship, cover
sufficient ground.[43] The range of equally legitimate propositions is inexhaustible. There is, to name only a few, Fellini's intense preoccupation
with the shelterless individual in quest for sympathy and purpose;[44] Buñuel's involvement in the cruelties and lusts which fill the lumber rooms of
our existence; Franju's dread of the abyss that is everyday life, the kind
of dread which befalls an adolescent who awakes by night and suddenly realizes the presence of death, the togetherness of pleasure and
slaughter . . .

Among the cinematic propositions one deserves special mention for
reflecting and endorsing the actual rapprochement between the peoples of
the world. Quite logically, Erich Auerbach hints of it in the wake of his
observation that the random moments of life represented by the modern
novel concern "the elementary things which men in general have in common."* "In this unprejudiced and exploratory type of representation,"
he continues, "we cannot but see to what an extent—below the surface
conflicts—the differences between men's ways of life and forms of thought
have already lessened. . . . Beneath the conflicts and also through them,
an economic and cultural leveling process is taking place. It is still a long
way to a common life of mankind on earth, but the goal begins to be
visible."[45]

Auerbach might have added that the task of rendering visible mankind on its way toward this goal is reserved for the photographic media;
they alone are in a position to record the material aspects of common
daily life in many places. It is not by accident that the idea of "The
Family of Man" was conceived by a born photographer. And one of the
reasons for the world-wide response to Edward Steichen's exhibition must
be laid precisely to the fact that it consists of photographs—images bound
to authenticate the reality of the vision they feature. Because of their
photographic nature films are predestined to take up this very theme.[46]
Some actually do. Thus WORLD WITHOUT END by Paul Rotha and Basil
Wright demonstrates the similarities between Mexican and Siamese
people, demonstrates them all the more convincingly since it acknowledges the limits of the leveling process: the dilapidated village church
manages to survive and the ancient Buddha meditates on the speed of the
motor trucks.**

Or think of Satyajit Ray's ARAPAJITO, an episode film crowded with
scenes such as these: The camera focuses on the ornamental bark of an

* Cf. p. 304.
** See pp. 205–6.

old tree and then slowly tilts down to the face of Apu's sick mother who yearns for her son in the big city. In the distance a train is passing by. The mother walks heavily back to the house where she imagines she hears Apu shout "Ma." Is he returning to her? She gets up and looks into the empty night aglow with water reflections and dancing will-o'-the-wisps. India is in this episode but not only India. [Illus. 61] "What seems to me to be remarkable about 'Arapajito,'" a reader of the *New York Times* writes to the editor of the film section, "is that you see this story happening in a remote land and see these faces with their exotic beauty and still feel that the same thing is happening every day somewhere in Manhattan or Brooklyn or the Bronx."[47]

Much as these propositions differ in terms of content, they all penetrate ephemeral physical reality and burn through it. But once again, their destination is no longer a concern of the present inquiry.

Notes

Unless otherwise specified, the translations in the text have been made by the author.

CHAPTER 1

1. Langer, *Philosophy in a New Key*, p. 210.
2. Whitehead, *Adventures of Ideas*, p. 27.
3. Quoted from Gay-Lussac's speech in the French House of Peers, July 30, 1839, by Eder, *History of Photography*, p. 242.
4. Quoted from same speech, ibid. p. 242.
5. Quoted from Arago's speech in the French Chamber of Deputies, July 3, 1839, ibid. p. 235.
6. Newhall, *The History of Photography* . . . , pp. 17–18.
7. Newhall, "Photography and the Development of Kinetic Visualization," *Journal of the Warburg and Courtauld Institutes*, 1944, vol. 7, p. 40. This paper is an important contribution to the history of instantaneous photography, which, says Mr. Newhall (p. 40), has not yet been written.
8. Ruskin, *Praeterita*, p. 341.
9. Quoted by Eder, op. cit. p. 341.
10. Newhall, *The History of Photography* . . . , p. 21.
11. For the references to Oliver Wendell Holmes and Darwin, see Newhall, "Photography and the Development of Kinetic Visualization," *Journal of the Warburg and Courtauld Institutes*, 1944, vol. 7, pp. 41–2.
12. Newhall, *The History of Photography* . . . , p. 27.
13. Cf., for instance, Ueberweg/Heinze, *Grundriss der Geschichte der Philosophie*, vol. 5, p. 27.
14. Freund, *La Photographie en France au dix-neuvième siècle*, pp. 102–7. For the Taine quote, see ibid. p. 103. In her excellent study Gisèle Freund traces the social and ideological trends that had a bearing on the development of photography. Her book is not free from lapses into commonplace materialism, but this minor shortcoming is compensated for by a wealth of source material.
15. Ibid. pp. 49, 53–7.
16. Hauser, *The Social History of Art*, vol. II, p. 775. (Translated by Stanley Godman.)
17. Ibid. pp. 775, 779; Freund, op. cit. pp. 106–7.
18. Newhall, *The History of Photography* . . . , p. 71.
19. Ibid. p. 71.
20. Weston, "Seeing Photographically," *The Complete Photographer*, 1943, vol. 9, issue 49:3200.
21. Newhall, op. cit. pp. 75–6; Freund, op. cit. p. 113.
22. Hauser, *The Social History of Art*, vol. II, p. 778.

23. Freund, op. cit. p. 96.
24. Ibid. p. 12; Newhall, op. cit. p. 43.
25. Freund, op. cit. pp. 78–9.
26. Ibid. p. 92.
27. Ibid. pp. 83, 85, 90.
28. Newhall, *The History of Photography* . . . , pp. 71–2.
29. Ibid. p. 76.
30. Ibid. p. 81.
31. Ibid. p. 75.
32. Ibid. pp. 71–2; Freund, *La Photographie en France* . . . , pp. 69, 101.
33. Freund, op. cit. pp. 107–8, 110–12.
34. Ibid. pp. 117–19.
35. Ibid. pp. 108–9.
36. Ibid. pp. 116–17.
37. So the painter and photographer Charles Sheeler in 1914; quoted by Newhall, *The History of Photography* . . . , p. 152.
38. Weston, "Seeing Photographically," *The Complete Photographer*, 1943, vol. 9, issue 49:3202. See also Moholy-Nagy, *Malerei, Photographie, Film*, p. 22.
39. Moholy-Nagy, *Vision in Motion*, pp. 206–7, 210.
40. Newhall, op. cit. p. 218. Moholy-Nagy, *Malerei, Photographie, Film*, p. 27.
41. Moholy-Nagy, *Vision in Motion*, p. 178.
42. Ibid. p. 178.
43. Moholy-Nagy, *Malerei, Photographie, Film*, p. 22.
44. Katz, "Dimensions in Photography," *The Complete Photographer*, 1942, vol. 4, issue 21:1354.
45. Newhall, op. cit. p. 131.
46. Moholy-Nagy, op. cit. p. 24.
47. Feininger, "Photographic Control Processes," *The Complete Photographer*, 1942, vol. 8, issue 43:2802.
48. Schmoll, "Vom Sinn der Photographie," in Steinert, *Subjective fotografie 2*, p. 38.
49. "Reaction to 'Creative Photography,'" *The New York Times*, Dec. 16, 1951.
50. Quoted by Newhall, *The History of Photography* . . . , p. 78, from H. P. Robinson. *Pictorial Effect in Photography* (1869), p. 109.
51. Newhall, ibid. pp. 157–8.
52. Cellini, *The Autobiography of Benvenuto Cellini*, p. 285.
53. Eisenstein, *Film Form*, p. 16.
54. Gasset, *The Dehumanization of Art* . . . . . . , p. 54. (Translator not named.)
55. Newhall, op. cit. p. 218. Cf. Moholy-Nagy, *Vision in Motion*, p. 177.
56. Freund, *La Photographie en France* . . . , pp. 105–6.
57. Proust, *Remembrance of Things Past*, vol. I, pp. 814–15. (Translated by C. K. Scott Moncrieff.)
58. Sherif and Cantril, *The Psychology of Ego-Involvements, passim*; e.g. pp. 30, 33, 34. Arnheim, "Perceptual Abstraction and Art," *Psychological Review*, March 1947, vol. 54, no. 2.
59. Mumford, *Technics and Civilization*, p. 339.
60. Freund, op. cit. p. 59.
61. Newhall, *The History of Photography* . . . , p. 47.

62. Ibid. p. 150.
63. Weston, "Seeing Photographically," *The Complete Photographer*, 1943, vol. 9, issue 49:3205.
64. Newhall, op. cit. p. 91.
65. Ibid. p. 139.
66. Moholy-Nagy, "Surrealism and the Photographer," *The Complete Photographer*, 1943, vol. 9, issue 52:3338.
67. I am greatly indebted to Mr. Edward Steichen for having this photograph brought to my attention.
68. Cf. Mumford, *Technics and Civilization*, p. 339.
69. Cf. Hajek-Halke, *Experimentelle Fotografie*, preface; p. 14. See also the above-quoted articles by Katz, Feininger, and Schmoll.
70. Quoted by Newhall, *The History of Photography* . . . , p. 213.
71. Mumford, op. cit. p. 340.
72. Newhall, "Photography and the Development of Kinetic Visualization," *Journal of the Warburg and Courtauld Institutes*, 1944, vol. 7, p. 40.
73. Newhall, *The History of Photography* . . . , p. 40; quoted from H. Fox Talbot, *The Pencil of Nature* (London, 1844), p. 40.
74. Quoted by Newhall, ibid. p. 144, from John A. Tennant's 1921 review of a New York Stieglitz exhibition.
75. Albert Londe, *La Photographie instantanée* (Paris, 1886), p. 139. I owe this reference to Mr. Beaumont Newhall who kindly let me have some of his notes on instantaneous photography.
76. Newhall, "Photography and the Development of Kinetic Visualization," *Journal of the Warburg and Courtauld Institutes*, 1944, vol. 7, p. 41.
77. McCausland, "Alfred Stieglitz," *The Complete Photographer*, 1943, vol. 9, issue 51:3321.
78. Newhall, *The History of Photography* . . . , p. 126.
79. Proust, *Remembrance of Things Past*, vol. I, p. 815. (Translated by C. K. Scott Moncrieff.)
80. Newhall, op. cit. p. 91.
81. Benjamin, "Ueber einige Motive bei Baudelaire," *Zeitschrift fuer Sozialforschung*, 1939, vol. VIII, nos. 1–2:82.
82. Cf. Newhall, op. cit. pp. 140, 143.
83. Quoted by Newhall, op. cit. p. 182, from H. Fox Talbot, *The Pencil of Nature* (London, 1844), p. 52.
84. Delluc, "Photographie," in Lapierre, ed., *Anthologie du cinéma*, p. 135.
85. Moholy-Nagy, *Vision in Motion*, p. 209.
86. Newhall, *The History of Photography* . . . , p. 198; quoted from Morgan & Lester, ed., *Graphic Graflex Photography* (1948), p. 218.

CHAPTER 2

1. Sadoul, *L'Invention du cinéma*, pp. 8, 49ff., 61–81 (about Marey). This book is a "must" for anyone interested in the complex developments that led up to Lumière. For Muybridge, see also Newhall, "Photography and the Development of Kinetic Visualization," *Journal of the Warburg and Courtauld Institutes*, 1944, vol. 7, pp. 42–3. T. Ra., "Motion Pictures," *Encyclopedia Britannica*, 1932, vol. 15, pp. 854–6, offers a short survey of the period.
2. Newhall, op. cit. p. 40.
3. Ibid. p. 40.
4. Sadoul, *L'Invention du cinéma*, p. 38.
5. Herschel, "Instantaneous Photography," *Photographic News*, 1860, vol. 4, no. 88:13. I am indebted to Mr. Beaumont Newhall for his reference to this quote.
6. Sadoul, *L'Invention du cinéma*, pp. 36–7, 86, 241–2.
7. It was Ducos du Hauron who, as far back as 1864, predicted these developments; see Sadoul, ibid. p. 37.
8. See, for instance, Balázs, *Der Geist des Films*; Arnheim, *Film*; Eisenstein, *The Film Sense* and *Film Form*; Pudovkin, *Film Technique and Film Acting*; Rotha, *The Film Till Now*; Spottiswoode, *A Grammar of the Film* and *Basic Film Techniques* (University of California Syllabus Series No. 303); Karel Reisz, *The Technique of Film Editing*, etc.
9. Caveing, "Dialectique du concept du cinéma," *Revue internationale de filmologie* (part I: July–Aug. 1947, no. 1; part II: Oct. 1948, nos. 3–4) applies, in a somewhat highhanded manner, the principles of Hegel's dialectics to the evolution of the cinema. The first dialectic stage, he has it, consists of Lumière's reproduction of reality and its antithesis—complete illusionism, as exemplified by Méliès (see especially part I, pp. 74–8). Similarly, Morin, *Le Cinéma ou l'homme imaginaire*, p. 58, conceives of Méliès's "absolute unreality" as the antithesis, in a Hegelian sense, of Lumière's "absolute realism." See also Sadoul, *Histoire d'un art*, p. 31.
10. Sadoul, *L'Invention du cinéma*, pp. 21–2, 241, 246.
11. Langlois, "Notes sur l'histoire du cinéma," *La Revue du cinéma*, July 1948, vol. III, no. 15:3.
12. Sadoul, op. cit. p. 247.
13. Ibid. pp. 249, 252, 300; and Sadoul, *Histoire d'un art*, p. 21.
14. Gorki, "You Don't Believe Your Eyes," *World Film News*, March 1938, p. 16.
15. Bessy and Duca, *Louis Lumière, inventeur*, p. 88. Sadoul, op. cit. pp. 23–4.
16. Quoted by Sadoul, *L'Invention du cinéma*, p. 208. See also, ibid. p. 253.
17. Sadoul, ibid. pp. 242–4, 248. Vardac, *Stage to Screen*, pp. 166–7. Vardac emphasizes that an ever-increasing concern with realism prompted the nineteenth-century stage to make elaborate use of special devices. For

instance, Steele MacKaye, a theatrical producer who died shortly before the arrival of the vitascope, invented a "curtain of light" so as to produce such effects as the fade-in, the fade-out, and the dissolve (p. 143).

18. Sadoul, op. cit. p. 246.
19. Bessy and Duca, *Louis Lumière, inventeur*, pp. 49–50. Sadoul, *Histoire d'un art*, p. 23.
20. Sadoul, *L'Invention du cinéma*, pp. 222–4, 227.
21. Sadoul, ibid. p. 332, and Sadoul, *Histoire d'un art*, p. 24.
22. Sadoul, *L'Invention du cinéma*, pp. 322, 328.
23. Ibid. p. 332. Langlois, "Notes sur l'histoire du cinéma," *La Revue du cinéma*, July 1948, vol. III, no. 15:10.
24. Quoted by Bardèche and Brasillach, *The History of Motion Pictures*, p. 10.
25. Sadoul, *L'Invention du cinéma*, p. 332.
26. Ibid. pp. 102, 201; esp. 205.
27. Ibid. pp. 324–6.
28. For Méliès's technical innovations, see Sadoul, *Les Pionniers du cinéma*, pp. 52–70.
29. Langlois, "Notes sur l'histoire du cinéma," *La Revue du cinéma*, July 1948, vol. III, no. 15:5.
30. Sadoul, op. cit. pp. 154, 166.
31. Sadoul, *L'Invention du cinéma*, pp. 330–31.
32. Cf. Meyerhoff, *Tonfilm und Wirklichkeit*, pp. 13, 22.
33. Clair, *Réflexion faite*, p. 96; he made this statement in 1924.
34. Ibid. p. 150.
35. Vuillermoz, "Réalisme et expressionisme," *Cinéma* (Les cahiers du mois, 16/17), 1925, pp. 78–9.
36. See Kracauer, *From Caligari to Hitler*, p. 240.
37. Berge, "Interview de Blaise Cendrars sur le cinéma," *Cinéma* (Les cahiers du mois, 16/17), 1925, p. 141. For the problems involved in the staging of actuality, see also Mauriac, *L'Amour du cinéma*, p. 36, and Obraszow, "Film und Theater," in *Von der Filmidee zum Drehbuch*, p. 54.
38. Scheffauer, "The Vivifying of Space," *The Freeman*, Nov. 24 and Dec. 1, 1920.
39. Eisenstein, *Film Form*, pp. 181–2.
40. See Kracauer, *From Caligari to Hitler*, p. 68.

CHAPTER 3

1. Quoted by Jacobs, *The Rise of the American Film*, p. 119.
2. "Core of the Movie—the Chase," *The New York Times Magazine*, Oct. 29, 1950. (An interview with Mr. Alfred Hitchcock.)
3. See Langlois, "Notes sur l'histoire du cinéma," *La Revue du cinéma*, July 1948, vol. III, no. 15:6. Sadoul, *Les Pionniers du cinéma*, pp. 264–5.
4. Rosenheimer, "They Make Documentaries . . . ," *Film News*, April 1946, vol. 7, no. 6:10. (An interview with Robert J. Flaherty.)
5. Knight, "Dancing in Films," *Dance Index*, 1947, vol. VI, no. 8:195; see also 185–6, 193. Among the best-known Astaire films are TOP HAT and SWING TIME.
6. Rotha, *The Film Till Now*, p. 370. Cf. Dard, *Valeur humaine du cinéma*, p. 17.
7. Cf. Arnheim, *Film*, p. 121.
8. Kracauer, *From Caligari to Hitler*, p. 189.
9. Léger, "A New Realism—The Object," *The Little Review*, 1926, p. 7.
10. Cohen-Séat, *Essai sur les principes d'une philosophie du cinéma*, p. 100.
11. Quoted by Henry, "Le film français," *Cinéma* (Les cahiers du mois, 16/17), 1925, pp. 197–8.
12. Doniol-Valcroze and Bazin, "Conversation with Buñuel," *Sight and Sound*, Spring 1955, vol. 24, no. 4:185.
13. Jacobs, *The Rise of the American Film*, p. 103. Referring to the close-up of Annie Lee, Sadoul, *Les Pionniers du cinéma*, pp. 555–7, compares Griffith's approach with that of Méliès.
14. See Jacobs, op. cit. p. 197, and Pudovkin, *Film Technique and Film Acting*, part I, pp. 118–19.
15. Eisenstein, *Film Form*, p. 238. Similarly, Pudovkin, op. cit. part I, p. 65.
16. Eisenstein, op. cit. p. 238.
17. Proust, *Remembrance of Things Past*, vol. I, pp. 978–9. (Translation by C. K. Scott Moncrieff.)
18. Benjamin, "L'Oeuvre d'art à l'époque de sa reproduction mécanisée," *Zeitschrift fuer Sozialforschung*, 1936, vol. V, no. 1:59–60.
19. Pudovkin, *Film Technique and Film Acting*, part I, pp. 60–61.
20. See Tyler, "The Film Sense and the Painting Sense," *Art Digest*, Feb. 15, 1954, p. 27.
21. Benjamin, "Ueber einige Motive bei Baudelaire," *Zeitschrift fuer Sozialforschung*, 1939, vol. VIII, nos. 1–2:59–60, 64–7, 68 n.
22. Cf. Faure, "Cinema," in *Le Rôle intellectuel du cinéma*, pp. 220–21.
23. Sadoul, *Les Pionniers du cinéma*, pp. 414–15.
24. Cf. Benjamin, "L'Oeuvre d'art . . . ," *Zeitschrift fuer Sozialforschung*, 1936, vol. V, no. 1:65 n.
25. See Epstein, *Cinéma*, Paris, 1921, pp. 99–100.

26. Pudovkin, op. cit. part I, pp. 53–4. See also Wright, "Handling the Camera," in Davy, ed., *Footnotes to the Film*, p. 49.

27. Cohen-Séat, *Essai sur les principes* . . . , pp. 117, 123–4, identifies the sequence long shot—close shot—long shot, etc. as a typically scientific procedure.

28. So Alexandre Arnoux, as quoted by Clair, *Reflexion faite*, p. 103.

29. Aragon, "Painting and Reality: A Discussion," *transition*, 1936, no. 25:98.

30. Epstein, "The Reality of Fairyland," in Bachmann, ed., *Jean Epstein, 1897–1953; Cinemages*, no. 2:44. For slow-motion pictures, see also Rotha, *The Film Till Now*, p. 370; Pudovkin, op. cit. part I, p. 153; Deren, *An Anagram of Ideas on Art* . . . , p. 47.

31. Cf. Epstein, *Le cinématographe vu de l'Etna*, p. 18; Deren, op. cit. p. 46.

32. Maddison, "Le cinéma et l'information mentale des peuples primitives," *Revue internationale de filmologie*, 1948, vol. I, nos. 3–4:307–8.

33. See Kracauer, "Jean Vigo," *Hollywood Quarterly*, April 1947, vol. II, no. 3:262.

34. Proust, *Remembrance of Things Past*, vol. I, pp. 630–31. (Translation by C. K. Scott Moncrieff.)

35. Clair, *Réflexion faite*, p. 77. (The quote dates from 1924.) See also Rotha, *The Film Till Now*, pp. 367–8.

36. Cf., for instance, Balázs, *Der sichtbare Mensch*, p. 120.

37. Cf. Bachmann, "The Films of Luis Buñuel," *Cinemages*, no. 1.

38. Quoted from Laffay, "Les grands thèmes de l'écran," *La Revue du cinéma*, April 1948, vol. II, no. 12:13. Cf. the reviews of the French film, WE ARE ALL MURDERERS, in *The New York Times*, Jan. 9, 1957; *New York Post*, Jan. 9, 1957; and *Cue*, Jan. 12, 1957. The reviewers unanimously praise this film about capital punishment in France for its grim realism and "pitiless candor" (N.Y. Times); and all of them clearly imply that it falls to the cinema to show horrors as they really are.

39. See Kracauer, *From Caligari to Hitler*, pp. 194–6. For an adequate rendering of such special modes of reality film makers may also have to draw on pictures belonging to "reality of another dimension."

CHAPTER 4

1. Stern, "D. W. Griffith and the Movies," *The American Mercury*, March 1944, vol. LXVIII, no. 303:318–19.

2. See Kracauer, *From Caligari to Hitler*, pp. 69–70.

3. Cf. Kracauer, "Silent Film Comedy," *Sight and Sound*, Aug.–Sept. 1951, vol. 21, no. 1:31.

4. Eisenstein, *Film Form*, p. 199.
5. Léger, "A propos du cinéma," in L'Herbier, ed., *Intelligence du cinémat-ographe*, p. 340.
6. Laffay, "Les grands thèmes de l'écran," *La Revue du cinéma*, April 1948, vol. II, no. 12:7, 9–10.
7. Kracauer, *From Caligari to Hitler*, p. 185. For Vertov, see also Rotha, *The Film Till Now*, p. 246.
8. Cf. Rotha, ibid. pp. 364–5.
9. Laffay, op. cit. pp. 10–11.
10. Cohen-Séat, *Essai sur les principes* . . . , p. 100.
11. Cf. Tyler, "The Film Sense and the Painting Sense," *Art Digest*, Feb. 15, 1954, p. 12.
12. Eisenstein, *Film Form*, pp. 99, 103–5, 106.
13. Sève, "Cinéma et méthode," *Revue internationale de filmologie*, July–Aug. 1947, vol. I, no. 1:45; see also 30–31.
14. Pudovkin, *Film Technique and Film Acting*, part I, p. 140.
15. Epstein, *Le Cinématographe vu de l'Etna*, p. 13.
16. Eisenstein, *Film Form*, pp. 64–8.
17. Scheffauer, "The Vivifying of Space," *The Freeman*, Nov. 24 and Dec. 1, 1920. See also Clair, *Réflexion faite*, p. 106. Rotha, *The Film Till Now*, p. 365, characterizes Feyder's THERESE RAQUIN as a film in which content grows out of images indulging in "subtle indirect suggestion."
18. Eisenstein, op. cit. p. 199.
19. Benjamin, "Ueber einige Motive bei Baudelaire," *Zeitschrift fuer Sozial-forschung* 1939, vol. VIII, nos. 1–2:60 n., 67, 88.
20. See Kracauer, *From Caligari to Hitler*, p. 121.

CHAPTER 5

1. Cavalcanti, "Sound in Films," *films*, Nov. 1939, vol. I, no. 1:37.
2. Laffay, "Les grands thèmes de l'écran," *La Revue du cinéma*, April 1948, vol. II, no. 12:8.
3. Cited from Faure, *L'Arbre d'Eden*, 1922, by Mauriac, *L'Amour du cinéma*, p. 213. Morin, *Le Cinéma ou l'homme imaginaire*, p. 68, also refers to Faure's idea.
4. Dreville, "Documentation: the Basis of Cinematography," *Close Up*, Sept. 1930, vol. VII, no. 3:206.
5. Cf. Rotha, *The Film Till Now*, p. 377.
6. T., H.H., "The Screen: 'Emperor and Golem,'" *The New York Times*, Jan. 10, 1955.

7. Clair, *Réflexion faite*, p. 79. Lindgren, *The Art of the Film*, p. 45, expresses himself in similar terms. There are exceptions, though. For instance, Obraszow, "Film and Theater," in *Von der Filmidee zum Drehbuch*, pp. 57–8, blames fantasy for being incompatible with the medium.
8. Pierre-Quint, "Signification du cinéma," *L'Art cinématographique*, 1927, vol. II, p. 24. Among the recent champions of this doctrine is Kyrou, *Le Surréalisme au cinéma*, *passim*.
9. Cf. Johnson, "The Tenth Muse in San Francisco," *Sight and Sound*, Jan.–March 1955, vol. 24, no. 3:154.
10. Gibbon, *The Red Shoes Ballet*, p. 12.
11. See Kracauer, *From Caligari to Hitler*, pp. 61–76.
12. Clair, *Réflexion faite*, p. 38. (This statement dates from 1922.)
13. Eisenstein, *Film Form*, p. 203.
14. Cavalcanti, "Sound in Films," *films*, Nov. 1939, vol. I, no. 1:38.
15. Neergaard, *Carl Dreyer* . . . , p. 29. (Translation by Marianne Helweg.)
16. See Clair, op. cit. p. 24.
17. Cf. Huff, *Charlie Chaplin*, p. 112.
18. Ibid. p. 133.
19. Cf. Kracauer, op. cit. pp. 77–9.
20. Cf. Lindgren, *The Art of the Film*, p. 28.
21. Cavalcanti, "Comedies and Cartoons," in Davy, ed., *Footnotes to the Film*, pp. 77–8, points to the near-documentary character of silent film comedy and its little dependence on cutting for pace.
22. Nicholl, *Film and Theatre*, p. 169; see also p. 93.
23. Quoted from Balázs, *Der sichtbare Mensch*, pp. 46–7.
24. Neergaard, *Carl Dreyer* . . . , p. 27. (Translation by Marianne Helweg.)
25. Ibid. p. 30.
26. Griffith, "The Film Since Then," in Rotha, *The Film Till Now*, p. 604.
27. Neergaard, op. cit. pp. 27–8.
28. Sadoul, *Histoire d'un art*, p. 180.

CHAPTER 6

1. See, for instance, Lindgren, *The Art of the Film*, pp. 156–7; Barbaro, "Le cinéma sans acteurs," in *Le Rôle intellectuel du cinéma*, p. 227; Barjavel, *Cinéma total* . . . , p. 81.
2. Quoted by Lyons, "The Lyons Den," *New York Post*, June 5, 1950.
3. Clair, *Réflexion faite*, p. 187.
4. "Film Crasher Hitchcock," *Cue*, May 19, 1951.
5. Cf. Barjavel, op. cit. pp. 84–5.

6. Clair, op. cit. p. 187.
7. Quoted by Rotha, *Documentary Film*, p. 143, from Pudovkin, "Acting—The Cinema *v.* the Theatre," *The Criterion*, vol. VIII, no. 1.
8. Sachs, "Film Psychology," *Close Up*, Nov. 1928, vol. III, no. 5:9.
9. Eisenstein, *Film Form*, p. 192.
10. Rossellini, "Dix ans de cinéma (I)," *Cahiers du cinéma*, Aug.–Sept. 1955, vol. IX, no. 50:9. See also Balázs, *Der sichtbare Mensch*, pp. 55–6.
11. Pudovkin, *Film Technique and Film Acting*, part I, p. 109.
12. Cf. Cooke, *Douglas Fairbanks*, p. 6.
13. Barjavel, *Cinéma total* . . . , p. 81.
14. Cited by Rotha, *Documentary Film*, p. 149. See also Rotha, *The Film Till Now*, p. 363.
15. Quoted by Marie Epstein, "Biographical Notes," in Bachmann, ed., *Jean Epstein, 1897–1953; Cinemages*, no. 2:8.
16. See Kracauer, *From Caligari to Hitler*, p. 175.
17. Chiaromonte, "Rome Letter: Italian Movies," *Partisan Review*, June 1944, vol. XVI, no. 6:628.
18. Rotha, *Documentary Film*, p. 148. See also Nicholl, *Film and Theatre*, p. 172.
19. Reynolds, *Leave It to the People*, p. 147.
20. Miles, "Are Actors Necessary?" *Documentary News Letter*, April 1941, vol. 2, no. 4:71.
21. Rossellini, "Dix ans de cinéma (I)," *Cahiers du cinéma*, Aug.–Sept. 1955, vol. IX, no. 50:9.
22. Chiaromonte, op. cit. p. 623.
23. Zinnemann, "On Using Non-Actors in Pictures," *The New York Times*, Jan. 8, 1950.
24. Ferguson, "Life Goes to the Pictures," *films*, Spring 1940, vol. 1, no. 2:22.

CHAPTER 7

1. Clair, *Réflexion faite*, p. 141. (A statement of 1928.)
2. Cf. Kracauer, *From Caligari to Hitler*, p. 205.
3. Eisenstein, *Film Form*, pp. 257–9.
4. Clair, op. cit. p. 116.
5. See, for instance, Charensol, "Le cinéma parlant," in L'Herbier, ed., *Intelligence du cinématographe*, p. 170; Adler, *Art and Prudence* . . . , p. 541; Lindgren, *The Art of the Film*, p. 106.
6. Clair, op. cit. p. 43.
7. Cavalcanti, "Sound in Films," *films*, Nov. 1939, vol. I, no. 1:29.

8. See Eisler, *Composing for the Films*, p. 77. Leech, "Dialogue for Stage and Screen," *The Penguin Film Review*, April 1948, no. 6:100, likewise rejects stage dialogue because "the epigrams, the patterned responses, the set speeches need the ceremonial ambiance of the playhouse and the living presence of the player . . ."

9. Barjavel, *Cinéma total* . . . , p. 29, remarks that the imagination of the spectator watching a dialogue film "builds from the words showered down on him and replaces the images on the screen by those which the dialogue suggests to him." See also Clair, *Réflexion faite*, pp. 146, 150, 158, 188.

10. Panofsky, "Style and Medium in the Motion Pictures," *Critique*, Jan.–Feb. 1947, vol. 1, no. 3:9.

11. Nicholl, *Film and Theatre*, pp. 178–80.

12. Cf. Balázs, "Das Drehbuch oder Filmszenarium," in *Von der Filmidee zum Drehbuch*, p. 77.

13. For instance, Balázs, ibid. pp. 76–7; Arnheim, *Film*, p. 213; Leech, op. cit. pp. 99–101.

14. Cavalcanti, "Sound in Films," *films*, Nov. 1939, vol. I, no. 1:31.

15. Cf. Meyerhoff, *Tonfilm und Wirklichkeit*, pp. 75–6; Arnheim, *Film*, p. 213.

16. Ruskin, *Praeterita*, p. 106.

17. Hardy, ed., *Grierson on Documentary*, pp. 115–16.

18. I am indebted to Mr. Arthur Knight for having this film brought to my attention.

19. Pudovkin, *Film Technique and Film Acting*, part I, pp. 157–8.

20. Reisz, *The Technique of Film Editing*, pp. 278–9.

21. Eisenstein, *Film Form*, p. 258. Cf. also Pudovkin, op. cit. p. 143.

22. Pudovkin, ibid. p. 157.

23. Arnheim, *Film*, p. 251, cautioned against this confusion as early as 1930.

24. For instance, Reisz, op. cit. *passim*.

25. Pudovkin, *Film Technique and Film Acting*, part I, pp. 159–60; part II, pp. 86–7.

26. Griffith, "Documentary Film Since 1939 . . . ," in Rotha, *Documentary Film*, p. 332, has it that the Canadian WORLD IN ACTION films followed a pattern which "already existed in the form of the *March of Time* . . ."

27. See Kracauer, *From Caligari to Hitler*, p. 220.

28. Knight, *The Liveliest Art* . . . , p. 178, observes that some of Hitchcock's "surprise effects on the sound track . . . such as the woman's scream in *The 39 Steps* that merges with a shriek of a locomotive's whistle, have become classics in the field."

29. Clair, *Réflexion faite*, p. 159.

30. Cf. Arnheim, *Film*, p. 267.

31. Cf. Panofsky, "Style and Medium in the Motion Pictures," *Critique*, Jan.–Feb. 1947, vol. 1, no. 3:16.

32. See Cavalcanti, "Sound in Films," *films*, Nov. 1939, vol. I, no. 1:36–7.

33. Ibid. p. 37.

34. So Clair in 1929; see his *Réflexion faite*, p. 145.

35. Quoted by MacDonald, "The Soviet Cinema: 1930–1938," *Partisan Review*, July 1938, vol. V, no. 2:46.

36. Clair, op. cit. p. 145.

37. Huff, *Charlie Chaplin*, pp. 256, 258.

38. Rosenheimer, "They Make Documentaries . . . ," *Film News*, April 1946, vol. 7, no. 6:10, 23. At the beginning of the sound era, Walter Ruttmann in his MELODY OF THE WORLD delighted in recording the din of traffic, the screech of a saw. These reproductions were as many discoveries.

39. Epstein, "Sound in Slow Motion," in Bachmann, ed., *Jean Epstein, 1897–1953; Cinemages*, no. 2:44.

40. Clair, *Réflexion faite*, p. 152.

41. Ibid. p. 152.

42. Rosenheimer, op. cit. p. 23.

43. Cf. Lindgren, *The Art of the Film*, pp. 104–5.

CHAPTER 8

1. Lindgren, *The Art of the Film*, p. 141, mentions that, "when the Lumière films were shown at the first public exhibition in this country [England] in February 1896, they were accompanied by piano improvisations on popular tunes." See also Cavalcanti, "Sound in Films," *films*, Nov. 1939, vol. I, no. 1:25.

2. Sadoul, *Les Pionniers du cinéma*, p. 485.

3. London, *Film Music*, pp. 27–8. Cavalcanti, op. cit. p. 27.

4. Landis and Bolles, *Textbook of Abnormal Psychology*, p. 68.

5. Cf. Eisler, *Composing for the Films*, p. 75.

6. Murphy, *Personality* . . . , p. 115 n. See also Meyerhoff, *Tonfilm und Wirklichkeit*, pp. 63ff.

7. Eisler, op. cit. p. 78. Cf. Vuillermoz, "La musique des images," *L'Art cinématographique*, vol. III, pp. 47–8, and Lindgren, op. cit. pp. 144–5.

8. Epstein, *Cinéma*, p. 106; Balázs, *Der sichtbare Mensch*, p. 143.

9. Cavalcanti, op. cit. p. 39.

10. Copland, "Tip to Moviegoers . . . ," *The New York Times Magazine*, Nov. 6, 1949.

11. Dahl, "Igor Stravinsky on Film Music," *Cinema*, June 1947, vol. 1, no. 1:8.

12. Mr. Paul Rotha tentatively advanced this interesting assumption in a personal discussion with me.

13. Lindgren, *The Art of the Film*, p. 141.

14. Eisler, *Composing for the Films*, p. 69.

15. Milano, "Music in the Film . . . ," *The Journal of Aesthetics and Art Criticism*, Spring 1941, no. 1:91.

16. Copland, op. cit.

17. Cf. Lindgren, op. cit. p. 147.

18. See Deren, *An Anagram of Ideas on Art* . . . , p. 40. Of course, such familiar melodies or visual clichés may be justified as short cuts in cases in which, were it not for their intervention, clumsy elaborations would be needed to advance the action.
19. Example volunteered by Marc Blitzstein in "Music in Films: A Symposium of Composers," *films*, 1940, vol. 1, no. 4:10.
20. Copland, "Tip to Moviegoers . . . ," *The New York Times Magazine*, Nov. 6, 1949.
21. Pudovkin. *Film Technique and Film Acting*, part I, pp. 162, 164–5.
22. London, *Film Music*, p. 135.
23. Lindgren, *The Art of the Film*, p. 146.
24. Eisler, *Composing for the Films*, p. 70.
25. Copland, op. cit.
26. Milano, "Music in the Film . . . ," *The Journal of Aesthetics and Art Criticism*, Spring 1941, no. 1:90.
27. Sargeant, "Music for Murder," *The New Yorker*, Oct. 30, 1954.
28. Cavalcanti, "Sound in Films," *films*, Nov. 1939, vol. I, no. 1:36.
29. Cf. Griffith, "The Film Since Then," in Rotha, *The Film Till Now*, pp. 443–4, 478.
30. Think of such musicals as ON THE TOWN, SEVEN BRIDES FOR SEVEN BROTHERS, LES GIRLS, etc.
31. Knight, "Dancing in Films," *Dance Index*, 1947, vol. VI, no. 8:193.
32. Eisler, *Composing for the Films*, pp. 73–4.
33. Cited by Benjamin, "L'oeuvre d'art . . . ," *Zeitschrift fuer Sozialforschung*, 1936–7, vol. V, no. 1:50–51, from a digest in *Lu*, Paris, Nov. 15, 1935, of Franz Werfel's article, "Ein Sommernachtstraum: Ein Film von Shakespeare und Reinhardt," *Neues Wiener Journal*. Eisler, op. cit. pp. 72–3, quotes this passage from Benjamin.
34. Cf. Erskine. "On Turning an Opera into a Film," *The New York Times*, Feb. 4, 1940.

CHAPTER 9

1. Clair, *Réflexion faite*, pp. 111–12.
2. For instance, Cohen-Séat, *Essai sur les principes* . . . , p. 92, assumes a continuity of effect, optimistically arguing that words, it is true, may partly "sterilize" the images but are powerless to overwhelm them.
3. Clair, op. cit. p. 112.
4. Wallon, "L'acte perceptif et le cinéma," *Revue internationale de filmologie*, April–June 1953, vol. IV, no. 13:107.

5. Quoted by Meyerhoff, *Tonfilm und Wirklichkeit*, p. 39, from Fr. Copei, "Psychologische Fragenzur Filmgestaltung," *Film und Bild*, 1944, Jahrgang 10, nos. 9–12.

6. Cohen-Séat, op. cit. pp. 154–5.

7. Barjavel, *Cinéma total*, p. 68, expresses himself in similar terms: "In the theater the spectator attends the spectacle. In the cinema he incorporates himself into it." See also Licart, *Théâtre et cinéma: Psychologie du spectateur, passim*; especially pp. 19, 20, 57. Licart discusses at length the different psychological effects of stage and screen, summarizing them graphically in two picturesque diagrams. The small volume is a curious mixture of shrewd and quaint observations. On the one hand, Licart fully acknowledges the cinema's unique impact on the senses; on the other, he frowns on it because of its alleged failure to "enrich" the mind (p. 57). This verdict is visibly in keeping with his exclusive devotion to the theater and traditional culture.

8. Wallon, op. cit. p. 110.

9. For the effects of darkness, see Mauerhofer, "Psychology of Film Experience," *The Penguin Film Review*, Jan. 1949, no. 8:103; Clair, op. cit. p. 111; Barjavel, op. cit. p. 68.

10. For references to the drugging effect of the cinema, see Maugé, "Qu'avez-vous appris au cinéma?" *Du cinéma*, May 1929, Série I, no. 3; Cranston, "The Prefabricated Daydream," *The Penguin Film Review*, 1949, no. 9:27; Epstein, *Cinéma*, p. 103; Wallon, "De quelques problèmes psycho-physiologiques que pose le cinéma," *Revue internationale de filmologie*, July–Aug. 1947, vol. I, no. 1:16.

11. Epstein, op. cit. p. 107; Wallon, op. cit. p. 16.

12. The hypnotic power of films is frequently mentioned and commented upon. See, for instance, Meyer Levin, "The Charge of the Light Brigade," in Cooke, ed., *Garbo and the Night Watchman*, pp. 124–6; L'Herbier, "Puissance de l'écran," in Ford, ed., *Bréviaire du cinéma*, p. 76; Epstein, *Cinéma*, p. 107; Cohen-Séat, *Essai sur les principes . . .* , p. 28; Quesnoy, *Littérature et cinéma* (Le Rouge et le Noir: Les essais, no. 9), p. 31.

13. Cf. L'Herbier, op. cit. p. 76.

14. See MacDonald, "The Soviet Cinema: 1930–1938," *Partisan Review*, July 1938, vol. V, no. 2:40; Pudovkin, *Film Technique and Film Acting*, part II, p. 44.

15. Hardy, ed., *Grierson on Documentary*, p. 77.

16. Waddington, "Two Conversations with Pudovkin," *Sight and Sound*, Winter 1948–9, vol. 17, no. 68:161.

17. See Kracauer, *From Caligari to Hitler*, p. 284, and Kracauer, "The Conquest of Europe on the Screen," *Social Research*, Sept. 1943, vol. 10, no. 3: *passim*.

18. Kracauer, *From Caligari to Hitler*, p. 280.

19. Cf. Rotha, *Documentary Film*, pp. 176, 195–6.

20. Kracauer, op. cit. p. 297.

21. Rotha, op. cit. p. 58.

22. Marcel, "Possibilités et limites de l'art cinématographique," *Revue internationale de filmologie*, July–Dec. 1954, vol. V, nos. 18–19:171. See also Meyerhoff, *Tonfilm und Wirklichkeit*, pp. 81–2.

23. Lebovici, "Psychanalyse et cinéma," *Revue internationale de filmologie*, vol. II, no. 5:54.

24. Mauerhofer, "Psychology of Film Experience," *The Penguin Film Review*, Jan. 1949, no. 8:107, says: "Film experience supplies countless people with acceptable material for their daydreams . . ." In their *Movies: A Psychological Study*, Wolfenstein and Leites stress throughout the daydream character of films.

25. This term, which of course applies to all centers of film production, even emerges in the titles of two books, *Die Traumfabrik: Chronik des Films* (Berlin, 1931) by Ilja Ehrenburg, a piece of tendentious, if clever, journalism, and *Hollywood: The Dream Factory* (Boston, 1950) by Hortense Powdermaker.

26. See Kracauer, "National Types as Hollywood Presents Them," *The Public Opinion Quarterly*, Spring 1949, vol. 13, no. 1:72.

27. Sève, "Cinéma et méthode," *Revue internationale de filmologie*, July–Aug. 1947, vol. I, no. 1:45–6.

28. Dard, *Valeur humaine du cinéma*, p. 10.

29. Berge, "Interview de Blaise Cendrars sur le cinéma," *Cinéma* (Les cahiers du mois, 16/17), 1925, p. 140.

30. Cf. Schachtel, "On Memory and Childhood Amnesia," *Psychiatry*, Feb. 1947, vol. X, no. 1, *passim*.

31. Hugo von Hofmannsthal, "Der Ersatz fuer Traeume," in his *Die Beruehrung der Sphaeren*, *passim*.

32. For the relations between audience desires and film content in the Germany of the late 'twenties, see Kracauer, "Der heutige Film und sein Publikum," *Frankfurter Zeitung*, Nov. 30 and Dec. 1, 1928.

33. Pordes, *Das Lichtspiel: Wesen—Dramaturgie—Regie*, p. 22.

34. Beucler, "L'homme cinéma," *La Revue du cinéma*, Nov. 1, 1930, vol. II, no. 10:20.

35. For further details of the research design, see Wilhelm, *Die Auftriebswirkung des Films*, pp. 6–9.

36. Ibid. pp. 19, 33, 34, 35.

37. Ibid. p. 47.

38. Chaperot, "Henri Chomette: Le poème d'images et le film parlé," *La Revue du cinéma*, Aug. 1, 1930, vol. II, no. 13:28.

39. Hofmannsthal, op. cit. p. 267.

40. Wilhelm, op. cit. p. 22.

CHAPTER 10

1. Maurois, "La poésie du cinéma," *L'art cinématographique*, 1927, vol. III, pp. 34–5.
2. Sève, "Cinéma et méthode," *Revue internationale de filmologie*, Sept.–Oct. 1947, vol. I, no. 2:172–3, and ibid. Oct. 1948, vol. I, nos. 3–4:352–3. See also Caveing, "Dialectique du concept du cinéma," ibid. Oct. 1948, vol. I, nos. 3–4:348. Valéry, "Le cinéma," in *Les techniques au service de la pensée*, pp. 161–2, too feels uneasy about the story film which he considers an awkward mixture of fiction and observation.
3. See Kracauer, *From Caligari to Hitler*, p. 68 n.
4. See Mekas, "The Experimental Film in America," *Film Culture*, May–June 1955, vol. I, no. 3:16, and Knight, *The Liveliest Art*, pp. 278–85.
5. Epstein, "Le sens 1 bis," in L'Herbier, ed., *Intelligence du cinématographe*, p. 259.
6. Dulac, "La cinégraphie intégrale," in Lapierre, ed., *Anthologie du cinéma*, pp. 159–60.
7. See Sadoul, *Les Pionniers du cinéma*, p. 541.
8. Cf. Brunius, "Experimental Film in France," in Manvell, ed., *Experiment in the Film*, pp. 68, 84–5.
9. See Dulac, "Le cinéma d'avant-garde," in L'Herbier, ed., *Intelligence du cinématographe*, pp. 346–7.
10. Clair, *Réflexion faite*, p. 53.
11. Dulac, op. cit. p. 348. According to Brunius, op. cit. p. 97, a 1924 screening of forgotten old science films at the Vieux Colombier, the famous Paris *avant-garde* moviehouse, greatly stimulated the trend in favor of documentaries. Cf. also Dulac, "L'essence du cinéma: L'idée visuelle," in *Cinéma* (Les cahiers du mois, 16/17), 1925, p. 62.
12. Brunius, op. cit. p. 69.
13. Ibid. p. 95.
14. Bardèche and Brasillach, *The History of Motion Pictures*, p. 243. (Translated by Iris Barry.)
15. Clair, *Réflexion faite*, p. 78.
16. Quoted by Brunius, op. cit. p. 71.
17. Chaperot, "Henri Chomette: Le poème d'images et le film parlé," *La Revue du cinéma*, Aug. 1, 1930, vol. 2, no. 13:29.
18. Dulac, "L'essence du cinéma: L'idée visuelle," *Cinéma* (Les cahiers du mois. 16/17), 1925, pp. 65–6.
19. Dulac, "La cinégraphie intégrale," in Lapierre, ed., *Anthologie du cinéma*, p. 165.
20. Dulac, ibid. p. 165.
21. Iris Barry, *Film Notes* . . . , p. 47.
22. Cf. ibid. p. 47.

23. Quoted by Richter, *Avantgarde: History and Dates* . . . , p. 5. I am indebted to Mr. Hans Richter for having put at my disposal a copy of this unpublished manuscript.
24. See Mekas, "The Experimental Film in America," *Film Culture*, May–June 1955, vol. I, no. 3:18, and Knight, "Self-Expression," *The Saturday Review of Literature*, May 27, 1950.
25. Cf. Mekas, op. cit. *passim*; Knight, op. cit. *passim*, and his *The Liveliest Art*, pp. 280–85; Jacobs, "Avant-Garde Production in America," in Manvell, ed., *Experiment in the Film, passim*.
26. Dard, *Valeur humaine du cinéma*, p. 11.
27. Artaud, "The Shell and the Clergyman: Film Scenario," *transition*, June 1930, nos. 19–20:63.
28. Deren, *An Anagram of Ideas on Art* . . . , p. 46.
29. Artaud, op. cit. p. 65.
30. Quoted from "Sang d'un poète (Le)," *Film Society Programmes*, April 2, 1933.
31. Allendy, "La valeur psychologique de l'image," in L'Herbier, ed., *Intelligence du cinématographe*, p. 318. (First published in 1926.) In the same year 1926 appeared the Pabst film, THE SECRETS OF A SOUL, whose dream sequences seemed to implement Dr. Allendy's idea. But their semblance of surrealism is deceptive, if only for the reason that they form part of a story which could not be more realistic.
32. Poisson, "Cinéma et psychanalyse," *Cinéma* (Les cahiers du mois, 16/17), 1925, p. 175.
33. Brunius, "Experimental Film in France," in Manvell, ed., *Experiment in the Film*, p. 100.
34. Morrison, "The French Avant-Garde: The Last Stage," *Sequence*, Winter 1948/9, no. 6:33. Wallis, "The Blood of a Poet," *Kenyon Review*, Winter 1944, vol. 6, no. 1, *passim*, goes still far beyond Morrison in reading symbolic meanings into the Cocteau film.
35. Cocteau, *The Blood of a Poet: A Film by Jean Cocteau*, p. 51. (Translated by Lily Pons.)
36. Richter, "The Avant-Garde Film Seen from Within," *Hollywood Quarterly*, Fall 1949, vol. IV, p. 38.
37. Clair, *Réflexion faite*, p. 107.
38. Cf. Brunius, op. cit. pp. 102–5; Knight, *The Liveliest Art*, pp. 108–9.

CHAPTER 11

1. Read, "The Film on Art as Documentary," *Film Culture*, Oct. 1957, vol. III, no. 3:6.
2. Cf. Rotha, *Documentary Film*, pp. 88, 117.
3. Ibid. p. 123.
4. For sociological comment on the typical U.S. newsreel, see Kracauer and Lyford, "A Duck Crosses Main Street," *The New Republic*, Dec. 13, 1948, and Meltzer, "Are Newsreels News?" *Hollywood Quarterly*, April 1947, vol. II, no. 3.
5. Arnheim, *Art and Visual Perception*, p. 202, means precisely this, but he is interested only in what happens to a painting if it is shown on the screen. "Pictorial superpositions," he argues, "are more effective on a projection screen than on paper or on canvas, because in a painting or drawing the visible flatness of the ground plane will counteract the three-dimensionality of the pattern."
6. Cf., for instance, Tyler, "The Film Sense and the Painting Sense," *Art Digest*, Feb. 15, 1954, p. 10.
7. Read, "The Film on Art as Documentary," *Film Culture*, Oct. 1957, vol. III, no. 3:7.
8. Tyler, op. cit. p. 12.
9. Ibid. p. 12.
10. So Herbert Matter's film, WORKS OF CALDER, and the Calder episode of Hans Richter's DREAMS THAT MONEY CAN BUY.
11. Bolen, "Films and the Visual Arts," in Bolen, ed., *Films on Art: Panorama 1953*. (Translated from the French edition of this UNESCO publication, p. 6.)
12. Ibid.
13. Read, op. cit. p. 7.
14. Tyler, op. cit. p. 12.
15. Cf. Iris Barry, "The Film of Fact," *Town & Country*, Sept. 1946, vol. 100, no. 4288:253–4.
16. Greene, "Nutrition," in Cooke, ed., *Garbo and the Night Watchman*, p. 228.
17. Ivens, "Borinage—A Documentary Experience," *Film Culture*, 1956, vol. II, no. 1:9.
18. Reynolds, *Leave It to the People*, p. 144.
19. Seton, *Sergei M. Eisenstein*, p. 357. Pudovkin, *Film Technique and Film Acting*, part I, pp. 133–34, also claims that nature should be adjusted, or indeed subordinated, to the film maker's compositional designs.
20. Grierson says of Flaherty that his "screen is . . . a magical opening in the theater wall, through which one may look out to the wide world . . ." Quoted from Hardy, ed., *Grierson on Documentary*, p. 60.

21. Rotha, "Presenting the World to the World," *Films and Filming*, April 1956, vol. 2, no. 7:17.
22. Dyke, "How 'Valley Town' Was Made," *Program Notes of Cinema 16*, Jan. 1950. (Reprinted from *U.S. Camera*, Winter 1940.)
23. Rotha, "It's in the Script," *World Film News*, Sept. 1938, vol. III, no. 5:205.
24. See Kracauer, *From Caligari to Hitler*, pp. 182–8.
25. Eisenstein, *Film Form*, p. 62.
26. See Rotha, *Documentary Film*, p. 175; Eisenstein, op. cit. p. 58.
27. Quoted by Kracauer, "The Conquest of Europe on the Screen," *Social Research*, Sept. 1943, vol. 10, no. 3:347–8.
28. Griffith, "Documentary Film Since 1939," in Rotha, *Documentary Film*, p. 335.
29. Hardy, ed., *Grierson on Documentary*, p. 215.
30. Rotha, *Documentary Film*, p. 106 n.
31. Ibid. p. 166 n.
32. Hardy, ed., *Grierson on Documentary*, p. 261.
33. Rotha, op. cit. p. 142.
34. Ibid. p. 147.
35. Ibid. p. 185. Road, "Documentary Film Since 1939," in Rotha, op. cit. p. 218, likewise submits that "maybe the individual human story has been rated too low."
36. Miles, "Are Actors Necessary?" *Documentary News Letter*, April 1941, vol. 2, no. 4:73.
37. Clair, *Réflexion faite*, p. 53.
38. Gasset, *The Dehumanization of Art* . . . , p. 80. (Translator not named.)

CHAPTER 12

1. Cf. Sadoul, *Les Pionniers du cinéma*, p. 540.
2. See ibid. pp. 540, 542; Langlois, "Notes sur l'histoire du cinéma," *La Revue du cinéma*, July 1948, vol. III, no. 15:13–14.
3. For this passage, see Jacobs, *The Rise of the American Film*, p. 9; Sadoul, op. cit. pp. 541–3, 573; Clair, "Le cinématographe contre l'esprit," in Lapierre, ed., *Anthologie du cinéma*, pp. 175–6.
4. Cf. Cohen-Séat, *Essai sur les principes* . . . , pp. 94–5.
5. See Auerbach, *Mimesis*, pp. 321–3.
6. Ibid. p. 548.
7. See Eisenstein, *Film Form*, pp. 7, 14, 17.
8. Ibid. p. 92.

9. Ibid. p. 254. It should be noted that Pudovkin, *Film Technique and Film Acting*, part I, p. 90, advances a similar opinion: "A film is only really significant when every one of its elements is firmly welded to a whole."

10. Balázs, *Der sichtbare Mensch*, p. 115.

11. Feyder, "Transposition visuelle," in *Cinéma* (Les cahiers du mois, 16/17), 1925, p. 71.

12. Griffith, "The Film Since Then," in Rotha, *The Film Till Now*, p. 483, characterizes THE INFORMER as a melodrama whose "pretentious, adolescent symbolism continued throughout the film."

13. Quoted by Bardèche and Brasillach, *The History of Motion Pictures*, p. 46, and Sadoul, *Les Pionniers du cinéma*, p. 530n.

14. Turner, "On Suspense and Other Film Matters: An Interview with Alfred Hitchcock," *Films in Review*, April 1950, vol. I, no. 3:22, 47.

15. Panofsky, "Style and Medium in the Moving Pictures," *transition*, 1937, no. 26:125.

16. Quoted from Eisenstein, *Film Form*, p. 182.

17. Lusk, "I Love Actresses!" *New Movies*, Jan. 1947, vol. XXII, no. 1:28, 30.

18. Ferguson, "Life Goes to the Pictures," *films*, Spring 1940, vol. I, no. 2:21.

19. Lewis, "Erich von Stroheim of the Movies . . . ," *The New York Times*, June 22, 1941.

20. Balázs, *Der sichtbare Mensch*, pp. 46–7. Cf. also Greene, "Subjects and Stories," in Davy, ed., *Footnotes to the Film*, p. 69, about incidental life in WE FROM KRONSTADT. Similarly, Ferguson, op. cit. *passim*, emphasizes the importance for films to incorporate fleeting moments of physical life.

21. Cf. Caveing, "Dialectique du concept du cinéma," *Revue internationale de filmologie*, Oct. 1948, vol. I, nos. 3–4:349–50.

22. Rotha, "A Foreword," in *Eisenstein, 1898–1948*.

23. Eisenstein, *Film Form*, pp. 162–3.

24. Seton, *Sergei M. Eisenstein*, pp. 74–5.

25. Eisenstein, op. cit. p. 132.

26. Marcel, "Possibilités et limites de l'art cinématographique," *Revue internationale de filmologie*, July–Dec. 1954, vol. V, nos. 18–9:170, applies the term "useless" in this sense. See also the passage on MOBY DICK in Bluestone, *Novels into Film*, p. 206.

27. Cf. Jacobs, *The Rise of the American Film*, pp. 105–6.

28. Pudovkin, *Film Technique and Film Acting*, part I, p. 19, believes the Griffith chase fully to live up to the significance of the action whose climax it marks. As for Eisenstein's oblique interpretation of this standardized chase sequence, see his *Film Form*, pp. 234–5.

29. Panofsky, "Style and Medium in the Motion Pictures," *Critique*, Jan.–Feb. 1947, vol. 1, no. 3:11.

30. Rawnsley, "Design by Inference," *The Penguin Film Review*, 1949, no. 9:34. Lindgren, *The Art of the Film*, p. 38, expresses a similar view.

31. Ferguson, "Hollywood's Half a Loaf," in Cooke, ed., *Garbo and the Night Watchman*, p. 257.

32. Longstreet, "Setting Back the Clock," *The Screen Writer*, Aug. 1945, vol. I, no. 3:12.

33. Kronenberger, "Meet One Day, Mate the Next," *PM*, May 4, 1945. There was the same division of opinions on occasion of Murnau's SUNRISE (1927),

with some critics enjoying the film's loose composition and others complaining about its lack of consistency.
34. Cf. Reisz, *The Technique of Film Editing*, pp. 24–5; Jacobs, *The Rise of the American Film*, pp. 111, 199.
35. Jacobs, ibid. pp. 185, 192.

CHAPTER 13

1. Forster, *Aspects of the Novel*, p. 45.
2. Ibid. p. 45. Gasset, *The Dehumanization of Art* . . . , pp. 60, 74, too considers the story something like a necessary evil.
3. Forster, op. cit. p. 133.
4. Ibid. p. 55.
5. Ibid. p. 55.
6. Ibid. p. 118.
7. Ibid. p. 118.
8. Ibid. p. 142.
9. Lukács, *Die Theorie des Romans, passim.*
10. Forster, op. cit. p. 145.
11. Ibid. p. 152.
12. Souriau, "Filmologie et esthétique comparée," *Revue internationale de filmologie*, April–June 1952, vol. III, no. 10:125–8.
13. Ibid. pp. 129–30.
14. Proust, *Remembrance of Things Past*, vol. II, pp. 459ff. (Translation by C. K. Scott Moncrieff.)
15. Ibid. vol. I, pp. 543–45.
16. Cf. Lefranc, "Radiguet et Stendhal à l'écran," in Astre, ed., *Cinéma et roman*, pp. 170–72.
17. Bluestone, *Novels into Film*, pp. 152–61, 163.
18. Ibid. p. 164.
19. Quoted by Moskowitz, " 'Gervaise': from Zola to Clément," *The New York Times*, Dec. 8, 1957.
20. This point is made by both Moskowitz, ibid., and Croce, "Gervaise," *Film Culture*, Dec. 1957, vol. III, no. 5.
21. Auerbach, *Mimesis*, p. 488. (Translated by Willard R. Trask.)
22. Ibid. p. 547.
23. Marcel, "Possibilités et limites de l'art cinématographique," *Revue internationale de filmologie*, July–Dec. 1954, vol. V, nos. 18–9:168–9.

CHAPTER 14

1. Rotha, *Documentary Film*, p. 106.
2. Quoted by Rosenheimer, "They Make Documentaries . . . ," *Film News*, April 1946, vol. 7, no. 6:9.
3. Flaherty's words. Quoted by Rosenheimer, ibid. p. 23.
4. See, for instance, Grierson, "Robert Flaherty: An Appreciation," *The New York Times*, July 29, 1951; Rotha, op. cit. p. 107; Manvell, *Film*, p. 84.
5. So Grierson, op. cit.
6. Quoted by Rosenheimer, op. cit. p. 10.
7. Grierson, op. cit. (His italics.)
8. Goodman, "Pioneer's Return . . . ," *The New York Times*, Aug. 31, 1947.
9. Jacobs, *The Rise of the American Film*, p. 173.
10. See, for instance, "Rossellini," *The New Yorker*, Feb. 19, 1949, p. 25.
11. Bachmann, "Federico Fellini: An Interview," in Hughes, ed., *Film: Book 1*, p. 103.
12. Rotha, "The Last Day of Summer," *Sight and Sound*, Autumn 1958, vol. 27, no. 6:315.
13. Manvell, *Film*, p. 107.
14. Rotha, *Documentary Film*, p. 195. Cf. also Road, "Documentary Film Since 1939," in Rotha, ibid. p. 250.
15. *Agee on Film*, p. 299. See Road, op. cit. p. 271.
16. Laffay, "Les grands thèmes de l'écran," *La Revue du cinéma*, April 1948, vol. II, no. 12:8.
17. Cf. Bachmann, "Federico Fellini: An Interview," in Hughes, ed., *Film: Book 1*, p. 97.
18. Ibid. p. 101.
19. Agel, "Du film en forme de chronicle," in Astre, ed., *Cinéma et roman*, p. 151.
20. Ibid. p. 150.
21. Ibid. p. 149. Cf. also Katulla, "Die Antwort des Moenchs: Bemerkungen zu Federico Fellini," *Film 1958*, vol. I, no. 2:150.
22. Quoted by Bluestone, "An Interview with Federico Fellini," *Film Culture*, Oct. 1957, vol. III, no. 3:3.
23. Quoted by Goodman, "Pioneer's Return . . . ," *The New York Times*, Aug. 31, 1947.
24. See Panofsky, "Style and Medium in the Motion Pictures," *Critique*, Jan.– Feb. 1947, vol. 1, no. 3:11.

CHAPTER 15

1. Marcel, "Possibilités et limites de l'art cinématographique," *Revue internationale de filmologie*, July–Dec. 1954, vol. V, nos. 18–19:168–9.
2. Caillois, "Le cinéma, le meurtre et la tragédie," *Revue internationale de filmologie*, vol. II, no. 5:191.
3. Ibid. p. 191.
4. Ibid. p. 191.
5. See Kracauer, *From Caligari to Hitler*, pp. 100–101, and *passim*.
6. Quoted by Bachmann, "Federico Fellini: An Interview," in Hughes, ed., *Film: Book 1*, pp. 101–2.
7. Cf. ibid. p. 100.
8. See Sadoul, *Les Pionniers du cinéma*, p. 392.
9. Conan Doyle, *The Complete Sherlock Holmes*, p. 13.
10. Poe, "The Mystery of Marie Rogêt," in *The Great Tales and Poems of Edgar Allan Poe*, pp. 212–13.
11. Conan Doyle, op. cit. p. 13.
12. W. K., " 'Trade Marks' That Identify Men," *The New York Times*, Jan. 2, 1949, quotes Dr. Francesco Ronchese, then dermatologist in chief at Rhode Island Hospital, as saying this.
13. See Kracauer, *From Caligari to Hitler*, p. 150.
14. Seton, *Sergei M. Eisenstein*, pp. 301–2.
15. Hitchcock, "Direction," in Davy, ed., *Footnotes to the Film*, pp. 13–14.
16. *Agee on Film*, pp. 71–2, 179, 295.
17. Hitchcock, op. cit. p. 12.
18. Knight, *The Liveliest Art*, p. 197.
19. Tyler, *Rashomon as Modern Art* (Cinema 16 Pamphlet One).
20. Personal communication to me.
21. Panofsky, "Style and Medium in the Motion Pictures," *Critique*, Jan.–Feb. 1947, vol. 1, no. 3:12.

CHAPTER 16

1. Valéry, "Cinématographe," in L'Herbier, ed., *Intelligence du cinématographe*, p. 35.
2. Quoted by Benjamin, "L'oeuvre d'art à l'époque de sa reproduction mécanisée," *Zeitschrift fuer Sozialforschung*, 1936, Jahrgang V, no. 1:62, from Duhamel, *Scènes de la vie future*, Paris, 1930.
3. Chiaromonto, "a note on the movies," *instead*, June 1948, no. 4.
4. Nietzsche, *Human, All-Too-Human*, p. 217. (Aphorism no. 234; translated by Helen Zimmern.)
5. Whitehead, *Science and the Modern World*, p. 187.
6. Freud, *The Future of an Illusion*, pp. 77–8, 96. (Translated by W. D. Robson-Scott.)
7. Dewey, *Art As Experience*, p. 340.
8. Durkheim, *Suicide*, p. 169. (Translated by John A. Spaulding and George Simpson.)
9. Ibid. p. 169.
10. Renan, *The Future of Science*, Preface, p. xviii, says: "The serious thing is that we fail to perceive a means of providing humanity in the future with a catechism that will be acceptable henceforth, except on the condition of returning to a state of credulity. Hence, it is possible that the ruin of idealistic beliefs may be fated to follow hard upon the ruin of supernatural beliefs and that the real abasement of the morality of humanity will date from the date it has seen the reality of things." (No translator named.) Written as early as 1848, *L'Avenir de la science* was published only in 1890, when Renan added the Preface.
11. Freud, op. cit. p. 98.
12. Freud, *Civilization and Its Discontents*, pp. 61, 75, 103. (Translated by Joan Riviere.)
13. Frankel, *The Case for Modern Man*, p. 20.
14. Cf. Toynbee, "Christianity and Civilization," in Toynbee, *Civilization on Trial* . . . , pp. 207, 209.
15. David Riesman's term. See his book, *The Lonely Crowd*.
16. Dewey, *Art as Experience*, p. 338.
17. Durkheim, *Suicide*, p. 168. See also Dewey, op. cit. pp. 340–41.
18. Toynbee, "Does History Repeat Itself?" in Toynbee, *Civilization on Trial* . . . , p. 45.
19. Whitehead, *Science and the Modern World*, p. 199.
20. Ibid. p. 200.
21. Proust, *Remembrance of Things Past*, *passim*; see, for instance, vol. I, pp. 15, 656.
22. Auerbach, *Mimesis*, p. 546. (Translated by Willard R. Trask.)
23. Ibid. p. 552.
24. Ibid. p. 551.

25. Mumford, *Technics and Civilization*, p. 340.
26. Ibid. p. 343.
27. Dewey, *Art as Experience*, p. 340.
28. Ibid. p. 339.
29. Quoted from Agel, "Du film en forme de chronicle," in Astre, ed., *Cinéma et roman*, p. 155.
30. Bachmann, "Federico Fellini: An Interview," in Hughes, ed., *Film: Book 1*, p. 103.
31. Dard, *Valeur humaine du cinéma*, p. 15.
32. Auerbach, *Mimesis*, p. 552.
33. Scheffauer, "The Vivifying of Space," *The Freeman*, Nov. 24 and Dec. 1, 1920.
34. Marcel, "Possibilités et limites de l'art cinématographique," *Revue internationale de filmologie*, July–Dec. 1954, vol. V, nos. 18–19:164.
35. See Graves, *The Greek Myths*, vol. I, pp. 127, 238–9.
36. Balázs, *Der Geist des Films*, pp. 215–17.
37. Dard, *Valeur humaine du cinéma*, p. 16.
38. Panofsky, "Style and Medium in the Motion Pictures," *Critique*, Jan.–Feb. 1947, vol. 1, no. 3:27. See also Hauser, *The Social History of Art*, vol. II, p. 955.
39. Sève, "Cinéma et méthode," *Revue internationale de filmologie*, July–Aug. 1947, vol. I, no. 1:46.
40. Dekeukeleire, *Le Cinéma et la pensée*, p. 15. Cf. also L'Herbier, "Théâtre et cinéma," in Ford, ed., *Bréviaire du cinéma*, p. 99.
41. Balázs, op. cit. pp. 215–17.
42. See, for instance, Faure, "Cinéma," in *Le Rôle intellectuel du cinéma*, pp. 216–20; Hauser, op. cit., vol. II, pp. 946–8.
43. Hardy, ed., *Grierson on Documentary*, *passim*.
44. Cf. Bachmann, "Federico Fellini: An Interview," in Hughes, ed., *Film: Book 1*, pp. 104–5.
45. Auerbach, *Mimesis*, p. 552.
46. Cf. Cohen-Séat, *Essai sur les principes* . . . , pp. 30, 180–81.
47. Laing, "Fine Fare," *The New York Times*, June 28, 1959. (A letter to the Screen Editor.)

Bibliography

This bibliography lists only such writings as are cited and referred to in the present book. The extensive background material consulted in the process could not be included.

Adler, Mortimer J., *Art and Prudence: A Study in Practical Philosophy*, New York, 1937.

Agee on Film: Reviews and Comments, New York, 1958.

Agel, Henri, "Du film en forme de chronicle," in G.-A. Astre, ed., *Cinéma et roman*, Paris, 1958, pp. 147–55. [La revue des lettres modernes, vol. V, nos. 36–8.]

Allendy, Dr., "La valeur psychologique de l'image," in Marcel L'Herbier, ed., *Intelligence du cinématographe*, Paris, 1946, pp. 304–18. [First published in 1926.]

Aragon, Louis, "Painting and Reality: A Discussion," *transition* (New York, Fall 1936), no. 25:93–103.

Arnheim, Rudolf, *Film*, London, 1933.

————, *Art and Visual Perception: A Psychology of the Creative Eye*, Berkeley and Los Angeles, 1954.

————, "Perceptual Abstraction and Art," *Psychological Review* (Princeton, March 1947), vol. 54, no. 2:66–82.

Artaud, Antonin, "The Shell and the Clergyman: Film Scenario," *transition* (Paris, June 1930), nos. 19–20:63–9.

Auerbach, Erich, *Mimesis: The Representation of Reality in Western Literature*, Princeton, 1953. Translated from the German by Willard R. Trask.

Bachmann, Gideon, "The Films of Luis Buñuel," *Cinemages* (New York, 1954), no. 1.

————, "Federico Fellini: An Interview," in Robert Hughes, ed., *Film: Book 1: The Audience and the Filmmaker*, New York, 1959, pp. 97–105.

————, ed., *Jean Epstein, 1897–1953; Cinemages* (New York, 1955), no. 2. A Jean Epstein memorial issue.

Balázs, Béla, *Der sichtbare Mensch, oder die Kultur des Films*, Wien/Leipzig, 1924.

————, *Der Geist des Films*, Halle, 1930.

————, "Das Drehbuch oder Filmszenarium," in *Von der Filmidee zum Drehbuch*, Berlin, 1949, pp. 60–80.

Barbaro, Umberto, "Le cinéma sans acteurs," in *Le Rôle intellectuel du cinéma*, Paris, 1937, pp. 225–34. [Published by the Institut de Coopération Intellectuelle, Société des Nations.]

Bardèche, Maurice, and Brasillach, Robert, *The History of Motion Pictures*, New York, 1938. Translated and edited by Iris Barry.

Barjavel, René, *Cinéma total: Essai sur les formes futures du cinéma*, Paris, 1944.

Barry, Iris, *Film Notes—Part I: The Silent Film*, New York, 1949. [Bulletin of The Museum of Modern Art, vol. XVI, nos. 2–3.]

————, "The Film of Fact," *Town & Country* (New York, Sept. 1946), vol. 100, no. 4288:142, 253–4, 256.

Benjamin, Walter, "L'oeuvre d'art à l'époque de sa reproduction mécanisée," *Zeitschrift fuer Sozialforschung* (Paris, 1936), vol. V, no. 1:40–68.

————, "Ueber einige Motive bei Baudelaire," *Zeitschrift fuer Sozialforschung* (Paris, 1939), vol. VIII, no. 1/2:50–91.

Berge, François, and André, "Interview de Blaise Cendrars sur le cinéma," in *Cinéma*, Paris, 1925, pp. 138–42. [Les cahiers du mois, 16/17.]

Bessy, Maurice, and Duca, Lo, *Louis Lumière, inventeur*, Paris, 1948.

Beucler, André, "L'homme cinéma," *La Revue du cinéma* (Paris, Nov. 1, 1930), vol. 2, no. 16:14–20.

Blitzstein, Marc: statement in "Music in Films: A Symposium of Composers," *films* (New York, Winter 1940), vol. I, no. 4.

Bluestone, George, *Novels into Film*, Baltimore, 1957.

————, "An Interview with Federico Fellini," *Film Culture* (New York, Oct. 1957), vol. III, no. 3:3–4, 21.

Bolen, Francis, "Films and the Visual Arts," in Bolen, ed., *Films on Art: Panorama 1953*, Paris, 1953. [See also the French edition of this UNESCO publication, pp. 5–10.]

Brunius, B. Jacques, "Experimental Film in France," in Roger Manvell, ed., *Experiment in the Film*, London, 1949, pp. 60–112.

Caillois, Roland, "Le cinéma, le meurtre et la tragédie," *Revue internationale de filmologie* (Paris), vol. II, no. 5:187–91.

Cavalcanti, Alberto, "Comedies and Cartoons," in Charles Davy, ed., *Footnotes to the Film*, London, 1937, pp. 71–86.

————, "Sound in Films," *films* (New York, Nov. 1939), vol. 1, no. 1:25–39.

Caveing, Maurice, "Dialectique du concept du cinéma," *Revue internationale de filmologie* (Paris), vol. I, July–Aug. 1947, no. 1:71–8, and Oct. 1948, nos. 3–4:343–50.

Cellini, Benvenuto, *The Autobiography of Benvenuto Cellini*, New York, 1927. [The Modern Library.]

Chaperot, Georges, "Henri Chomette: Le poème d'images et le film parlé," *La Revue du cinéma* (Paris, Aug. 1, 1930), vol. 2, no. 13:26–36.

Charensol, Georges, "Le cinéma parlant," in Marcel L'Herbier, ed., *Intelligence du cinématographe*, Paris, 1946, pp. 169–71. [First published in 1935.]

Chavance, Louis, "Les conditions d'existence du cinéma muet," ibid. pp. 141–4. [First published in 1929.]

Chiaromonte, Nicola, "a note on the movies," *instead* (New York, June 1948), no. 4.

————, "Rome Letter: Italian Movies," *Partisan Review* (New York, June 1949), vol. XVI, no. 6:621–30.

Clair, René, *Réflexion faite: Notes pour servir à l'histoire de l'art cinématographique de 1920 à 1950*, Paris, 1951.

————, "Le cinématographe contre l'esprit," in Marcel Lapierre, ed., *Anthologie du cinéma*, Paris, 1946, pp. 175–82. [Lecture given in 1927.]

Cocteau, Jean, *The Blood of a Poet: A Film by Jean Cocteau*, New York, 1949. Translated from the French by Lily Pons.

Cohen-Séat, Gilbert, *Essai sur les principes d'une philosophie du cinéma. I. Introduction générale: Notions fondamentales et vocabulaire de filmologie*, Paris, 1946.

Cooke, Alistair, *Douglas Fairbanks: The Making of a Screen Character*, New York, 1940.

Copland, Aaron, "Tip to Moviegoers: Take off Those Ear-Muffs," *The New York Times Magazine*, Nov. 6, 1949.

"Core of the Movies—the Chase: Answers by Alfred Hitchcock," *The New York Times Magazine*, Oct. 29, 1950.

Cranston, Maurice, "The Pre-Fabricated Daydream," *The Penguin Film Review* (London, 1949), no. 9:26–31.

Croce, Arlene, "Gervaise," *Film Culture* (New York, Dec. 1957), vol. III, no. 5:14–15.

Crowther, Bosley, "Seen in Close-up," *The New York Times*, Sept. 23, 1951.

Dahl, Ingohf, "Igor Stravinsky on Film Music," *Cinema* (Hollywood, June 1947), vol. 7, no. 1:8–9, 21.

Dard, Michel, *Valeur humaine du cinéma*, Paris, 1928. [Le rouge et le noir: Les essais, no. 10.]

Dekeukeleire, Charles, *Le Cinéma et la pensée*, Bruxelles, 1947. [Collection Savoir, no. 13.]

Delluc, Louis, *Photogénie*, Paris, 1920.

————, "Photographie," in Marcel Lapierre, ed., *Anthologie du cinéma*, Paris, 1946, pp. 134–6.

Deren, Maya, *An Anagram of Ideas on Art, Form, and Film*, Yonkers, New York, 1946.

Dewey, John, *Art As Experience*, New York, 1934.

Doniol-Valcroze, Jacques, and Bazin, André, "Conversation with Bunuel," *Sight and Sound* (London, Spring 1955), vol. 24, no. 4:181–5.

Doyle, A. Conan, *The Complete Sherlock Holmes*, Garden City, New York, 1938.

Dreville, Jean, "Documentation: The Basis of Cinematography," *Close Up* (Territet, Switzerland, Sept. 1930), vol. VII, no. 3:202–6.

Dulac, Germaine, "L'essence du cinéma l'idée visuelle," in *Cinéma*, Paris, 1925, pp. 57–66. [Les cahiers du mois, 16/17.]

————, "La cinégraphie intégrale," in Marcel Lapierre, ed., *Anthologie du cinéma*, Paris, 1946, pp. 157–68. [First published in 1927.]

————, "Le cinéma d'avant-garde," in Marcel L'Herbier, ed., *Intelligence du cinématographe*, Paris, 1946, pp. 341–53. [First published in 1932.]

Durkheim, Emile, *Suicide: A Study in Sociology*, London, 1952. Translated by John A. Spaulding and George Simpson. [Original French edition: Paris, 1897.]

Eder, Josef Maria, *History of Photography*, New York, 1945. Translated by Edward Epstean.

Ehrenburg, Ilja, *Die Traumfabrik: Chronik des Films*, Berlin, 1931.

Eisenstein, Sergei M., *The Film Sense*, New York, 1942. Translated and edited by Jay Leyda.

————, *Film Form: Essays in Film Theory*, New York, 1949. Edited and translated by Jay Leyda.

Eisenstein, 1898–1948, London, 1949. [A British pamphlet in commemoration of Eisenstein, issued by the Film Section of the Society for Cultural Relations with the U.S.S.R.]

Eisler, Hanns, *Composing for the Films*, New York, 1947.

Epstein, Jean, *Cinéma*, Paris, 1921.

————, *Le Cinématographe vu de l'Etna*, Paris, 1926.

————, "Le sens 1 bis," in Marcel L'Herbier, ed., *Intelligence du cinématographe*, Paris, 1946, pp. 257–65. [First published in 1921.]

————, "The Reality of Fairyland," in Bachmann, ed., *Jean Epstein, 1897–1953; Cinemages*, no. 1:43–4. [See Bachmann. The article is drawn from an unpublished manuscript of Epstein's.]

————, "Sound in Slow Motion," ibid. p. 44. [An unpublished manuscript.]

Epstein, Marie, "Biographical Notes," ibid. pp. 7–8.

Erskine, John, "On Turning an Opera into a Film," *The New York Times*, Feb. 4, 1940.

Faure, Elie, "Cinéma," in *Le Rôle intellectuel du cinéma*, Paris, 1937, pp. 195–221. [Published by the Institut de Coopération Intellectuelle, Société des Nations.]

Feininger, Andreas, "Photographic Control Processes," *The Complete Photographer* (New York, 1942), vol. 8, issue 43:2795–2804.

"Fellini ueber Fellini," *Film 1958* (Frankfurt a.M., 1958), vol. I, no. 2:160–62.

Ferguson, Otis, "Hollywood's Half a Loaf," in Alistair Cooke, ed., *Garbo and the Night Watchman*, London, 1937, pp. 255–9.

————, "Life Goes to the Pictures," *films* (New York, Spring 1940), vol. 1, no. 2:19–29.

Feyder, Jacques, "Transposition visuelle," in *Cinéma*, Paris, 1925, pp. 67–71. [Les cahiers du mois, 16/17.]

"Film Crasher Hitchcock," *Cue* (New York), May 19, 1951.

Fondane, Benjamin, "Du muet au parlant: Grandeur et décadence du cinéma," in Marcel L'Herbier, ed., *Intelligence du cinématographe*, Paris, 1946, pp. 145–58. [First published in 1930.]

Forster, E. M., *Aspects of the Novel*, New York, 1927.

Frankel, Charles, *The Case for Modern Man*, Boston, 1959. [A Beacon Paperback edition.]

Freud, Sigmund, *The Future of an Illusion*, New York, 1957. Translated by W. D. Robson-Scott. [A Doubleday Anchor Book. First published in 1927.]

————, *Civilization and Its Discontents*, New York, 1958. Translated by Joan Riviere. [A Doubleday Anchor Book. First published in 1929.]

Freund, Gisèle, *La Photographie en France au dix-neuvième siècle: Essai de sociologie et d'esthétique*, Paris, 1936.

Gasset, José Ortega y, *The Dehumanization of Art and Other Writings on Art and Culture*, Garden City, New York, 1956. Translator not named. [A Doubleday Anchor Book.]

Gibbon, Monk, *The Red Shoes Ballet*, London, 1948.

Goodman, Ezra, "Pioneer's Return: Robert Flaherty Discusses His Latest Documentary, 'The Louisiana Story,'" *The New York Times*, Aug. 31, 1947.

Gorki, Maxim, "You Don't Believe Your Eyes," *World Film News* (London, March 1938), vol. 2, no. 12:16.

Graves, Robert, *The Greek Myths*, Baltimore, Maryland, 1955. 2 vols. [Penguin Books.]

Greene, Graham, "Nutrition," in Alistair Cooke, ed., *Garbo and the Night Watchman*, London, 1937, pp. 228–30.

————, "Subjects and Stories," in Charles Davy, ed., *Footnotes to the Film*, London, 1937, pp. 57–70.

Grierson, John, "Eisenstein and Documentary," in *Eisenstein, 1898–1948*, London, 1949, pp. 15–16. (See this title.)

————, "Robert Flaherty: An Appreciation," *The New York Times*, July 29, 1951.

Griffith, Richard, "The Film Since Then," in Rotha, *The Film Till Now*, New York, 1950.

————, "Documentary Film Since 1939 (II. National Developments, section ii)," in Rotha, *Documentary Film*, London, 1952.

————, "The Use of Films By the U.S. Armed Services," in Rotha, *Documentary Film*, London, 1952.

Hajek-Halke, H., *Experimentelle Fotografie*, Bonn, 1955.

Hardy, Forsyth, ed., *Grierson on Documentary*, New York, 1947.

Hauser, Arnold, *The Social History of Art*, London, 1951. 2 vols. Translated from the German by Stanley Godman in collaboration with the author.

————, *The Philosophy of Art History*, New York, 1958.

Herschel, Sir J. F. W., "Instantaneous Photography," *Photographic News* (London, May 11, 1860), vol. 4, no. 88:13.

Hitchcock, Alfred, "Direction," in Charles Davy, ed., *Footnotes to the Film*, London, 1937, pp. 3–15.

Hofmannsthal, Hugo von, "Der Ersatz fuer Traeume," in *Die Beruehrung der Sphaeren*, Berlin, 1931, pp. 263–8. [First published in *Neue Freie Presse*, March 27, 1921.]

Huff, Theodore, *Charlie Chaplin*, New York, 1951.

Ivens, Joris, "Borinage—A Documentary Experience," *Film Culture* (New York, 1956), vol. II, no. 1:6–9.

Jacobs, Lewis, *The Rise of the American Film*, New York, 1939.

————, "Avant-Garde Production in America," in Roger Manvell, ed., *Experiment in the Film*, London, 1949, pp. 113–52.

Johnson, Albert, "The Tenth Muse in San Francisco," *Sight and Sound* (London, Jan.–March, 1955), vol. 24, no. 3:152–6.

K., W., " 'Trade Marks' That Identify Men," *The New York Times*, Jan. 2, 1949.

Kast, Pierre, "Une fonction de constat: Notes sur l'œuvre de Buñuel," *Cahiers du cinéma* (Paris, Dec. 1951), vol. II, no. 7:6–16.

Katulla, Theodor, "Die Antwort des Moenchs: Bemerkungen zu Federico Fellini," *Film 1958* (Frankfurt a.M., 1958), vol. I, no. 2:139–59.

Katz, Leo, "Dimensions in Photography," *The Complete Photographer* (New York, 1942), vol. 4, issue 21:1331–55.

Knight, Arthur, *The Liveliest Art: A Panoramic History of the Movies*, New York, 1957.

————, "Dancing in Films," *Dance Index* (New York, 1947), vol. VI, no. 8:179–99.

————, "Self-Expression," *The Saturday Review of Literature*, May 27, 1950.

Kracauer, Siegfried, *From Caligari to Hitler*, Princeton, 1947.

————, "Der heutige Film und sein Publikum," *Frankfurter Zeitung*, Nov. 30 and Dec. 1, 1928.

————, "The Conquest of Europe on the Screen: The Nazi Newsreel 1939–1940," *Social Research* (New York, Sept. 1943), vol. 10, no. 3:337–57.

————, "Jean Vigo," *Hollywood Quarterly* (Berkeley and Los Angeles, April 1947), vol. II, no. 3:261–3.

————, "National Types as Hollywood Presents Them," *The Public Opinion Quarterly* (Princeton, Spring 1949), vol. 13, no. 1:53–72.

————, "Silent Film Comedy," *Sight and Sound* (London, Aug.–Sept. 1951), vol. 21, no. 1:31–2.

————, and Lyford, Joseph, "A Duck Crosses Main Street," *The New Republic* (New York, Dec. 13, 1948), vol. 119, no. 24:13–15.

Kronenberger, Louis, "Meet One Day, Mate the Next," *PM*, May 4, 1945, p. 16.

Kyrou, Ado, *Le Surréalisme au cinéma*, Paris, 1953.

Laffay, Albert, "Les grands thèmes de l'écran," *La Revue du cinéma* (Paris, April 1948), vol. II, no. 12:3–19.

Laing, Frederick, "Fine Fare," *The New York Times*, June 28, 1959. [A letter to the Screen Editor.]

Landis, Carney, and Bolles, M. Marjorie, *Textbook of Abnormal Psychology*, New York, 1950.

Langer, Susanne K., *Philosophy in a New Key: A Study in the Symbolism of Reason, Rite, and Art*, New York, 1953. [A Mentor Book.] First published by Harvard University Press, Cambridge, Mass., 1951.

Langlois, Henri, "Notes sur l'histoire du cinéma," *La Revue du cinéma* (Paris, July 1948), vol. III, no. 15:3–15.

Lebovici, Dr. Serge, "Psychanalyse et cinéma," *Revue internationale de filmologie* (Paris), vol. II, no. 5:49–55.

Leech, Clifford, "Dialogue for Stage and Screen," *The Penguin Film Review* (London, April 1948), no. 6:97–103.

Lefranc, Ph., "Radiguet et Stendhal à l'écran," in G.-A. Astre, ed., *Cinéma et roman*, Paris, 1958, pp. 170–75. [La revue des lettres modernes, vol. V, nos. 36–8.]

Léger, Fernand, "A New Realism—The Object," *The Little Review* (New York, Winter 1926), pp. 7–8.

––––––, "A propos du cinéma," in Marcel L'Herbier, ed., *Intelligence du cinématographe*, Paris, 1946, pp. 337–40. [First published in 1931.]

Levin, Meyer, "The Charge of the Light Brigade," in Alistair Cooke, ed., *Garbo and the Night Watchman*, London, 1937, pp. 124–8.

Lewis, Lloyd, "Erich von Stroheim of the Movies Now is a Vicious Brewster of Chicago's 'Arsenic and Old Lace,' " *The New York Times*, June 22, 1941.

L'Herbier, Marcel, "Puissance de l'écran," in Charles Ford, ed., *Bréviaire du cinéma*, Paris, 1945, p. 76.

––––––, "Théâtre et cinéma," ibid. p. 99.

Licart, Albert, *Théâtre et cinéma: Psychologie du spectateur*, Bruxelles, 1937.

Lindgren, Ernest, *The Art of the Film*, London, 1948.

Londe, Albert, *La Photographie instantanée*, Paris, 1886.

London, Kurt, *Film Music*, London, 1936.

Longstreet, Stephen, "Setting Back the Clock," *The Screen Writer* (Hollywood, Aug. 1945), vol. I, no. 3:9–13.

Lukács, George, *Die Theorie des Romans*, Berlin, 1920.

Lusk, Norbert, "I Love Actresses!" *New Movies* (New York, Jan. 1947), vol. XXII, no. 1:24–30.

Lyons, Leonard, "The Lyons Den," *New York Post*, June 5, 1950.

McCausland, Elizabeth, "Alfred Stieglitz," *The Complete Photographer* (New York, 1943), vol. 9, issue 51:3319–22.

Macdonald, Dwight, "The Soviet Cinema: 1930–1938," *Partisan Review* (New York), vol. V, July 1938, no. 2:37–50, and Aug.–Sept. 1938, no. 3:35–62.

Maddison, John, "Le cinéma et l'information mentale des peuples primitifs," *Revue internationale de filmologie* (Paris, Oct. 1948), vol. I, nos. 3–4:305–10.

Manvell, Roger, *Film*, London, 1944.

Marcel, Gabriel, "Possibilités et limites de l'art cinématographique," *Revue internationale de filmologie* (Paris, July–Dec. 1954), vol. V, nos. 18–19:163–76.

Mauerhofer, Hugo, "Psychology of Film Experience," *The Penguin Film Review* (London, Jan. 1949), no. 8:103–9.

Maugé, André R., "Qu'avez-vous appris au cinéma?" *Du cinéma* (Paris, May 1929), vol. I, no. 3.

Mauriac, Claude, *L'Amour du cinéma*, Paris, 1954.

Maurois, André, "La poésie du cinéma," in *L'Art cinématographique*, Paris, 1927, vol. III, pp. 1–37.

Mekas, Jonas, "The Experimental Film in America," *Film Culture* (New York, May–June 1955), vol. 1, no. 3:15–19.

Meltzer, Newton E., "Are Newsreels News?" *Hollywood Quarterly* (Berkeley and Los Angeles, April 1947), vol. II, no. 3:270–72.

Metzner, Ernö, "A Mining Film," *Close Up* (London, March 1932), vol. IX, no. 1:3–9.

Meyerhoff, Horst, *Tonfilm und Wirklichkeit: Grundlagen zur Psychologie des Films*, Berlin, 1949.

Milano, Paolo, "Music in the Film: Notes for a Morphology," *The Journal of Aesthetics and Art Criticism* (New York, Spring 1941), no. 1:89–94.

Miles, Bernard, "Are Actors Necessary?" *Documentary News Letter* (London, April 1941), vol. 2, no. 4:70–74.

Moholy-Nagy, László, *Vision in Motion*, Chicago, 1947.

———, *Malerei, Photographie, Film*, Munich, 1925. [In the series "Bauhausbuecher."]

———, "Surrealism and the Photographer," *The Complete Photographer* (New York, 1943), vol. 9, issue 52:3337–42.

Morin, Edgar, *Le Cinéma ou l'homme imaginaire*, Paris, 1956.

Morrison, George, "The French Avant-Garde," *Sequence* (London): part 1: Summer 1948, no. 4:30–34; part 2: Autumn 1948, no. 5:29–34; part 3: Winter 1948/9, no. 6:32–7.

Moskowitz, Gene, " 'Gervaise': From Zola to Clément," *The New York Times*, Dec. 8, 1957.

Mumford, Lewis, *Technics and Civilization*, New York, 1934.

Murphy, Gardner, *Personality: A Biosocial Approach to Origins and Structure*, New York, 1947.

"Music in Films: A Symposium of Composers," *films* (New York, Winter 1940), vol. 1, no. 4:5–20.

Neergaard, Ebbe, *Carl Dreyer: A Film Director's Work*, London, 1950. Translated from the Danish by Marianne Helweg. [The British Film Institute: New Index Series No. 1.]

Newhall, Beaumont, *The History of Photography from 1839 to the Present Day*, New York, 1949.

———, "Photography and the Development of Kinetic Visualization," *Journal of the Warburg and Courtauld Institutes* (London, 1944), vol. 7, pp. 40–45.

Nicoll, Allardyce, *Film and Theatre*, New York, 1936.

Nietzsche, Friedrich, *Human, All-Too-Human*, part I, Edinburgh and London, 1910. [The Complete Works of Friedrich Nietzsche, vol. 6.] Translated by Helen Zimmern.

Obraszow, Sergej, "Film und Theater," in *Von der Filmidee zum Drehbuch*, Berlin, 1949, pp. 41–59.

Panofsky, Erwin, "Style and Medium in the Moving Pictures," *transition* (Paris, 1937), no. 26:121–33.

———, "Style and Medium in the Motion Pictures," *Critique* (New York, Jan.–Feb. 1947), vol. 1, no. 3:5–28. [Revised and enlarged edition of the 1937 article.]

Pierre-Quint, Léon, "Signification du cinéma," in *L'Art cinématographique*, Paris, 1927, vol. II, pp. 1–28.

Poe, Edgar Allan, "The Mystery of Marie Rogêt," in *The Great Tales and*

Poems of Edgar Allan Poe, New York, 1940, pp. 178–237. [Pocket Books, Inc.]

Poisson, Jacques, "Cinéma et psychanalyse," in *Cinéma*, Paris, 1925, pp. 175–6. [Les cahiers du mois, 16/17.]

Pordes, Dr. Victor E., *Das Lichtspiel: Wesen–Dramaturgie–Regie*, Wien, 1919.

Powdermaker, Hortense, *Hollywood: The Dream Factory*, Boston, 1950.

Proust, Marcel, *Remembrance of Things Past*, New York, 1932 and 1934, 2 vols. Translated by C. K. Scott Moncrieff, except for the last part, "The Past Recaptured," which has been translated by Frederick A. Blossom.

Pudovkin, V. I., *Film Technique and Film Acting*, New York, 1949. Part I: Film Technique; part II: Film Acting. Translated by Ivor Montagu.

Quesnoy, Pierre-F., *Littérature et cinéma*, Paris, 1928. [Le Rouge et le Noir: Les essais, no. 9.]

Ra., T., "Motion Pictures," in *Encyclopedia Britannica*, London & New York, 1932, vol. 15, pp. 854–6.

Rawnsley, David, "Design by Inference," *The Penguin Film Review* (London, 1949), no. 9:32–8. [An interview with Oswell Blakeston.]

"Reaction to 'Creative Photography,'" *The New York Times*, Dec. 16, 1951.

Read, John, "The Film on Art as Documentary," *Film Culture* (New York, Oct. 1957), vol. III, no. 3:6–7.

Reisz, Karel, *The Technique of Film Editing*, London and New York, 1953.

Renan, Ernest, *The Future of Science*, Boston, 1891. Translator not named.

Reynolds, Quentin, *Leave It to the People*, New York, 1948.

Richter, Hans, *Avantgarde: History and Dates of the Only Independent Artistic Film Movement, 1921–1931.* [Unpublished manuscript.]

———, "The Avant-Garde Film Seen from Within," *Hollywood Quarterly* (Los Angeles, Fall 1949), vol. IV, pp. 34–41.

Road, Sinclair, "Documentary Film Since 1939 (I. The General Scene, and II. National Developments, section i)," in Rotha, *Documentary Film*, London, 1952.

Rosenheimer, Arthur, Jr., "They Make Documentaries: Number One–Robert J. Flaherty," *Film News* (New York, April 1946), vol. 7, no. 6:1–2, 8–10, 23.

Rossellini, Roberto, "Dix ans de cinéma (I)," *Cahiers du cinéma* (Paris, Aug.–Sept. 1955), vol. IX, no. 50:3–9.

"Rossellini," *The New Yorker*, Feb. 19, 1949, p. 25.

Rotha, Paul, *The Film Till Now*. With an additional section, "The Film Since Then," by Richard Griffith. New York, 1950.

———, *Documentary Film*. With contributions by Sinclair Road and Richard Griffith. London, 1952.

———, "It's in the Script," *World Film News* (London, Sept. 1938), vol. III, no. 5:204–5.

———, "A Foreword," in *Eisenstein 1898–1948*, London, 1949, pp. 1–4. [See this title.]

———, "Presenting the World to the World," *Films and Filming* (London, April 1956), vol. 2, no. 7:8, 17.

———, "The Last Day of Summer," *Sight and Sound* (London, Autumn 1958), vol. 27, no. 6:314–15.

Ruskin, John, *Praeterita: Outlines of Scenes and Thoughts Perhaps Worthy of Memory in My Past Life*, London, 1949. [First published during 1885–9.]

Sachs, Hanns, "Film Psychology," *Close Up* (Territet, Switzerland, Nov. 1928), vol. III, no. 5:8–15.

Sadoul, Georges, *L'Invention du cinéma, 1832–1897* (Histoire générale du cinéma, I), Paris, 1946.

———, *Les Pionniers du cinéma: De Méliès à Pathé, 1897–1909* (Histoire générale du cinéma, II), Paris, 1947.

———, *Histoire d'un art: Le cinéma des origines à nos jours*, Paris, 1949.

"Sang d'un poète (Le)," *Film Society Programmes*, London, April 2, 1933.

Sargeant, Winthrop, "Music for Murder," *The New Yorker*, Oct. 30, 1954.

Schachtel, Ernest G., "On Memory and Childhood Amnesia," *Psychiatry* (Washington, Feb. 1947), vol. X, no. 1:1–26.

Scheffauer, Herman G., "The Vivifying of Space," *The Freeman* (New York), Nov. 24, 1920, pp. 248–50, and Dec. 1, 1920, pp. 275–6. (Republished in Lewis Jacobs, ed., *Introduction to the Art of the Movies*, New York, 1960, pp. 76–85. A Noonday Press paperback.)

Schenk, Gustav, *Schoepfung aus dem Wassertropfen*, Berlin, 1954.

Schmoll, J. A., gen. Eisenwerth, "Vom Sinn der Fotografie," in Otto Steinert, *Subjective fotografie 2: ein Bildband moderner Fotografie*, Munich, 1955.

Seton, Marie, *Sergei M. Eisenstein*, New York, 1952.

Sève, Lucien, "Cinéma et méthode," *Revue internationale de filmologie* (Paris), vol. I: July–Aug. 1947, no. 1:42–6; Sept.–Oct. 1947, no. 2:171–4; and Oct. 1948, nos. 3–4:351–5.

Sherif, Muzafer, and Cantril, Hadley, *The Psychology of Ego-Involvements: Social Attitudes and Identifications*, New York, 1947.

Souriau, Etienne, "Filmologie et esthétique comparée," *Revue internationale de filmologie* (Paris, April–June 1952), vol. III, no. 10:113–41.

Spottiswoode, Raymond, *A Grammar of the Film: An Analysis of Film Technique*, London, 1935.

———, *Basic Film Techniques*, Berkeley and Los Angeles, 1948. [University of California Syllabus Series No. 303.]

Stern, Seymour, "D. W. Griffith and the Movies," *The American Mercury* (New York, March 1949), vol. LXVIII, no. 303:308–19.

Stifter, Adalbert, *Bunte Steine/Nachlese*, Insel Verlag, Leipzig.

T., H. H., "The Screen: 'Emperor and Golem,' " *The New York Times*, Jan. 10, 1955.

Toynbee, Arnold, "Christianity and Civilization," in Toynbee, *Civilization on Trial*, and *The World and the West*, New York, 1958, pp. 198–220. [Meridian Books, Inc.]

———, "Does History Repeat Itself?" ibid. pp. 37–46.

Turner, John B., "On Suspense and Other Film Matters: An Interview with Alfred Hitchcock," *Films in Review* (New York, April 1950), vol. I, no. 3:21–2, 47.

Tyler, Parker, "The Film Sense and the Painting Sense," *Art Digest* (New York, Feb. 15, 1954), pp. 10–12, 27–8.
————, *Rashomon as Modern Art.* New York, 1952. [Cinema 16 Pamphlet One.]

Ueberweg/Heinze, *Grundriss der Geschichte der Philosophie.* Band V. Basel, 1953.

Valéry, Paul, "Le retour de Hollande," in *Variété II*, Paris, 1930, pp. 19–41.
————, "Le cinéma," in *Les Techniques au service de la pensée*, Paris, 1938, pp. 157–64.
————, "Cinématographe," in Marcel L'Herbier, ed., *Intelligence du cinématographe*, Paris, 1946, pp. 35–6.
————, *Degas, danse, dessin*, Paris, 1938.
Van Dyke, Willard, "How 'Valley Town' Was Made," *Program Notes of Cinema 16*, Jan. 1950. [Reprinted from *U.S. Camera*, Winter 1940.]
Vardac, A. Nicholas, *Stage to Screen: Theatrical Method from Garrick to Griffith*, Cambridge, 1949.
Vuillermoz, Emile, "Réalisme et expressionisme," in *Cinéma*, Paris, 1925, pp. 72–80. [Les cahiers du mois, 16/17.]
————, "La musique des images," in *L'Art cinématographique*, Paris, 1927, vol. III, pp. 39–66.

Waddington, Prof. C. H., "Two Conversations with Pudovkin," *Sight and Sound* (London, Winter 1948–9), vol. 17, no. 68:159–61.
Wallis, C. G., "The Blood of a Poet," *Kenyon Review* (Gambier, Ohio, Winter 1944), vol. 6, no. 1:24–42.
Wallon, Henri, "De quelques problèmes psycho-physiologiques que pose le cinéma," *Revue internationale de filmologie* (Paris, July–Aug. 1947), vol. I, no. 1:15–18.
————, "L'acte perceptif et le cinéma," ibid. (April–June 1953), vol. IV, no. 13:97–110.
Weston, Edward, "Seeing Photographically," *The Complete Photographer* (New York, 1943), vol. 9, issue 49:3200–3206.
Whitehead, Alfred North, *Science and the Modern World*, New York, 1948. [A Mentor Book. First published in 1925.]
————, *Adventures of Ideas*, New York, 1955. [A Mentor Book. First Published in 1933.]
Wilhelm, Wolfgang, *Die Auftriebswirkung des Films*, Bremen, 1940. [Inaugural-Dissertation, Leipzig.]
Wolf-Czapek, K. W., *Die Kinematographie: Wesen, Entstehung und Ziele des lebenden Bildes*, Berlin, 1911.
Wolfenstein, Martha, and Leites, Nathan, *Movies: A Psychological Study*, Glencoe, Ill., 1950.
Wright, Basil, "Handling the Camera," in Charles Davy, ed., *Footnotes to the Film*, London, 1937, pp. 37–53.

Zinnemann, Fred, "On Using Non-Actors in Pictures," *The New York Times*, Jan. 8, 1950.

Each film title is followed by the year of release and the country of production. It should be noted, though, that the sources available do not permit one to establish all these data with absolute certainty. Whenever a subject is mentioned without being explicitly named, the page number referring to it is put in parentheses.